# MASTER THE
# POSTAL EXAMS

### 8th Edition

John Gosney
Dawn Rosenberg McKay

**PETERSON'S**
A nelnet COMPANY

# PETERSON'S

A ⓝelnet COMPANY

**About Peterson's, a Nelnet company**

Peterson's (www.petersons.com) is a leading provider of education information and advice, with books and online resources focusing on education search, test preparation, and financial aid. Its Web site offers searchable databases and interactive tools for contacting educational institutions, online practice tests and instruction, and planning tools for securing financial aid. Peterson's serves 110 million education consumers annually.

---

**Petersons.com/publishing**

Check out our Web site at www.petersons.com/publishing to see if there is any new information regarding the test and any revisions or corrections to the content of this book. We've made sure the information in this book is accurate and up-to-date; however, the test format or content may have changed since the time of publication.

---

For more information, contact Peterson's, 2000 Lenox Drive, Lawrenceville, NJ 08648; 800-338-3282; or find us on the World Wide Web at www.petersons.com/about.

© 2008 Peterson's, a Nelnet company

Previous editions published as *24 Hours to the Postal Exam* © 2001, 2003; as *Postal Exams* © 1992, 1993, 1994, 1997, 2001; and as *Master the Postal Exams,* © 2005

Stephen Clemente, President; Fern A. Oram, Content Director; Bernadette Webster, Operations Director; Roger S. Williams, Sales and Marketing; Therese DeAngelis, Editor; Jill Schwartz, Production Editor; Ray Golaszewski, Manufacturing Manager; Linda M. Williams, Composition Manager

ISBN-13: 978-0-7689-2716-0
ISBN-10: 0-7689-2716-1

Printed in the United States of America

10  9  8  7  6  5  4  3  2  1     10  09  08

Eighth Edition

# Contents

## PART II: FAMILIARIZE YOURSELF WITH THE TESTS

# Contents

## OTHER RECOMMENDED TITLES

*Master the Civil Service Exams*
*Civil Service Handbook*
*Civil Service Arithmetic & Vocabulary Review*

# Before You Begin

Congratulations! You have in your hands a powerful tool to ensure your best chances of getting a great score on the United States Postal Service (USPS) exams. By working through this book, taking time to practice the sample exercises, and studying the various strategies and techniques for tackling all the various question types, you will put yourself at a significant advantage for achieving a top-notch score.

This book contains information on:

- Every exam given by the USPS for maintenance, operations, and transportation positions including Exam 473/473-C and Exam 460
- Job requirements
- Salary and benefits
- Working conditions

## HOW TO USE THIS BOOK

This book is designed as a teach-yourself training course, complete with test-taking tips and strategies, exercises, and nine full-length practice tests.

**Part I** provides a quick overview of important information you need to know about the USPS job market, working conditions, and job requirements.

**Part II** explains the exams required for specific USPS positions. It also has exercises to prepare you for the question types you will encounter on the actual exams.

**Part III** provides nine full-length practice tests, including detailed answer explanations, for Exams 473/473-C, 460, 710, 230, 238, and 240, as well as exams to test your ability to follow oral instructions and a review of basic skills tested in exams such as 710 and 916.

The **Glossary** at the end of the book provides definitions of some of the most important and frequently used terms you can expect to see during the application process.

## SPECIAL STUDY FEATURES

*Master the Postal Exams* is designed to be as user friendly as it is complete. To this end, it includes several features to make your preparation more efficient.

### Overview

Each chapter begins with a bulleted overview listing the topics covered in the chapter. This will allow you to quickly target the areas in which you are most interested.

### Summing It Up

Each chapter ends with a point-by-point summary that reviews the most important items in the chapter. The summaries offer a convenient way to review key points.

### Bonus Information

As you work your way through the book, look for bonus information and advice in the margins of the pages. Information is in the following forms:

#### NOTE

*Notes* highlight need-to-know information about the Postal Exams, whether it's details about application and scoring or the structure of the question type.

#### TIP

*Tips* provide valuable strategies and insider information to help you score your best on the Postal Exams.

#### ALERT!

*Alerts* do just what they say—alert you to common pitfalls and misconceptions you might face or hear regarding the Postal Exams.

## YOU'RE WELL ON YOUR WAY TO SUCCESS

You've made the decision to apply to the U.S. Postal Service. *Master the Postal Exams* will help prepare you for the steps you'll need to take to achieve your goal—from scoring high on the exams to finding the best Postal Service job for you. Good luck!

## GIVE US YOUR FEEDBACK

Peterson's publishes a full line of resources to help guide you through the exam process. Peterson's publications can be found at your local bookstore or library, and you can access us online at www.petersons.com.

We welcome any comments or suggestions you may have about this publication and invite you to complete our online survey at www.petersons.com/survey. Or you can fill out the survey at the back of this book, tear it out, and mail it to us at:

Publishing Department

Peterson's, a Nelnet Company

2000 Lenox Drive

Lawrenceville, NJ 08648

Your feedback will help us make your education and career dreams come true.

# PART I

## A CAREER WITH THE U.S. POSTAL SERVICE

# Benefits of Working for the U.S. Postal Service

## OVERVIEW

- Salary and benefits
- Training and qualifications
- Finding more information about USPS positions
- Summing it up

Remember when you were a kid and you took a field trip to your local post office? More than likely, a friendly employee gave you a tour of the mail-sorting area, demonstrated how the various computers are used (depending, of course, on your age at the time of the tour), and perhaps gave you a peek into one of the mail trucks. And, if you're like many people, you left with the impression that the only thing postal employees do is sort mail.

Most people are familiar with the duties of the city carrier and window clerk, the same friendly employees who may have given you the tour when you were young. However, very few people are aware of the many different tasks required in "sorting the mail," not to mention the enormous variety of occupations within the U.S. Postal Service (USPS). Twenty-four hours a day, mail moves through the typical large post office. It takes a lot of hard work to keep that mail moving, and that hard work requires the involvement of many people performing a broad array of tasks.

The USPS employs nearly 800,000 people, operates more than 37,000 post offices, and handles more than 212 billion pieces of mail per year, or about 8,000 per second. This group includes city carriers; data conversion operators; electronic technicians; mail handlers; mail processing clerks; rural carrier associates; and sales, services, and distribution associates. Postmasters and supervisors make up nearly 10 percent of total employment; and maintenance workers, which include automotive mechanics, building equipment mechanics, custodians, mail processing equipment mechanics, and maintenance mechanics, comprise about 4 percent. The remainder includes postal inspectors, guards, personnel workers, and secretaries.

chapter 1

## SALARY AND BENEFITS

The USPS is an independent agency of the federal government. As such, USPS employees are federal employees who enjoy the very generous benefits offered by the government. These benefits include an automatic raise at least once a year, regular cost-of-living adjustments, liberal paid vacation and sick leave, life insurance, hospitalization, and the opportunity to join a credit union.

### Salary

Salaries within the USPS are graded. The amount of time you've been employed, any promotions you might have received, which shift you work, and whether you work full- or part-time all determine your salary. The following tables illustrate salary levels for various positions with the USPS.

### CITY CARRIER GRADE 1 PAY SCHEDULE
### EFFECTIVE 2006

| STEP | ANNUAL SALARY | HOURLY WAGE | REGULAR OVERTIME |
|------|---------------|-------------|------------------|
| A | $38,527 | $18.52 | $27.78 |
| B | 42,025 | 20.20 | 30.31 |
| C | 43,381 | 20.86 | 31.28 |
| D | 45,979 | 22.11 | 33.16 |
| E | 46,338 | 22.28 | 33.42 |
| F | 46,697 | 22.45 | 33.68 |
| G | 47,050 | 22.62 | 33.93 |
| H | 47,408 | 22.79 | 34.19 |
| I | 47,766 | 22.96 | 34.45 |
| J | 48,119 | 23.13 | 34.70 |
| K | 48,478 | 23.31 | 34.96 |
| L | 48,834 | 23.48 | 35.22 |
| M | 49,193 | 23.65 | 35.48 |
| N | 49,552 | 23.82 | 35.73 |
| O | 49,907 | 23.99 | 35.99 |

### CITY CARRIER GRADE 2 PAY SCHEDULE
### EFFECTIVE 2006

| STEP | ANNUAL SALARY | HOURLY WAGE | REGULAR OVERTIME |
|------|---------------|-------------|------------------|
| A | $40,315 | $19.38 | $29.07 |
| B | 44,034 | 21.17 | 31.76 |
| C | 44,119 | 21.21 | 31.82 |
| D | 46,780 | 22.49 | 33.74 |
| E | 47,166 | 22.68 | 34.01 |
| F | 47,555 | 22.86 | 34.29 |
| G | 47,937 | 23.05 | 34.57 |
| H | 48,321 | 23.23 | 34.85 |
| I | 48,710 | 23.42 | 35.13 |
| J | 49,086 | 23.60 | 35.40 |

| STEP | ANNUAL SALARY | HOURLY WAGE | REGULAR OVERTIME |
|------|---------------|-------------|------------------|
| K | 49,475 | 23.79 | 35.68 |
| L | 49,862 | 23.97 | 35.96 |
| M | 50,244 | 24.16 | 36.23 |
| N | 50,637 | 24.34 | 36.52 |
| O | 51,021 | 24.53 | 36.79 |

## MAIL HANDLERS (RSC M) SCHEDULE
## FULL-TIME ANNUAL BASIC RATES
## EFFECTIVE 2008
### FULL-TIME REGULAR—LEVEL 4

| STEP | ANNUAL SALARY | HOURLY WAGE | REGULAR OVERTIME |
|------|---------------|-------------|------------------|
| AA | $29,017 | $13.95 | $20.93 |
| A | 33,256 | 15.99 | 23.99 |
| B | 38,568 | 18.54 | 27.81 |
| C | 41,079 | 19.75 | 29.63 |
| D | 44,775 | 21.53 | 32.30 |
| E | 45,072 | 21.67 | 32.51 |
| F | 45,376 | 21.82 | 32.73 |
| G | 45,671 | 21.96 | 32.94 |
| H | 45,973 | 22.10 | 33.15 |
| I | 46,272 | 22.25 | 33.38 |
| J | 46,577 | 22.39 | 33.59 |
| K | 46,873 | 22.50 | 33.81 |
| L | 47,174 | 22.68 | 34.02 |
| M | 47,474 | 22.82 | 34.23 |
| N | 47,772 | 22.97 | 34.46 |
| O | 48,071 | 23.11 | 34.67 |
| P | 48,372 | 23.26 | 34.89 |

## MAIL HANDLERS (RSC M) SCHEDULE
## FULL-TIME ANNUAL BASIC RATES
## EFFECTIVE 2008
### FULL-TIME REGULAR—LEVEL 5

| STEP | ANNUAL SALARY | HOURLY WAGE | REGULAR OVERTIME |
|------|---------------|-------------|------------------|
| AA | $30,509 | $14.67 | $22.01 |
| A | 34,750 | 16.71 | 25.07 |
| B | 40,426 | 19.44 | 29.16 |
| C | 43,007 | 20.68 | 31.02 |
| D | 45,503 | 21.88 | 32.82 |
| E | 45,825 | 22.03 | 33.05 |
| F | 46,152 | 22.19 | 33.29 |
| G | 46,468 | 22.34 | 33.51 |
| H | 46,793 | 22.50 | 33.75 |
| I | 47,119 | 22.65 | 33.98 |
| J | 47,439 | 22.81 | 34.22 |
| K | 47,761 | 22.96 | 34.44 |
| L | 48,080 | 23.12 | 34.68 |
| M | 48,407 | 23.27 | 34.91 |

| STEP | ANNUAL SALARY | HOURLY WAGE | REGULAR OVERTIME |
|------|---------------|-------------|------------------|
| N | 48,730 | 23.43 | 35.15 |
| O | 49,050 | 23.58 | 35.37 |
| P | 49,372 | 23.74 | 35.61 |

**NOTE**

As you advance in your selected position within the USPS, you will become eligible for pay increases.

To be eligible for a periodic step increase, an employee must meet the following criteria:

- Must have received and currently be serving under a career appointment
- Must have performed in a satisfactory or outstanding manner during the waiting period
- Cannot have received an equivalent increase during the waiting period
- Must have completed the required waiting period

## Health Benefits

The Federal Employees Health Benefits (FEHB) Program, administered by the Office of Personnel Management, is among the most generous and popular of all postal benefit plans. Depending on the employee's craft and selected health-care plan, the USPS pays from 71 percent to about 88 percent of the premium.

Virtually all career USPS employees (and eligible family members) are covered by the FEHB Plan. Employees who are not eligible (with certain exceptions) include those serving in a temporary position lasting less than a year, such as casual and temporary employees, substitute rural carriers, and rural carrier associates. Other exclusions include noncitizens and employees paid on a contract or fee basis, including contract job cleaners and contract carriers.

Several types of plans are available, including traditional insurance coverage and Health Maintenance Organizations (HMOs). In addition, employee premium contributions are not subject to most taxes.

## Vacation

Vacation is provided to employees for paid time off from regularly scheduled work hours. The charts on page 8 show how much vacation is accrued for full-time and part-time employees. Vacation for full-time employees is credited at the beginning of the year, while vacation for part-time employees is accrued in units of 20, 13, or 10 hours worked. Military service time (in most cases) counts towards USPS service time for determining vacation per year. (For example, if you served four years in the U.S. military prior to your employment with the USPS, your initial vacation amount would be in the 3- to 15-year category. However, military retirees do not qualify for this time except under certain conditions.)

## FULL-TIME REGULAR APWU SALARY SCHEDULE (CLERK, MAINTENANCE, MOTOR VEHICLE, SUPPORT SERVICES)

### Effective 2008

| Old Grade | New Grade | Pay Step | | | | | | | | | | | | | | | | | | Step Increase |
|---|---|---|---|---|---|---|---|---|---|---|---|---|---|---|---|---|---|---|---|---|
| | | BB | AA | A | B | C | D | E | F | G | H | I | J | K | L | M | N | O | P | |
| 2 | 3 | 30,801 | 31,806 | 32,811 | 33,816 | 34,821 | 35,826 | 36,831 | 37,836 | 38,841 | 39,846 | 40,851 | 41,856 | 42,861 | 43,866 | 44,871 | 45,876 | 47,006 | | 1,005 |
| 3 | 4 | 31,979 | 32,974 | 33,969 | 34,964 | 35,959 | 36,954 | 37,949 | 38,944 | 39,939 | 40,934 | 41,929 | 42,924 | 43,919 | 44,914 | 45,909 | 46,904 | 47,899 | | 995 |
| 4 | 5 | | | 35,735 | 36,672 | 37,609 | 38,546 | 39,483 | 40,420 | 41,357 | 42,294 | 43,231 | 44,168 | 45,105 | 46,042 | 46,979 | 47,916 | 48,853 | | 937 |
| 5 | 6 | | | 37,480 | 38,366 | 39,252 | 40,138 | 41,024 | 41,910 | 42,796 | 43,682 | 44,568 | 45,454 | 46,340 | 47,226 | 48,112 | 48,998 | 49,884 | | 886 |
| 6 | 7 | | | 39,322 | 40,158 | 40,994 | 41,830 | 42,666 | 43,502 | 44,338 | 45,174 | 46,010 | 46,846 | 47,682 | 48,518 | 49,354 | 50,190 | 51,026 | | 836 |
| 7 | 8 | | | 40,160 | 41,022 | 41,884 | 42,746 | 43,608 | 44,470 | 45,332 | 46,194 | 47,056 | 47,918 | 48,780 | 49,642 | 50,504 | 51,366 | 52,228 | | 862 |
| 8 | 9 | | | | | | 46,478 | 47,123 | 47,768 | 48,413 | 49,058 | 49,703 | 50,348 | 50,993 | 51,638 | 52,283 | 52,928 | 53,573 | 54,218 | 645 |
| 11 | 10 | | | | | | 49,656 | 50,423 | 51,190 | 51,957 | 52,724 | 53,491 | 54,258 | 55,025 | 55,792 | 56,559 | 57,326 | 58,093 | 58,860 | 767 |
| 12 | 11 | | | | | | 50,831 | 51,645 | 52,459 | 53,273 | 54,087 | 54,901 | 55,715 | 56,529 | 57,343 | 58,157 | 58,971 | 59,785 | 60,599 | 814 |

### Step Increase Waiting Period (In Weeks)

| Steps (From–To) | BB-AA | AA-A | A-B | B-C | C-D | D-E | E-F | F-G | G-H | H-I | I-J | J-K | K-L | L-M | M-N | N-O | O-P | Years |
|---|---|---|---|---|---|---|---|---|---|---|---|---|---|---|---|---|---|---|
| Grade 3 | 44 | 44 | 44 | 44 | 44 | 44 | 44 | 44 | 44 | 44 | 44 | 44 | 44 | 44 | 44 | 44 | | 13.5 |
| Grade 4 | 36 | 36 | 36 | 36 | 36 | 36 | 36 | 36 | 36 | 36 | 36 | 36 | 36 | 36 | 36 | 36 | | 11.1 |
| Grades 5–7 | | | 36 | 36 | 36 | 36 | 36 | 36 | 36 | 36 | 36 | 36 | 36 | 36 | 36 | 36 | | 9.7 |
| Grade 8 | | | 30 | 30 | 30 | 30 | 30 | 30 | 30 | 30 | 30 | 30 | 30 | 30 | 30 | 30 | | 8.1 |
| Grades 9–11 | | | | | | 30 | 30 | 30 | 30 | 30 | 30 | 30 | 30 | 30 | 30 | 30 | 30 | 6.9 |

## ANNUAL VACATION FOR FULL-TIME EMPLOYEES

| YEARS OF EMPLOYMENT | VACATION |
| --- | --- |
| Less than 3 years | 13 days |
| 3 to 15 years | 20 days |
| 15 years or more | 26 days |

## ANNUAL VACATION FOR PART-TIME EMPLOYEES

| YEARS OF EMPLOYMENT | VACATION |
| --- | --- |
| Less than 3 years | 13 days per 26-period leave year or 4 hours for each biweekly pay period; one hour for each unit of 20 hours in pay status |
| 3 to 15 years | 20 days per 26-period leave year or 6 hours for each full biweekly pay period, plus 4 hours in last pay period in leave year; one hour for each unit of 13 hours in pay status |
| 15 years or more | 26 days per 26-period leave year or 8 hours for each full biweekly pay period; one hour for each unit of 10 hours in pay status |

## Sick Leave

Sick leave is provided to employees for paid time off from regularly scheduled work hours due to illness, injury, pregnancy, and medical examinations and treatment (including dental and optical). Sick leave is accrued and credited at the end of each biweekly pay period in which it is earned. Both full- and part-time employees receive thirteen sick days per year.

## Court Leave

An employee is entitled to paid time off without charge to leave for service as a juror or witness. An employee is responsible for informing his or her supervisor if he or she is excused from jury or witness service for one day or more or for a substantial part of a day. To avoid undue hardship, an agency may adjust the schedule of an employee who works nights or weekends and is called to jury duty. (If there is no jury/witness service, there is no court leave. The employee would be charged annual leave, sick leave, or leave without pay, as appropriate.)

## Family and Medical Leave

Under the Family and Medical Leave Act of 1993 (FMLA), most federal employees are entitled to a total of up to twelve weeks of unpaid leave during any twelve-month period for the following purposes:

- Birth of a son or daughter of the employee and the care of such son or daughter
- Placement of a son or daughter with the employee for adoption or foster care
- Care of spouse, son, daughter, or parent of the employee who has a serious health condition

- Serious health condition of the employee that makes the employee unable to perform the essential functions of his or her position

## Military Leave

An employee is entitled to time off at full pay for certain types of active or inactive duty in the National Guard or as a Reserve of the Armed Forces. Any full-time federal civilian employee whose appointment is not limited to one year is entitled to military leave.

## Organ Donor Leave

An employee may use up to seven days of paid leave each calendar year to serve as a bone-marrow donor. An employee also may use up to thirty days of paid leave each calendar year to serve as an organ donor. Leave for bone marrow and organ donation is a separate category of leave that is in addition to annual and sick leave.

## Leave Transfer

An employee may donate annual leave directly to another federal employee who has a personal or family medical emergency and who has exhausted his or her available paid leave. Each agency must administer a voluntary leave transfer program for its employees. There is no limit on the amount of donated annual leave a leave recipient may receive from the leave donor(s). However, any unused donated leave must be returned to the leave donor(s) when the medical emergency ends.

## Federal Holidays

The following ten days are observed as holidays by the USPS:

- New Year's Day
- Martin Luther King Jr.'s Birthday
- Washington's Birthday
- Memorial Day
- Independence Day
- Labor Day
- Columbus Day
- Veterans' Day
- Thanksgiving Day
- Christmas Day

## Workers' Compensation Benefits

All USPS employees are covered by the Federal Employee's Compensation Act (FECA), which is administered by the Office of Workers' Compensation Program (OWCP)—United States Department of Labor. FECA entitles employees who have suffered a job-related disability to:

- Continuation of regular pay for the period of the disability, up to a maximum of forty-five calendar days, for a traumatic job-related injury

- Compensation for wages lost as a result of job-related injury or illness

- Medical care for disability due to personal injuries sustained while in the performance of duty or diseases caused, aggravated, or accelerated by postal employment

- Vocational rehabilitation

## TRAINING AND QUALIFICATIONS

An applicant for a postal service job must meet minimum age requirements. Generally, the minimum age is 18 years, but a high school graduate may begin work at 16 years if the job is not hazardous and does not require use of a motor vehicle. Many postal service jobs do not require formal education or special training. Applicants for these jobs are hired on the basis of their examination scores.

Some postal jobs do have special education or experience requirements, while some are open only to veterans.

**NOTE**

Any special requirements will be stated on the announcement of examination.

### Additional Qualifying Issues for USPS Positions

- Male applicants born after December 31, 1959, must be registered with the Selective Service System, unless for some reason they are exempt.

- The Immigration Reform and Control Act of 1986 applies to postal workers. All postal workers must be citizens of the United States, lawful permanent resident aliens (i.e., possessing "green cards"), or citizens of American Samoa or any other territory owing permanent allegiance to the United States.

- Applicants should apply at the post office where they wish to work and take the entrance examination for the job they want.

- A medical assessment, including drug screening, is required.

- Applicants for jobs that require strength and stamina may require a special test. For example, mail handlers must be able to lift mail sacks weighing up to 70 pounds. The names of applicants who pass the examinations are placed on a list in the order of their scores.

- Examinations for some jobs include a written test.

- A local criminal check is required before employment. (A more extensive criminal history check is completed at the time of employment.)

When a job opens, the appointing officer chooses one of the top three applicants. Other applications are kept on file so those applicants can be considered for future openings.

New employees are trained either on the job by supervisors and other experienced employees or in local training centers. Training ranges from a few days to several months, depending on the job. Advancement opportunities are available for most postal workers because a management commitment provides career development. Employees also can get preferred assignments, such as the day shift or a more desirable delivery route, as their seniority increases. When an opening occurs, employees may submit written requests, called "bids," for assignment to the vacancy. The bidder who meets the qualifications and who has the most seniority gets the job.

## FINDING MORE INFORMATION ABOUT USPS POSITIONS

National job listings for the United States Postal Service can be found at the USPS Web site at www.usps.gov. Employment opportunities are broken into these categories:

- Mail Processing Jobs: maintenance, operations, transportation
- Corporate Jobs: administrative/clerical, customer service, economics, emergency preparedness, engineering, facilities, finance, human resources, information technology, law enforcement, labor relations, legal, sales, purchasing, transportation, and other corporate areas
- Sales and Marketing Jobs: sales managers, account managers
- USPS Employees: internal positions for those who already work for the USPS
- Bargaining Unit Reassignment: This Web-based application, also known as eReassign, allows USPS employees to electronically:
  - Submit a reassignment request via the Internet
  - View the status of a request
  - View offices and positions within each district

**TIP**

You also can visit www.jobsfed.com and www.usps.gov/hrisp for additional information about career opportunities with the USPS.

## SUMMING IT UP

- USPS employees enjoy very generous benefits, including:
  - Automatic raises at least once a year
  - Regular cost-of-living adjustments
  - Liberal paid vacation, sick leave, and other forms of leave
  - Life insurance
  - Hospitalization
  - Opportunity to join a credit union
- Applicants for USPS jobs must meet minimum age requirements and other qualifications, such as being a U.S. citizen or lawful resident alien and passing a medical assessment, including a drug screening.

# Postal Service Job Descriptions

## chapter 2

## OVERVIEW

- Post office clerk
- City or special carrier/special delivery messenger
- Distribution clerk—machine
- Flat sorting machine operator
- Mail handler
- Mail processor
- Mark-up clerk—automated
- Rural carrier
- Data conversion operator
- Cleaner, custodian, laborer—custodial
- Building equipment mechanic
- Electronic technician
- Motor vehicle operator, tractor-trailer operator
- Garageman
- Summing it up

Deciding on a job with the USPS is like deciding on any other job. Each position is unique and will appeal to different individuals for different reasons. Do you enjoy a specific type of work? If you don't really like being outdoors, then a courier route is probably not the right position for you. Perhaps you enjoy a position that is more structured compared to one that changes every minute. If that's the case, a mail sorting position might be the best fit for you.

The point is that you should try to match the job descriptions listed in this chapter with your own interests. Keep in mind, however, that all positions within the USPS are competitive, so you may need to find two or three positions that interest you, in case your position of choice doesn't open up right away.

The U.S. Postal Service divides mail processing jobs into three broad categories:

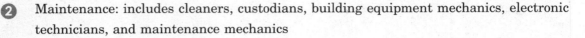

①  Operations: includes post office clerks, city or special carriers, distribution clerks, sorting machine operators, mail handlers, mail processors, mark-up clerks, rural carriers, clerk-typists and clerk-stenographers, and data conversion operators

②  Maintenance: includes cleaners, custodians, building equipment mechanics, electronic technicians, and maintenance mechanics

③  Transportation: includes motor vehicle operators; tractor trailer operators; automotive mechanics, and automotive technicians

Here's a review of the duties, working conditions, qualifications, and testing requirements of representative jobs in each of these categories.

## POST OFFICE CLERK

### Job Duties

Think back to that trip to the post office we talked about earlier. You might remember thinking that the only duties of a postal clerk are to sell stamps and to process your packages. Actually, the majority of postal clerks are distribution clerks who sort incoming and outgoing mail in workrooms, away from the public eye. Only in a small post office will a postal clerk perform the double duties of sitting behind the counter and sorting mail. Generally speaking, a post office clerk performs the following tasks:

• Sorts and distributes mail to post offices and carrier routes

• Performs services at public windows of post offices, post office branches, or stations (again, usually only in small post offices)

• Performs related duties as assigned

### Working Conditions

A postal clerk may have to perform manual work, depending on the size of the post office and the equipment it has (such as chutes and sorting machines) to help with this task. Generally speaking, work involves continuous standing, stretching, and reaching. In addition, the postal clerk may be required to handle sacks of letter mail or parcel post weighing up to 70 pounds.

As we mentioned earlier, different jobs will appeal to different people—for different reasons. However, be aware that some people may become bored with the routine of sorting mail. Also, postal clerks may be required to work at night (especially in large post offices where sorting and distributing the mail is a 24/7 activity).

However, if your duties also include those of a window clerk, you will more than likely experience a wider variety of duties. You will have frequent contact with the public (which may be viewed as a benefit or drawback, depending on the type of person you are), your work will (usually) be less physically strenuous, and you won't have to work at night very often. Again, each post office differs in the particular duties that are assigned to the postal clerk.

## Qualifications

Qualification requirements for the position of postal clerk closely mirror the working conditions just described. Candidates must demonstrate the following:

- Ability to perform the physical duties of the position, including prolonged standing, walking, and reaching

- Ability to lift heavy sacks of mail up to 70 pounds

- 20/40 (Snellen) vision in at least one eye (corrective lenses are permitted)

- Ability to read, without strain, printed material the size of typewritten characters (corrective lenses are permitted)

- Ability to hear the conversational voice with or without a hearing aid (for window positions)

- Emotional and mental stability

- No irremediable defect or incurable disease that prevents efficient performance of duty or that renders a worker a hazard to himself or herself, fellow employees, or others

## Testing Requirement

Applicants must pass Exam 473/473-C.

Postal clerks are represented by:

The American Postal Workers Union (APWU), AFL-CIO
1300 L St. NW
Washington, D.C. 20005
202-842-4200
www.apwu.org

# CITY OR SPECIAL CARRIER/SPECIAL DELIVERY MESSENGER

Perhaps the most familiar position within the postal service is that of mail carrier. Indeed, the mailperson is a fixture in our culture. Despite the rise in popularity of e-mail, it's difficult to imagine a world where there is no daily mail. You might be surprised to learn, however, that much of the postal carrier's work is done before and after they deliver the mail. Often as early as 6 a.m., mail carriers start their shifts at the post office, where they spend a few hours arranging their mail for delivery, readdressing letters to be forwarded, and handling other details.

## Job Duties

A mail carrier typically covers a route on foot, toting a heavy load of mail in a satchel or pushing it in a cart. In suburban or outlying areas, a mail carrier may drive a car or small truck. Mail carriers and special delivery messengers perform the following tasks:

- Promptly and efficiently deliver and collect mail on foot or by vehicle under varying conditions in a prescribed area or on various routes

- Deliver parcel post from trucks and make collections of mail from various postal boxes or other locations

- Maintain pleasant and effective public relations with customers

## Working Conditions

The mail is always delivered, regardless of the weather conditions. In fact, there must be an extreme weather situation for the mail to be postponed for an entire day (it may be late, of course, but that's different from it not going out at all).

Carriers must be able to perform the following tasks:

- Drive motor vehicles in all kinds of traffic and road conditions

- Carry mail in shoulder satchels weighing as much as 35 pounds

- Load and unload sacks of mail weighing up to 70 pounds

- Serve in all types of weather

Despite these tough requirements, the job does have many advantages. Carriers who begin work early in the morning are finished by early afternoon. They are also free to work at their own pace, as long as they cover their routes within a reasonable period of time.

## Qualifications

As is the case with many positions with the USPS, carriers must be able to perform physically taxing work. Candidates must demonstrate the following:

- Ability to perform the physical duties of the position, including prolonged standing, walking, and reaching

- Ability to lift heavy sacks of mail up to 70 pounds

- 20/40 (Snellen) vision in at least one eye (corrective lenses are permitted)

- Ability to read, without strain, printed material the size of typewritten characters (corrective lenses are permitted)

- Ability to hear the conversational voice with or without a hearing aid (for window positions)

- Emotional and mental stability

- No irremediable defect or incurable disease that prevents efficient performance of duty or that renders a worker a hazard to himself or herself, fellow employees, or others

For positions that require driving, applicants must have a valid state driver's license and must demonstrate and maintain a safe driving record. Applicants must pass the Postal Service road test to show their ability to safely drive a vehicle of the type used on the job.

If driving a vehicle weighing less than 10,000 pounds (GVW), candidates must have vision of 20/40 in at least one eye and the ability to read, without strain, printed material the size of typewritten characters (corrective lenses are permitted). The ability to hear is not required to operate a vehicle weighing less than 10,000 pounds (GVW).

## Testing Requirement

Applicants must pass Exam 473/473-C.

City or Special Carrier/Special Delivery Messengers are represented by:

National Association of Letter Carriers (NALC), AFL-CIO
100 Indiana Ave. NW
Washington, D.C. 20001-2144
202-393-4695
www.nalc.org

# DISTRIBUTION CLERK—MACHINE

## Job Duties

The work of the distribution clerk is more routine than that of other postal clerks, but the starting salary is higher. However, you should realize that as a distribution clerk, you may be on your feet all day. In addition, you must be able to occasionally handle sacks of mail weighing up to 70 pounds.

Perhaps the most challenging aspect of the job (and an aspect that will either greatly appeal to you or greatly discourage you, depending on your personality type) is the way in which you must sort mail. You must memorize a complicated scheme that enables you to quickly and efficiently sort mail. For example, you must be able to quickly read a ZIP Code and then determine how each piece of mail is to be directed.

## Qualifications

The distribution clerk—machine applicant must possess sufficient levels of the following Knowledge, Skills, and Abilities (KSAs):

- Knowledge of multi-position letter sorting machine
- Ability to work without immediate supervision

**TIP**

Increased automation within the USPS has made the job of the distribution clerk quite secure. Although nothing is ever 100 percent guaranteed, this is a fact you might consider when investigating USPS positions.

- Ability to work in cooperation with follow employees to efficiently perform the duties of the position
- Ability to observe and act on visual information such as names, addresses, numbers, and shapes
- Ability to learn and recall pairings of addresses with numbers, letters, or positions
- Ability to sequence (place) mail in the proper numerical, alphabetical, or geographic order
- Ability to efficiently perform the physical duties of the position
- 20/40 (Snellen) vision in at least one eye, near acuity of 7 or higher in either eye (Titmus or Bausch & Lomb), and the ability to read, without strain, printed material the size of typewritten characters (corrective lenses are permitted)
- Ability to distinguish basic colors and shades

## Testing Requirements

Applicants must pass Exam 473/473-C and successfully complete dexterity training as required by management.

Distribution Clerks—Machine are represented by:

The American Postal Workers Union (APWU), AFL-CIO
1300 L St. NW
Washington, D.C. 20005
202-842-4200
www.apwu.org

# FLAT SORTING MACHINE OPERATOR

## Job Duties

A flat sorting machine operator's work is very similar to that of a distribution clerk. However, a flat sorting machine operator works with large, bulky packages.

As you might guess, you will have to possess greater physical strength and stamina than you would if you were a distribution clerk. As with the machine operator's position, increasing automation adds a good degree of security to this position.

## Qualifications

The flat sorting machine operator applicant must possess sufficient levels of the following Knowledge, Skills, and Abilities (KSAs):

- Knowledge of all recall pairings of addresses with numbers, letters, or positions
- Ability to work without immediate supervision

- Ability to work in cooperation with fellow employees to efficiently perform the duties of the position
- Ability to observe and act on visual information such as names, addresses, numbers, and shapes
- Ability to sequence (place) mail in the proper numerical, alphabetical, or geographic order
- Ability to perform routine troubleshooting such as removing machine jams
- Ability to efficiently perform the physical duties of the position
- 20/40 (Snellen) vision in at least one eye, near acuity of 7 or higher in either eye (Titmus or Bausch & Lomb), and the ability to read, without strain, printed material the size of typewritten characters (corrective lenses are permitted)
- Ability to distinguish basic colors and shades

## Testing Requirements

Applicants must pass Exam 473/473-C, successfully complete the appropriate training program for the flat sorting machine operation, and be able to key 45 items per minute with 98 percent accuracy.

Flat Sorting Machine Operators are represented by:

The American Postal Workers Union (APWU), AFL-CIO
1300 L St. NW
Washington, D.C. 20005
202-842-4200
www.apwu.org

# MAIL HANDLER

## Job Duties

Mail handlers unload loads, move bulk mail, and perform other duties incidental to the movement and processing of mail.

## Qualifications

Mail handler applicants must possess sufficient levels of the following Knowledge, Skills, and Abilities (KSAs):

- Minimum competency for senior-qualified positions
- Ability to perform efficiently the physical duties of the position
- Because of the extreme physical nature of this job, certain physical conditions can preclude you from taking the strength and stamina test without prior approval from your doctor (which is a requirement for this position). These conditions include hernia or

rupture, back trouble, heart trouble, pregnancy, or any other condition that makes it dangerous for you to lift and carry 70-pound weights.

- 20/40 (Snellen) vision in at least one eye and the ability to read, without strain, printed material the size of typewritten characters (corrective lenses are permitted)

- Ability to hear the conversational voice in at least one ear (hearing aid is permitted)

## Testing Requirements

Applicants must pass Exam 473/473-C and physical ability test.

Mail Handlers are represented by:

National Postal Mail Handlers Union (NPMHU), AFL-CIO
1101 Connecticut Ave. NW, Suite 500
Washington, D.C. 20036
202-833-9095
www.npmhu.org

**ALERT!**

If you fail to qualify on the strength and stamina test, you won't be tested again in the same group of hires. If you fail the test a second time, your eligibility for the position is canceled.

# MAIL PROCESSOR

## Job Duties

Mail processors perform a combination of tasks required to process the mail by using a variety of mail processing equipment.

## Working Conditions

You won't find the physical requirements for this position as tough as those required for mail handlers. However, mail processors start at lower salaries than mail handlers.

## Qualifications

The mail processor applicant must possess sufficient levels of the following Knowledge, Skills, and Abilities (KSAs):

- Ability to perform efficiently the physical duties of the position

- 20/40 (Snellen) vision in at least one eye and the ability to read, without strain, printed material the size of typewritten characters (corrective lenses are permitted)

- Ability to distinguish basic colors and shades

## Testing Requirements

Applicants must pass Exam 473/473-C and a physical ability test.

Mail Processors are represented by:

The American Postal Workers Union (APWU), AFL-CIO
1300 L St. NW
Washington, D.C. 20005
202-842-4200
www.apwu.org

# MARK-UP CLERK—AUTOMATED

## Job Duties

A mark-up clerk—automated operates an electro-mechanical, operator-paced machine to process mail that is undeliverable as addressed. In doing so, the clerk operates the keyboard of a computer terminal to enter and extract data to several databases. Although you don't have to be a computer programmer to qualify for this position, you should feel comfortable working with computers, because you will need to work in several different computer programs to enter, view, and change data.

## Qualifications

The mark-up clerk—automated applicant must possess sufficient levels of the following Knowledge, Skills, and Abilities (KSAs):

- Ability to use reference materials and manuals relevant to the position
- Ability to perform effectively under the pressures of the position
- Ability to operate any office equipment appropriate to the position
- Ability to work with others
- Six months of clerical or office machine operating experience (successful completion of business school may be substituted)
- Ability to type
- Successful completion of a four-year high school course
- Ability to perform efficiently the physical duties of the position
- 20/40 (Snellen) vision in at least one eye and the ability to read, without strain, printed material the size of typewritten characters (corrective lenses are permitted)
- Ability to distinguish basic colors and shades

## Testing Requirements

Given the clerically oriented requirements of this position, you'll need to demonstrate the ability to key data codes on a computer terminal at a rate of 14 correct lines per minute. This is determined by successful completion of Exam 710. You'll also need to pass Exam 473/473-C.

Mark-up Clerks—Automated are represented by:

> The American Postal Workers Union (APWU), AFL-CIO
> 1300 L St. NW
> Washington, D.C. 20005
> 202-842-4200
> www.apwu.org

# RURAL CARRIER

## Job Duties

The work of the rural carrier combines the jobs of window clerk and letter carrier. However, the position also has its own special characteristics.

A rural carrier begins the day by sorting and loading the mail for delivery. Then comes delivery, which may require driving over rough roads and through tough weather. Most rural carriers deliver much of the mail from a vehicle. At the end of the day, the carrier returns to the post office with outgoing mail and money he or she has collected from various transactions.

As you might guess, rural carriers enjoy a great deal of independence, because there is no one directly supervising them. However, the work can be taxing, and you will have to endure the inherent dilemmas that come with spending a lot of time driving.

Because many of the rural carrier's patrons live in remote locations, this employee occasionally is also required to perform all the duties of a window clerk, including accepting, collecting, and delivering all classes of mail and selling stamp supplies and money orders.

## Working Conditions

In general, rural carriers must meet the following conditions:

- Load and deliver parcels weighing up to 70 pounds
- Place letters and parcels in mailboxes while carefully handling the vehicle and frequently shifting from one side of the vehicle to the other

## Qualifications

The rural carrier applicant must possess sufficient levels of the following Knowledge, Skills, and Abilities (KSAs):

- Ability to read, understand, and apply written instructions
- Ability to perform basic arithmetic computations
- Ability to prepare reports and maintain records
- Ability to communicate effectively with customers
- Ability to work effectively without close supervision
- Ability to perform efficiently the arduous physical duties of the position
- 20/40 (Snellen) vision in at least one eye and the ability to read, without strain, printed material the size of typewritten characters (corrective lenses are permitted)

## Testing Requirements

Applicants must pass Exam 460.

In addition to completing Exam 460, applicants must also have a valid state driver's license and a safe driving record and must pass the Postal Service road test. In addition, rural carriers must furnish all necessary vehicle equipment for prompt handling of the mail, unless supplied by the employer.

Rural carriers are represented by:

National Rural Letter Carriers Association (NLRCA)
1630 Duke St.
Alexandria, VA 22314-3465
703-684-5545
www.nrlca.org

# DATA CONVERSION OPERATOR

## Job Duties

Data conversion operators use computer terminals to prepare mail for automated sorting equipment. They read typed or handwritten addresses from an envelope image on the terminal screen and then select and type essential information so that an address bar code can be applied to the letter. Depending on the quality of the address information shown on the image, data conversion operators are prompted to key a five-number ZIP Code or an abbreviated version of the street and city address. Abbreviated addresses must conform to strict encoding rules so that the computer can expand the abbreviation to a full address and find the correct ZIP + 4. Unlike some other types of data entry, this job is not just "key what you see."

**NOTE**

Working with the public requires maintaining pleasant and effective working relations with customers and keeping an acceptable appearance.

## REMOTE BAR CODING SYSTEM

Data conversion operators are vital components of the Remote Bar Coding System (RBCS), designed to allow letter mail that cannot be read by a machine to be bar-coded and processed in the automated mail stream. RBCS technology has created a new operation called a remote encoding center (REC). RBCS has two major elements: an input subsystem (ISS) and an output subsystem (OSS).

At the processing plant, ISS takes a video picture or image of each letter and then looks up the address to find a ZIP + 4. For letters for which the ISS computer cannot find a ZIP + 4, corresponding images are transmitted by telephone lines to data conversion operators at the remote encoding center for further processing. At the REC, data conversion operators working at video display terminals are presented with images one at a time. Using specific rules, operators key data for each image so that the computers can find the correct ZIP + 4.

At the plant, the OSS sprays letters with correct ZIP + 4 bar codes and performs initial sorting. Letters are then processed by bar code sorters. These elements are linked by a communication system consisting of cabling and telephone or microwave telecommunications.

NOTE

Remote encoding centers offer the possibility of flexible scheduling. Basic work hours are between 3 p.m. and 1 a.m. Individual work schedules range between four and eight hours. RECs operate seven days a week.

## Qualifications

The data conversion operator applicant must possess sufficient levels of the following Knowledge, Skills, and Abilities (KSAs):

- Ability to perform efficiently the physical duties of the position

- 20/40 (Snellen) vision in at least one eye and the ability to read, without strain, printed material the size of typewritten characters (corrective lenses are permitted)

- Ability to distinguish basic colors and shades

- Ability to hear the conversational voice (hearing aid is permitted)

## Testing Requirement

Applicants must pass Exam 710 at a high standard. This demonstrates the applicant's ability to key data on a computer terminal at a rate of 35 correct lines within five minutes.

Data Conversion Operators are represented by:

The American Postal Workers Union (APWU), AFL-CIO
1300 L St. NW
Washington, D.C. 20005
202-842-4200
www.apwu.org

# CLEANER, CUSTODIAN, LABORER—CUSTODIAL

## Job Duties

Workers who serve as cleaners, custodians, or custodial laborers are charged with the maintenance of postal buildings. These positions include routine and periodic heavy cleaning, routine maintenance (such as replacing light bulbs), and responsibility for noticing when specialized maintenance or repair work is called for and then following through to be certain that it is done at the proper time.

While the work of custodial laborers, cleaners, and custodians is not generally noticed by the public, it is vital to the operation of post offices and to the health and safety of postal workers and patrons.

### FOR VETERANS ONLY

The positions of cleaner, custodian, and custodial laborer are restricted to applicants eligible for Veterans' preference when hiring externally. Although these positions are at the low end of the USPS pay scale, they afford veterans an opportunity to earn a steady wage and to enjoy all the benefits and security of other postal employees.

The person who starts a career with the Postal Service as a cleaner, custodian, or custodial laborer can advance to positions of greater responsibility within the custodial service. He or she can also prepare for examinations for other positions, either in more specialized jobs within building maintenance or in completely different jobs such as mail handler or letter clerk.

People who already work for the Postal Service in any capacity need not wait for an announcement that a position is open. After a USPS employee has been at his or her present position for a year, the person may ask to take an exam at any time. The request may or may not be granted, but this is one of the advantages that makes the veterans-only feature of these positions worthwhile.

## Qualifications

The cleaner, custodian, laborer—custodial applicant must possess sufficient levels of the following Knowledge, Skills, and Abilities (KSAs):

- Ability to use hand tools, such as power cleaning equipment (waxers, polishers, mowers, and similar equipment)

- Ability to work without immediate supervision

- Ability to handle weights and loads beyond normal functions of a position (for custodian and laborer)

- Ability to perform efficiently the physical duties of the position, including standing, walking, climbing, bending, reaching, and stooping for prolonged periods of time

**NOTE**

A veteran who wants to begin a postal career may start at a low level, but he or she has the opportunity to rise rapidly.

- 20/40 (Snellen) vision in at least one eye and the ability to read, without strain, printed material the size of typewritten characters (corrective lenses are permitted)

Cleaner, Custodian, Laborer–Custodial employees are represented by:

The American Postal Workers Union (APWU), AFL-CIO
1300 L St. NW
Washington, D.C. 20005
202-842-4200
www.apwu.org

# BUILDING EQUIPMENT MECHANIC

## Job Duties

Building equipment mechanics perform a variety of tasks (some highly specialized), including:

- Troubleshooting and performing complex maintenance work on building and building equipment systems

- Performing preventive maintenance inspections of building, building equipment, and building systems

- Maintaining and operating large, automated air conditioning systems and large heating systems

## Working Conditions

Building equipment mechanics for the USPS may be required to work irregular hours. The work involves prolonged standing, walking, climbing, bending, reaching, and stooping. Employees must be able to lift heavy objects on level surfaces, on ladders, and/or on stairways. Applicants for these positions may also be required to qualify on industrial powered lifting equipment.

For building equipment mechanic positions that require driving, applicants must have a valid state driver's license and a safe driving record, and they may be required to pass the USPS road test to demonstrate an ability to safely drive a vehicle of the type used on the job. The position also requires that applicants drive motor vehicles in all kinds of traffic and under varied road conditions.

## Qualifications

Given the nature of the job, applicants are required to have at least a basic understanding of several maintenance-related topics, including:

- Basic mechanics

- Basic electricity

- Basic electronics

- Safety procedures and equipment
- Lubrication materials and procedures
- Cleaning materials and procedures
- National Electrical Code (NEC)
- Refrigeration
- Heating, ventilation, and air conditioning (HVAC)
- Plumbing

In addition, the building equipment mechanic applicant must possess sufficient levels of the following Knowledge, Skills, and Abilities (KSAs):

- Knowledge of basic and complex mathematics
- Ability to apply theoretical knowledge to practical applications
- Ability to detect patterns
- Ability to use written reference materials
- Ability to write and communicate effectively
- Ability to follow instructions
- Ability to work under pressure
- Ability to work with others
- Ability to work without immediate supervision
- Ability to work at heights
- Ability to use hand tools and portable power tools
- Ability to read and understand technical drawings
- Ability to use test equipment
- Ability to solder
- 20/40 (Snellen) vision in at least one eye and the ability to read, without strain, printed material the size of typewritten characters (corrective lenses are permitted)
- Ability to distinguish basic colors and shades
- Ability to hear the conversational voice in a noisy environment and to identify environmental sounds such as equipment running or unusual noises (hearing aids are permitted)

## Testing Requirements

Applicants must pass Exam 931.

In addition, applicants must complete a prescribed training course (for some positions).

Building Equipment Mechanic employees are represented by:

> The American Postal Workers Union (APWU), AFL-CIO
> 1300 L St. NW
> Washington, D.C. 20005
> 202-842-4200
> www.apwu.org

# ELECTRONIC TECHNICIAN

## Job Duties

**NOTE**

Similar to the maintenance position mentioned previously, the electronic technician may be called upon to possess a specific knowledge base.

An electronic technician must independently perform the full range of diagnostic preventive maintenance, alignment, and calibrations, as well as overhaul tasks on both hardware and software on a variety of mail processing, customer service, and building equipment and systems. These workers also apply advanced technical knowledge to solve complex problems. The position requires highly skilled and experienced individuals.

## Working Conditions

Electronic technicians for the USPS may be required to work irregular hours. The work involves prolonged standing, walking, climbing, bending, reaching and stooping. Employees must be able to lift heavy objects on level surfaces, on ladders, and/or on stairways. Applicants for these positions may also be required to qualify on industrial powered lifting equipment. Qualified applicants must successfully pass a pre-employment drug screening.

For electronic technician positions that require driving, applicants must have a valid state driver's license and a safe driving record. These positions also require that applicants drive motor vehicles in all kinds of traffic and under varied road conditions.

## Qualifications

In addition, the electronic technician applicant must possess sufficient levels of the following Knowledge, Skills, and Abilities (KSAs):

- Knowledge of basic mechanics, electricity, electronics, and digital electronics
- Knowledge of safety procedures and equipment
- Knowledge of basic computer concepts
- Knowledge of basic and complex mathematics
- Ability to apply theoretical knowledge to practical applications

- Ability to detect patterns
- Ability to use written reference materials
- Ability to write and communicate effectively
- Ability to follow instructions
- Ability to work under pressure
- Ability to work with others
- Ability to work without immediate supervision
- Ability to work at heights
- Ability to use hand tools and portable power tools
- Ability to use technical drawings
- Ability to use test equipment
- Ability to solder
- 20/40 (Snellen) vision in at least one eye and the ability to read, without strain, printed material the size of typewritten characters (corrective lenses are permitted)
- Ability to distinguish basic colors and shades
- Ability to hear the conversational voice in a noisy environment and to identify environmental sounds such as equipment running or unusual noises (hearing aids are permitted)

## Testing Requirements

Applicants must pass Exam 932. In addition, applicants may be required to complete a prescribed training course at the National Center for Employee Development (NCED) in Norman, Oklahoma.

Electronic Technicians are represented by:

The American Postal Workers Union (APWU), AFL-CIO
1300 L St. NW
Washington, D.C. 20005
202-842-4200
www.apwu.org

# MOTOR VEHICLE OPERATOR, TRACTOR-TRAILER OPERATOR

## Job Duties

What do these jobs have in common? The answer is driving various Postal Service vehicles on highways and within the lots and properties of the Postal Service.

Motor vehicle operators operate a mail truck on a regularly scheduled route to pick up and transport mail in bulk. Tractor-trailer operators operate heavy-duty tractor-trailers in over-the-road service, city shuttle service, or trailer spotting operations.

## Qualifications

Given the specific technical training inherent in these positions (knowing how to handle a large vehicle), you'll need to have one year or more of full-time or equivalent employment driving 7-ton (or larger) trucks or buses of at least 16 passengers. At least six months of that experience must be in driving a tractor-trailer for the position of Tractor-Trailer Operator. In addition, the motor vehicle or tractor-trailer operator applicant must possess sufficient levels of the following Knowledge, Skills, and Abilities (KSAs):

- Knowledge of safety procedures for the duties common to the position

- Ability to drive under varied conditions

- Ability to follow instructions and to prepare trip reports and other reports

- Ability to perform efficiently the physical duties of the position

- 30/30 (Snellen) vision in at least one eye and 20/50 (Snellen) vision in the other eye, with or without corrective lenses; the ability to read, without strain, printed material the size of typewritten characters (corrective lenses are permitted) (for applicants required to drive vehicles 10,000 pounds [CVW] or more)

- Ability to hear the conversational voice in one ear (hearing aids are permitted)

- Emotional and mental stability

**NOTE**

In most instances, an amputation of the leg or foot will not disqualify an applicant, although it may be necessary that this condition be compensated for by use of a suitable prosthesis.

## Testing Requirements

These positions are filled by rated application. Applicants must successfully complete Exam 230 (Motor Vehicle Operator), 240 (Tractor-Trailer Operator), or 238 (Motor Vehicle Operator-Tractor-Trailer Operator), which demonstrates an applicant's ability to understand instructions and fill out forms. Applicants must also pass the Postal Service road test to demonstrate their ability to safely drive a vehicle of the type used on the job.

In addition, applicants:

- Must have a valid state driver's license

- Must demonstrate and maintain a safe driving record

Motor Vehicle Operator employees are represented by:

The American Postal Workers Union (APWU), AFL-CIO
1300 L St. NW
Washington, D.C. 20005
202-842-4200
www.apwu.org

# GARAGEMAN

## Job Duties

The position of garageman requires that the worker perform routine maintenance to keep USPS motor vehicles in working condition.

## Qualifications

The garageman applicant must possess sufficient levels of the following Knowledge, Skills, and Abilities (KSAs):

- Ability to assemble and disassemble mechanical equipment
- Ability to troubleshoot and diagnose more complex malfunctions using computerized test equipment
- Ability to work without immediate supervision
- Ability to work with others
- 20/40 (Snellen) vision in at least one eye and the ability to read, without strain, printed material the size of typewritten characters (corrective lenses are permitted)
- Ability to distinguish basic colors and shades
- Ability to hear the conversational voice (hearing aids are permitted)

## Testing Requirements

This position is filled by rated application. Applicants must pass Automotive Mechanic Exam 943 or 944. They must also pass a bench test for Career Automotive Mechanic or Technician positions.

In addition, applicants:

- Must have a valid state driver's license
- Must have and maintain a safe driving record

Garagemen are represented by:

The American Postal Workers Union (APWU), AFL-CIO
1300 L St. NW
Washington, D.C. 20005
202-842-4200
www.apwu.org

## SUMMING IT UP

- Each USPS job has unique working conditions, qualifications, and testing requirements. Try to match the requirements, working conditions, and required skills with your own interests.

- All USPS positions are competitive, so you may want to apply for two or three positions that interest you, in case your position of choice doesn't open up right away.

# PART II
## FAMILIARIZE YOURSELF WITH THE TESTS

# What You Need to Know

## OVERVIEW

- What's it all about?
- Exam 473
- Exam 460
- Exam 710
- Exams 916, 931, 932, and 933
- Exams 230, 238, and 240
- Finding information on specific exams
- Test-taking instructions
- Filling in answer sheets
- Score determination and reporting
- General test-taking strategies
- Summing it up

## WHAT'S IT ALL ABOUT?

Anxiety before taking a test is normal. You've spent many hours studying and preparing for the exam, and you want to get the best score possible. In addition, you probably think (and rightly so) that this test may be just a bit more important than some of those spelling tests you took in elementary school. This is your career, and you want to prove to yourself and others that you're capable of achieving the highest performance.

Although the postal exams are a bit unusual compared to other tests, there really is no reason for you to be overly nervous. If you've put in the time studying for the exam, if you use common sense, and if you don't panic, you'll be well on your way to achieving a good score.

This chapter is designed to help alleviate some of your pre-test anxiety by introducing you to the formats of the tests. Then, as you study the rest of this book, you'll have plenty of opportunity to practice answering the various question types. By test day, you might still be a bit nervous, but you shouldn't encounter any surprises.

chapter 3

This chapter provides you with an introduction to the most commonly administered postal exams, with a focus on Exams 473/473-C and 460. These two exams are used to fill more than 90 percent of all full-time USPS positions.

# EXAM 473

Exam 473/473-C replaced old Exam 470 in 2004. The exam is called Exam 473 when it is given to fill all entry-level Processing, Distribution, Delivery, and Retail positions. But because the City Carrier position is in highest demand, that test is occasionally given to fill this one job classification. When the test is given just to fill City Carrier positions, it is called Exam 473-C. Regardless of which of these exams you may take, the content is identical. The only difference is the name. As a result, in this book we will refer to Exam 473/473-C simply as Exam 473.

Exam 473 contains traditional topics such as address checking and coding and memory, but it also includes testing for other job-related skills such as:

- Forms completion
- Customer service and interpersonal skills

The following table describes the Exam parts and the subject matter covered, time allotted for each part, and number of questions in each part.

| EXAM PART | TIME ALLOTTED | NUMBER OF QUESTIONS | SUBJECT MATTER |
| --- | --- | --- | --- |
| Part A: Address Checking | 11 Minutes | 60 | Determine whether two addresses are the same. |
| Part B: Forms Completion | 15 Minutes | 30 | Identify information for correctly completing forms. |
| Part C: Section 1—Coding | 6 Minutes | 36 | Identify the correct code to assign for an address. |
| Part C: Section 2—Memory | 7 Minutes | 36 | Memorize codes to be assigned to a range of addresses. |
| Part D: Personal Characteristics and Experience Inventory | 90 Minutes | 236 | Tendencies toward job-related characteristics and experience. |

Don't fall into the trap of thinking that you must possess certain innate talents to get a high score. On the contrary, preparing well for this test will definitely increase your chances of scoring high. The question types are extremely coachable and will seem easier with practice. Use your desire for getting hired as a key motivator throughout the test preparation process.

The remaining chapters of this book and the full-length practice tests will help you become familiar with the various question types you'll see on Exam 473.

Like every Postal Service exam, Exam 473 is opened to the public to meet local staffing needs. Entry-level tests examine general aptitude and/or characteristics, not specific knowledge of facts. USPS employees deliver billions of pieces of mail each day and provide service to millions of customers. Moving this volume of mail quickly and accurately requires certain skills and abilities related to providing such service, including checking addresses and sorting and delivering mail. Exam 473 helps identify individuals who have matching job-related experience, abilities, and personal characteristics.

You must take Exam 473 if you wish to apply for any of the following positions with the Postal Service:

- City Carrier
- Mail Processing Clerk
- Mail Handler
- Sales, Services, and Distribution Associate

## Part A: Address Checking

Part A of Exam 473 includes 60 questions, which must be completed in 11 minutes. This section tests your ability to compare the content of two lists quickly and accurately. You will see a correct list of addresses and ZIP Codes, and a list that must be checked against the correct list. The list you need to check is supposed to be exactly the same as the correct list, but it contains errors that you must find.

You will be asked to compare the information in each row of the list to be checked against the correct list and decide whether the former contains errors. Your choices will be to decide whether:

- no errors are present
- there is an error in the address only
- there is an error in the ZIP Code only
- there are errors in both the address and ZIP Code

Each row of information is considered one item (or question). This section requires that you work quickly and accurately.

### SCORING

The partial score for this section of Exam 473 is based on the number of items that you answer correctly, minus one third of the number of items that you answer incorrectly. The score depends on how many items in the lists you accurately compare in the 11 minutes allowed. You may not be able to finish all of the items before time runs out, but do your best to complete as many as you can, remembering to be as accurate as possible.

In the scoring for Part A, you'll be penalized for guessing wrong, so be sure not to guess randomly. However, if you can eliminate one or more responses as obviously incorrect, it may be a good idea to make an educated guess from among the remaining responses.

## AVOIDING MISTAKES

Here are a few tips to help you avoid making mistakes on this part of the exam:

- **Work quickly but accurately.** You're not expected to answer all the questions in the allotted 11 minutes, but try to answer as many as possible.

- **Mark your place.** Because you're working quickly to answer questions, it may be easy to lose your place. Be sure to figure out a way to mark your place as you work so that this doesn't happen.

- **Focus on the question at hand.** Try not to let your eyes wander. From time to time, check to see that you are working on the same item that you are marking on your answer sheet.

## Part B: Forms Completion

Part B is made up of 30 questions that you must complete in 15 minutes. This section tests your ability to identify the information required to complete forms that are similar to those used by the Postal Service. On the exam, you'll see several forms, along with several items about what information is required to complete each one. Each part of the form will be labeled.

## SCORING

Your score for Part B is based on the number of items that you answer correctly. There is no penalty for wrong answers, so it's a good idea to answer every question possible, even if you have to guess.

## AVOIDING MISTAKES

Follow these tips to help you avoid making mistakes on this part of the exam:

- **Study each form carefully**. Every form is different and requires different pieces of information. Examine the forms carefully before you respond, so you're sure that you know what information is requested.

- **Answer easier questions first.** If you're not sure of an answer, consider returning to it later if time permits. You won't be penalized for incorrect answers in this section, so if you can make an educated guess, do so. But be absolutely sure that you're marking the correct answer on your answer sheet—when you're skipping ahead, it's easy to lose your place and mark the wrong circle.

## Part C: Coding and Memory

Part C consists of two sections: Coding, which includes 36 items to be completed in 6 minutes; and Memory, which includes 36 items to be completed in 7 minutes. Part C assesses your ability to use codes quickly and accurately, both with a coding guide and from memory.

On the exam, you'll see a coding guide and several items for which you must assign proper codes. You are to look up the correct code for each item and record your response on the answer sheet accurately and quickly. During the first section of Part C, you'll be permitted to look at the coding guide while assigning codes. During the second section, however, you must assign codes based on your memory of the same coding guide. While the coding guide is visible (in the first section), try to memorize as many of the codes as you can, because these same codes will be used in the Memory section.

During the actual test, you are NOT permitted to look at the codes when answering the items in the Memory section, and you may NOT write down any addresses during the Coding period.

### SCORING

Your score for Part C is based on the number of items you answer correctly, minus one-third of the number of items you answer incorrectly. In both sections of this test part, your score depends on how many items you can accurately code in the time allowed. You may not have time to assign a code to all of the items in the time allotted, but do your best to answer as many items as you can, as accurately as you can.

Because you're penalized for wrong answers in this section, avoid guessing randomly. However, if you can make an educated guess by eliminating obviously wrong answers, do so.

### AVOIDING MISTAKES

In the actual Exam 473, you have several opportunities to work with the coding guide and to practice memorizing the codes for each range of addresses before you answer questions based on your memory. Here are a few tips to help you reduce errors on Part C of Exam 473:

- **Answer easiest questions first.** If you're not sure of an answer, plan to return to it later if time permits. If you do return to an item, be sure that you're marking the correct answer on your answer sheet. It is easy to lose your place and mark the wrong circle.

- **Avoid random guessing.** If you can eliminate one or more answer choices, however, it may be to your advantage to guess.

- **Work as quickly and accurately as possible.** You're not expected to answer all items in the time allotted, but try to answer as many as possible.

## Part D: Personal Characteristics and Experience Inventory

Part D of Exam 473 consists of 236 test items to be completed in 90 minutes. This part is divided into three sections. One section includes items with four response choices ranging from "Strongly agree" to "Strongly disagree." A second section includes items with four response choices ranging from "Very often" to "Rarely or never." The third section includes items that have four to nine response choices. The items in Part D are designed to assess personal characteristics, tendencies, or experiences related to being an effective employee of the Postal Service.

Read each item carefully and decide which of the response choices is most true about you. For some items, more than one response may describe you, but be sure to mark only one response for each item. Answer every question, even if you're not completely certain which response is most true about you—but try to work as quickly as you can without making mistakes.

Whenever possible, base your answer choices on what you have done, felt, or believed in a work setting. If you cannot relate the item to your own work experiences, base your response on experiences that may have been similar to those of work, such as school or volunteer activities.

### SCORING

Part D is different from the other sections of Exam 473 because it calls for honest responses from you about your own experiences. Your score is based on these responses. Do not try to guess the "correct" response; if you are dishonest or offer distorted descriptions of yourself, you may score poorly. All of your responses are considered in the score for this section.

### AVOIDING MISTAKES

Follow these tips to help you reduce errors in this section of Exam 473:

- **Read each statement carefully before marking your responses.**
- **Don't "practice" your responses.** There's no advantage to having pre-set responses to the questions in this section. Instead, read each statement carefully and respond honestly based on your personal experiences or preferences.

# EXAM 460

You must take Exam 460 if you wish to apply for a position as a Rural Carrier with the USPS. Most Postal Service opportunities involve sorting and delivering mail. Rural Carrier employees sort mail into delivery sequence for an assigned route and deliver mail along a prescribed rural route by vehicle, but they also provide customers with a variety of postal-related services.

The following table describes the Exam parts and the subject matter covered, time allotted for each part, and number of questions in each part.

| EXAM PART | TIME ALLOTTED | NUMBER OF QUESTIONS | SUBJECT MATTER |
| --- | --- | --- | --- |
| Section A: Address Checking | 6 minutes | 95 | Determine whether two addresses are the same. |
| Section B: Memory for Addresses | 5 minutes | 88 | Memorize locations of addresses. |
| Section C: Number Series | 20 minutes | 24 | Identify next two numbers in an incomplete number series. |
| Section D: Following Oral Directions | 25 minutes | N/A | Follow directions by writing in test book and then on the answer sheet. |

## Section A: Address Checking

This section of Exam 460 is similar to Part A of Exam 473. It consists of 95 questions to be completed in 6 minutes. For each question, you are to determine whether two addresses are:

- exactly alike
- different in any way

If they are exactly alike, darken circle (A); if they are different in any way, darken circle (D). There are no (B) or (C) circles. It's important to work quickly and accurately in this section.

### SCORING

Section A is scored by subtracting the number of wrong answers from the number of correct answers. Because you are penalized for incorrect responses, it's a good idea NOT to guess randomly.

### AVOIDING MISTAKES

Follow these tips to help you avoid mistakes in this section of Exam 460:

- **Work as quickly and accurately as possible.** You're not expected to answer all items in the time allotted, but try to answer as many as possible.
- **Mark your place.** Because you're working quickly to answer questions, it may be easy to lose your place. Be sure to figure out a way to mark your place as you work, so that this doesn't happen.
- **Focus on the question at hand.** Try not to let your eyes wander. From time to time, check to see that you are working on the same item that you are marking on your answer sheet.
- **Avoid random guessing.** You are penalized for wrong answers, so it's in your best interest not to guess.

- **Avoid making stray marks on the answer sheet.** The exam is scored by machine, and any stray marks may be read as incorrect responses.

## Section B: Memory for Addresses

Section B of Exam 460 includes 88 questions to be completed in 5 minutes. You must memorize the locations of addresses from a set of 5 boxes labeled A, B, C, D, and E, each of which contains five addresses.

You have three opportunities in this section to memorize the location of the addresses in the boxes. Then you must complete questions about the locations of these addresses. For each address, you must determine which box it came from. You don't need to know where in the box the address was; only which box it is in.

During the actual test, you are NOT permitted to refer to the boxes when answering the questions, and you may NOT write down any addresses during the memorization period.

### SCORING

Section B is scored by taking the number of right answers and subtracting one-quarter point for each wrong answer.

### AVOIDING MISTAKES

In the actual 460 exam, you have several opportunities to practice memorizing the location of each address before you answer questions based on your memory. Here are a few tips to help you reduce errors on Section B of Exam 460:

- **Answer easiest questions first.** If you're not sure of an answer, plan to return to it later if time permits. Remember, though: You have only 5 minutes to complete your questions. If you do return to an item, be sure that you're marking the correct answer on your answer sheet. It is easy to lose your place and mark the wrong circle.

- **Avoid random guessing.** You are penalized for wrong answers, so it's in your best interest not to guess.

- **Work as quickly and accurately as possible.** You're not expected to answer all items in the time allotted, but try to answer as many as possible.

## Section C: Number Series

This section of Exam 460 includes 24 questions to be completed in 20 minutes. You are permitted to mark your test book for this section.

For each question, you identify the next two missing numbers in an incomplete number series. As you work, try to identify a pattern in the number series. Keep trying different combinations until you see a pattern, and then answer the question based on that pattern.

Some are more difficult than others, so try not to become frustrated and remain relaxed and focused.

## SCORING

Section C is scored based on the number of questions you answer correctly. Because there is no penalty for wrong answers, try to answer every question, even if you have to guess.

## AVOIDING MISTAKES

Here are a few tips to help you reduce errors on Section C of Exam 460:

- **Look for repeated numbers and alternating series first.** If you don't recognize a pattern quickly in a number series, try different ways of approaching the problem. For example, you may want to try sounding it out (silently) or making notes on the test guide. Keep focused and relaxed.

- **Answer easiest questions first.** If you're not sure of an answer, plan to return to it later if time permits. If you do return to an item, be sure that you're marking the correct answer on your answer sheet. It is easy to lose your place and mark the wrong circle.

- **Feel free to guess.** You won't be penalized for wrong answers, so try to answer every question in this section—but don't spend too much time on any one question.

## Section D: Following Oral Directions

This section of Exam 460 is designed to assess how well you listen to and follow directions. The examiner reads instructions to you only once; he or she will not repeat them. You must then follow directions according to the instructions the examiner reads or gives you. After each set of instructions, you will be given time to mark your test book and record your answers on the answer sheet.

## SCORING

The score for this section of the exam is based on the number of questions you answer correctly in the time allotted (25 minutes).

## AVOIDING MISTAKES

Here are a few tips to help you reduce errors on Section D of Exam 460:

- **Be sure you have no more than one space darkened for each answer.** If more than one space is darkened, the answer will be counted as incorrect.

- **Feel free to guess.** Because you aren't penalized for wrong answers, answer every question in this section, even if you have to guess.

## EXAM 710

You must take Exam 710 if you wish to apply for a Data Conversion Operator position with the Postal Service. This position is a temporary data entry job that may lead to full-time work.

Data Conversion Operators use a computer terminal to prepare mail for automated sorting equipment. They read typed or handwritten addresses from an envelope image on the terminal screen, and then select and type essential information so that an address bar code can be applied to the envelope.

The Postal Service has several facilities where Data Conversion Operators work. Usually these facilities are staffed by a greater number of temporary employees than full-time employees. As full-time positions become available, they are offered to temporary workers who scored highest on Exam 710. Promotions to higher positions are also based on Exam 710 scores.

Exam 710 consists of two sections: Clerical Abilities and Verbal Abilities. These sections are divided into smaller parts.

### Clerical Abilities

The first half of Exam 710 consists of four timed sections:

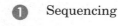 Sequencing

**2** Comparison

**3** Spelling

**4** Mathematics

#### SEQUENCING

This subsection of Exam 710 includes 20 questions to be completed in 3 minutes. Each question in this section consists of a list of four names or codes arranged alphabetically or in numeric order. Some codes are made up of numbers and letters; others are only numbers. You are provided with a fifth name or code and instructed to determine where in the list this fits numerically or alphabetically. Speed and accuracy are very important.

#### COMPARISON

This subsection includes 30 questions to be completed in 5 minutes. Each question consists of a list of three names, addresses, or codes that are exactly alike or are similar. You must compare the three names, addresses, or codes in each question and determine whether:

- they are exactly alike

- only the first and second items are exactly alike

- only the first and third items are exactly alike

- only the second and third items exactly alike
- all three items are different

As with the Sequencing subsection, you're not expected to answer all the questions in the allotted time, but you should try to answer as many as possible as accurately as you can.

## SPELLING

This subsection includes 20 questions to be completed in 3 minutes. Each question provides three answer choices as possible ways to spell a word. You must select the answer choice—(A), (B), or (C)—in which the word is spelled correctly, or choose (D) if none of the other choices are spelled correctly.

## MATHEMATICS

This subsection includes 15 questions to be completed in 8 minutes. Each question consists of a math problem you must solve, working with whole numbers, decimals, fractions, and percentages. You are not permitted to have or use a calculator.

## Verbal Abilities

The second half of Exam 710 includes 55 questions to be completed in 50 minutes. This section assesses your ability to understand and carry out instructions, as you would on the job. The 55 questions are divided into three sections:

1. Following Written Instructions
2. Grammar, Usage, and Punctuation
3. Vocabulary and Reading Comprehension

## FOLLOWING WRITTEN INSTRUCTIONS

In this subsection, you are instructed to create an answer code consisting of a letter and number. You then find this code on the table provided, and find the answer choice it matches—(A), (B), (C), (D), or (E)—and darken the appropriate circle on the answer sheet.

## GRAMMAR, USAGE, AND PUNCTUATION

This subsection consists of 20 (of the total 55) questions. Each item consists of four similar sentences. You must choose the one that is most correct in terms of grammar, word usage, and punctuation.

## VOCABULARY AND READING COMPREHENSION

As the name suggests, this subsection of Exam 710 assesses your knowledge of vocabulary and your reading comprehension skills. For the vocabulary questions, you are presented with a sentence in which one word is highlighted. For each question, you must choose from four answer choices the one that most nearly matches the definition of the highlighted word.

For the reading comprehension questions, you must first read a paragraph of text and then four sentences related to that text. You must choose the sentence that best summarizes or supports the theme of the paragraph.

## EXAMS 916, 931, 932, AND 933

These four Postal Service exams are administered to fill custodial and maintenance positions.

### Exam 916

Exam 916 is administered for Custodian and Laborer–Custodial positions. Custodian duties include manual cleaning and buildings and grounds maintenance. Laborer–Custodial duties include manual labor in connection with maintaining and cleaning USPS buildings and grounds. The test consists of four sections:

**NOTE**

Exam 916 was suspended until September 30, 2008, for all purposes. At press time, there was no word on whether the exam would be reinstated or waived completely. If you are interested in a custodial position with the Postal Service, be sure to check on whether you will need to take this exam.

1 **Vocabulary and Reading:** assesses your ability to read and understand written materials as used in product labels, instructions and warnings, material safety data sheets, equipment operating instructions, and cleaning route sheets.

2 **Basic Safety:** assesses your knowledge of basic safety principles and practices, including proper lifting techniques, using personal protective equipment, and awareness of electrical, chemical, and other health hazards in cleaning and building maintenance.

3 **General Cleaning:** assesses your knowledge of general cleaning and disinfecting resources as well as techniques, equipment, and tools commonly used by custodial workers.

4 **Following Written Instructions:** assesses how well you understand and carry out instructions similar to those you will encounter on the job.

### Exam 931

Exam 931 is administered for positions related to building maintenance and building equipment maintenance. These include building equipment mechanic, maintenance mechanic, building maintenance custodian, carpenter, painter, and plumber. Such positions require highly skilled and experienced individuals. The Postal Service provides on-the-job and on-site training for these employees, as well as continuous training at the National Center for Employee Development (NCED) in Norman, Oklahoma.

This exam consists of two sections:

1 **Following Oral Instructions:** assesses how well you understand and carry out oral instructions similar to those you will encounter on the job.

**2** **Knowledge, Skills, and Abilities**: tests your knowledge, skills, and abilities related to the position you're seeking. These include knowledge of basic mechanics; basic electricity and electronics; safety procedures and equipment; refrigeration; and heating, ventilation, and air conditioning (HVAC) equipment operation. You are also tested on your ability to perform basic and more complex math computations, apply theoretical knowledge to practice, detect patterns, use written reference materials and follow instructions, read and comprehend technical drawings (such as diagrams, schematics, flow charts, and blueprints), use hand tools proficiently, use test equipment properly, and solder.

## Exam 932

Exam 932 is administered for Electronic Technician positions. Employees must perform a full range of diagnostic, preventive maintenance, alignment and calibration, and overhaul tasks. These tasks are performed on hardware and software on a variety of mail processing, customer service, and building equipment and systems.

Electronic Technicians must apply advanced technical knowledge to solve complex problems. As with building and equipment maintenance positions, these jobs require highly skilled and experienced individuals. The Postal Service provides on-the-job and on-site training for these employees, as well as continuous training at the National Center for Employee Development (NCED) in Norman, Oklahoma.

This exam consists of two sections:

**1** **Following Oral Instructions:** assesses how well you understand and carry out oral instructions similar to those you will encounter on the job.

**2** **Knowledge, Skills, and Abilities**: tests your knowledge, skills, and abilities related to the position you're seeking. These include knowledge of basic mechanics, basic electricity and electronics, digital electronics, safety procedures and equipment, and basic computer concepts. You are also tested on your ability to perform basic and more complex math computations, apply theoretical knowledge to practice, detect patterns, and use written reference materials and follow instructions. You will be assessed for your proficiency with hand tools, your ability to read and comprehend technical drawings (such as diagrams, schematics, flow charts, and blueprints), your ability to use test equipment properly, and your ability to solder.

### Exam 933

Exam 933 is administered for full-time Mail Processing Equipment Mechanic positions. Employees must perform semiskilled preventive, corrective, and predictive maintenance tasks. These tasks are associated with the upkeep and operation of various types of mail processing equipment, buildings and their equipment, and customer service and delivery equipment.

The Postal Service provides on-the-job and on-site training for these employees, as well as continuous training at the National Center for Employee Development (NCED) in Norman, Oklahoma.

This exam consists of two sections:

**1** **Following Oral Instructions:** assesses how well you understand and carry out oral instructions similar to those you will encounter on the job.

**2** **Knowledge, Skills, and Abilities**: tests your knowledge, skills, and abilities related to the position you're seeking. These include knowledge of basic mechanics, basic electricity and electronics, safety procedures and equipment, and lubrication materials and procedures. You are also tested on your ability to perform basic and more complex math computations, apply theoretical knowledge to practice, detect patterns, and use written reference materials and follow instructions. You will be assessed for your proficiency with hand tools and portable power tools, your ability to read and comprehend technical drawings (such as diagrams, schematics, flow charts, and blueprints), your ability to use test equipment properly, and your ability to solder.

## EXAMS 230, 238, AND 240

These Postal Service exams are administered to fill motor vehicle and tractor-trailer operator positions. Exam 230 is the Motor Vehicle Operator (MVO) exam; Exam 238 is the MVO/Tractor-Trailer Operator (TTO) exam; and Exam 240 is the TTO exam. These tests replace the former Exam 91.

Applicants for MVO or TTO employment opportunities with the Postal Service must complete an assessment questionnaire online or by phone to be considered for any of these positions. You have a choice of the following two methods for completing the questionnaire:

**1**     Online via the Web: Go to www.usps.com/employment.

**2**     Interactive voice response system: Call 1–866-999-8777 (TTY 1–800-800-8776) and follow the prompts. (You must have an announcement number to apply by phone.)

The questionnaire requires specific information about your driving history and safety record. Before you go online or call, you can print out an assessment worksheet to help you complete the questionnaire. Use PS Form 5999, Motor Vehicle Operator and Tractor-Trailer Operator

Assessment Worksheet, dated July 2004, available on the USPS Web site at http://www.usps.com/forms/_pdf/ps5999.pdf.

You must receive a passing score of 70 on the assessment to be considered for employment. If the Postal Service determines that you are eligible, you will be contacted to continue the process for employment.

## FINDING INFORMATION ON SPECIFIC EXAMS

Test dates for all Postal Service exams are publicized widely. Here are some sources of information:

- The Postal Service Internet home page: www.usps.com/employment
- Public bulletin boards in post offices
- Local, federal, and state municipal buildings
- State employment offices
- Local television, newspaper, and radio advertisements
- Community groups, including minority, women's, and veterans' organizations

### Arranging to Take Your Exam

During the opening period indicated on the exam announcement, schedule yourself to take the exam by accessing the job posting on www.usps.com/employment or by calling the toll-free phone number provided. The Internet and phone system prompt you through the application process. The prompt will request the announcement number of the job in which you're interested and will ask for other required application information.

At least one week before the exam date, the USPS will mail you a scheduling package that indicates when and where you report for your exam. The package will also include applicant instructions and sample questions.

## TEST-TAKING INSTRUCTIONS

Do not underestimate the importance of following all the rules and procedures required at the test center. This includes following all of the examiner's test-taking instructions and filling in the answer sheets correctly.

Instructions read by the examiner are intended to ensure that neither you nor any other applicant has an unfair advantage when taking the exam. Any infraction of the rules is considered cheating.

- Listen to what the examiner says at all times. Be prepared to immediately act on any changes to content, question type, directions, or time limits.

**ALERT!**

If you cheat, your test paper will not be scored and you will not be eligible for appointment.

- Follow all the instructions the examiner gives you. If you do not understand something, ask for clarification.

- Don't begin working on any part of the test until told to do so.

- Stop working as soon as the examiner tells you to do so. Remember that your ability to follow instructions is considered in the hiring process.

- If you finish a test part before time is called, review your work for that test part. Although you cannot go ahead or back to any other part of the test, you do have the chance to review answers that you are unsure of, or to guess answers, if guessing is a good strategy for that test part. Use whatever extra time you have wisely.

- Don't work on any part of the test other than the one you are told to work on. Be certain to check that you're working on the right test part. While working in the wrong section could be an inadvertent error on your part, it would not leave a favorable impression and probably would put you out of the running for the position you seek.

## FILLING IN ANSWER SHEETS

To be admitted to the test center you will be required to provide personal information on the sample answer sheet that is sent to you by the Postal Service. You cannot take the test without doing this. You will be instructed to transfer the personal information you filled in on the sample answer sheet to the actual answer sheet.

### How to Enter Your Answer

Most exams are machine-scored, so be careful to fill in your answer sheets clearly and accurately. You will be given instructions in the test kit the Postal Service sends you before exam day. You will also be given ample opportunity to perfect your skills in the practice material in this book.

**TIP**

As you answer each question check that you are marking your answer in the space with the correct number.

## SCORE DETERMINATION AND REPORTING

When the exam is over, the examiner will collect your test booklet and answer sheet. Your answer sheet will be sent to the National Test Administration Center in Merrifield, Virginia, where a machine will scan your answers and mark them as either right or wrong.

### Reporting Scaled Scores

Your raw score is not your final score. Here's how scoring works:

- The Postal Service determines your raw scores for each test part.

- Your part scores are combined according to a certain formula.

- Your raw score is converted to a scaled score, on a scale of 1 to 100.

The entire process of conversion from raw to scaled score is confidential.

A total scaled score of 70 is a passing score. The names of all persons who score 70 or higher are placed on an eligibility list (called the register) that remains valid for two years. The register is ordered according to score rankings—the people with the highest scores are at the top of the list. Positions are filled from the top of the list as vacancies occur. Many candidates prepare rigorously for this test and strive for perfect scores. In fact, most applicants who are hired score between 90 percent and 100 percent.

## How Did I Do?

The scoring process may take six to ten weeks or longer. Be patient. The entire process could take many months, but you remain eligible for employment for two years after taking the test. If you pass the exam, you will receive notice of your scaled score. As your name rises on the list, you will be notified to appear for the remaining steps of the hiring process, which may include:

- Drug testing
- Psychological interview
- Physical performance tests, according to the requirements of the position
- Alphanumeric typing test

If you fail the exam, you will not be informed of your score. You will simply be notified that you have failed and will not be considered for postal employment. Of course, your score may vary with each exam administration. Use this number as a reality check for setting a serious study schedule. Don't let a failure shake your confidence. Your preparation will give you better odds of getting a higher score than many other candidates.

# GENERAL TEST-TAKING STRATEGIES

## Learn the Directions for Each Question Type

Don't waste time reading directions during the actual test. You will be given the instructions by the Postal Service in your exam kit; learn them inside and out. This book also provides the most recent directions used on the exams. Remember, though, to listen to the examiner in case something has changed.

## Skip Questions When Stumped

When you cannot answer a question, skip the question and return to it after finishing the other questions in that part of the test. Circle the number of the question in your test booklet to remind yourself to return—and remember to skip the appropriate space on your answer sheet. In a later section, we'll discuss when it's safe to guess.

**NOTE**

A total scaled score of 70 is considered passing, but it will probably not get you hired. Aim to score at least 90.

**TIP**

Use the practice tests in this book to get used to the quick pace of the tests and the stringent time limitations for each test part. Adhere to these time limitations without exception.

### Avoid Perfectionism

You are not expected to answer every question. Don't be a perfectionist and waste time on questions you cannot answer. This kind of attitude limits the number of questions you attempt to answer, which will lower your score. Come back to the difficult questions if you have time to spare.

When practicing, use a stopwatch or a kitchen timer for accurate measurement; this will give you a sense of your optimal pace.

### Know How Much Time You Have

To do well on any of the postal exams, you must work quickly within the time limits allowed. The examiner will inform you at periodic intervals of how much time you have left. Check your wristwatch as a backup, but don't become obsessed by the clock. Your time is better spent answering the questions. This means practicing for the test as much as possible, knowing what to expect, and following the strategies provided in this book.

### Develop a Test-Smart Attitude

By practicing as much as you can for your exam, you will gain confidence, which in turn will help you succeed on the actual test. Developing a test-smart attitude also will help boost your competitive spirit—an essential factor in scoring well on these highly competitive examinations.

### Use the Test Booklet as Scratch Paper

You may find it beneficial to make notes or draw lines or arrows in the test booklet to help solve certain test questions. This can help you organize your thoughts. However, don't spend too much time doing this. If it doesn't help you, just go on to the next question.

### Eliminate Obviously Incorrect Answers

This common test-taking strategy is useful to different degrees on each test part except Part A, which has only two answer choices. Read all the answer choices and try to eliminate obviously incorrect answers before you choose the correct answer. This improves your chances for recognizing the correct answer.

**NOTE**

Although you must keep a steady pace, do not rush through a section and answer questions carelessly. You must be in control to do your best.

# SUMMING IT UP

- The Postal Service exams are somewhat unusual compared with the types of tests you're accustomed to, but familiarizing yourself with the sorts of questions and exercises you'll encounter will help you stay relaxed and focused on exam day.

- Postal Service exams are designed to evaluate knowledge, skills, and abilities related to the jobs for which you're applying. You need not possess specific innate talents to score high.

- Exam 473/473-C is the most commonly administered Postal Service exam. Along with Exam 460, it is used to fill more than 90 percent of all full-time USPS positions.

- Exam 473 is used to test applicants for City Carrier; Mail Processing Clerk; Mail Handler; and Sales, Services, and Distribution Associate positions. Exam 460 tests applicants for Rural Carrier positions.

- Exam 710 is used to test applicants for Data Conversion Operator positions. These are temporary positions with the Postal Service that may lead to full-time work.

- Exams 916, 931, 932, and 933 are administered to fill custodial and maintenance positions with the Postal Service.

- Exams 230, 238, and 240 are administered to fill Motor Vehicle Operator and Tractor-Trailer Operator positions with the Postal Service. Applicants for MVO or TTO employment opportunities with the Postal Service must complete an assessment questionnaire online or by phone to be considered for any of these positions. If the Postal Service determines that an applicant is eligible, he or she is then contacted to continue the process for employment, which includes an exam.

- You can find more information on openings with the Postal Service by checking the USPS Web page; checking the public bulletin board at your local post office; visiting local, federal, and municipal offices in your area; contacting your state employment office; watching for local TV, newspaper, and radio announcements; or visiting local community centers.

- On exam day, be sure to follow all the rules and procedures required at the test center. Listen carefully to the examiner's instructions and fill in all answer sheets completely and accurately.

- The exam scoring process may take several months. However, remember that you remain eligible for employment for two years after taking the test. If you pass the exam, you'll receive notification of your score. Once your name rises to the top of the list of candidates, you will be contacted with information on the remaining steps of the hiring process.

# Strategies for Address-Checking Questions

## OVERVIEW

- **Tips and techniques**
- **Summing it up**

## TIPS AND TECHNIQUES

Although everyone responds differently to taking tests, you can use the following tips and guidelines to assist you in answering address-checking questions.

- **Read for differences only.** Once you spot a difference between the two given addresses, mark your answer sheet with a "D" and go immediately to the next question.

- **Vocalize your reading.** This doesn't mean reading out loud, but reading exactly what is listed. For example, if you see "St.," don't read it as "Street" but as "ess–t." This will help you to focus on the exact details.

- **Know your state and territory abbreviations.** You should be familiar with conventional abbreviations as well as the two-letter capitalized abbreviations used with ZIP Codes.

- **Use your hands.** Don't be afraid to use your index finger under or alongside the addresses you're comparing. This will help you to keep your place and focus on just one line at a time.

- **Take the question apart.** Try to break the addresses into parts: For example, first compare the street name, then the ZIP Code, and so on for each of the two items to be compared. This will help to make the comparison more manageable.

- **Read from right to left.** This can be very difficult for people who read left to right in their native language. However, you might be surprised at how well this forces your brain to focus on the details instead of on extraneous information.

- **Play the numbers game.** You can expect to find many differences in numbers, so keep a close eye on this when you are making your comparison. Questions with two items that are not alike will often differ in the number of digits as well as in the order of digits.

- **Watch for differences in abbreviations.** As with differences in numbers, you'll find that it's very easy to misread these, especially when comparing two items.

TIP

Remember, you aren't expected to answer all the questions in the time given. Just try to work as quickly and as accurately as possible, and avoid guessing if you start to run out of time.

## Vocalizing

Sound out the following abbreviations and numbers:

NY (example: "en–why")

CA

OR

VA

AL

HA

MT

MA

IL

TX

68919

10001

3694

Ct

Pkwy

Cir

## Sample Questions

**Directions:** Use your index finger to compare the following addresses. Are they alike or different? For each question, compare the address in the left column with the address in the right column. If the two addresses are **ALIKE** in every way, write "A" next to the question number. If the two addresses are **DIFFERENT** in any way, write "D" next to the question number.

| | |
|---|---|
| **1.** 5115 Colchester Rd | 5115 Calchester Rd |
| **2.** 4611 N Randall Pl | 4611 N Randall Pl |
| **3.** 17045 Pascack Cir | 17045 Pascack Cir |
| **4.** 3349 Palma del Mar Blvd | 3346 Palma del Mar Blvd |
| **5.** 13211 E 182nd Ave | 13211 E 182nd Ave |
| **6.** Francisco WY 82636 | Francisco WI 82636 |
| **7.** 6198 N Albritton Rd | 6198 N Albretton Rd |
| **8.** 11230 Twinflower Cir | 11230 Twintower Cir |
| **9.** 6191 MacDonald Station Rd | 6191 MacDonald Station Rd |
| **10.** 1587 Vanderbilt Dr N | 1587 Vanderbilt Dr S |

## Answer Key

| | | | | |
|---|---|---|---|---|
| 1. D | 3. A | 5. A | 7. D | 9. A |
| 2. A | 4. D | 6. D | 8. D | 10. D |

## Sample Questions

**Directions:** Break the following addresses into parts. Are they alike or different? For each question, compare the address in the left column with the address in the right column. If the two addresses are **ALIKE** in every way, write "A" next to the question number. If the two addresses are **DIFFERENT** in any way, write "D" next to the question number.

| | | |
|---|---|---|
| **1.** 3993 S Freemont Ter | | 3993 S Freemount Ter |
| **2.** 3654 S Urbane Dr | | 3564 S Urbane Cir |
| **3.** 1408 Oklahoma Ave NE | | 1408 Oklahoma Ave NE |
| **4.** 6201 Meadowland Ln | | 6201 Meadowlawn Ln |
| **5.** 5799 S Rockaway Ln | | 15799 S Rockaway Ln |
| **6.** 3782 SE Verrazanno Bay | | 37872 SE Verrazanno Bay |
| **7.** 2766 N Thunderbird Ct | | 2766 N Thunderbird Ct |
| **8.** 2166 N Elmmorado Ct | | 2166 N Eldorado Ct |
| **9.** 10538 Innsbruck Ln | | 10538 Innsbruck Ln |
| **10.** 888 Powerville Rd | | 883 Powerville Rd |

## Answer Key

| 1. D | 3. A | 5. D | 7. A | 9. A |
|---|---|---|---|---|
| 2. D | 4. D | 6. D | 8. D | 10. D |

## Sample Questions

**Directions:** Reading from right to left, compare the following addresses. Are they alike or different? For each question, compare the address in the left column with the address in the right column. If the two addresses are **ALIKE** in every way, write "A" next to the question number. If the two addresses are **DIFFERENT** in any way, write "D" next to the question number.

| | | |
|---|---|---|
| **1.** 4202 N Bainbridge Rd | | 4202 N Bainbridge Rd |
| **2.** 300 E Roberta Ave | | 3000 E Roberta Ave |
| **3.** Quenemo KS 66528 | | Quenemo KS 66528 |
| **4.** 13845 Donahoo St | | 13345 Donahoo St |
| **5.** 10466 Gertrude NE | | 10466 Gertrude NE |
| **6.** 2733 N 105th Ave | | 2773 N 105th Ave |
| **7.** 3100 N Wyandotte Cir | | 3100 N Wyandottte Ave |
| **8.** 11796 Summerville Dr | | 11769 Summerville Dr |
| **9.** Wilburnum Miss 65566 | | Vilburnum Miss 65566 |
| **10.** 9334 Kindleberger Rd | | 9334 Kindleberger Rd |

## Answer Key

| | | | | |
|---|---|---|---|---|
| 1. A | 3. A | 5. A | 7. D | 9. D |
| 2. D | 4. D | 6. D | 8. D | 10. A |

## Sample Questions

**Directions:** Answer "A" if the two numbers are exactly **ALIKE** and "D" if the two numbers are **DIFFERENT** in any way.

1. 2003                          2003
2. 75864                         75864
3. 7300                          730
4. 50105                         5016
5. 2184                          2184
6. 8789                          8789
7. 36001                         3601
8. 1112                          1112
9. 89900                         8990
10. 07035                        07035

## Answer Key

| 1. A | 3. D | 5. A | 7. D | 9. D |
| 2. A | 4. D | 6. A | 8. A | 10. A |

## EXERCISE

**Directions:** For each question, compare the address in the left column with the address in the right column. If the two addresses are **ALIKE** in every way, write "A" next to the question number. If the two addresses are **DIFFERENT** in any way, write "D" next to the question number.

1. 8690 W 134th St                8960 W 134th St

2. 1912 Berkshire Rd              1912 Berkshire Wy

3. 5331 W Professor St            5331 W Proffesor St

4. Philadelphia PA 19124          Philadelphia PN 19124

5. 7450 Gaguenay St               7450 Saguenay St

6. 8650 Christy St                8650 Christey St

7. Lumberville PA 18933           Lumberville PA 1998333

8. 114 Alabama Ave NW             114 Alabama Av NW

9. 1756 Waterford St              1756 Waterville St

10. 2214 Wister Wy                2214 Wister Wy

11. 2974 Repplier Rd              2974 Repplier Dr

12. Essex CT 06426                Essex CT 06426

13. 7676 N Bourbon St             7616 N Bourbon St

14. 2762 Rosengarten Wy           2762 Rosengarden Wy

15. 239 Windell Ave               239 Windell Ave

16. 4667 Edgeworth Rd             4677 Edgeworth Rd

17. 2661 Kennel St Se             2661 Kennel St Sw

18. Alamo TX 78516                Alamo TX 78516

19. 3709 Columbine St             3709 Columbine St

20. 9699 W 14th St                9699 W 14th Rd

21. 2207 Markland Ave             2207 Markham Ave

| | | |
|---|---|---|
| **22.** | Los Angeles CA 90013 | Los Angeles CA 90018 |
| **23.** | 4608 N Warnock St | 4806 N Warnock St |
| **24.** | 7718 S Summer St | 7718 S Sumner St |
| **25.** | New York NY 10016 | New York NY 10016 |
| **26.** | 4514 Ft Hamilton Pk | 4514 Ft Hamilton Pk |
| **27.** | 5701 Kosciusko St | 5701 Koscusko St |
| **28.** | 5422 Evergreen St | 4522 Evergreen St |
| **29.** | Gainsville FL 43611 | Gainsville FL 32611 |
| **30.** | 5018 Church St | 5018 Church Ave |
| **31.** | 1079 N Blake St | 1097 N Blake St |
| **32.** | 8072 W 20th Rd | 80702 W 20th Dr |
| **33.** | Onoro ME 04473 | Orono ME 04473 |
| **34.** | 2175 Kimbell Rd | 2175 Kimball Rd |
| **35.** | 1243 Mermaid St | 1243 Mermaid St |
| **36.** | 4904 SW 134th St | 4904 SW 134th St |
| **37.** | 1094 Hancock St | 1049 Hancock St |
| **38.** | Des Moines IA 50311 | Des Moines IA 50311 |
| **39.** | 4832 S Rinaldi Rd | 48323 S rinaldo Rd |
| **40.** | 2015 Dorchester Rd | 2015 Dorchester Rd |
| **41.** | 5216 Woodbine St | 5216 Woodburn St |
| **42.** | Boulder CO 80302 | Boulder CA 80302 |
| **43.** | 4739 N Marion St | 479 N Marion St |
| **44.** | 3720 Nautilus Wy | 3270 Nautilus Way |
| **45.** | 3636 Gramercy Pk | 3636 Gramercy Pk |
| **46.** | 757 Johnson Ave | 757 Johnston Ave |

**47.** 3045 Brighton 12th St        3045 Brighton 12th St

**48.** 237 Ovington Ave        237 Ovington Ave

**49.** Kalamazoo MI 49007        Kalamazoo MI 49007

**50.** Lissoula MT 59812        Missoula MS 59812

**51.** Stillwater OK 74704        Stillwater OK 47404

**52.** 47446 Empire Blvd        4746 Empire Bldg

**53.** 6321 St Johns Pl        6321 St Johns Pl

**54.** 2242 Vanderbilt Ave        2242 Vanderbilt Ave

**55.** 542 Ditmas Blvd        542 Ditmars Blvd

**56.** 4603 W Argyle Rd        4603 W Argyle Rd

**57.** 653 Knickerbocker Ave NE        653 Knickerbocker Ave NE

**58.** 3651 Midwood Terr        3651 Midwood Terr

**59.** Chapel Hill NC 27514        Chaple Hill NC 27514

**60.** 3217 Vernon Pl NW        3217 Vernon Dr NW

**61.** 1094 Rednor Pkwy        1049 Rednor Pkwy

**62.** 986 S Doughty Blvd        986 S Douty Blvd

**63.** Lincoln NE 68508        Lincoln NE 65808

**64.** 1517 LaSalle Ave        1517 LaSalle Ave

**65.** 3857 S Morris St        3857 S Morriss St

**66.** 6104 Saunders Expy        614 Saunders Expy

**67.** 2541 Appleton St        2541 Appleton Rd

**68.** Washington DC 20052        Washington DC 20052

**69.** 6439 Kessler Blvd S        6439 Kessler Blvd S

**70.** 4786 Catalina Dr        4786 Catalana Dr

**71.** 132 E Hampton Pkwy        1322 E Hampton Pkwy

72. 1066 Goethe Sq S               1066 Geothe Sq S

73. 1118 Jerriman Wy               1218 Jerriman Wy

74. 5798 Grand Central Pkwy        57998 Grand Central Pkwy

75. Delaware OH 43015              Delaware OK 43015

76. Corvallis OR 973313            Corvallis OR 97331

77. 4231 Keating Ave N             4231 Keating Av N

78. 5689 Central Pk Pl             5869 Central Pk Pl

79. 1108 Lyndhurst Dr              1108 Lyndhurst Dr

80. 842 Chambers Ct                842 Chamber Ct

81. Athens OH 45701                Athens GA 45701

82. Tulsa OK 74171                 Tulsa OK 71471

83. 6892 Beech Grove Ave           6892 Beech Grove Ave

84. 2939 E Division St             2929 W Division St

85. 1554 Pitkin Ave                1554 Pitkin Ave

86. 905 St Edwards Plz             950 St Edwards Plz

87. 1906 W 152nd St                1906 W 152nd St

88. 3466 Glenmore Ave              3466 Glenville Ave

89. Middlebury VT 05753            Middleberry VT 05753

90. Evanston IL 60201              Evanston IN 60201

91. 9401 W McDonald Ave            9401 W MacDonald Ave

92. 55527 Albermarle Rd            5527 Albermarle Rd

93. 9055 Carter Dr                 9055 Carter Dr

94. Greenvale NY 11548             Greenvale NY 11458

95. 1149 Cherry Gr S               1149 Cherry Gr S

## ANSWER KEY

| | | | | |
|---|---|---|---|---|
| 1. D | 20. D | 39. D | 58. A | 77. D |
| 2. D | 21. D | 40. A | 59. D | 78. D |
| 3. D | 22. D | 41. D | 60. D | 79. A |
| 4. D | 23. D | 42. D | 61. D | 80. D |
| 5. D | 24. D | 43. D | 62. D | 81. D |
| 6. D | 25. A | 44. D | 63. D | 82. D |
| 7. D | 26. A | 45. A | 64. A | 83. A |
| 8. D | 27. D | 46. D | 65. D | 84. D |
| 9. D | 28. D | 47. A | 66. D | 85. A |
| 10. A | 29. D | 48. A | 67. D | 86. D |
| 11. D | 30. D | 49. A | 68. A | 87. A |
| 12. A | 31. D | 50. D | 69. A | 88. D |
| 13. D | 32. D | 51. D | 70. D | 89. D |
| 14. D | 33. D | 52. D | 71. D | 90. D |
| 15. A | 34. D | 53. A | 72. D | 91. D |
| 16. D | 35. A | 54. A | 73. D | 92. D |
| 17. D | 36. A | 55. D | 74. D | 93. A |
| 18. A | 37. D | 56. A | 75. D | 94. D |
| 19. A | 38. A | 57. A | 76. D | 95. A |

answers

## SUMMING IT UP

- Address-checking questions on Postal Service exams carry the highest penalties for guessing.

- Reading for differences and vocalization are the two best techniques for answering address-checking questions more accurately.

# Strategies for Forms Completion Questions

## OVERVIEW

- Tips and techniques
- Summing it up

## TIPS AND TECHNIQUES

Your score on the forms completion section is based on the number of items you answer correctly. There is no penalty for wrong answers on this part of the Postal Service exams, so it is to your advantage to respond to each item, even if you have to guess.

Here are some proven tips to help you do your best on forms completion questions:

- **Study each form carefully.** Every form is different and calls for different information in various sections. Take time to study the forms carefully before responding to the items related to them, so you are sure you know what information is requested.

- **Answer the easiest questions first.** Once you answer the easiest questions, return to those you skipped the first time around.

- **If time permits, go back and try to answer the more difficult questions.** Be careful, however: If you return to an item, make sure you mark the correct answer on your answer sheet. It is easy to lose your place and darken the wrong circle. If you can make an educated guess, it's to your benefit, since you are not penalized for incorrect answers.

chapter 5

## EXERCISE

**Directions:** Answer each question based on the information in the sample forms provided.

---

**Authorization to Hold Mail**

NOTE: Complete and give to your letter carrier or mail to the post office that delivers your mail.

We can hold your mail for a minimum of **3**, but not for more than **30 days.**

**Postmaster: Please hold mail for:**

Name(s)

Address (Number, street, apt./suite no., city, state, ZIP + 4)

☐ **A.** Please deliver all accumulated mail and resume normal delivery on the ending date shown below.

☐ **B.** I will pick up all accumulated mail when I return and understand that mail delivery will not resume until I do.

| Beginning Date | Ending Date (May only be changed by the customer in writing) | Customer Signature |
|---|---|---|

**For Post Office Use Only**

| Date Received **1.** | | |
|---|---|---|
| Clerk **2.** | Bin Number **3.** | |
| Carrier **4.** | Route Number **5.** | |

(Complete this section only if customer selected option B)

| **6.** ☐ Accumulated mail has been picked up. | Resume Delivery of Mail (Date) **7.** | By **8.** |
|---|---|---|

---

1. Which of these would be a proper entry for Box 2?
   (A) Rural Route 3
   (B) $2.90
   (C) 9/12/08
   (D) Josh Kidd

2. Where would you enter 7/27/08?
   (A) Box 1
   (B) Box 2
   (C) Box 3
   (D) Box 4

3. Which of these would be a correct entry for Box 6?
   (A) A check mark
   (B) 10/07/08
   (C) 1/13/08 to 2/27/08
   (D) Amy McDonnell

4. Which of these would be a correct entry for Box 7?
   (A) A check mark
   (B) 12/20/08
   (C) 6351 Hardin Road
   (D) 19134

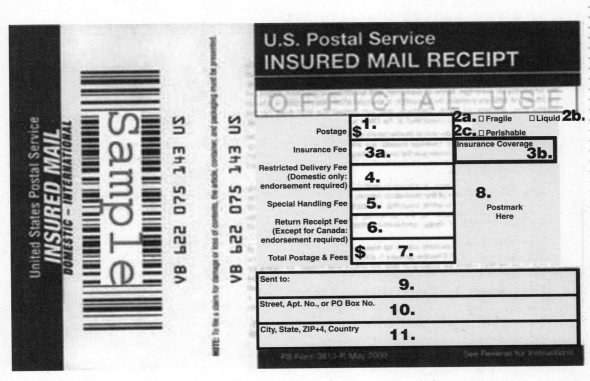

**5.** Where would you check that the item is liquid?
- **(A)** Box 2a
- **(B)** Box 2b
- **(C)** Box 2c
- **(D)** Box 3b

**6.** Where would you enter the special handling fee?
- **(A)** Box 1
- **(B)** Box 3a
- **(C)** Box 5
- **(D)** Box 7

**7.** What would be the correct entry for Box 1?
- **(A)** A check mark
- **(B)** A postmark
- **(C)** $2.50
- **(D)** 12456

**8.** You could enter fees in all of the following boxes EXCEPT
- **(A)** Box 1
- **(B)** Box 4
- **(C)** Box 7
- **(D)** Box 11

## ANSWER KEY AND EXPLANATIONS

### Exercise

| | | | |
|---|---|---|---|
| 1. D | 3. A | 5. B | 7. C |
| 2. A | 4. B | 6. C | 8. D |

1. **The correct answer is (D).** Box 2 is labeled "Clerk." Therefore, Josh Kidd is the correct answer.

2. **The correct answer is (A).** Box 1 is labeled "Date Received." Therefore, 7/27/08 would be entered in Box 1.

3. **The correct answer is (A).** Box 6 contains a check box. Therefore, a check mark is the correct answer.

4. **The correct answer is (B).** Box 7 is labeled "Resume Delivery of Mail *(Date).*" Therefore, 12/20/08 is the correct answer.

5. **The correct answer is (B).** Box 2b is a check box labeled "Liquid." Therefore, Box 2b is where you would place a check mark indicating an item contains liquid.

6. **The correct answer is (C).** Box 5 is labeled "Special Handling Fee." Therefore, Box 5 is the correct answer.

7. **The correct answer is (C).** Box 1 is labeled "Postage." Therefore, $2.50 is the correct answer.

8. **The correct answer is (D).** Boxes 1, 4, and 7 are all fee boxes. Box 11 is labeled "City, State, ZIP+4, Country." Therefore, Box 11 is the correct answer.

# SUMMING IT UP

- Your score on the forms completion section is based on the number of items you answer correctly. There is no penalty for incorrect answers on this part of the test.

- Learn the proven tips to help you do your best on forms completion questions:
  - Study each form carefully.
  - Answer the easiest questions first.
  - If time permits, go back and try to answer the more difficult questions.

# Strategies for Coding and Memory Questions

## OVERVIEW

- Tips and techniques
- Explanation of coding guide
- Summing it up

## TIPS AND TECHNIQUES

Exam 473 includes a section on Coding and Memory, and Exam 460 includes a section on Memory for Addresses. These are tests of your ability to use codes quickly and accurately, both with a coding guide visible and from memory, without using a guide. In Coding and Memory questions, you will be shown a coding guide and several items that must be assigned a code. To the best of your ability, you must look up the correct code for each item and record your responses. During the first section, you will be allowed to look at the coding guide while you assign codes. During the second section, however, you must assign codes based on your memory of the same coding guide. While the coding guide is visible, try to memorize as many of the codes as you can. These are the same codes that will be used in the memory section.

During the actual test, you are not permitted to look at the codes when answering the items in the Memory section, nor are you permitted to write down addresses during the memorization period.

## SCORING

Your score is based on the number of items you answer correctly minus one third of the number of items you answer incorrectly. In both parts of the Coding and Memory section, your score depends on how many items you can accurately assign a code to in the time allowed. You may not be able to assign a code to all of the items before time runs out, but you should do your best to assign codes to as many items as possible with a high degree of accuracy.

During the actual test, you will have several opportunities to work with the coding guide and practice memorizing the codes for each range of addresses

chapter 6

before you must answer questions based on memory. Here are some techniques for scoring high on coding and memory questions:

- **Answer the easiest questions first.** You have a set amount of time to answer all the questions. Do not waste time on a question you can't immediately answer.

- **Narrow it down to a couple of possible answers.** If you can do this, it might be advantageous to make an educated guess.

- **Work as quickly and as accurately as possible.** You are not expected to answer all the items in the time allowed, but do your best to work quickly while avoiding careless mistakes.

- **Take advantage of the practice time and memorization periods available to you.**

## EXPLANATION OF THE CODING GUIDE

The first column of the coding guide shows each **Address Range.** The second column of the coding guide shows a one-letter code for the **Delivery Route** that serves the address ranges listed in that row. You may assume that addresses run in order from lowest to highest.

## EXERCISE 1

**Directions:** Circle the correct delivery route for each address based on the following coding guide. Work as quickly and as accurately as possible. Time yourself on this exercise. Stop after 2 minutes to give yourself a feel for taking this part of the exam under timed conditions.

### CODING GUIDE

| ADDRESS RANGE | DELIVERY ROUTE |
|---|---|
| 1–99 Washington Avenue<br>10–200 Cedar Street<br>5–15 Tyson Avenue | A |
| 100–200 Washington Avenue<br>16–30 Tyson Avenue | B |
| 10000–12000 Agate Street<br>1–10 Lancaster Avenue<br>201–1500 Hardin Road | C |
| All mail that doesn't fall into one of the address ranges listed above | D |

| Address | Delivery Route | | | |
|---|---|---|---|---|
| **1.** 12 Washington Avenue | A | B | C | D |
| **2.** 11500 Agate Street | A | B | C | D |
| **3.** 1256 Hardin Road | A | B | C | D |
| **4.** 11 Lancaster Avenue | A | B | C | D |
| **5.** 24 Cedar Street | A | B | C | D |
| **6.** 9 Tyson Avenue | A | B | C | D |
| **7.** 3035 Aramingo Avenue | A | B | C | D |
| **8.** 1187 Lancaster Avenue | A | B | C | D |
| **9.** 456 Hardin Road | A | B | C | D |
| **10.** 176 Washington Avenue | A | B | C | D |
| **11.** 2880 Tulip Street | A | B | C | D |
| **12.** 157 Cedar Street | A | B | C | D |
| **13.** 84 Washington Avenue | A | B | C | D |
| **14.** 15400 Agate Street | A | B | C | D |
| **15.** 27 Glenn Drive | A | B | C | D |

## ANSWER KEY

| | | | | |
|---|---|---|---|---|
| 1. A | 4. D | 7. D | 10. B | 13. A |
| 2. C | 5. A | 8. D | 11. D | 14. D |
| 3. C | 6. A | 9. C | 12. A | 15. D |

## EXERCISE 2

**Directions:** Take 3 minutes to memorize the coding guide on page 75. You may not take any notes when memorizing the coding guide, but you can write in the test booklet while you are answering the questions. Then circle the correct delivery route for each address based on that coding guide. DO NOT refer to the coding guide when working through the exercise. Work as quickly and as accurately as possible. Time yourself on this exercise. Stop after 3 minutes to give yourself a feel for taking this portion of the test under timed conditions.

| Address | Delivery Route | | | |
|---|---|---|---|---|
| 1. 10320 Agate Street | A | B | C | D |
| 2. 203 Hardin Road | A | B | C | D |
| 3. 215 Cedar Street | A | B | C | D |
| 4. 7 Lancaster Avenue | A | B | C | D |
| 5. 27 Tyson Avenue | A | B | C | D |
| 6. 14 Lancaster Avenue | A | B | C | D |
| 7. 56 Pacific Street | A | B | C | D |
| 8. 1217 Edge Hill Road | A | B | C | D |
| 9. 942 Hardin Road | A | B | C | D |
| 10. 98 Washington Avenue | A | B | C | D |
| 11. 3012 Mercer Street | A | B | C | D |
| 12. 914 Agate Street | A | B | C | D |
| 13. 172 Washington Avenue | A | B | C | D |
| 14. 11000 Agate Street | A | B | C | D |
| 15. 300 Hardin Road | A | B | C | D |

## ANSWER KEY

| | | | | |
|---|---|---|---|---|
| 1. C | 4. C | 7. D | 10. A | 13. B |
| 2. C | 5. B | 8. D | 11. D | 14. C |
| 3. D | 6. D | 9. C | 12. D | 15. C |

## SUMMING IT UP

- Your score on the memory and coding sections of a Postal Service exam is based on the number of items you answer correctly minus one third of the number of items you answer incorrectly.

- There is a wrong-answer penalty for this section of the test, so avoid guessing.

- The same coding guide is used in both the coding and memory sections of the test.

# Strategies for Number
# Series Questions

## OVERVIEW

- **Tips and techniques**
- **Summing it up**

## TIPS AND TECHNIQUES

Don't worry too much about these types of questions, especially if you don't have advanced math skills. You're not going to be asked to do algebra. The Postal Service exams on which you're tested for number series require only a knowledge of simple addition, subtraction, multiplication, and division. Best of all, you can solve most of these questions quickly, and there is no penalty for wrong answers.

If you must guess, make all your guesses the same letter. By the law of averages, doing so may give you a better chance of hitting the right answer.

So you're a bit anxious about working with numbers. Well, put your fears aside. Remember, the test isn't going to ask you to break out the calculus (or even a simple calculator, for that matter). As usual, you'll need to work with as much speed and efficiency as you can muster. However, if you try to use the following six tips, you may find that this type of question isn't as frightening as you thought.

1. **In number series with one pattern,** look for the following number arrangements:
   - Simple ascending (increasing) or descending (decreasing) numbers, in which the same number is added to or subtracted from each number in a series
   - Alternating ascending or descending numbers, in which two different numbers are alternately added to or subtracted from each number in a series
   - Simple or alternating multiplication or division

- Simple repetition, in which one or more numbers in the series are repeated immediately before or after addition, subtraction, or another arithmetic operation
- Repetition of a number pattern by itself
- Unusual pattern

**2** **In number series with two or more patterns,** look for the following kinds of patterns:
- Random number (not one of the numbers in the series)
- Introduced and repeated number in a one-pattern series
- Two or more alternating series of two or more distinct patterns
- Two or more alternating series of patterns, plus repetitive or random numbers
- Two or more alternating patterns that include simple multiplication and division
- Unusual alternating or combination arrangements

**3** **Solve at a glance.** Look for simple number series that jump out at you, such as 1 2 3 1 2 3. Also be on the lookout for patterns in which you either add or subtract to get the next number, such as 20 21 22 23 or 35 34 33 32.

**4** **Vocalize for meaning.** With all those numbers on the page, it's easy for your eye (and your brain) to get confused, mistakenly reading one number for another. That's why it sometimes helps to vocalize (say quietly to yourself) what you are reading. You might be able to *hear* a pattern more quickly and more accurately than if you simply look at it.

**5** **When you spot a difference, mark it down.** By "difference," we mean any change in the number series. For example, if you notice that the series is increasing by 2 (for example, 2 4 6 8), write down that difference in the numbers of the series (again, in this case, 2). If you can't figure it out using addition or subtraction, try multiplication or division. Number series that use multiplication and division are fairly rare, but don't discount them entirely—just remember to try addition and subtraction first.

**6** **Know how to spot repeating and random numbers.** Repeating and random numbers may not be very obvious. Be sure to mark the question in your test booklet to help you spot these types of numbers.

## EXERCISE 1

**Directions:** To the left of the answer choices in each row is a series of numbers, each of which follows some definite order. Look at the numbers in the series on the left and determine what order they follow. Then decide what the next two numbers in the series would be if the same order were continued. Circle the letter of the correct answer.

| | | | | | |
|---|---|---|---|---|---|
| **1.** 8 9 10 8 9 10 8 | **(A)** 8 9 | **(B)** 9 10 | **(C)** 9 8 | **(D)** 10 8 | **(E)** 8 10 |
| **2.** 16 16 15 15 14 14 13 | **(A)** 12 13 | **(B)** 14 13 | **(C)** 12 11 | **(D)** 12 10 | **(E)** 13 12 |
| **3.** 2 6 10 2 14 18 2 | **(A)** 2 22 | **(B)** 2 26 | **(C)** 22 26 | **(D)** 22 2 | **(E)** 26 2 |
| **4.** 30 28 27 25 24 22 21 | **(A)** 21 20 | **(B)** 19 18 | **(C)** 20 19 | **(D)** 20 18 | **(E)** 21 21 |
| **5.** 25 25 22 22 19 19 16 | **(A)** 18 18 | **(B)** 16 16 | **(C)** 16 13 | **(D)** 15 15 | **(E)** 15 13 |
| **6.** 9 17 24 30 35 39 42 | **(A)** 43 44 | **(B)** 44 46 | **(C)** 44 45 | **(D)** 45 49 | **(E)** 46 50 |
| **7.** 28 31 34 37 40 43 46 | **(A)** 49 52 | **(B)** 47 49 | **(C)** 50 54 | **(D)** 49 53 | **(E)** 51 55 |
| **8.** 17 17 24 24 31 31 38 | **(A)** 38 39 | **(B)** 38 17 | **(C)** 38 45 | **(D)** 38 44 | **(E)** 39 50 |
| **9.** 87 83 79 75 71 67 63 | **(A)** 62 61 | **(B)** 63 59 | **(C)** 60 56 | **(D)** 59 55 | **(E)** 59 54 |
| **10.** 8 9 11 14 18 23 29 | **(A)** 35 45 | **(B)** 32 33 | **(C)** 38 48 | **(D)** 34 40 | **(E)** 36 44 |
| **11.** 4 8 12 16 20 24 | **(A)** 26 28 | **(B)** 28 30 | **(C)** 30 28 | **(D)** 28 32 | **(E)** 28 29 |
| **12.** 3 4 1 3 4 1 3 | **(A)** 4 1 | **(B)** 4 5 | **(C)** 4 3 | **(D)** 1 2 | **(E)** 4 4 |

# ANSWER KEY AND EXPLANATIONS

| | | | |
|---|---|---|---|
| 1. B | 4. B | 7. A | 10. E |
| 2. E | 5. C | 8. C | 11. D |
| 3. C | 6. C | 9. D | 12. A |

1. **The correct answer is (B).** The series is simply a repetition of the sequence 8 9 10.

2. **The correct answer is (E).** This series is a simple descending series combined with repetition. Each number is first repeated and then decreased by 1.

3. **The correct answer is (C).** This pattern is +4, +4, then repeat the number 2.

4. **The correct answer is (B).** This pattern is not as easy to spot as the ones in the previous questions. If you write in the direction and degree of change between each number, you can see that this is an alternating descending series with the pattern $-2, -1, -2, -1$, etc.

5. **The correct answer is (C).** The rule here is: repeat, $-3$, repeat, $-3$, repeat, $-3$.

6. **The correct answer is (C).** The rule here is: +8, +7, +6, +5, +4, +3, +2.

7. **The correct answer is (A).** This is a simple +3 rule.

8. **The correct answer is (C).** Each number repeats itself, then increases by +7.

9. **The correct answer is (D).** Here the rule is: $-4$.

10. **The correct answer is (E).** The rule here is: +1, +2, +3, +4, +5, +6, +7, +8.

11. **The correct answer is (D).** This is a simple ascending series, where each number increases by 4.

12. **The correct answer is (A).** This series is simply a repetition of the sequence 3 4 1.

## EXERCISE 2

**Directions:** To the left of the answer choices in each row is a series of numbers, each of which follows some definite order. Look at the numbers in the series on the left and determine what order they follow. Then decide what the next two numbers in the series would be if the same order were continued. Circle the letter of the correct answer.

1. 12 26 15 26 18 26 21    **(A)** 21 24    **(B)** 24 26    **(C)** 21 26    **(D)** 26 24    **(E)** 26 25

2. 72 67 69 64 66 61 63    **(A)** 58 60    **(B)** 65 62    **(C)** 60 58    **(D)** 65 60    **(E)** 60 65

3. 81 10 29 81 10 29 81    **(A)** 29 10    **(B)** 81 29    **(C)** 10 29    **(D)** 81 10    **(E)** 29 81

4. 91 91 90 88 85 81 76    **(A)** 71 66    **(B)** 70 64    **(C)** 75 74    **(D)** 70 65    **(E)** 70 63

5. 22 44 29 37 36 30 43    **(A)** 50 23    **(B)** 23 50    **(C)** 53 40    **(D)** 40 53    **(E)** 50 57

6. 0 1 1 0 2 2 0    **(A)** 0 0    **(B)** 0 3    **(C)** 3 3    **(D)** 3 4    **(E)** 2 3

7. 32 34 36 34 36 38 36    **(A)** 34 32    **(B)** 36 34    **(C)** 36 38    **(D)** 38 40    **(E)** 38 36

8. 26 36 36 46 46 56 56    **(A)** 66 66    **(B)** 56 66    **(C)** 57 57    **(D)** 46 56    **(E)** 26 66

9. 64 63 61 58 57 55 52    **(A)** 51 50    **(B)** 52 49    **(C)** 50 58    **(D)** 50 47    **(E)** 51 49

10. 4 6 8 7 6 8 10 9 8    **(A)** 7 9    **(B)** 11 12    **(C)** 12 14    **(D)** 7 10    **(E)** 10 12

11. 57 57 52 47 47 42 37    **(A)** 32 32    **(B)** 37 32    **(C)** 37 37    **(D)** 32 27    **(E)** 27 27

12. 13 26 14 25 16 23 19    **(A)** 20 21    **(B)** 20 22    **(C)** 20 23    **(D)** 20 24    **(E)** 22 25

13. 15 27 39 51 63 75 87    **(A)** 97 112    **(B)** 99 111    **(C)** 88 99    **(D)** 89 99    **(E)** 90 99

14. 2 0 2 2 2 4 2 6 2 8    **(A)** 2 2    **(B)** 2 8    **(C)** 2 10    **(D)** 2 12    **(E)** 2 16

15. 19 18 18 17 17 17 16    **(A)** 16 16    **(B)** 16 15    **(C)** 15 15    **(D)** 15 14    **(E)** 16 17

16. 55 53 44 51 49 44 47    **(A)** 45 43    **(B)** 46 45    **(C)** 46 44    **(D)** 44 44    **(E)** 45 44

17. 100 81 64 49 36 25 16    **(A)** 8 4    **(B)** 8 2    **(C)** 9 5    **(D)** 9 4    **(E)** 9 3

18. 2 2 4 6 8 18 16    **(A)** 32 64    **(B)** 32 28    **(C)** 54 32    **(D)** 32 54    **(E)** 54 30

19. 47 43 52 48 57 53 62    **(A)** 58 54    **(B)** 67 58    **(C)** 71 67    **(D)** 58 67    **(E)** 49 58

20. 38 38 53 48 48 63 58    **(A)** 58 58    **(B)** 58 73    **(C)** 73 73    **(D)** 58 68    **(E)** 73 83

21. 12 14 16 13 15 17 14    **(A)** 17 15    **(B)** 15 18    **(C)** 17 19    **(D)** 15 16    **(E)** 16 18

22. 30 30 30 37 37 37 30    **(A)** 30 30    **(B)** 30 37    **(C)** 37 37    **(D)** 37 30    **(E)** 31 31

23. 75 52 69 56 63 59 57    **(A)** 58 62    **(B)** 55 65    **(C)** 51 61    **(D)** 61 51    **(E)** 63 55

24. 176 88 88 44 44 22 22    **(A)** 22 11    **(B)** 11 11    **(C)** 11 10    **(D)** 11 5    **(E)** 22 10

## ANSWER KEY AND EXPLANATIONS

| | | | | |
|---|---|---|---|---|
| 1. D | 6. C | 11. B | 16. E | 21. E |
| 2. A | 7. D | 12. C | 17. D | 22. A |
| 3. C | 8. A | 13. B | 18. C | 23. D |
| 4. E | 9. E | 14. C | 19. D | 24. B |
| 5. B | 10. E | 15. A | 20. B | |

1. **The correct answer is (D).** This is a +3 series, with the number 26 between terms.
$$12 \; ^{+3} \; 26 \; 15 \; ^{+3} \; 26 \; 18 \; ^{+3} \; 26 \; 21 \; ^{+3} \; 26 \; 24$$

2. **The correct answer is (A).** You may read this as a −5, +2 series:
$$72 \; ^{-5} \; 67 \; ^{+2} \; 69 \; ^{-5} \; 64 \; ^{+2} \; 66 \; ^{-5} \; 61 \; ^{+2} \; 63 \; ^{-5} \; 58 \; ^{+2} \; 60$$
or as two alternating −3 series.

   $$\overset{-3 \qquad -3 \qquad -3 \qquad -3}{72 \; 67 \; 69 \; 64 \; 66 \; 61 \; 63 \; 58 \; 60}$$
   $$\underset{\quad -3 \qquad -3 \qquad -3}{}$$

3. **The correct answer is (C).** By inspection or grouping, the sequence 81 10 29 repeats itself.

4. **The correct answer is (E).** Write in the numbers for this one.
$$91 \; ^{-0} \; 91 \; ^{-1} \; 90 \; ^{-2} \; 88 \; ^{-3} \; 85 \; ^{-4} \; 81 \; ^{-5} \; 76 \; ^{-6} \; 70 \; ^{-7} \; 63$$

5. **The correct answer is (B).** Here we have two distinct alternating series.

   $$\overset{+7 \qquad +7 \qquad +7 \qquad +7}{22 \; 44 \; 29 \; 37 \; 36 \; 30 \; 43 \; 23 \; 50}$$
   $$\underset{\quad -7 \qquad -7 \qquad -7}{}$$

6. **The correct answer is (C).** The digit 0 intervenes after each repeating number of a simple +1 and repeat series.
$$0 \; 1 \; ^{r} \; 1 \; ^{+1} \; 0 \; 2 \; ^{r} \; 2 \; ^{+1} \; 0 \; 3 \; ^{r} \; 3$$

7. **The correct answer is (D).** Group the numbers into threes. Each succeeding group of three begins with a number two higher than the first number of the preceding group of three. Within each group, the pattern is +2, +2, −2; +2, +2, −2.

8. **The correct answer is (A).** The pattern is +10, repeat the number, +10, repeat the number.
$$26 \; ^{+10} \; 36 \; ^{r} \; 36 \; ^{+10} \; 46 \; ^{r} \; 46 \; ^{+10} \; 56 \; ^{r} \; 56 \; ^{+10} \; 66 \; ^{r} \; 66$$

9. **The correct answer is (E).** The pattern is −1, −2, −3; −1, −2, −3, and so on. If you can't see it, write it in for yourself.

10. **The correct answer is (E).** Here the pattern is +2, +2, −1, −1; +2, +2, −1, −1.
$$4 \; ^{+2} \; 6 \; ^{+2} \; 8 \; ^{-1} \; 7 \; ^{-1} \; 6 \; ^{+2} \; 8 \; ^{+2} \; 10 \; ^{-1} \; 9 \; ^{-1} \; 8 \; ^{+2} \; 10 \; ^{+2} \; 12$$
The series that is given to you is a little bit longer than most to better assist you in establishing this extra long pattern.

11. **The correct answer is (B).** This is a −5 pattern with every other term repeated.
$$57 \; ^{r} \; 57 \; ^{-5} \; 52 \; ^{-5} \; 47 \; ^{r} \; 47 \; ^{-5} \; 42 \; ^{-5} \; 37 \; ^{r} \; 37 \; ^{-5} \; 32$$

12. **The correct answer is (C).** This series consists of two alternating series.

   $$\overset{+1 \qquad +2 \qquad +3 \qquad +4}{13 \; 26 \; 14 \; 25 \; 16 \; 23 \; 19 \; 20 \; 23}$$
   $$\underset{\quad -1 \qquad -2 \qquad -3}{}$$

13. **The correct answer is (B).** This is a simple +12 series.

14. **The correct answer is (C).** The digit 2 intervenes before each number of a simple +2 series.
$$2 \; 0 \; ^{+2} \; 2 \; 2 \; ^{+2} \; 2 \; 4 \; ^{+2} \; 2 \; 6 \; ^{+2} \; 2 \; 8 \; ^{+2} \; 2 \; 10$$

15. **The correct answer is (A).** Each number is repeated one time more than the number before it: 19 appears only once, 18 twice, 17 three times and, if the series were extended beyond the question, 16 would appear four times.

16. **The correct answer is (E).** This is a −2 series, with the number 44 appearing after every two numbers of the series. You probably can see this now without writing it out.

17. **The correct answer is (D).** The series consists of the squares of the numbers from 4 to 10, in descending order.

18. **The correct answer is (C).** This is a tricky alternating series question.

$$\overset{\times 2 \quad \times 2 \quad \times 2 \quad \times 2}{2\ 2\ 4\ 6\ 8\ 18\ 16\ 54\ 32}$$
$$\underset{\times 3 \quad \times 3 \quad \times 3}{}$$

19. **The correct answer is (D).** The progress of this series is −4, +9; −4, +9.

20. **The correct answer is (B).** This series is not really difficult, but you may have to write it out to see it.
38 ʳ 38 ⁺¹⁵ 53 ⁻⁵ 48 ʳ 48 ⁺¹⁵ 63 ⁻⁵ 58 ʳ 58 ⁺¹⁵ 73
You may also see this as two alternating +10 series, with the numbers ending in 8 repeated.

21. **The correct answer is (E).** Group into groups of three numbers. Each +2 group begins one step up from the previous group.

22. **The correct answer is (A).** By inspection, you can see that this series is nothing more than the number 30 repeated three times and the number 37 repeated three times. You have no further clues, so you must assume that the series continues with the number 30 repeated three times.

23. **The correct answer is (D).** Here are two alternating series:

$$\overset{-6 \qquad -6 \qquad -6 \qquad -6}{75\ 52\ 69\ 56\ 63\ 59\ 57\ 61\ 51}$$
$$\underset{+4 \qquad +3 \qquad +2}{}$$

24. **The correct answer is (B).** The pattern is divide by 2 and repeat the number, divide by 2 and repeat the number.
176 ÷² 88 ʳ 88 ÷² 44 ʳ 44 ÷² 22 ʳ 22 ÷² 11 ʳ 11

## SUMMING IT UP

- Number series questions do not require advanced math skills.

- There is no penalty for wrong answers on this section of the test, so you may want to take educated guesses.

- Follow the proven techniques in this chapter to score high on number series questions.

# Strategies for Oral Instruction Questions

## OVERVIEW

- Tips and techniques
- Summing it up

## TIPS AND TECHNIQUES

It always pays to be a good listener, and you'll find that Oral Instruction questions on Postal Service exams are no exception. Unlike other types of questions you'll encounter on these exams, Oral Instruction questions require you to focus your attention on another individual (or more precisely, the sound of his or her voice) rather than simply on questions in the test booklet. However, like all questions on the exam, you'll score your highest if you concentrate and relax and if you are well prepared. The information in this chapter will help you do just that.

- **Pay attention to the instructions.** We've stressed in previous chapters that concentration is important. Well, with Oral Instruction questions, attention is paramount! Unlike other questions, if you "space out" during this portion of the exam, you can't simply re-read the question in your booklet. Try to stay focused!

- **Mark your answer sheet as instructed.** Unlike other question types, Oral Instruction questions are not answered in sequential order on your answer sheet. In fact, you will skip around the page, filling in answers in the order specified. Actually, you will not even use all the answer spaces provided.

- **Work from left to right.** If the instructions say to mark the "fourth letter," it means the fourth letter from the left, with no exceptions. Of course, if the instructions tell you differently (for example, if they say, "Please put a circle around the fifth letter from the right"), then you'll obviously need to make an exception. Again, it's extremely important to listen closely.

## chapter 8

- **Don't waste time changing answers.** If you are about to enter a choice on your answer sheet and suddenly realize you've already filled in that choice (i.e., you've made that choice from another question), don't make a change. Wait for the next set of instructions, and move on.

  If you find that you've blackened two answer spaces for the same question, erase one of them only if you have time and if it won't distract you and cause you to fall behind in the instructions.

## EXERCISE 1 ANSWER SHEET

| | | | |
|---|---|---|---|
| 1. Ⓐ Ⓑ Ⓒ Ⓓ Ⓔ | 23. Ⓐ Ⓑ Ⓒ Ⓓ Ⓔ | 45. Ⓐ Ⓑ Ⓒ Ⓓ Ⓔ | 67. Ⓐ Ⓑ Ⓒ Ⓓ Ⓔ |
| 2. Ⓐ Ⓑ Ⓒ Ⓓ Ⓔ | 24. Ⓐ Ⓑ Ⓒ Ⓓ Ⓔ | 46. Ⓐ Ⓑ Ⓒ Ⓓ Ⓔ | 68. Ⓐ Ⓑ Ⓒ Ⓓ Ⓔ |
| 3. Ⓐ Ⓑ Ⓒ Ⓓ Ⓔ | 25. Ⓐ Ⓑ Ⓒ Ⓓ Ⓔ | 47. Ⓐ Ⓑ Ⓒ Ⓓ Ⓔ | 69. Ⓐ Ⓑ Ⓒ Ⓓ Ⓔ |
| 4. Ⓐ Ⓑ Ⓒ Ⓓ Ⓔ | 26. Ⓐ Ⓑ Ⓒ Ⓓ Ⓔ | 48. Ⓐ Ⓑ Ⓒ Ⓓ Ⓔ | 70. Ⓐ Ⓑ Ⓒ Ⓓ Ⓔ |
| 5. Ⓐ Ⓑ Ⓒ Ⓓ Ⓔ | 27. Ⓐ Ⓑ Ⓒ Ⓓ Ⓔ | 49. Ⓐ Ⓑ Ⓒ Ⓓ Ⓔ | 71. Ⓐ Ⓑ Ⓒ Ⓓ Ⓔ |
| 6. Ⓐ Ⓑ Ⓒ Ⓓ Ⓔ | 28. Ⓐ Ⓑ Ⓒ Ⓓ Ⓔ | 50. Ⓐ Ⓑ Ⓒ Ⓓ Ⓔ | 72. Ⓐ Ⓑ Ⓒ Ⓓ Ⓔ |
| 7. Ⓐ Ⓑ Ⓒ Ⓓ Ⓔ | 29. Ⓐ Ⓑ Ⓒ Ⓓ Ⓔ | 51. Ⓐ Ⓑ Ⓒ Ⓓ Ⓔ | 73. Ⓐ Ⓑ Ⓒ Ⓓ Ⓔ |
| 8. Ⓐ Ⓑ Ⓒ Ⓓ Ⓔ | 30. Ⓐ Ⓑ Ⓒ Ⓓ Ⓔ | 52. Ⓐ Ⓑ Ⓒ Ⓓ Ⓔ | 74. Ⓐ Ⓑ Ⓒ Ⓓ Ⓔ |
| 9. Ⓐ Ⓑ Ⓒ Ⓓ Ⓔ | 31. Ⓐ Ⓑ Ⓒ Ⓓ Ⓔ | 53. Ⓐ Ⓑ Ⓒ Ⓓ Ⓔ | 75. Ⓐ Ⓑ Ⓒ Ⓓ Ⓔ |
| 10. Ⓐ Ⓑ Ⓒ Ⓓ Ⓔ | 32. Ⓐ Ⓑ Ⓒ Ⓓ Ⓔ | 54. Ⓐ Ⓑ Ⓒ Ⓓ Ⓔ | 76. Ⓐ Ⓑ Ⓒ Ⓓ Ⓔ |
| 11. Ⓐ Ⓑ Ⓒ Ⓓ Ⓔ | 33. Ⓐ Ⓑ Ⓒ Ⓓ Ⓔ | 55. Ⓐ Ⓑ Ⓒ Ⓓ Ⓔ | 77. Ⓐ Ⓑ Ⓒ Ⓓ Ⓔ |
| 12. Ⓐ Ⓑ Ⓒ Ⓓ Ⓔ | 34. Ⓐ Ⓑ Ⓒ Ⓓ Ⓔ | 56. Ⓐ Ⓑ Ⓒ Ⓓ Ⓔ | 78. Ⓐ Ⓑ Ⓒ Ⓓ Ⓔ |
| 13. Ⓐ Ⓑ Ⓒ Ⓓ Ⓔ | 35. Ⓐ Ⓑ Ⓒ Ⓓ Ⓔ | 57. Ⓐ Ⓑ Ⓒ Ⓓ Ⓔ | 79. Ⓐ Ⓑ Ⓒ Ⓓ Ⓔ |
| 14. Ⓐ Ⓑ Ⓒ Ⓓ Ⓔ | 36. Ⓐ Ⓑ Ⓒ Ⓓ Ⓔ | 58. Ⓐ Ⓑ Ⓒ Ⓓ Ⓔ | 80. Ⓐ Ⓑ Ⓒ Ⓓ Ⓔ |
| 15. Ⓐ Ⓑ Ⓒ Ⓓ Ⓔ | 37. Ⓐ Ⓑ Ⓒ Ⓓ Ⓔ | 59. Ⓐ Ⓑ Ⓒ Ⓓ Ⓔ | 81. Ⓐ Ⓑ Ⓒ Ⓓ Ⓔ |
| 16. Ⓐ Ⓑ Ⓒ Ⓓ Ⓔ | 38. Ⓐ Ⓑ Ⓒ Ⓓ Ⓔ | 60. Ⓐ Ⓑ Ⓒ Ⓓ Ⓔ | 82. Ⓐ Ⓑ Ⓒ Ⓓ Ⓔ |
| 17. Ⓐ Ⓑ Ⓒ Ⓓ Ⓔ | 39. Ⓐ Ⓑ Ⓒ Ⓓ Ⓔ | 61. Ⓐ Ⓑ Ⓒ Ⓓ Ⓔ | 83. Ⓐ Ⓑ Ⓒ Ⓓ Ⓔ |
| 18. Ⓐ Ⓑ Ⓒ Ⓓ Ⓔ | 40. Ⓐ Ⓑ Ⓒ Ⓓ Ⓔ | 62. Ⓐ Ⓑ Ⓒ Ⓓ Ⓔ | 84. Ⓐ Ⓑ Ⓒ Ⓓ Ⓔ |
| 19. Ⓐ Ⓑ Ⓒ Ⓓ Ⓔ | 41. Ⓐ Ⓑ Ⓒ Ⓓ Ⓔ | 63. Ⓐ Ⓑ Ⓒ Ⓓ Ⓔ | 85. Ⓐ Ⓑ Ⓒ Ⓓ Ⓔ |
| 20. Ⓐ Ⓑ Ⓒ Ⓓ Ⓔ | 42. Ⓐ Ⓑ Ⓒ Ⓓ Ⓔ | 64. Ⓐ Ⓑ Ⓒ Ⓓ Ⓔ | 86. Ⓐ Ⓑ Ⓒ Ⓓ Ⓔ |
| 21. Ⓐ Ⓑ Ⓒ Ⓓ Ⓔ | 43. Ⓐ Ⓑ Ⓒ Ⓓ Ⓔ | 65. Ⓐ Ⓑ Ⓒ Ⓓ Ⓔ | 87. Ⓐ Ⓑ Ⓒ Ⓓ Ⓔ |
| 22. Ⓐ Ⓑ Ⓒ Ⓓ Ⓔ | 44. Ⓐ Ⓑ Ⓒ Ⓓ Ⓔ | 66. Ⓐ Ⓑ Ⓒ Ⓓ Ⓔ | 88. Ⓐ Ⓑ Ⓒ Ⓓ Ⓔ |

answer sheet

## WORKSHEET

**Directions:** Listen carefully to the instructions read to you from page 93 and mark each item on this worksheet as directed. Then complete each question by marking the answer sheet on the previous page as directed. For each direction, you will darken the answer sheet for an appropriate number-letter combination.

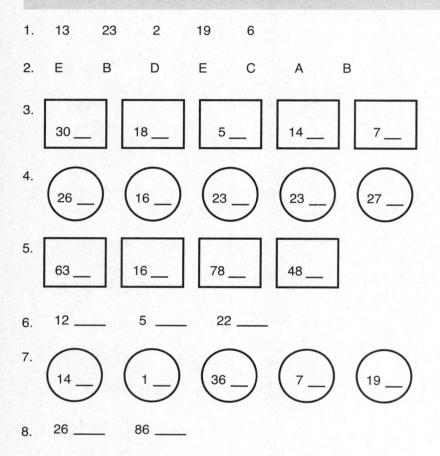

1.   13     23     2     19     6

2.   E     B     D     E     C     A     B

3.   30 __     18 __     5 __     14 __     7 __

4.   26 __     16 __     23 __     23 __     27 __

5.   63 __     16 __     78 __     48 __

6.   12 ____     5 ____     22 ____

7.   14 __     1 __     36 __     7 __     19 __

8.   26 ____     86 ____

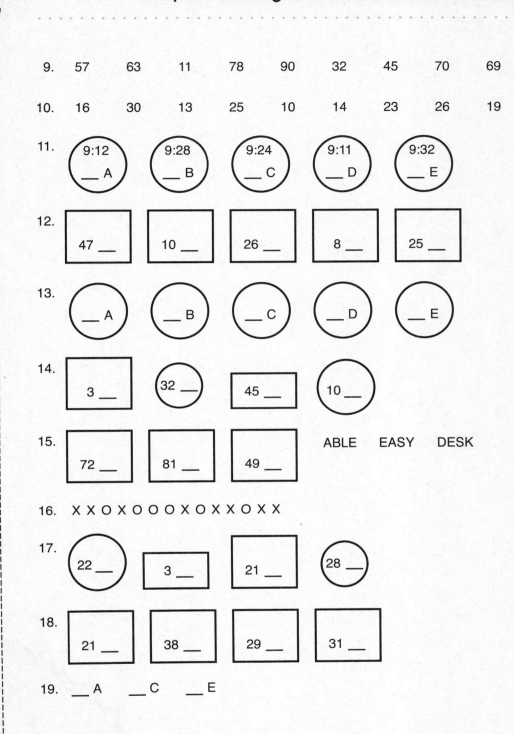

9.   57     63     11     78     90     32     45     70     69

10.  16     30     13     25     10     14     23     26     19

11.  (9:12 __ A)   (9:28 __ B)   (9:24 __ C)   (9:11 __ D)   (9:32 __ E)

12.  [47 __]   [10 __]   [26 __]   [8 __]   [25 __]

13.  (__ A)   (__ B)   (__ C)   (__ D)   (__ E)

14.  [3 __]   (32 __)   [45 __]   (10 __)

15.  [72 __]   [81 __]   [49 __]     ABLE     EASY     DESK

16.  X  X  O  X  O  O  O  X  O  X  X  O  X  X

17.  (22 __)   [3 __]   [21 __]   (28 __)

18.  [21 __]   [38 __]   [29 __]   [31 __]

19.  __ A     __ C     __ E

answer sheet

## EXERCISE 1

**Directions:** Give the following instructions to a friend and have him or her read them aloud to you at the rate of 80 words per minute. (They should NOT read aloud the words in parentheses.) Do NOT read them to yourself. Your friend will need a watch with a second hand. Listen carefully and do exactly what your friend tells you to do with the worksheet and answer sheet. Your friend will tell you what to do with each item on the worksheet. After each set of instructions, you will have time to mark your answer by darkening a circle on the sample answer sheet. Since B and D sound very much alike, ask your friend to say "B as in baker" when he or she means B, and "D as in dog" when he or she means D.

**Look at line 1 on the worksheet.** (Pause briefly.) Draw a line under the fourth number in the line. (Pause 2 seconds.) Now, on your answer sheet, find the number under which you just drew the line and darken space A for that number. (Pause 5 seconds.)

**Look at the letters in line 2 on the worksheet.** (Pause briefly.) Draw a line under the fifth letter in the line. Now, on your answer sheet, find number 59 (pause 2 seconds) and darken the space for the letter under which you drew a line. (Pause 5 seconds.)

**Look at the letters in line 2 on the worksheet again.** (Pause briefly.) Now draw two lines under the third letter in the line. (Pause 2 seconds.) Now, on your answer sheet, find number 65 (pause 2 seconds) and darken the space for the letter under which you drew two lines. (Pause 5 seconds.)

**Look at line 3 on the worksheet.** (Pause briefly.) Write an E in the last box. (Pause 2 seconds.) Now, on your answer sheet, find the number in that box and darken space E for that number. (Pause 5 seconds.)

**Now look at line 3 again.** (Pause briefly.) Write an A in the first box. (Pause 2 seconds.) Now, on your answer sheet, find the number in that box and darken space A for that number. (Pause 5 seconds.)

**Look at line 4.** The number in each circle is the number of packages in a mail sack. In the circle for the sack holding the largest number of packages, write a B as in baker. (Pause 2 seconds.) Now, on your answer sheet, darken the space for the number-letter combination that is in the circle you just wrote in. (Pause 5 seconds.)

**Look at line 4 again.** In the circle for the sack holding the smallest number of packages, write an E. (Pause 2 seconds.) Now, on your answer sheet, darken the space for the number-letter combination that is in the circle you just wrote in. (Pause 5 seconds.)

**Look at line 5 on the worksheet.** The four boxes are trucks for carrying mail. (Pause briefly.) The truck with the highest number is to be loaded first. Write B as in baker on the line beside the highest number. (Pause 2 seconds.) Now, on your answer sheet, darken the space for the number-letter combination that is in the box you just wrote in. (Pause 5 seconds.)

**Look at line 6 on the worksheet.** (Pause briefly.) Next to the middle number write the letter D as in dog. (Pause 2 seconds.) Now, on your answer sheet, find the space for the number beside which you wrote and darken space D as in dog. (Pause 5 seconds.)

**Look at the five circles in line 7 on the worksheet.** Write B as in baker on the blank in the second circle. (Pause 2 seconds.) Now, on your answer sheet, darken the space for the number-letter combination that is in the circle you just wrote in. (Pause 5 seconds.)

**Now take the worksheet again and write C on the blank in the third circle on line 7.** (Pause 2 seconds.) Now, on your answer sheet, darken the space for the number-letter combination that is in the circle you just wrote in. (Pause 5 seconds.)

**Now look at line 8 on the worksheet.** (Pause briefly.) Write an A on the line next to the right-hand number. (Pause 2 seconds.) Now, on your answer sheet, find the space for the number beside which you wrote and darken box A. (Pause 5 seconds.)

**Look at line 9 on the worksheet.** (Pause briefly.) Draw a line under every number that is more than 60 but less than 70. (Pause 12 seconds.) Now, on your answer sheet, for each number that you drew a line under, darken space C. (Pause 25 seconds.)

**Look at line 10 on the worksheet.** (Pause briefly.) Draw a line under every number that is more than 5 and less than 15. (Pause 10 seconds.) Now, on your answer sheet, for each number that you drew a line under, darken space D as in dog. (Pause 25 seconds.)

**Look at line 11 on the worksheet.** (Pause briefly.) In each circle there is a time when the mail must leave. In the circle for the latest time, write on the line the last two figures of the time. (Pause 5 seconds.) Now, on your answer sheet, darken the space for the number-letter combination that is in the circle you just wrote in. (Pause 5 seconds.)

**Look at the five boxes in line 12 on your worksheet.** (Pause briefly.) If 6 is less than 3, put an E in the fourth box. (Pause briefly.) If 6 is not less than 3, put a B as in baker in the first box. (Pause 10 seconds.) Now, on your answer sheet, darken the space for the number-letter combination that is in the box you just wrote in. (Pause 5 seconds.)

**Now look at line 13 on the worksheet.** (Pause briefly.) There are five circles. Each circle has a letter. (Pause briefly.) In the second circle, write the answer to this question: Which of the following numbers is smallest: 72, 51, 88, 71, 58? (Pause 10 seconds.) Now, on your answer sheet, darken the space for the number-letter combination that is in the circle you just wrote in. (Pause 5 seconds.) In the third circle on the same line, write 28. (Pause 2 seconds.) Now, on your answer sheet, darken the space for the number-letter combination that is in the circle you just wrote in. (Pause 5 seconds.) In the fourth circle do nothing. In the fifth circle write the answer to this question: How many months are there in a year? (Pause 5 seconds.) Now, on your answer sheet, darken the space for the number-letter combination that is in the circle you just wrote in. (Pause 5 seconds.)

**Look at line 14 on your worksheet.** (Pause briefly.) There are two circles and two boxes of different sizes with numbers in them. (Pause briefly.) If 2 is smaller than 4 and if 7 is less than 3, write A in the larger circle. (Pause briefly.) Otherwise write B as in baker in the smaller box. (Pause 10 seconds.) Now, on your answer sheet, darken the space for the number-letter combination in the box or circle in which you just wrote. (Pause 5 seconds.)

**Look at the boxes and words in line 15 on the worksheet.** (Pause briefly.) Write the second letter of the first word in the third box. (Pause 5 seconds.) Write the first letter of the second word in the first box. (Pause 5 seconds.) Write the first letter of the third word in the second box. (Pause 5 seconds.) Now, on your answer sheet, darken the spaces for the number-letter combinations that are in the three boxes you just wrote in. (Pause 15 seconds.)

**Look at line 16 on the worksheet.** (Pause briefly.) Draw a line under every "0" in the line. (Pause 5 seconds.) Count the number of lines that you have drawn, subtract 2, and write that number at the end of the line. (Pause 5 seconds.) Now, on your answer sheet, find that number and darken space D as in dog for that number. (Pause 5 seconds.)

**Look at line 17 on the worksheet.** (Pause briefly.) If the number in the left-hand circle is smaller than the number in the right-hand circle, add 2 to the number in the left-hand circle, and change the number in that circle to this number. (Pause 8 seconds.) Then write B as in baker next to the new number. (Pause briefly.) Next, write E beside the number in the smaller box. (Pause 3 seconds.) Then, on your answer sheet, darken the spaces for the number-letter combinations that are in the box and circle you just wrote in. (Pause 5 seconds.)

**Look at line 18 on the worksheet.** (Pause briefly.) If in a year October comes before September, write A in the box with the smallest number. (Pause briefly.) If it does not, write C in the box with the largest number. (Pause 10 seconds.) Now, on your answer sheet, darken the space for the number-letter combination that is in the box you just wrote in. (Pause 5 seconds.)

**Look at line 19 on the worksheet.** (Pause briefly.) On the line beside the second letter, write the highest of these numbers: 12, 56, 42, 39, 8. (Pause 2 seconds.) Now, on your answer sheet, darken the space of the number-letter combination you just wrote. (Pause 5 seconds.)

# ANSWER KEY

## Correctly Completed Answer Sheet

| # | A | B | C | D | E |
|---|---|---|---|---|---|
| 1. | | ● | | | |
| 2. | | | | | |
| 3. | | | | | ● |
| 4. | | | | ● | |
| 5. | | | | ● | |
| 6. | | | | | |
| 7. | | | | | ● |
| 8. | | | | | |
| 9. | | | | | |
| 10. | | | | ● | |
| 11. | | | | | |
| 12. | | | | | ● |
| 13. | | | | ● | |
| 14. | | | | ● | |
| 15. | | | | | |
| 16. | | | | | ● |
| 17. | | | | | |
| 18. | | | | | |
| 19. | ● | | | | |
| 20. | | | | | |
| 21. | | | | | |
| 22. | | | | | |

| # | A | B | C | D | E |
|---|---|---|---|---|---|
| 23. | | | | | |
| 24. | | ● | | | |
| 25. | | | | | |
| 26. | | | | | |
| 27. | | ● | | | |
| 28. | | | ● | | |
| 29. | | | | | |
| 30. | ● | | | | |
| 31. | | | | | |
| 32. | | | | | ● |
| 33. | | | | | |
| 34. | | | | | |
| 35. | | | | | |
| 36. | | | ● | | |
| 37. | | | | | |
| 38. | | | ● | | |
| 39. | | | | | |
| 40. | | | | | |
| 41. | | | | | |
| 42. | | | | | |
| 43. | | | | | |
| 44. | | | | | |

| # | A | B | C | D | E |
|---|---|---|---|---|---|
| 45. | | ● | | | |
| 46. | | | | | |
| 47. | | ● | | | |
| 48. | | | | | |
| 49. | | ● | | | |
| 50. | | | | | |
| 51. | | ● | | | |
| 52. | | | | | |
| 53. | | | | | |
| 54. | | | | | |
| 55. | | | | | |
| 56. | | | ● | | |
| 57. | | | | | |
| 58. | | | | | |
| 59. | | | ● | | |
| 60. | | | | | |
| 61. | | | | | |
| 62. | | | | | |
| 63. | | | ● | | |
| 64. | | | | | |
| 65. | | | | ● | |
| 66. | | | | | |

| # | A | B | C | D | E |
|---|---|---|---|---|---|
| 67. | | | | | |
| 68. | | | | | |
| 69. | | | ● | | |
| 70. | | | | | |
| 71. | | | | | |
| 72. | | | | | ● |
| 73. | | | | | |
| 74. | | | | | |
| 75. | | | | | |
| 76. | | | | | |
| 77. | | | | | |
| 78. | | ● | | | |
| 79. | | | | | |
| 80. | | | | | |
| 81. | | | | ● | |
| 82. | | | | | |
| 83. | | | | | |
| 84. | | | | | |
| 85. | | | | | |
| 86. | ● | | | | |
| 87. | | | | | |
| 88. | | | | | |

## Correctly Completed Worksheet

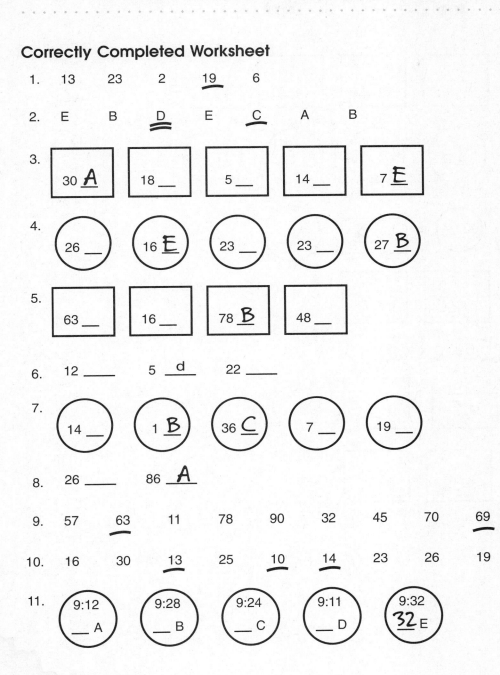

1.  13    23    2    19    6

2.  E    B    D    E    C    A    B

3.  | 30 A | 18 __ | 5 __ | 14 __ | 7 E |

4.  ( 26 __ )  ( 16 E )  ( 23 __ )  ( 23 __ )  ( 27 B )

5.  | 63 __ | 16 __ | 78 B | 48 __ |

6.  12 ___    5 d    22 ___

7.  ( 14 __ )  ( 1 B )  ( 36 C )  ( 7 __ )  ( 19 __ )

8.  26 ___    86 A

9.  57    63    11    78    90    32    45    70    69

10.  16    30    13    25    10    14    23    26    19

11.  ( 9:12 __ A )  ( 9:28 __ B )  ( 9:24 __ C )  ( 9:11 __ D )  ( 9:32 32 E )

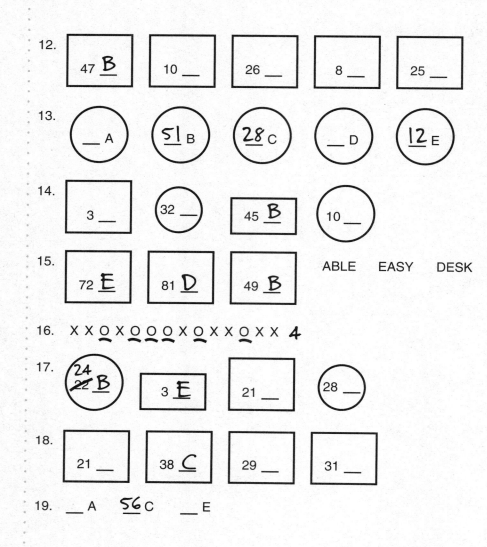

12. [47 B] [10 __] [26 __] [8 __] [25 __]

13. (__ A) (51 B) (28 C) (__ D) (12 E)

14. [3 __] (32 __) [45 B] (10 __)

15. [72 E] [81 D] [49 B]    ABLE    EASY    DESK

16. X X O X O O O X O X X O X X 4

17. (24 22 B) [3 E] [21 __] (28 __)

18. [21 __] [38 C] [29 __] [31 __]

19. __ A    56 C    __ E

## EXERCISE 2 ANSWER SHEET

| | | | |
|---|---|---|---|
| 1. Ⓐ Ⓑ Ⓒ Ⓓ Ⓔ | 23. Ⓐ Ⓑ Ⓒ Ⓓ Ⓔ | 45. Ⓐ Ⓑ Ⓒ Ⓓ Ⓔ | 67. Ⓐ Ⓑ Ⓒ Ⓓ Ⓔ |
| 2. Ⓐ Ⓑ Ⓒ Ⓓ Ⓔ | 24. Ⓐ Ⓑ Ⓒ Ⓓ Ⓔ | 46. Ⓐ Ⓑ Ⓒ Ⓓ Ⓔ | 68. Ⓐ Ⓑ Ⓒ Ⓓ Ⓔ |
| 3. Ⓐ Ⓑ Ⓒ Ⓓ Ⓔ | 25. Ⓐ Ⓑ Ⓒ Ⓓ Ⓔ | 47. Ⓐ Ⓑ Ⓒ Ⓓ Ⓔ | 69. Ⓐ Ⓑ Ⓒ Ⓓ Ⓔ |
| 4. Ⓐ Ⓑ Ⓒ Ⓓ Ⓔ | 26. Ⓐ Ⓑ Ⓒ Ⓓ Ⓔ | 48. Ⓐ Ⓑ Ⓒ Ⓓ Ⓔ | 70. Ⓐ Ⓑ Ⓒ Ⓓ Ⓔ |
| 5. Ⓐ Ⓑ Ⓒ Ⓓ Ⓔ | 27. Ⓐ Ⓑ Ⓒ Ⓓ Ⓔ | 49. Ⓐ Ⓑ Ⓒ Ⓓ Ⓔ | 71. Ⓐ Ⓑ Ⓒ Ⓓ Ⓔ |
| 6. Ⓐ Ⓑ Ⓒ Ⓓ Ⓔ | 28. Ⓐ Ⓑ Ⓒ Ⓓ Ⓔ | 50. Ⓐ Ⓑ Ⓒ Ⓓ Ⓔ | 72. Ⓐ Ⓑ Ⓒ Ⓓ Ⓔ |
| 7. Ⓐ Ⓑ Ⓒ Ⓓ Ⓔ | 29. Ⓐ Ⓑ Ⓒ Ⓓ Ⓔ | 51. Ⓐ Ⓑ Ⓒ Ⓓ Ⓔ | 73. Ⓐ Ⓑ Ⓒ Ⓓ Ⓔ |
| 8. Ⓐ Ⓑ Ⓒ Ⓓ Ⓔ | 30. Ⓐ Ⓑ Ⓒ Ⓓ Ⓔ | 52. Ⓐ Ⓑ Ⓒ Ⓓ Ⓔ | 74. Ⓐ Ⓑ Ⓒ Ⓓ Ⓔ |
| 9. Ⓐ Ⓑ Ⓒ Ⓓ Ⓔ | 31. Ⓐ Ⓑ Ⓒ Ⓓ Ⓔ | 53. Ⓐ Ⓑ Ⓒ Ⓓ Ⓔ | 75. Ⓐ Ⓑ Ⓒ Ⓓ Ⓔ |
| 10. Ⓐ Ⓑ Ⓒ Ⓓ Ⓔ | 32. Ⓐ Ⓑ Ⓒ Ⓓ Ⓔ | 54. Ⓐ Ⓑ Ⓒ Ⓓ Ⓔ | 76. Ⓐ Ⓑ Ⓒ Ⓓ Ⓔ |
| 11. Ⓐ Ⓑ Ⓒ Ⓓ Ⓔ | 33. Ⓐ Ⓑ Ⓒ Ⓓ Ⓔ | 55. Ⓐ Ⓑ Ⓒ Ⓓ Ⓔ | 77. Ⓐ Ⓑ Ⓒ Ⓓ Ⓔ |
| 12. Ⓐ Ⓑ Ⓒ Ⓓ Ⓔ | 34. Ⓐ Ⓑ Ⓒ Ⓓ Ⓔ | 56. Ⓐ Ⓑ Ⓒ Ⓓ Ⓔ | 78. Ⓐ Ⓑ Ⓒ Ⓓ Ⓔ |
| 13. Ⓐ Ⓑ Ⓒ Ⓓ Ⓔ | 35. Ⓐ Ⓑ Ⓒ Ⓓ Ⓔ | 57. Ⓐ Ⓑ Ⓒ Ⓓ Ⓔ | 79. Ⓐ Ⓑ Ⓒ Ⓓ Ⓔ |
| 14. Ⓐ Ⓑ Ⓒ Ⓓ Ⓔ | 36. Ⓐ Ⓑ Ⓒ Ⓓ Ⓔ | 58. Ⓐ Ⓑ Ⓒ Ⓓ Ⓔ | 80. Ⓐ Ⓑ Ⓒ Ⓓ Ⓔ |
| 15. Ⓐ Ⓑ Ⓒ Ⓓ Ⓔ | 37. Ⓐ Ⓑ Ⓒ Ⓓ Ⓔ | 59. Ⓐ Ⓑ Ⓒ Ⓓ Ⓔ | 81. Ⓐ Ⓑ Ⓒ Ⓓ Ⓔ |
| 16. Ⓐ Ⓑ Ⓒ Ⓓ Ⓔ | 38. Ⓐ Ⓑ Ⓒ Ⓓ Ⓔ | 60. Ⓐ Ⓑ Ⓒ Ⓓ Ⓔ | 82. Ⓐ Ⓑ Ⓒ Ⓓ Ⓔ |
| 17. Ⓐ Ⓑ Ⓒ Ⓓ Ⓔ | 39. Ⓐ Ⓑ Ⓒ Ⓓ Ⓔ | 61. Ⓐ Ⓑ Ⓒ Ⓓ Ⓔ | 83. Ⓐ Ⓑ Ⓒ Ⓓ Ⓔ |
| 18. Ⓐ Ⓑ Ⓒ Ⓓ Ⓔ | 40. Ⓐ Ⓑ Ⓒ Ⓓ Ⓔ | 62. Ⓐ Ⓑ Ⓒ Ⓓ Ⓔ | 84. Ⓐ Ⓑ Ⓒ Ⓓ Ⓔ |
| 19. Ⓐ Ⓑ Ⓒ Ⓓ Ⓔ | 41. Ⓐ Ⓑ Ⓒ Ⓓ Ⓔ | 63. Ⓐ Ⓑ Ⓒ Ⓓ Ⓔ | 85. Ⓐ Ⓑ Ⓒ Ⓓ Ⓔ |
| 20. Ⓐ Ⓑ Ⓒ Ⓓ Ⓔ | 42. Ⓐ Ⓑ Ⓒ Ⓓ Ⓔ | 64. Ⓐ Ⓑ Ⓒ Ⓓ Ⓔ | 86. Ⓐ Ⓑ Ⓒ Ⓓ Ⓔ |
| 21. Ⓐ Ⓑ Ⓒ Ⓓ Ⓔ | 43. Ⓐ Ⓑ Ⓒ Ⓓ Ⓔ | 65. Ⓐ Ⓑ Ⓒ Ⓓ Ⓔ | 87. Ⓐ Ⓑ Ⓒ Ⓓ Ⓔ |
| 22. Ⓐ Ⓑ Ⓒ Ⓓ Ⓔ | 44. Ⓐ Ⓑ Ⓒ Ⓓ Ⓔ | 66. Ⓐ Ⓑ Ⓒ Ⓓ Ⓔ | 88. Ⓐ Ⓑ Ⓒ Ⓓ Ⓔ |

answer sheet

# WORKSHEET

> **Directions:** Listen carefully to the instructions read to you from page 103 and mark each item on the worksheet as directed. Then complete each question by marking the answer sheet on the previous page as directed. For each direction, you will darken the answer sheet for an appropriate number-letter combination.

1.   A        B        B        D        C        D        E        D

2.   24        12        17        11        14        20

3.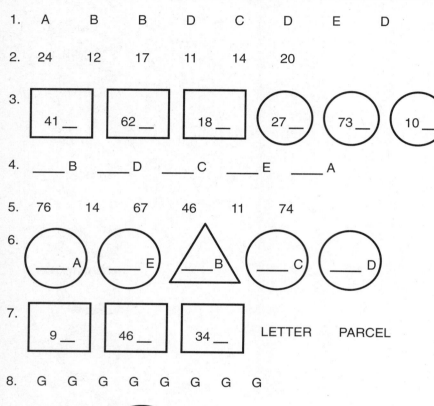

4.   ____ B        ____ D        ____ C        ____ E        ____ A

5.   76        14        67        46        11        74

6.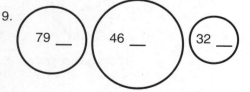

7. 
| 9 __ | 46 __ | 34 __ |

LETTER        PARCEL

8.   G   G   G   G   G   G   G   G

9. 
79 __        46 __        32 __

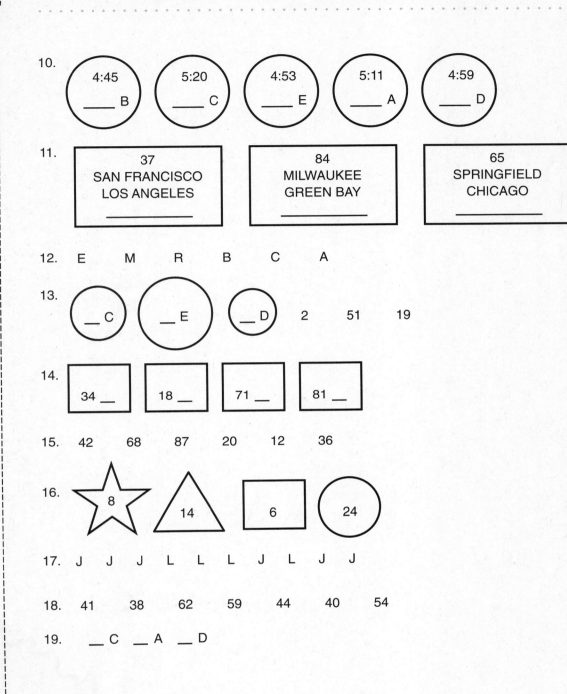

10.

4:45 ___ B    5:20 ___ C    4:53 ___ E    5:11 ___ A    4:59 ___ D

11.

| 37 SAN FRANCISCO LOS ANGELES _____ | 84 MILWAUKEE GREEN BAY _____ | 65 SPRINGFIELD CHICAGO _____ |

12.    E    M    R    B    C    A

13.    __ C    __ E    __ D    2    51    19

14.    34 __    18 __    71 __    81 __

15.    42    68    87    20    12    36

16.    ⭐ 8    △ 14    ▢ 6    ◯ 24

17.    J    J    J    L    L    L    J    L    J    J

18.    41    38    62    59    44    40    54

19.    __ C    __ A    __ D

answer sheet

## EXERCISE 2

**Directions:** Give the following instructions to a friend and have him or her read them aloud to you at the rate of 80 words per minute. (They should NOT read aloud the words in parentheses.) Do NOT read them to yourself. Your friend will need a watch with a second hand. Listen carefully and do exactly what your friend tells you to do with the worksheet and answer sheet. Your friend will tell you what to do with each item on the worksheet. After each set of instructions, you will have time to mark your answer by darkening a circle on the sample answer sheet. Since B and D sound very much alike, ask your friend to say "B as in baker" when he or she means B, and "D as in dog" when he or she means D.

**Look at line 1 on your worksheet.** (Pause briefly.) Circle the seventh letter on line 1. (Pause 5 seconds.) Now, on your answer sheet, find number 83 and for number 83 darken the space for the letter you just circled. (Pause 5 seconds.)

**Look at line 2 on your worksheet.** (Pause briefly.) Draw a line under all the odd numbers between 12 and 20. (Pause 5 seconds.) Now, on your answer sheet, darken space B as in baker for all the numbers under which you drew a line. (Pause 5 seconds.)

**Look at line 2 again.** (Pause briefly.) Find the number that is two times another number on line 2 and circle it. (Pause 5 seconds.) Now, on your answer sheet, darken space A for the number you just circled. (Pause 5 seconds.)

**Look at line 3 on your worksheet.** (Pause briefly.) Write the letter C in the middle box. (Pause 2 seconds.) Now, on your answer sheet, darken the space for the number-letter combination in the figure you just wrote in. (Pause 5 seconds.)

**Look at line 3 again.** (Pause briefly.) Write the letter D as in dog in the left-hand circle. (Pause 2 seconds.) Now, on your answer sheet, darken the space for the number-letter combination in the figure you just wrote in. (Pause 5 seconds.)

**Look at line 4 on your worksheet.** (Pause briefly.) If first-class mail costs more than bulk-rate mail, write the number 22 on the third line; if not, write the number 19 on the fourth line. (Pause 5 seconds.) Now, on your answer sheet, darken the space for the number-letter combination on the line you just wrote on. (Pause 5 seconds.)

**Look at line 4 again.** (Pause briefly.) Write the number 31 on the second line from the left. (Pause 2 seconds.) Now, on your answer sheet, darken the space for the number-letter combination on the line on which you just wrote. (Pause 5 seconds.)

**Look at line 5 on your worksheet.** (Pause briefly.) Find the highest number on line 5 and draw a line under the number. (Pause 2 seconds.) Now, on your answer sheet, find the number under which you just drew a line and darken space E for that number. (Pause 5 seconds.)

**Look at line 5 again.** (Pause briefly.) Find the lowest number on line 5 and draw two lines under the number. (Pause 2 seconds.) Now, on your answer sheet, find the number under which you just drew two lines and darken space A for that number. (Pause 5 seconds.)

**Look at line 6 on your worksheet.** (Pause briefly.) Write the number 57 in the figure that differs from the others on line 6. (Pause 2 seconds.) Now, on your answer sheet, darken the number-letter combination that is in the figure in which you just wrote. (Pause 5 seconds.)

**Look at line 7 on your worksheet.** (Pause briefly.) Write the second letter of the second word in the first box. (Pause 5 seconds.) Write the fifth letter of the first word in the third box. (Pause 5 seconds.) Write the fourth letter of the second word in the second box. (Pause 5 seconds.) Now, on your answer sheet, darken the number-letter combinations in all three boxes. (Pause 15 seconds.)

**Look at line 8 on your worksheet.** (Pause briefly.) Count the number of G's on line 8 and divide the number of G's by 2. Write that number at the end of the line. (Pause 5 seconds.) Now, on your answer sheet, darken space D as in dog for the number you wrote at the end of line 8. (Pause 5 seconds.)

**Look at line 9 on your worksheet.** (Pause briefly.) Write the letter B as in baker in the middle-sized circle. (Pause 2 seconds.) Now, on your answer sheet, darken the space for the number-letter combination in the circle in which you just wrote. (Pause 5 seconds.)

**Look at line 10 on your worksheet.** (Pause briefly.) The time in each circle represents the last scheduled pickup of the day from a street letterbox. Find the circle with the earliest pickup time and write the last two figures of that time on the line in the circle. (Pause 10 seconds.) Now, on your answer sheet, darken the space for the number-letter combination in the circle you just wrote in. (Pause 5 seconds.)

**Look at line 10 again.** (Pause briefly.) Find the circle with the latest pickup time and write the last two figures of that time on the line in the circle. (Pause 10 seconds.) Now, on your answer sheet, darken the space for the number-letter combination in the circle in which you just wrote. (Pause 5 seconds.)

**Look at line 11 on your worksheet.** (Pause briefly.) Mail directed for San Francisco and Los Angeles is to be placed in box 37; mail for Milwaukee and Green Bay, in box 84; mail for Springfield and Chicago, in box 65. Find the box for mail being sent to Green Bay and write the letter A in the box. (Pause 2 seconds.) Now, on your answer sheet, darken the number-letter combination for the box you just wrote in. (Pause 5 seconds.)

**Look at line 11 again.** (Pause briefly.) Mr. Green lives in Springfield. Find the box in which to put Mr. Green's mail and write E on the line. (Pause 2 seconds.) Now, on your answer sheet, darken the space for the number-letter combination in the box in which you just wrote. (Pause 5 seconds.)

**Look at line 12 on your worksheet.** (Pause briefly.) Find the letter on line 12 that is not in the word CREAM and draw a line under the letter. (Pause 2 seconds.) Now, on your answer sheet, find number 38 and darken the space for the letter under which you just drew a line. (Pause 5 seconds.)

**Look at line 13 on your worksheet.** (Pause briefly.) Write the smallest number in the largest circle. (Pause 2 seconds.) Write the largest number in the left-hand circle. (Pause 2 seconds.) Now, on your answer sheet, darken the number-letter combinations that are in the circles in which you just wrote. (Pause 10 seconds.)

**Look at line 14 on your worksheet.** (Pause briefly.) If there are 36 inches in a foot, write B as in baker in the first box; if not, write D as in dog in the third box. (Pause 5 seconds.) Now, on your answer sheet, darken the number-letter combination that is in the box in which you just wrote. (Pause 5 seconds.)

**Look at line 14 again.** (Pause briefly.) Find the box that contains a number in the teens and write B as in baker in that box. (Pause 2 seconds.) Now, on your answer sheet, darken the number-letter combination that is in the box in which you just wrote. (Pause 5 seconds.)

**Look at line 15 on your worksheet.** (Pause briefly.) Circle the only number on line 15 that is not divisible by 2. (Pause 2 seconds.) Now, on your answer sheet, darken space A for the number you circled. (Pause 5 seconds.)

**Look at line 16 on your worksheet.** (Pause briefly.) If the number in the circle is greater than the number in the box, write the letter E in the box; if not, write the letter E in the circle. (Pause 5 seconds.) Now, on your answer sheet, darken the number-letter combination that is in the figure in which you just wrote. (Pause 5 seconds.)

**Look at line 16 again.** (Pause briefly.) If the number in the triangle is smaller than the number in the figure directly to its left, write the letter A in the triangle; if not, write the letter C in the triangle. (Pause 5 seconds.) Now, on your answer sheet, darken the number-letter combination that is in the figure you just wrote in. (Pause 5 seconds.)

**Look at line 17 on your worksheet.** (Pause briefly.) Count the number of J's on line 17, multiply the number of J's by 5, and write that number at the end of the line. (Pause 5 seconds.) Now, on your answer sheet, find the number you just wrote at the end of the line and darken space C for that number. (Pause 5 seconds.)

**Look at line 18 on your worksheet.** (Pause briefly.) Draw one line under the number that is at the middle of line 18. (Pause 5 seconds.) Now, on your answer sheet, darken space B as in baker for the number under which you just drew a line. (Pause 5 seconds.)

**Look at line 18 again.** (Pause briefly.) Draw two lines under each odd number that falls between 35 and 45. (Pause 10 seconds.) Now, on your answer sheet, darken space D as in dog for each number under which you drew two lines. (Pause 5 seconds.)

**Look at line 19 on your worksheet.** (Pause briefly.) Next to the last letter on line 19, write the first number you hear: 53, 18, 6, 75. (Pause 2 seconds.) Now, on your answer sheet, darken the space for the number-letter combination you just wrote. (Pause 5 seconds.)

## ANSWER KEY

### Correctly Completed Answer Sheet

| | | | |
|---|---|---|---|
| 1. Ⓐ Ⓑ Ⓒ Ⓓ Ⓔ | 23. Ⓐ Ⓑ Ⓒ Ⓓ Ⓔ | 45. Ⓐ ● Ⓒ Ⓓ Ⓔ | 67. Ⓐ Ⓑ Ⓒ Ⓓ Ⓔ |
| 2. Ⓐ Ⓑ Ⓒ Ⓓ ● | 24. ● Ⓑ Ⓒ Ⓓ Ⓔ | 46. Ⓐ Ⓑ ● Ⓓ Ⓔ | 68. Ⓐ Ⓑ Ⓒ Ⓓ Ⓔ |
| 3. Ⓐ Ⓑ Ⓒ Ⓓ Ⓔ | 25. Ⓐ Ⓑ Ⓒ Ⓓ Ⓔ | 47. Ⓐ Ⓑ Ⓒ Ⓓ Ⓔ | 69. Ⓐ Ⓑ Ⓒ Ⓓ Ⓔ |
| 4. Ⓐ Ⓑ Ⓒ ● Ⓔ | 26. Ⓐ Ⓑ Ⓒ Ⓓ Ⓔ | 48. Ⓐ Ⓑ Ⓒ Ⓓ Ⓔ | 70. Ⓐ Ⓑ Ⓒ Ⓓ Ⓔ |
| 5. Ⓐ Ⓑ Ⓒ Ⓓ Ⓔ | 27. Ⓐ Ⓑ Ⓒ ● Ⓔ | 49. Ⓐ Ⓑ Ⓒ Ⓓ Ⓔ | 71. Ⓐ Ⓑ Ⓒ ● Ⓔ |
| 6. Ⓐ Ⓑ Ⓒ Ⓓ ● | 28. Ⓐ Ⓑ Ⓒ Ⓓ Ⓔ | 50. Ⓐ Ⓑ Ⓒ Ⓓ Ⓔ | 72. Ⓐ Ⓑ Ⓒ Ⓓ Ⓔ |
| 7. Ⓐ Ⓑ Ⓒ Ⓓ Ⓔ | 29. Ⓐ Ⓑ Ⓒ Ⓓ Ⓔ | 51. Ⓐ Ⓑ ● Ⓓ Ⓔ | 73. Ⓐ Ⓑ Ⓒ Ⓓ Ⓔ |
| 8. Ⓐ Ⓑ Ⓒ Ⓓ Ⓔ | 30. Ⓐ Ⓑ ● Ⓓ Ⓔ | 52. Ⓐ Ⓑ Ⓒ Ⓓ Ⓔ | 74. Ⓐ Ⓑ Ⓒ Ⓓ Ⓔ |
| 9. ● Ⓑ Ⓒ Ⓓ Ⓔ | 31. Ⓐ Ⓑ Ⓒ ● Ⓔ | 53. Ⓐ Ⓑ Ⓒ ● Ⓔ | 75. Ⓐ Ⓑ Ⓒ Ⓓ Ⓔ |
| 10. Ⓐ Ⓑ Ⓒ Ⓓ Ⓔ | 32. Ⓐ Ⓑ Ⓒ Ⓓ Ⓔ | 54. Ⓐ Ⓑ Ⓒ Ⓓ Ⓔ | 76. Ⓐ Ⓑ Ⓒ Ⓓ ● |
| 11. ● Ⓑ Ⓒ Ⓓ Ⓔ | 33. Ⓐ Ⓑ Ⓒ Ⓓ Ⓔ | 55. Ⓐ Ⓑ Ⓒ Ⓓ Ⓔ | 77. Ⓐ Ⓑ Ⓒ Ⓓ Ⓔ |
| 12. Ⓐ Ⓑ Ⓒ Ⓓ Ⓔ | 34. Ⓐ Ⓑ Ⓒ Ⓓ ● | 56. Ⓐ Ⓑ Ⓒ Ⓓ Ⓔ | 78. Ⓐ Ⓑ Ⓒ Ⓓ Ⓔ |
| 13. Ⓐ Ⓑ Ⓒ Ⓓ Ⓔ | 35. Ⓐ Ⓑ Ⓒ Ⓓ Ⓔ | 57. Ⓐ ● Ⓒ Ⓓ Ⓔ | 79. Ⓐ ● Ⓒ Ⓓ Ⓔ |
| 14. Ⓐ Ⓑ ● Ⓓ Ⓔ | 36. Ⓐ Ⓑ Ⓒ Ⓓ Ⓔ | 58. Ⓐ Ⓑ Ⓒ Ⓓ Ⓔ | 80. Ⓐ Ⓑ Ⓒ Ⓓ Ⓔ |
| 15. Ⓐ Ⓑ Ⓒ Ⓓ Ⓔ | 37. Ⓐ Ⓑ Ⓒ Ⓓ Ⓔ | 59. Ⓐ ● Ⓒ Ⓓ Ⓔ | 81. Ⓐ Ⓑ Ⓒ Ⓓ Ⓔ |
| 16. Ⓐ Ⓑ Ⓒ Ⓓ Ⓔ | 38. Ⓐ ● Ⓒ Ⓓ Ⓔ | 60. Ⓐ Ⓑ Ⓒ Ⓓ Ⓔ | 82. Ⓐ Ⓑ Ⓒ Ⓓ Ⓔ |
| 17. Ⓐ ● Ⓒ Ⓓ Ⓔ | 39. Ⓐ Ⓑ Ⓒ Ⓓ Ⓔ | 61. Ⓐ Ⓑ Ⓒ Ⓓ Ⓔ | 83. Ⓐ Ⓑ Ⓒ Ⓓ ● |
| 18. Ⓐ ● Ⓒ Ⓓ Ⓔ | 40. Ⓐ Ⓑ Ⓒ Ⓓ Ⓔ | 62. Ⓐ Ⓑ ● Ⓓ Ⓔ | 84. ● Ⓑ Ⓒ Ⓓ Ⓔ |
| 19. Ⓐ Ⓑ Ⓒ Ⓓ Ⓔ | 41. Ⓐ Ⓑ Ⓒ ● Ⓔ | 63. Ⓐ Ⓑ Ⓒ Ⓓ Ⓔ | 85. Ⓐ Ⓑ Ⓒ Ⓓ Ⓔ |
| 20. Ⓐ Ⓑ ● Ⓓ Ⓔ | 42. Ⓐ Ⓑ Ⓒ Ⓓ Ⓔ | 64. Ⓐ Ⓑ Ⓒ Ⓓ Ⓔ | 86. Ⓐ Ⓑ Ⓒ Ⓓ Ⓔ |
| 21. Ⓐ Ⓑ Ⓒ Ⓓ Ⓔ | 43. Ⓐ Ⓑ Ⓒ Ⓓ Ⓔ | 65. Ⓐ Ⓑ Ⓒ Ⓓ ● | 87. ● Ⓑ Ⓒ Ⓓ Ⓔ |
| 22. Ⓐ Ⓑ ● Ⓓ Ⓔ | 44. Ⓐ Ⓑ Ⓒ Ⓓ Ⓔ | 66. Ⓐ Ⓑ Ⓒ Ⓓ Ⓔ | 88. Ⓐ Ⓑ Ⓒ Ⓓ Ⓔ |

## Correctly Completed Worksheet

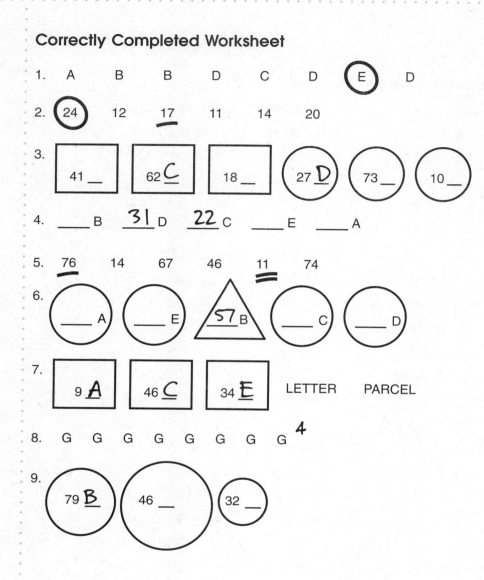

1.  A    B    B    D    C    D    (E)    D

2.  (24)    12    17    11    14    20

3.  [41 __]    [62 C]    [18 __]    (27 D)    (73 __)    (10 __)

4.  ___ B    31 D    22 C    ___ E    ___ A

5.  76    14    67    46    11    74

6.  (___ A)    (___ E)    △57 B    (___ C)    (___ D)

7.  [9 A]    [46 C]    [34 E]    LETTER    PARCEL

8.  G    G    G    G    G    G    G    G⁴

9.  (79 B)    (46 __)    (32 __)

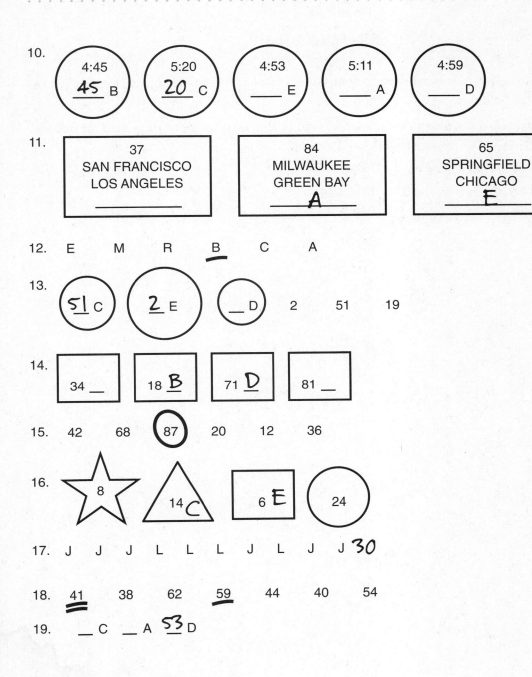

10.

4:45 _45_ B  5:20 _20_ C  4:53 ___ E  5:11 ___ A  4:59 ___ D

11.

| 37 SAN FRANCISCO LOS ANGELES _____ | 84 MILWAUKEE GREEN BAY _A_ | 65 SPRINGFIELD CHICAGO _E_ |

12. E   M   R   B   C   A

13. 51 C   2 E   __ D   2   51   19

14. 34 __   18 B   71 D   81 __

15. 42   68   (87)   20   12   36

16. ★ 8   △ 14 C   6 E   ◯ 24

17. J   J   J   L   L   L   J   L   J   J 30

18. 41   38   62   59   44   40   54

19. __ C   __ A   53 D

# SUMMING IT UP

- Oral instruction questions require that you focus your attention on directions given by another individual.

- Be sure to learn the four techniques reviewed in this chapter for scoring high on the oral instruction section of your Postal Service exam.

  ○ Pay attention to the instructions

  ○ Mark your answer sheet as instructed

  ○ Work from left to right

  ○ Don't waste time changing answers

# Personal Characteristics and Experience Inventory

## OVERVIEW

- **Tips and techniques**
- **Personal characteristics and experience inventory techniques**
- **Summing it up**

One of the most interesting aspects of Exam 473 is a section called the Personal Characteristics and Experience Inventory. Understanding its role as a service provider, the USPS has developed this section in an effort to identify potential employees who have the customer service and interpersonal skills necessary to succeed in certain positions with the USPS.

You will be asked to answer 236 questions in 90 minutes. The items in this section assess personal characteristics, tendencies, or experiences related to performing effectively as an USPS employee.

## TIPS AND TECHNIQUES

- **Read each item carefully and decide which of the responses is most true about you.** For some items, more than one response may fit. However, be sure to mark only one response for each item.

- **Whenever possible, respond to the questions or statements in terms of what you have done, felt, or believed in a work setting.** If you cannot relate the questions or statements to your work experiences, base your responses on other similar experiences, such as school or volunteer opportunities. Simply stated, draw on whatever experiences you have had to respond to the item.

This part of the test is divided into three sections. One section includes items with four choices ranging from "Strongly agree" to "Strongly disagree." A second section includes items with four response choices, ranging from "Very often" to "Rarely" or "Never." The third section includes items that have four to nine response choices.

## PERSONAL CHARACTERISTICS AND EXPERIENCE INVENTORY TECHNIQUES

NOTE

This section of the test calls for honest responses. Dishonest or distorted descriptions of yourself will not help you score higher.

Although you cannot "practice" for this section of the exam, you can take steps to help reduce potential errors.

- **Read each statement carefully before choosing a response.**

- **Do not try to out-think the question or statement.** Respond to each item based on your personal experiences, not on what you think is the "correct" answer.

Here are samples of questions you can expect to see on this section of Exam 473:

Q  You work best with minimal supervison.
- **(A)**  Strongly agree
- **(B)**  Agree
- **(C)**  Disagree
- **(D)**  Strongly disagree

Q  You plan things carefully and in advance.
- **(A)**  Very often
- **(B)**  Often
- **(C)**  Sometimes
- **(D)**  Rarely

Q  What type of work do you like best?
- **(A)**  Tasks that require sitting or standing for long periods of time
- **(B)**  Tasks that require working at a very fast pace
- **(C)**  Tasks that require decision making
- **(D)**  Tasks that involve repetitive activity
- **(E)**  I like all types of work
- **(F)**  Not sure

## SUMMING IT UP

- The Personal Characteristics and Experience Inventory section was developed to identify potential employees who have the requisite customer service and interpersonal skills to work for the USPS.

- The questions in this section of Exam 473 assess one's personal experiences related to work situations. Although you cannot practice for this section of the exam, you can take steps to help reduce potential errors.

# PART III

## NINE PRACTICE TESTS

**answer sheet**

## PRACTICE TEST 1: EXAMS 473/473-C AND 460

### Part A: Address Checking

| | | | | |
|---|---|---|---|---|
| 1. Ⓐ Ⓑ Ⓒ Ⓓ | 13. Ⓐ Ⓑ Ⓒ Ⓓ | 25. Ⓐ Ⓑ Ⓒ Ⓓ | 37. Ⓐ Ⓑ Ⓒ Ⓓ | 49. Ⓐ Ⓑ Ⓒ Ⓓ |
| 2. Ⓐ Ⓑ Ⓒ Ⓓ | 14. Ⓐ Ⓑ Ⓒ Ⓓ | 26. Ⓐ Ⓑ Ⓒ Ⓓ | 38. Ⓐ Ⓑ Ⓒ Ⓓ | 50. Ⓐ Ⓑ Ⓒ Ⓓ |
| 3. Ⓐ Ⓑ Ⓒ Ⓓ | 15. Ⓐ Ⓑ Ⓒ Ⓓ | 27. Ⓐ Ⓑ Ⓒ Ⓓ | 39. Ⓐ Ⓑ Ⓒ Ⓓ | 51. Ⓐ Ⓑ Ⓒ Ⓓ |
| 4. Ⓐ Ⓑ Ⓒ Ⓓ | 16. Ⓐ Ⓑ Ⓒ Ⓓ | 28. Ⓐ Ⓑ Ⓒ Ⓓ | 40. Ⓐ Ⓑ Ⓒ Ⓓ | 52. Ⓐ Ⓑ Ⓒ Ⓓ |
| 5. Ⓐ Ⓑ Ⓒ Ⓓ | 17. Ⓐ Ⓑ Ⓒ Ⓓ | 29. Ⓐ Ⓑ Ⓒ Ⓓ | 41. Ⓐ Ⓑ Ⓒ Ⓓ | 53. Ⓐ Ⓑ Ⓒ Ⓓ |
| 6. Ⓐ Ⓑ Ⓒ Ⓓ | 18. Ⓐ Ⓑ Ⓒ Ⓓ | 30. Ⓐ Ⓑ Ⓒ Ⓓ | 42. Ⓐ Ⓑ Ⓒ Ⓓ | 54. Ⓐ Ⓑ Ⓒ Ⓓ |
| 7. Ⓐ Ⓑ Ⓒ Ⓓ | 19. Ⓐ Ⓑ Ⓒ Ⓓ | 31. Ⓐ Ⓑ Ⓒ Ⓓ | 43. Ⓐ Ⓑ Ⓒ Ⓓ | 55. Ⓐ Ⓑ Ⓒ Ⓓ |
| 8. Ⓐ Ⓑ Ⓒ Ⓓ | 20. Ⓐ Ⓑ Ⓒ Ⓓ | 32. Ⓐ Ⓑ Ⓒ Ⓓ | 44. Ⓐ Ⓑ Ⓒ Ⓓ | 56. Ⓐ Ⓑ Ⓒ Ⓓ |
| 9. Ⓐ Ⓑ Ⓒ Ⓓ | 21. Ⓐ Ⓑ Ⓒ Ⓓ | 33. Ⓐ Ⓑ Ⓒ Ⓓ | 45. Ⓐ Ⓑ Ⓒ Ⓓ | 57. Ⓐ Ⓑ Ⓒ Ⓓ |
| 10. Ⓐ Ⓑ Ⓒ Ⓓ | 22. Ⓐ Ⓑ Ⓒ Ⓓ | 34. Ⓐ Ⓑ Ⓒ Ⓓ | 46. Ⓐ Ⓑ Ⓒ Ⓓ | 58. Ⓐ Ⓑ Ⓒ Ⓓ |
| 11. Ⓐ Ⓑ Ⓒ Ⓓ | 23. Ⓐ Ⓑ Ⓒ Ⓓ | 35. Ⓐ Ⓑ Ⓒ Ⓓ | 47. Ⓐ Ⓑ Ⓒ Ⓓ | 59. Ⓐ Ⓑ Ⓒ Ⓓ |
| 12. Ⓐ Ⓑ Ⓒ Ⓓ | 24. Ⓐ Ⓑ Ⓒ Ⓓ | 36. Ⓐ Ⓑ Ⓒ Ⓓ | 48. Ⓐ Ⓑ Ⓒ Ⓓ | 60. Ⓐ Ⓑ Ⓒ Ⓓ |

### Part B: Forms Completion

| | | | | |
|---|---|---|---|---|
| 1. Ⓐ Ⓑ Ⓒ Ⓓ | 7. Ⓐ Ⓑ Ⓒ Ⓓ | 13. Ⓐ Ⓑ Ⓒ Ⓓ | 19. Ⓐ Ⓑ Ⓒ Ⓓ | 25. Ⓐ Ⓑ Ⓒ Ⓓ |
| 2. Ⓐ Ⓑ Ⓒ Ⓓ | 8. Ⓐ Ⓑ Ⓒ Ⓓ | 14. Ⓐ Ⓑ Ⓒ Ⓓ | 20. Ⓐ Ⓑ Ⓒ Ⓓ | 26. Ⓐ Ⓑ Ⓒ Ⓓ |
| 3. Ⓐ Ⓑ Ⓒ Ⓓ | 9. Ⓐ Ⓑ Ⓒ Ⓓ | 15. Ⓐ Ⓑ Ⓒ Ⓓ | 21. Ⓐ Ⓑ Ⓒ Ⓓ | 27. Ⓐ Ⓑ Ⓒ Ⓓ |
| 4. Ⓐ Ⓑ Ⓒ Ⓓ | 10. Ⓐ Ⓑ Ⓒ Ⓓ | 16. Ⓐ Ⓑ Ⓒ Ⓓ | 22. Ⓐ Ⓑ Ⓒ Ⓓ | 28. Ⓐ Ⓑ Ⓒ Ⓓ |
| 5. Ⓐ Ⓑ Ⓒ Ⓓ | 11. Ⓐ Ⓑ Ⓒ Ⓓ | 17. Ⓐ Ⓑ Ⓒ Ⓓ | 23. Ⓐ Ⓑ Ⓒ Ⓓ | 29. Ⓐ Ⓑ Ⓒ Ⓓ |
| 6. Ⓐ Ⓑ Ⓒ Ⓓ | 12. Ⓐ Ⓑ Ⓒ Ⓓ | 18. Ⓐ Ⓑ Ⓒ Ⓓ | 24. Ⓐ Ⓑ Ⓒ Ⓓ | 30. Ⓐ Ⓑ Ⓒ Ⓓ |

### Part C: Coding and Memory

**CODING SECTION: SEGMENT 3**

| | | | | |
|---|---|---|---|---|
| 1. Ⓐ Ⓑ Ⓒ Ⓓ | 9. Ⓐ Ⓑ Ⓒ Ⓓ | 16. Ⓐ Ⓑ Ⓒ Ⓓ | 23. Ⓐ Ⓑ Ⓒ Ⓓ | 30. Ⓐ Ⓑ Ⓒ Ⓓ |
| 2. Ⓐ Ⓑ Ⓒ Ⓓ | 10. Ⓐ Ⓑ Ⓒ Ⓓ | 17. Ⓐ Ⓑ Ⓒ Ⓓ | 24. Ⓐ Ⓑ Ⓒ Ⓓ | 31. Ⓐ Ⓑ Ⓒ Ⓓ |
| 3. Ⓐ Ⓑ Ⓒ Ⓓ | 11. Ⓐ Ⓑ Ⓒ Ⓓ | 18. Ⓐ Ⓑ Ⓒ Ⓓ | 25. Ⓐ Ⓑ Ⓒ Ⓓ | 32. Ⓐ Ⓑ Ⓒ Ⓓ |
| 4. Ⓐ Ⓑ Ⓒ Ⓓ | 12. Ⓐ Ⓑ Ⓒ Ⓓ | 19. Ⓐ Ⓑ Ⓒ Ⓓ | 26. Ⓐ Ⓑ Ⓒ Ⓓ | 33. Ⓐ Ⓑ Ⓒ Ⓓ |
| 5. Ⓐ Ⓑ Ⓒ Ⓓ | 13. Ⓐ Ⓑ Ⓒ Ⓓ | 20. Ⓐ Ⓑ Ⓒ Ⓓ | 27. Ⓐ Ⓑ Ⓒ Ⓓ | 34. Ⓐ Ⓑ Ⓒ Ⓓ |
| 6. Ⓐ Ⓑ Ⓒ Ⓓ | 14. Ⓐ Ⓑ Ⓒ Ⓓ | 21. Ⓐ Ⓑ Ⓒ Ⓓ | 28. Ⓐ Ⓑ Ⓒ Ⓓ | 35. Ⓐ Ⓑ Ⓒ Ⓓ |
| 7. Ⓐ Ⓑ Ⓒ Ⓓ | 15. Ⓐ Ⓑ Ⓒ Ⓓ | 22. Ⓐ Ⓑ Ⓒ Ⓓ | 29. Ⓐ Ⓑ Ⓒ Ⓓ | 36. Ⓐ Ⓑ Ⓒ Ⓓ |
| 8. Ⓐ Ⓑ Ⓒ Ⓓ | | | | |

**MEMORY SECTION: SEGMENT 4**

| | | | | |
|---|---|---|---|---|
| 1. Ⓐ Ⓑ Ⓒ Ⓓ | 9. Ⓐ Ⓑ Ⓒ Ⓓ | 16. Ⓐ Ⓑ Ⓒ Ⓓ | 23. Ⓐ Ⓑ Ⓒ Ⓓ | 30. Ⓐ Ⓑ Ⓒ Ⓓ |
| 2. Ⓐ Ⓑ Ⓒ Ⓓ | 10. Ⓐ Ⓑ Ⓒ Ⓓ | 17. Ⓐ Ⓑ Ⓒ Ⓓ | 24. Ⓐ Ⓑ Ⓒ Ⓓ | 31. Ⓐ Ⓑ Ⓒ Ⓓ |
| 3. Ⓐ Ⓑ Ⓒ Ⓓ | 11. Ⓐ Ⓑ Ⓒ Ⓓ | 18. Ⓐ Ⓑ Ⓒ Ⓓ | 25. Ⓐ Ⓑ Ⓒ Ⓓ | 32. Ⓐ Ⓑ Ⓒ Ⓓ |
| 4. Ⓐ Ⓑ Ⓒ Ⓓ | 12. Ⓐ Ⓑ Ⓒ Ⓓ | 19. Ⓐ Ⓑ Ⓒ Ⓓ | 26. Ⓐ Ⓑ Ⓒ Ⓓ | 33. Ⓐ Ⓑ Ⓒ Ⓓ |
| 5. Ⓐ Ⓑ Ⓒ Ⓓ | 13. Ⓐ Ⓑ Ⓒ Ⓓ | 20. Ⓐ Ⓑ Ⓒ Ⓓ | 27. Ⓐ Ⓑ Ⓒ Ⓓ | 34. Ⓐ Ⓑ Ⓒ Ⓓ |
| 6. Ⓐ Ⓑ Ⓒ Ⓓ | 14. Ⓐ Ⓑ Ⓒ Ⓓ | 21. Ⓐ Ⓑ Ⓒ Ⓓ | 28. Ⓐ Ⓑ Ⓒ Ⓓ | 35. Ⓐ Ⓑ Ⓒ Ⓓ |
| 7. Ⓐ Ⓑ Ⓒ Ⓓ | 15. Ⓐ Ⓑ Ⓒ Ⓓ | 22. Ⓐ Ⓑ Ⓒ Ⓓ | 29. Ⓐ Ⓑ Ⓒ Ⓓ | 36. Ⓐ Ⓑ Ⓒ Ⓓ |
| 8. Ⓐ Ⓑ Ⓒ Ⓓ | | | | |

## Part D: Personal Characteristics and Experience Inventory

**SECTION 1: AGREE/DISAGREE**

| | | | | |
|---|---|---|---|---|
| 1. Ⓐ Ⓑ Ⓒ Ⓓ | 22. Ⓐ Ⓑ Ⓒ Ⓓ | 43. Ⓐ Ⓑ Ⓒ Ⓓ | 63. Ⓐ Ⓑ Ⓒ Ⓓ | 83. Ⓐ Ⓑ Ⓒ Ⓓ |
| 2. Ⓐ Ⓑ Ⓒ Ⓓ | 23. Ⓐ Ⓑ Ⓒ Ⓓ | 44. Ⓐ Ⓑ Ⓒ Ⓓ | 64. Ⓐ Ⓑ Ⓒ Ⓓ | 84. Ⓐ Ⓑ Ⓒ Ⓓ |
| 3. Ⓐ Ⓑ Ⓒ Ⓓ | 24. Ⓐ Ⓑ Ⓒ Ⓓ | 45. Ⓐ Ⓑ Ⓒ Ⓓ | 65. Ⓐ Ⓑ Ⓒ Ⓓ | 85. Ⓐ Ⓑ Ⓒ Ⓓ |
| 4. Ⓐ Ⓑ Ⓒ Ⓓ | 25. Ⓐ Ⓑ Ⓒ Ⓓ | 46. Ⓐ Ⓑ Ⓒ Ⓓ | 66. Ⓐ Ⓑ Ⓒ Ⓓ | 86. Ⓐ Ⓑ Ⓒ Ⓓ |
| 5. Ⓐ Ⓑ Ⓒ Ⓓ | 26. Ⓐ Ⓑ Ⓒ Ⓓ | 47. Ⓐ Ⓑ Ⓒ Ⓓ | 67. Ⓐ Ⓑ Ⓒ Ⓓ | 87. Ⓐ Ⓑ Ⓒ Ⓓ |
| 6. Ⓐ Ⓑ Ⓒ Ⓓ | 27. Ⓐ Ⓑ Ⓒ Ⓓ | 48. Ⓐ Ⓑ Ⓒ Ⓓ | 68. Ⓐ Ⓑ Ⓒ Ⓓ | 88. Ⓐ Ⓑ Ⓒ Ⓓ |
| 7. Ⓐ Ⓑ Ⓒ Ⓓ | 28. Ⓐ Ⓑ Ⓒ Ⓓ | 49. Ⓐ Ⓑ Ⓒ Ⓓ | 69. Ⓐ Ⓑ Ⓒ Ⓓ | 89. Ⓐ Ⓑ Ⓒ Ⓓ |
| 8. Ⓐ Ⓑ Ⓒ Ⓓ | 29. Ⓐ Ⓑ Ⓒ Ⓓ | 50. Ⓐ Ⓑ Ⓒ Ⓓ | 70. Ⓐ Ⓑ Ⓒ Ⓓ | 90. Ⓐ Ⓑ Ⓒ Ⓓ |
| 9. Ⓐ Ⓑ Ⓒ Ⓓ | 30. Ⓐ Ⓑ Ⓒ Ⓓ | 51. Ⓐ Ⓑ Ⓒ Ⓓ | 71. Ⓐ Ⓑ Ⓒ Ⓓ | 91. Ⓐ Ⓑ Ⓒ Ⓓ |
| 10. Ⓐ Ⓑ Ⓒ Ⓓ | 31. Ⓐ Ⓑ Ⓒ Ⓓ | 52. Ⓐ Ⓑ Ⓒ Ⓓ | 72. Ⓐ Ⓑ Ⓒ Ⓓ | 92. Ⓐ Ⓑ Ⓒ Ⓓ |
| 11. Ⓐ Ⓑ Ⓒ Ⓓ | 32. Ⓐ Ⓑ Ⓒ Ⓓ | 53. Ⓐ Ⓑ Ⓒ Ⓓ | 73. Ⓐ Ⓑ Ⓒ Ⓓ | 93. Ⓐ Ⓑ Ⓒ Ⓓ |
| 12. Ⓐ Ⓑ Ⓒ Ⓓ | 33. Ⓐ Ⓑ Ⓒ Ⓓ | 54. Ⓐ Ⓑ Ⓒ Ⓓ | 74. Ⓐ Ⓑ Ⓒ Ⓓ | 94. Ⓐ Ⓑ Ⓒ Ⓓ |
| 13. Ⓐ Ⓑ Ⓒ Ⓓ | 34. Ⓐ Ⓑ Ⓒ Ⓓ | 55. Ⓐ Ⓑ Ⓒ Ⓓ | 75. Ⓐ Ⓑ Ⓒ Ⓓ | 95. Ⓐ Ⓑ Ⓒ Ⓓ |
| 14. Ⓐ Ⓑ Ⓒ Ⓓ | 35. Ⓐ Ⓑ Ⓒ Ⓓ | 56. Ⓐ Ⓑ Ⓒ Ⓓ | 76. Ⓐ Ⓑ Ⓒ Ⓓ | 96. Ⓐ Ⓑ Ⓒ Ⓓ |
| 15. Ⓐ Ⓑ Ⓒ Ⓓ | 36. Ⓐ Ⓑ Ⓒ Ⓓ | 57. Ⓐ Ⓑ Ⓒ Ⓓ | 77. Ⓐ Ⓑ Ⓒ Ⓓ | 97. Ⓐ Ⓑ Ⓒ Ⓓ |
| 16. Ⓐ Ⓑ Ⓒ Ⓓ | 37. Ⓐ Ⓑ Ⓒ Ⓓ | 58. Ⓐ Ⓑ Ⓒ Ⓓ | 78. Ⓐ Ⓑ Ⓒ Ⓓ | 98. Ⓐ Ⓑ Ⓒ Ⓓ |
| 17. Ⓐ Ⓑ Ⓒ Ⓓ | 38. Ⓐ Ⓑ Ⓒ Ⓓ | 59. Ⓐ Ⓑ Ⓒ Ⓓ | 79. Ⓐ Ⓑ Ⓒ Ⓓ | 99. Ⓐ Ⓑ Ⓒ Ⓓ |
| 18. Ⓐ Ⓑ Ⓒ Ⓓ | 39. Ⓐ Ⓑ Ⓒ Ⓓ | 60. Ⓐ Ⓑ Ⓒ Ⓓ | 80. Ⓐ Ⓑ Ⓒ Ⓓ | 100. Ⓐ Ⓑ Ⓒ Ⓓ |
| 19. Ⓐ Ⓑ Ⓒ Ⓓ | 40. Ⓐ Ⓑ Ⓒ Ⓓ | 61. Ⓐ Ⓑ Ⓒ Ⓓ | 81. Ⓐ Ⓑ Ⓒ Ⓓ | 101. Ⓐ Ⓑ Ⓒ Ⓓ |
| 20. Ⓐ Ⓑ Ⓒ Ⓓ | 41. Ⓐ Ⓑ Ⓒ Ⓓ | 62. Ⓐ Ⓑ Ⓒ Ⓓ | 82. Ⓐ Ⓑ Ⓒ Ⓓ | 102. Ⓐ Ⓑ Ⓒ Ⓓ |
| 21. Ⓐ Ⓑ Ⓒ Ⓓ | 42. Ⓐ Ⓑ Ⓒ Ⓓ | | | |

## SECTION 2: FREQUENCY

103. Ⓐ Ⓑ Ⓒ Ⓓ
104. Ⓐ Ⓑ Ⓒ Ⓓ
105. Ⓐ Ⓑ Ⓒ Ⓓ
106. Ⓐ Ⓑ Ⓒ Ⓓ
107. Ⓐ Ⓑ Ⓒ Ⓓ
108. Ⓐ Ⓑ Ⓒ Ⓓ
109. Ⓐ Ⓑ Ⓒ Ⓓ
110. Ⓐ Ⓑ Ⓒ Ⓓ
111. Ⓐ Ⓑ Ⓒ Ⓓ
112. Ⓐ Ⓑ Ⓒ Ⓓ
113. Ⓐ Ⓑ Ⓒ Ⓓ
114. Ⓐ Ⓑ Ⓒ Ⓓ
115. Ⓐ Ⓑ Ⓒ Ⓓ
116. Ⓐ Ⓑ Ⓒ Ⓓ
117. Ⓐ Ⓑ Ⓒ Ⓓ
118. Ⓐ Ⓑ Ⓒ Ⓓ
119. Ⓐ Ⓑ Ⓒ Ⓓ
120. Ⓐ Ⓑ Ⓒ Ⓓ
121. Ⓐ Ⓑ Ⓒ Ⓓ
122. Ⓐ Ⓑ Ⓒ Ⓓ
123. Ⓐ Ⓑ Ⓒ Ⓓ

124. Ⓐ Ⓑ Ⓒ Ⓓ
125. Ⓐ Ⓑ Ⓒ Ⓓ
126. Ⓐ Ⓑ Ⓒ Ⓓ
127. Ⓐ Ⓑ Ⓒ Ⓓ
128. Ⓐ Ⓑ Ⓒ Ⓓ
129. Ⓐ Ⓑ Ⓒ Ⓓ
130. Ⓐ Ⓑ Ⓒ Ⓓ
131. Ⓐ Ⓑ Ⓒ Ⓓ
132. Ⓐ Ⓑ Ⓒ Ⓓ
133. Ⓐ Ⓑ Ⓒ Ⓓ
134. Ⓐ Ⓑ Ⓒ Ⓓ
135. Ⓐ Ⓑ Ⓒ Ⓓ
136. Ⓐ Ⓑ Ⓒ Ⓓ
137. Ⓐ Ⓑ Ⓒ Ⓓ
138. Ⓐ Ⓑ Ⓒ Ⓓ
139. Ⓐ Ⓑ Ⓒ Ⓓ
140. Ⓐ Ⓑ Ⓒ Ⓓ
141. Ⓐ Ⓑ Ⓒ Ⓓ
142. Ⓐ Ⓑ Ⓒ Ⓓ
143. Ⓐ Ⓑ Ⓒ Ⓓ
144. Ⓐ Ⓑ Ⓒ Ⓓ

145. Ⓐ Ⓑ Ⓒ Ⓓ
146. Ⓐ Ⓑ Ⓒ Ⓓ
147. Ⓐ Ⓑ Ⓒ Ⓓ
148. Ⓐ Ⓑ Ⓒ Ⓓ
149. Ⓐ Ⓑ Ⓒ Ⓓ
150. Ⓐ Ⓑ Ⓒ Ⓓ
151. Ⓐ Ⓑ Ⓒ Ⓓ
152. Ⓐ Ⓑ Ⓒ Ⓓ
153. Ⓐ Ⓑ Ⓒ Ⓓ
154. Ⓐ Ⓑ Ⓒ Ⓓ
155. Ⓐ Ⓑ Ⓒ Ⓓ
156. Ⓐ Ⓑ Ⓒ Ⓓ
157. Ⓐ Ⓑ Ⓒ Ⓓ
158. Ⓐ Ⓑ Ⓒ Ⓓ
159. Ⓐ Ⓑ Ⓒ Ⓓ
160. Ⓐ Ⓑ Ⓒ Ⓓ
161. Ⓐ Ⓑ Ⓒ Ⓓ
162. Ⓐ Ⓑ Ⓒ Ⓓ
163. Ⓐ Ⓑ Ⓒ Ⓓ
164. Ⓐ Ⓑ Ⓒ Ⓓ
165. Ⓐ Ⓑ Ⓒ Ⓓ

166. Ⓐ Ⓑ Ⓒ Ⓓ
167. Ⓐ Ⓑ Ⓒ Ⓓ
168. Ⓐ Ⓑ Ⓒ Ⓓ
169. Ⓐ Ⓑ Ⓒ Ⓓ
170. Ⓐ Ⓑ Ⓒ Ⓓ
171. Ⓐ Ⓑ Ⓒ Ⓓ
172. Ⓐ Ⓑ Ⓒ Ⓓ
173. Ⓐ Ⓑ Ⓒ Ⓓ
174. Ⓐ Ⓑ Ⓒ Ⓓ
175. Ⓐ Ⓑ Ⓒ Ⓓ
176. Ⓐ Ⓑ Ⓒ Ⓓ
177. Ⓐ Ⓑ Ⓒ Ⓓ
178. Ⓐ Ⓑ Ⓒ Ⓓ
179. Ⓐ Ⓑ Ⓒ Ⓓ
180. Ⓐ Ⓑ Ⓒ Ⓓ
181. Ⓐ Ⓑ Ⓒ Ⓓ
182. Ⓐ Ⓑ Ⓒ Ⓓ
183. Ⓐ Ⓑ Ⓒ Ⓓ
184. Ⓐ Ⓑ Ⓒ Ⓓ
185. Ⓐ Ⓑ Ⓒ Ⓓ
186. Ⓐ Ⓑ Ⓒ Ⓓ

**answer sheet**

## SECTION 3: EXPERIENCE

187. Ⓐ Ⓑ Ⓒ Ⓓ Ⓔ Ⓕ Ⓖ Ⓗ Ⓘ
188. Ⓐ Ⓑ Ⓒ Ⓓ Ⓔ Ⓕ Ⓖ Ⓗ Ⓘ
189. Ⓐ Ⓑ Ⓒ Ⓓ Ⓔ Ⓕ Ⓖ Ⓗ Ⓘ
190. Ⓐ Ⓑ Ⓒ Ⓓ Ⓔ Ⓕ Ⓖ Ⓗ Ⓘ
191. Ⓐ Ⓑ Ⓒ Ⓓ Ⓔ Ⓕ Ⓖ Ⓗ Ⓘ
192. Ⓐ Ⓑ Ⓒ Ⓓ Ⓔ Ⓕ Ⓖ Ⓗ Ⓘ
193. Ⓐ Ⓑ Ⓒ Ⓓ Ⓔ Ⓕ Ⓖ Ⓗ Ⓘ
194. Ⓐ Ⓑ Ⓒ Ⓓ Ⓔ Ⓕ Ⓖ Ⓗ Ⓘ
195. Ⓐ Ⓑ Ⓒ Ⓓ Ⓔ Ⓕ Ⓖ Ⓗ Ⓘ
196. Ⓐ Ⓑ Ⓒ Ⓓ Ⓔ Ⓕ Ⓖ Ⓗ Ⓘ
197. Ⓐ Ⓑ Ⓒ Ⓓ Ⓔ Ⓕ Ⓖ Ⓗ Ⓘ
198. Ⓐ Ⓑ Ⓒ Ⓓ Ⓔ Ⓕ Ⓖ Ⓗ Ⓘ
199. Ⓐ Ⓑ Ⓒ Ⓓ Ⓔ Ⓕ Ⓖ Ⓗ Ⓘ
200. Ⓐ Ⓑ Ⓒ Ⓓ Ⓔ Ⓕ Ⓖ Ⓗ Ⓘ
201. Ⓐ Ⓑ Ⓒ Ⓓ Ⓔ Ⓕ Ⓖ Ⓗ Ⓘ
202. Ⓐ Ⓑ Ⓒ Ⓓ Ⓔ Ⓕ Ⓖ Ⓗ Ⓘ
203. Ⓐ Ⓑ Ⓒ Ⓓ Ⓔ Ⓕ Ⓖ Ⓗ Ⓘ

204. Ⓐ Ⓑ Ⓒ Ⓓ Ⓔ Ⓕ Ⓖ Ⓗ Ⓘ
205. Ⓐ Ⓑ Ⓒ Ⓓ Ⓔ Ⓕ Ⓖ Ⓗ Ⓘ
206. Ⓐ Ⓑ Ⓒ Ⓓ Ⓔ Ⓕ Ⓖ Ⓗ Ⓘ
207. Ⓐ Ⓑ Ⓒ Ⓓ Ⓔ Ⓕ Ⓖ Ⓗ Ⓘ
208. Ⓐ Ⓑ Ⓒ Ⓓ Ⓔ Ⓕ Ⓖ Ⓗ Ⓘ
209. Ⓐ Ⓑ Ⓒ Ⓓ Ⓔ Ⓕ Ⓖ Ⓗ Ⓘ
210. Ⓐ Ⓑ Ⓒ Ⓓ Ⓔ Ⓕ Ⓖ Ⓗ Ⓘ
211. Ⓐ Ⓑ Ⓒ Ⓓ Ⓔ Ⓕ Ⓖ Ⓗ Ⓘ
212. Ⓐ Ⓑ Ⓒ Ⓓ Ⓔ Ⓕ Ⓖ Ⓗ Ⓘ
213. Ⓐ Ⓑ Ⓒ Ⓓ Ⓔ Ⓕ Ⓖ Ⓗ Ⓘ
214. Ⓐ Ⓑ Ⓒ Ⓓ Ⓔ Ⓕ Ⓖ Ⓗ Ⓘ
215. Ⓐ Ⓑ Ⓒ Ⓓ Ⓔ Ⓕ Ⓖ Ⓗ Ⓘ
216. Ⓐ Ⓑ Ⓒ Ⓓ Ⓔ Ⓕ Ⓖ Ⓗ Ⓘ
217. Ⓐ Ⓑ Ⓒ Ⓓ Ⓔ Ⓕ Ⓖ Ⓗ Ⓘ
218. Ⓐ Ⓑ Ⓒ Ⓓ Ⓔ Ⓕ Ⓖ Ⓗ Ⓘ
219. Ⓐ Ⓑ Ⓒ Ⓓ Ⓔ Ⓕ Ⓖ Ⓗ Ⓘ
220. Ⓐ Ⓑ Ⓒ Ⓓ Ⓔ Ⓕ Ⓖ Ⓗ Ⓘ

221. Ⓐ Ⓑ Ⓒ Ⓓ Ⓔ Ⓕ Ⓖ Ⓗ Ⓘ
222. Ⓐ Ⓑ Ⓒ Ⓓ Ⓔ Ⓕ Ⓖ Ⓗ Ⓘ
223. Ⓐ Ⓑ Ⓒ Ⓓ Ⓔ Ⓕ Ⓖ Ⓗ Ⓘ
224. Ⓐ Ⓑ Ⓒ Ⓓ Ⓔ Ⓕ Ⓖ Ⓗ Ⓘ
225. Ⓐ Ⓑ Ⓒ Ⓓ Ⓔ Ⓕ Ⓖ Ⓗ Ⓘ
226. Ⓐ Ⓑ Ⓒ Ⓓ Ⓔ Ⓕ Ⓖ Ⓗ Ⓘ
227. Ⓐ Ⓑ Ⓒ Ⓓ Ⓔ Ⓕ Ⓖ Ⓗ Ⓘ
228. Ⓐ Ⓑ Ⓒ Ⓓ Ⓔ Ⓕ Ⓖ Ⓗ Ⓘ
229. Ⓐ Ⓑ Ⓒ Ⓓ Ⓔ Ⓕ Ⓖ Ⓗ Ⓘ
230. Ⓐ Ⓑ Ⓒ Ⓓ Ⓔ Ⓕ Ⓖ Ⓗ Ⓘ
231. Ⓐ Ⓑ Ⓒ Ⓓ Ⓔ Ⓕ Ⓖ Ⓗ Ⓘ
232. Ⓐ Ⓑ Ⓒ Ⓓ Ⓔ Ⓕ Ⓖ Ⓗ Ⓘ
233. Ⓐ Ⓑ Ⓒ Ⓓ Ⓔ Ⓕ Ⓖ Ⓗ Ⓘ
234. Ⓐ Ⓑ Ⓒ Ⓓ Ⓔ Ⓕ Ⓖ Ⓗ Ⓘ
235. Ⓐ Ⓑ Ⓒ Ⓓ Ⓔ Ⓕ Ⓖ Ⓗ Ⓘ
236. Ⓐ Ⓑ Ⓒ Ⓓ Ⓔ Ⓕ Ⓖ Ⓗ Ⓘ

# Practice Test 1: Exams 473/473-C and 460

**NOTE:** Practice Tests 1–5 are a combination of the types of questions test-takers will see on Exam 473 and Exam 460.

Exam 473 consists of four parts:

A.  Address Checking

B.  Forms Completion

C.  Coding and Memory

D.  Personal Characteristics and Experience Inventory

Exam 460 consists of four parts:

A.  Address Checking

B.  Memory for Addresses

C.  Number Series

D.  Following Oral Instructions

If you are practicing to take Exam 460, you may want to follow these tips:

- Skip Part B (Forms Completion) of Practice Tests 1 through 5. This material will not be included on your actual exam; it is only on Exam 473.

- Skip Part D (Personal Characteristics and Experience Inventory) of Practice Test 1. This material will not be included on your actual exam; it is only on Exam 473.

- To practice for Part D of Exam 460 (Following Oral Instructions), take Practice Test 7 in this book.

practice test 1

# PART A: ADDRESS CHECKING

**60 QUESTIONS • 11 MINUTES**

**Directions:** Compare the **List to be Checked** with the **Correct List.** Decide if there are **(A) NO ERRORS,** an error in the **(B) ADDRESS ONLY,** an error in the **(C) ZIP CODE ONLY,** or an error in the **(D) BOTH** the address and ZIP Code. Record your answers on the answer sheet.

| | Correct List | | List to be Checked | |
|---|---|---|---|---|
| | *Address* | *ZIP Code* | *Address* | *ZIP Code* |
| **1.** | 462 Midland Avenue<br>Wappingers Falls, NY | 12590-7287 | 462 Midland Avenue<br>Wappingers Falls, NY | 12590-7287 |
| **2.** | 2319 Sherry Dr.<br>Worcester, MA | 01610-0010 | 3219 Sherry Dr.<br>Worcester, ME | 01610-0010 |
| **3.** | 1015 Kimball Ave.<br>Miami Beach, FL | 33139-4242 | 1015 Kimball Ave.<br>Miami Beach, FL | 33193-4242 |
| **4.** | 1255 North Avenue<br>Palm Springs, CA | 92262-0777 | 1225 North Avenue<br>Palm Springs, CA | 92262-0777 |
| **5.** | 1826 Tibbets Road<br>Buffalo, New York | 42113-6281 | 1826 Tibetts Road<br>Buffulo, New York | 42113-6281 |
| **6.** | 603 N. Division Street<br>Watertown, MA | 02172-3975 | 603 N. Division Street<br>Watertown, MA | 02172-3975 |
| **7.** | 2304 Manhattan Avenue<br>West Chester, PA | 19380-4201 | 2034 Manhattan Avenue<br>West Chester, PA | 19830-4201 |
| **8.** | 1186 Vernon Drive, Apt. B<br>Sunrise, FL | 33313-6223 | 186 Vernon Drive, Apt. B<br>Sunrise, FL | 33133-6223 |
| **9.** | 209 Peter Bont Rd<br>Dover, DE | 19901-8781 | 209 Peter Bent Rd<br>Dover, DL | 19901-8781 |
| **10.** | 1100 West Ave<br>Purchase, NY | 10577-9001 | 1100 East Ave<br>Purchase, NY | 10577-9001 |
| **11.** | 2063 Winyah Terrace<br>Elmhurst, NY | 11373-6112 | 2036 Winyah Terrace<br>Elmherst, NY | 11373-6112 |
| **12.** | 3483 Suncrest Avenue<br>Wilmington, DE | 19810-8638 | 3483 Suncrest Drive<br>Wilmington, DE | 19810-8638 |

**Directions:** Compare the **List to be Checked** with the **Correct List.** Decide if there are **(A) NO ERRORS,** an error in the **(B) ADDRESS ONLY,** an error in the **(C) ZIP CODE ONLY,** or an error in **(D) BOTH** the address and ZIP Code. Record your answers on the answer sheet.

| | | | | |
|---|---|---|---|---|
| **13.** | 234 Rochambeau Road<br>Bronxville, NY | 10708-1089 | 234 Roshambeau Road<br>Bronxville, NJ | 10708-1089 |
| **14.** | 306 N. Terrace Blvd.<br>Baltimore, MD | 21215-1121 | 306 N. Terrace Blvd.<br>Baltimore, MD | 21215-1121 |
| **15.** | 1632 Paine Street, P.O. Box 17374<br>Miami Beach, FL | 33179-3111 | 1632 Pain Street, P.O. Box 17374<br>Miami, FL | 33179-3111 |
| **16.** | 286 Marietta Avenue<br>Indianapolis, IN | 46260-3974 | 286 Marrietta Avenue<br>Indianapolis, IN | 46260-3974 |
| **17.** | 2445 Pigott Road, Apt. C210<br>Jamaica, NY | 11435-5627 | 2445 Pigott Road, Apt. C210<br>Jamiaca, NY | 11435-5627 |
| **18.** | 2204 PineBrook Boulevard<br>Kew Gardens, NY | 11415-6002 | 2204 Pinebrook Boulevard<br>Kew Garden, NY | 11415-6002 |
| **19.** | 487 Warburton Avenue<br>Bronx, New York | 10475-7881 | 487 Warburton Avenue<br>Bronx, New York | 10475-7881 |
| **20.** | 9386 North Street<br>Darien, CT | 06820-9000 | 9386 North Avenue<br>Darien, CT | 06820-9000 |
| **21.** | 2272 Glandale Rd.<br>Ontarioville, IL | 60103-1421 | 2772 Glandale Rd.<br>Ontarioville, IL | 60103-1421 |
| **22.** | 9236 Puritan Drive<br>Quickley, MA | 09821-1692 | 9236 Puritan Place<br>Quickley, ME | 09821-1692 |
| **23.** | 7803 Kimball Avenue<br>Walden, Colorado | 80480-8171 | 7803 Kimbal Avenue<br>Waldon, Colorado | 08480-8171 |
| **24.** | 1362 Colonial Pkwy<br>Muscle Shoals, AL | 35660-1498 | 1362 Colonial Pkwy<br>Muscle Shoals, AL | 35660-1498 |
| **25.** | 115 Rolling Hills Road<br>Daytona Beach, Fla | 32016-0749 | 115 Rolling Hills Road<br>Daytona Beach, FL | 32016-0749 |
| **26.** | 218 Rockledge Road<br>Hammond, GA | 31785-0414 | 2181 Rockledge Road<br>Hammond, GA | 31785-0414 |
| **27.** | 8346 N. Broadnax Street<br>Francisco, Wyoming | 82636-1227 | 8346 W. Broadnax Street<br>Francisco, Wyoming | 82636-1227 |

**Directions:** Compare the **List to be Checked** with the **Correct List.** Decide if there are **(A) NO ERRORS,** an error in the **(B) ADDRESS ONLY,** an error in the **(C) ZIP CODE ONLY,** or an error in **(D) BOTH** the address and ZIP Code. Record your answers on the answer sheet.

| | | | | | |
|---|---|---|---|---|---|
| **28.** | 9224 Highland Way, Box 321 Centralville, MT | 08869-0102 | 9244 Highland Way, Box 321 Centralville, MT | 08869-0102 | |
| **29.** | 8383 Mamaroneck Avenue Quenemo, Kansas | 66528-0322 | 8383 Mamaroneck Avenue Quenemo, Kansas | 66528-0322 | |
| **30.** | 276 Furnace Dock Road Wilburnum, MS | 65566-1217 | 276 Furnace Dock Road Vilburnum, MS | 65566-1217 | |
| **31.** | 4137 Loockerman St Ware, MA | 08215-0323 | 4137 Lockerman St Ware, MA | 08215-0323 | |
| **32.** | 532 Broadhollow Rd. Scarsdale, NY | 10583-0720 | 532 Broadhollow Rd. Scarsdale, NY | 10583-0720 | |
| **33.** | 148 Cortlandt Road Milwaukee, Wisconsin | 53202-0929 | 148 Cortland Road Milwaukee, Wisconsin | 53202-0929 | |
| **34.** | 5951 W. Hartsdale Road Portland, OR | 97208-0602 | 5951 W. Hartsdale Avenue Portland, OR | 97208-0602 | |
| **35.** | 5231 Alta Vista Circle Omaha, NE | 68127-0928 | 5321 Alta Vista Circle Omaha, NE | 68127-0928 | |
| **36.** | 6459 Chippewa Rd Dallas, Texas | 75234-0127 | 6459 Chippewa Rd Dallas, Texas | 75224-0127 | |
| **37.** | 1171 S. Highland Road San Francisco, CA | 94108-0124 | 1771 S. Highland Road San Francisco, CA | 94108-0124 | |
| **38.** | 2363 Old Farm Ln Westport, CT | 06880-0203 | 2363 Old Farm Ln Westport, CT | 06888-0203 | |
| **39.** | 1001 Hemingway Drive Noquochoke, MA | 02790-1227 | 1001 Hemmingway Drive Noquochoke, MA | 02790-1227 | |
| **40.** | 1555 Morningside Ave Kingsfield, Maine | 04947-1010 | 1555 Morningslide Ave Kingsfield, Maine | 04947-1010 | |
| **41.** | 1189 E. 9th Street Seattle, WA | 98102-0724 | 1189 E. 9th Street Seattle, WY | 98102-0724 | |
| **42.** | 168 Old Lyme Road Boiceville, NY | 12412-0710 | 186 Old Lyme Road Boiceville, NY | 12412-0710 | |

> **Directions:** Compare the **List to be Checked** with the **Correct List.** Decide if there are **(A) NO ERRORS,** an error in the **(B) ADDRESS ONLY,** an error in the **(C) ZIP CODE ONLY,** or an error in **(D) BOTH** the address and ZIP Code. Record your answers on the answer sheet.

**43.** 106 Notingham Rd
New Orleans, LA    70153-0114      106 Nottingham Rd
New Orleans, LA    70153-0114

**44.** 1428 Midland Avenue
Charlotte, VT    05445-0229      1428 Midland Avenue
Charlotte, VA    05445-0229

**45.** 1450 West Chester Pike
Havertown, PA    19083-1020      1450 West Chester Pike
Havertown, PA    19883-1020

**46.** 3357 Main St.
Freeport, ME    04033-0528      3357 Main St.
Freeport, NE    04033-0528

**47.** 5062 Marietta Ave.
Natick, MA    01760-0607      5062 Marrietta Ave.
Natick, MA    01760-0607

**48.** 1890 3rd Court
Irvington, NY    10533-0811      1980 3rd Court
Irvington, NY    10533-0811

**49.** 1075 Park Avenue
Sea Island, GA    31561-0412      1075 W. Park Avenue
Sea Inland, GA    31561-0412

**50.** 672 Bacon Hill Rd.
Providence, RI    02903-0510      672 Beacon Hill Rd.
Providence, RI    02903-0510

**51.** 1725 W. 17th Street
Arundel, ME    04046-0727      1725 W. 17th Street
Anurdel, ME    04046-0727

**52.** 2066 Old Wilmot Road
Oakland, Calif.    94604-6801      2066 Old Wilmont Road
Oakland, Calif.    94604-6801

**53.** 3333 State Road
Philadelphia, PA    19124-4211      3333 State Road
Philadelphia, PN    19124-4211

**54.** 1483 Meritoria Drive
Essex, CT    06426-3007      1438 Meritoria Drive
Essex, CT    06426-3007

**55.** 2327 E. 23rd St
Alamo, TX    78516-7321      2327 E. 27th St
Alamo, TX    78516-7321

**56.** 137 Clarence Rd.
Los Angeles, CA    90013-6111      137 Claremont Rd.
Los Angeles, CA    90018-6111

**57.** 3516 N. Ely Avenue
New York, NY    10016-8090      3516 N. Ely Avenue
New York, NY    10016-8090

practice test

**Directions:** Compare the **List to be Checked** with the **Correct List.** Decide if there are **(A) NO ERRORS,** an error in the **(B) ADDRESS ONLY,** an error in the **(C) ZIP CODE ONLY,** or an error in **(D) BOTH** the address and ZIP Code. Record your answers on the answer sheet.

| | | | | |
|---|---|---|---|---|
| **58.** | 111 Beechwood Street<br>Gainesville, Florida | 43611-9176 | 1111 Beechwood Street<br>Gainsville, Florida | 32611-9176 |
| **59.** | 143 N. Highland Avenue<br>Onoro, ME | 04473-7467 | 143 N. Highland Avenue<br>Orono, ME | 04473-7467 |
| **60.** | 6430 Spring Mill Road<br>Des Moines, Iowa | 50311-0001 | 6340 Spring Mill Road<br>Des Moines, Iowa | 50311-0001 |

# PART B: FORMS COMPLETION

**30 QUESTIONS • 15 MINUTES**

**Directions:** Read each form and answer the items based on the information provided. Mark your answers on the answer sheet.

1. Which of these would be a correct entry for Box 5?
   - **(A)** A check mark
   - **(B)** $13.85
   - **(C)** 12 and 20
   - **(D)** 08530

2. Where would you enter the insurance fee?
   - **(A)** Box 3
   - **(B)** Box 6
   - **(C)** Box 10
   - **(D)** Box 12

3. A check mark would be the correct entry for every box EXCEPT
   - **(A)** Box 6
   - **(B)** Box 7a
   - **(C)** Box 8a
   - **(D)** Box 11b

4. Where would you indicate that the package was delivered?
   - **(A)** Box 16
   - **(B)** Box 18
   - **(C)** Box 19
   - **(D)** Box 22

5. All of the following boxes indicate employee signatures are needed EXCEPT
   (A) Box 4
   (B) Box 18
   (C) Box 21
   (D) Box 24

6. Which of these would be a correct entry for Box 13b?
   (A) A check mark
   (B) 3 lbs. 6 oz.
   (C) 4/11
   (D) $13.85

7. Which box would you check to show 2nd day delivery to the military?
   (A) Box 2a
   (B) Box 2b
   (C) Box 8a
   (D) Box 11a

8. The country code for mail being sent out of the United States is entered in which box?
   (A) Box 1
   (B) Box 14
   (C) Box 15
   (D) Box 16

9. Which of these would be the correct entry for Box 15?
   (A) A check mark
   (B) $1.60
   (C) Initials
   (D) 6/12/08

| 1a | 1b | 1c | 1d | 1e | 1f |
|----|----|----|----|----|----|

| | | | | | | |
|---|---|---|---|---|---|---|
| Item Description (Nature de l'envoi) | Registered □ Article (Envoi recommandé) | □ Letter (Lettre) | Printed □ Matter (imprimé) | □ Other (Autre) | Recorded Delivery □ (Envoi à livraison attestée) | Express □ Mail International |
| Insured Parcel  2 □ (Colis avec valeur déclarée) | | Insured Value (Valeur déclarée)  3 | | | Article Number  4 | |
| Office of Mailing (Bureau de dépôt)  5 | | | | Date of Posting (Date de dépôt)  6 | | |
| Addressee Name or Firm (Nom ou raison sociale du destinataire)  7 | | | | | | |
| Street and No. (Rue et No.)  8 | | | | | | |
| Place and Country (Localité et pays)  9 | | | | | | |

This receipt must be signed by: (1) the addressee; or, (2) a person authorized to sign under the regulations of the country of destination; or, (3) if those regulations so provide, by the employee of the office of destination. This signed form will be returned to the sender by the first mail.

(Cet avis doit être signé par le destinataire ou par une personne y autorisée en vertu des règlements du pays de destination, ou, si ces règlements le comportent, par l'agent du bureau de destination, et renvoyé par le premier courrier directement à expéditeur).

Postmark of the office of destination (Timbre du bureau de destination)  14

□ The article mentioned above was duly delivered. (L'envoi mentionné ci-dessus a été dûment livré.)  10   Date  11

Signature of Addressee (Signature du destinataire)  12

Office of Destination Employee Signature (Signature de l'agent du bureau du destination)  13

PS Form **2865**, February 1997 (Reverse)

10. Which of these would be a correct entry for Box 9?
    (A) Paris, France
    (B) Ms. Marie Hrouda
    (C) 10/21/09
    (D) $100

11. Where would you indicate that the item is Express Mail International?
    (A) Box 1a
    (B) Box 1b
    (C) Box 1c
    (D) Box 1f

12. Which of these would be a correct entry for Box 7?
   (A) A check mark
   (B) Computer Programmers World-wide
   (C) 14 Piccadilly Lane
   (D) 9/30/08

13. How would you indicate that the piece of mail was a letter?
   (A) Check Box 1a
   (B) Check Box 1b
   (C) Write "letter" in Box 3
   (D) Write "letter" in Box 5

14. Where would you enter the Article Number?
   (A) Box 2
   (B) Box 3
   (C) Box 4
   (D) Box 6

15. Which of these would be the correct entry for Box 3?
   (A) A check mark
   (B) Peoria, IL
   (C) London, England
   (D) $250

16. Where would you enter the check number for the COD package?
   (A) Box 2
   (B) Box 3
   (C) Box 4
   (D) Box 5

17. Which of the following would be a correct entry for Box 2?
   (A) 2/22/09
   (B) A check mark
   (C) #2345
   (D) Mr. Steve Krasowski

18. You could enter a date in each of the following boxes EXCEPT
   (A) Box 1
   (B) Box 4
   (C) Box 5
   (D) Box 6

U.S. Postal Service™
CERTIFIED MAIL™ RECEIPT
(Domestic Mail Only; No Insurance Coverage Provided)

For delivery information vist our website at www.usps.com.

OFFICIAL USE

| | | |
|---|---|---|
| Postage | $ **1** | |
| Certified Fee | **2** | **6** |
| Return Receipt Fee (Endorsement Required) | **3** | Postmark Here |
| Restricted Delivery Fee (Endorsement Required) | **4** | |
| Total Postage & Fees | $ **5** | |

Sent To:                           **7**

Street, Apt No.;
or PO Box No.                    **8**

City, State, ZIP+ 4            **9**

PS Form 3800, June 2002          See Reverse for Instructions

CERTIFIED MAIL™

PLACE STICKER AT TOP OF ENVELOPE TO THE RIGHT OF RETURN ADDRESS  FOLD AT DOTTED LINE

7000 0520 0017 2917 7637

**19.** Which of these would be a correct entry for Box 7?
- **(A)** A check mark
- **(B)** $1,000
- **(C)** Ms. Dy Anne Going
- **(D)** 3/22/09

**20.** Where would you stamp the receipt?
- **(A)** Box 1
- **(B)** Box 2
- **(C)** Box 6
- **(D)** Box 9

**21.** Where would you indicate that the item is being sent to Boston?
- **(A)** Box 2
- **(B)** Box 4
- **(C)** Box 6
- **(D)** Box 9

**Authorization to Hold Mail**

NOTE: *Complete and give to your letter carrier or mail to the post office that delivers your mail.*

➤ We can hold your mail for a minimum of **3**, but not for more than **30 days.**

**Postmaster: Please hold mail for:**

Name(s)

☐ **A.** Please deliver all accumulated mail and resume normal delivery on the ending date shown below.

Address *(Number, street, apt./suite no., city, state, ZIP + 4)*

☐ **B.** I will pick up all accumulated mail when I return and understand that mail delivery will not resume until I do.

| Beginning Date | Ending Date *(May only be changed by the customer in writing)* | Customer Signature |
|---|---|---|

**For Post Office Use Only**

| Date Received **1.** | | Bin Number **3.** |
|---|---|---|
| Clerk **2.** | | |
| Carrier **4.** | | Route Number **5.** |

*(Complete this section only if customer selected option B)*

| **6.** ☐ Accumulated mail has been picked up. | Resume Delivery of Mail *(Date)* **7.** | By **8.** |
|---|---|---|

PS Form **8076,** April 2001

---

**22.** Which of these would be a correct entry for Box 5?
 **(A)** Rural Route 5
 **(B)** $1.60
 **(C)** 6/5/08
 **(D)** Tim Criswell

**23.** Where would you enter the mail carrier's name?
 **(A)** Box 1
 **(B)** Box 2
 **(C)** Box 3
 **(D)** Box 4

**24.** Which of these would be a correct answer for Box 6?
 **(A)** A check mark
 **(B)** 5/20/09
 **(C)** 5/20/09 to 6/1/09
 **(D)** Michelle McDermott

**25.** Which of these would be a correct answer for Box 7?
 **(A)** A check mark
 **(B)** 1/20/09
 **(C)** 510 Crescent Boulevard
 **(D)** 07046

26. Where would you check that the item is perishable?
    (A) Box 2a
    (B) Box 2b
    (C) Box 2c
    (D) Box 3b

27. Where would you enter the total postage and fees?
    (A) Box 1
    (B) Box 3a
    (C) Box 5
    (D) Box 7

28. What would be the correct entry for Box 8?
    (A) A check mark
    (B) A postmark
    (C) $2.50
    (D) 12456

29. If the item was being mailed to a foreign country, which box could NOT be completed?
    (A) Box 1
    (B) Box 3b
    (C) Box 4
    (D) Box 5

30. You could enter fees in all of the following boxes EXCEPT
    (A) Box 1
    (B) Box 2a
    (C) Box 3a
    (D) Box 4

## PART C: CODING AND MEMORY

### Coding Section: Segment 1

**4 QUESTIONS • 2 MINUTES**

**Directions:** Segment 1 is *not* scored and does not count toward your total exam score. It is a practice exercise to help you with the Coding Section under a time constraint similar to the one used in the scored Coding Section. Use the coding guide below to match each address to a delivery route. Mark your answers on the answer section at the bottom of this page.

### CODING GUIDE

| ADDRESS RANGE | DELIVERY ROUTE |
|---|---|
| 100–199 N. Broad Avenue<br>50–250 E. 12th Street<br>10–25 E. Chestnut Street | A |
| 200–500 N. Broad Avenue<br>26–70 E. Chestnut Street | B |
| 20–35 Rural Route 2<br>7000–15000 S. Broad Avenue<br>300–1000 S. Chester Road | C |
| All mail that doesn't fall into one of the address ranges listed above. | D |

| | Address | Delivery Route | | | |
|---|---|---|---|---|---|
| 1. | 37 Rural Route 2 | A | B | C | D |
| 2. | 115 E. 12th Street | A | B | C | D |
| 3. | 8742 S. Broad Avenue | A | B | C | D |
| 4. | 62 E. Chestnut Street | A | B | C | D |

### Sample Answer Sheet

1. Ⓐ Ⓑ Ⓒ Ⓓ      3. Ⓐ Ⓑ Ⓒ Ⓓ

2. Ⓐ Ⓑ Ⓒ Ⓓ      4. Ⓐ Ⓑ Ⓒ Ⓓ

## Coding Section: Segment 2

**8 QUESTIONS • 1.5 MINUTES (90 SECONDS)**

**Directions:** Segment 2 is *not* scored and does not count toward your total exam score. It is a practice exercise to help you with the Coding Section under a time constraint similar to the one used in the scored Coding Section. Use the coding guide below to match each address to a delivery route. Mark your answers on the answer section at the bottom of this page.

### CODING GUIDE

| ADDRESS RANGE | DELIVERY ROUTE |
| --- | --- |
| 100−199 N. Broad Avenue<br>50−250 E. 12th Street<br>10−25 E. Chestnut Street | A |
| 200−500 N. Broad Avenue<br>26−70 E. Chestnut Street | B |
| 20−35 Rural Route 2<br>7000−15000 S. Broad Avenue<br>300−1000 S. Chester Road | C |
| All mail that doesn't fall into one of the address ranges listed above. | D |

| Address | Delivery Route | | | |
| --- | --- | --- | --- | --- |
| 1. 421 S. Chester Road | A | B | C | D |
| 2. 326 N. Broad Avenue | A | B | C | D |
| 3. 13131 S. Broad Avenue | A | B | C | D |
| 4. 16000 S. Broad Avenue | A | B | C | D |
| 5. 115 E. 12th Street | A | B | C | D |
| 6. 62 E. Chestnut Street | A | B | C | D |
| 7. 555 S. Chester Road | A | B | C | D |
| 8. 12 E. Chestnut Street | A | B | C | D |

## Sample Answer Sheet

1. Ⓐ Ⓑ Ⓒ Ⓓ     4. Ⓐ Ⓑ Ⓒ Ⓓ     7. Ⓐ Ⓑ Ⓒ Ⓓ

2. Ⓐ Ⓑ Ⓒ Ⓓ     5. Ⓐ Ⓑ Ⓒ Ⓓ     8. Ⓐ Ⓑ Ⓒ Ⓓ

3. Ⓐ Ⓑ Ⓒ Ⓓ     6. Ⓐ Ⓑ Ⓒ Ⓓ

## Coding Section: Segment 3

**36 QUESTIONS • 6 MINUTES**

**Directions:** This is the actual *scored* Coding Section of the exam. Work through items 1 through 36, assigning a code to each item based on the Coding Guide below. Mark your answers on the answer sheet. Work quickly and accurately.

### CODING GUIDE

| ADDRESS RANGE | DELIVERY ROUTE |
|---|---|
| 100–199 N. Broad Avenue<br>50–250 E. 12th Street<br>10–25 E. Chestnut Street | A |
| 200–500 N. Broad Avenue<br>26–70 E. Chestnut Street | B |
| 20–35 Rural Route 2<br>7000–15000 S. Broad Avenue<br>300–1000 S. Chester Road | C |
| All mail that doesn't fall into one of the address ranges listed above. | D |

| | Address | Delivery Route | | | |
|---|---|---|---|---|---|
| 1. | 105 N. Broad Avenue | A | B | C | D |
| 2. | 52 E. Chestnut Street | A | B | C | D |
| 3. | 220 N. Brook Street | A | B | C | D |
| 4. | 195 E. 12th Street | A | B | C | D |
| 5. | 68 E. Chestnut Street | A | B | C | D |
| 6. | 28 Rural Route 2 | A | B | C | D |
| 7. | 7801 S. Broad Avenue | A | B | C | D |
| 8. | 10 Rural Route 2 | A | B | C | D |
| 9. | 42 Rural Route 2 | A | B | C | D |
| 10. | 72 E. 12th Street | A | B | C | D |
| 11. | 152 N. Brook Street | A | B | C | D |
| 12. | 9500 S. Broad Avenue | A | B | C | D |
| 13. | 900 S. Chester Road | A | B | C | D |
| 14. | 1000 N. Broad Avenue | A | B | C | D |
| 15. | 401 N. Broad Avenue | A | B | C | D |
| 16. | 76 E. Chestnut Street | A | B | C | D |

## CODING GUIDE

| ADDRESS RANGE | DELIVERY ROUTE |
|---|---|
| 100−199 N. Broad Avenue<br>50−250 E. 12th Street<br>10−25 E. Chestnut Street | A |
| 200−500 N. Broad Avenue<br>26−70 E. Chestnut Street | B |
| 20−35 Rural Route 2<br>7000−15000 S. Broad Avenue<br>300−1000 S. Chester Road | C |
| All mail that doesn't fall into one of the address ranges listed above. | D |

| # | Address | | | | |
|---|---|---|---|---|---|
| 17. | 368 N. Broad Avenue | A | B | C | D |
| 18. | 8620 S. Broad Avenue | A | B | C | D |
| 19. | 1201 S. Clement Street | A | B | C | D |
| 20. | 14 Rural Route 2 | A | B | C | D |
| 21. | 15 E. Chestnut Street | A | B | C | D |
| 22. | 1250 E. 12th Street | A | B | C | D |
| 23. | 59 W. Chestnut Street | A | B | C | D |
| 24. | 28 Rural Route 2 | A | B | C | D |
| 25. | 1400 S. Broad Avenue | A | B | C | D |
| 26. | 305 S. Chester Road | A | B | C | D |
| 27. | 178 N. Broad Avenue | A | B | C | D |
| 28. | 15101 N. Broad Avenue | A | B | C | D |
| 29. | 59 E. Chestnut Street | A | B | C | D |
| 30. | 99 E. 12th Street | A | B | C | D |
| 31. | 7000 S. Brook Street | A | B | C | D |
| 32. | 249 N. Broad Avenue | A | B | C | D |
| 33. | 30 Rural Route 2 | A | B | C | D |
| 34. | 1049 S. Chester Road | A | B | C | D |
| 35. | 19 E. Chestnut Street | A | B | C | D |
| 36. | 1000 S. Broad Avenue | A | B | C | D |

## Memory Section: Segment 1

**3 MINUTES**

> **Directions:** Segment 1 is *not* scored. This is a study period during which you will attempt to memorize the Coding Guide you used in the Coding Section of this exam. There are no answers to mark during this period.
>
> Begin the study period whenever you're ready.

### CODING GUIDE

| ADDRESS RANGE | DELIVERY ROUTE |
|---|---|
| 100–199 N. Broad Avenue<br>50–250 E. 12th Street<br>10–25 E. Chestnut Street | A |
| 200–500 N. Broad Avenue<br>26–70 E. Chestnut Street | B |
| 20–35 Rural Route 2<br>7000–15000 S. Broad Avenue<br>300–1000 S. Chester Road | C |
| All mail that doesn't fall into one of the address ranges listed above. | D |

practice test

## Memory Section: Segment 2

**8 QUESTIONS • 1.5 MINUTES (90 SECONDS)**

**Directions:** Segment 2 is *not* scored and does not count toward your total exam score. It is an exercise to help you practice coding addresses from memory under a time constraint similar to the one used in the scored Memory Section of the actual exam. You will *not* see the Coding Guide during this segment of the exam. Based on your memory of the Coding Guide, match each address to a delivery route. Mark your answers on the answer section at the bottom of this page.

| Address | Delivery Route | | | |
|---|---|---|---|---|
| 1.  6234 Broad Avenue | A | B | C | D |
| 2.  27 Rural Route 2 | A | B | C | D |
| 3.  52 E. Chestnut Street | A | B | C | D |
| 4.  298 S. Chester Road | A | B | C | D |
| 5.  100 E. 12th Street | A | B | C | D |
| 6.  301 N. Broad Avenue | A | B | C | D |
| 7.  13300 S. Broad Avenue | A | B | C | D |
| 8.  225 E. 12th Street | A | B | C | D |

## Sample Answer Sheet

1. Ⓐ Ⓑ Ⓒ Ⓓ          4. Ⓐ Ⓑ Ⓒ Ⓓ          7. Ⓐ Ⓑ Ⓒ Ⓓ
2. Ⓐ Ⓑ Ⓒ Ⓓ          5. Ⓐ Ⓑ Ⓒ Ⓓ          8. Ⓐ Ⓑ Ⓒ Ⓓ
3. Ⓐ Ⓑ Ⓒ Ⓓ          6. Ⓐ Ⓑ Ⓒ Ⓓ

## Memory Section: Segment 3

**5 MINUTES**

> **Directions:** Segment 3 is *not* scored. This is another study period during which you will attempt to memorize the Coding Guide you used in the Coding Section of this exam. There are no answers to mark during this period.

Begin the study period whenever you're ready.

### CODING GUIDE

| ADDRESS RANGE | DELIVERY ROUTE |
|---|:---:|
| 100–199 N. Broad Avenue<br>50–250 E. 12th Street<br>10–25 E. Chestnut Street | A |
| 200–500 N. Broad Avenue<br>26–70 E. Chestnut Street | B |
| 20–35 Rural Route 2<br>7000–15000 S. Broad Avenue<br>300–1000 S. Chester Road | C |
| All mail that doesn't fall into one of the address ranges listed above. | D |

practice test

## Memory Section: Segment 4

**36 QUESTIONS • 7 MINUTES**

**Directions:** This is the actual *scored* Memory Section of the exam. Take 3 minutes to memorize the Coding Guide on page 139. Work through items 1 through 36, assigning a code based on your memory of the Coding Guide. Mark your answers on the answer sheet. Work quickly and accurately.

- You may NOT write down any addresses during the memorization period.
- You may NOT look at the Coding Guide when answering the items.

| Address | Delivery Route | | | |
|---|---|---|---|---|
| 1.  250 E. 12th Street | A | B | C | D |
| 2.  12501 S. Broad Avenue | A | B | C | D |
| 3.  205 N. Broad Avenue | A | B | C | D |
| 4.  601 N. Broad Avenue | A | B | C | D |
| 5.  20 Rural Route 10 | A | B | C | D |
| 6.  30 Rural Route 2 | A | B | C | D |
| 7.  51 E. 12th Street | A | B | C | D |
| 8.  25 E. 12th Street | A | B | C | D |
| 9.  36 Belmont Lane | A | B | C | D |
| 10.  300 E. 12th Street | A | B | C | D |
| 11.  137 N. Broad Avenue | A | B | C | D |
| 12.  301 N. Broad Avenue | A | B | C | D |
| 13.  400 E. 12th Street | A | B | C | D |
| 14.  900 S. Chester Road | A | B | C | D |
| 15.  13040 S. Broad Street | A | B | C | D |
| 16.  406 S. Chester Road | A | B | C | D |
| 17.  6700 S. Broad Avenue | A | B | C | D |
| 18.  48 E. 14th Street | A | B | C | D |
| 19.  51 E. Chestnut Street | A | B | C | D |
| 20.  15 E. Chestnut Street | A | B | C | D |
| 21.  115 E. 12th Street | A | B | C | D |
| 22.  1000 S. Brook Street | A | B | C | D |
| 23.  210 E. 12th Street | A | B | C | D |
| 24.  105 N. Broad Avenue | A | B | C | D |

| 25. | 15 Rural Route 2 | A | B | C | D |
|-----|------------------|---|---|---|---|
| 26. | 68 E. Chestnut Street | A | B | C | D |
| 27. | 28 Rural Route 2 | A | B | C | D |
| 28. | 325 N. Broad Avenue | A | B | C | D |
| 29. | 1000 E. Chestnut Street | A | B | C | D |
| 30. | 14 North Broad Avenue | A | B | C | D |
| 31. | 117 S. 12th Street | A | B | C | D |
| 32. | 717 S. Chester Road | A | B | C | D |
| 33. | 14 N. Broad Avenue | A | B | C | D |
| 34. | 25 Belmont Lane | A | B | C | D |
| 35. | 67 E. Chestnut Street | A | B | C | D |
| 36. | 608 S. Chester Road | A | B | C | D |

practice test

## PART D: PERSONAL CHARACTERISTICS AND EXPERIENCE INVENTORY

**236 QUESTIONS • 90 MINUTES**

### Section 1: Agree/Disagree

**Directions:** Read each item carefully. Decide which of the four responses, ranging from **Strongly Agree** to **Strongly Disagree,** fits you best. For some items, more than one response may describe you, but choose the best description and mark only one answer on the answer sheet. It is important to answer each item, even if you are not certain which response is best for you. Try to work at a fairly rapid pace.

1. You like to work at a fast pace.
   (A) Strongly Agree
   (B) Agree
   (C) Disagree
   (D) Strongly Disagree

2. You like a job where you are in contact with people.
   (A) Strongly Agree
   (B) Agree
   (C) Disagree
   (D) Strongly Disagree

3. You like to have others give you directions about what to do.
   (A) Strongly Agree
   (B) Agree
   (C) Disagree
   (D) Strongly Disagree

4. You are very organized about your work and work area.
   (A) Strongly Agree
   (B) Agree
   (C) Disagree
   (D) Strongly Disagree

5. You believe in performing every task to the best of your ability.
   (A) Strongly Agree
   (B) Agree
   (C) Disagree
   (D) Strongly Disagree

6. You like looking for answers to problems.
   (A) Strongly Agree
   (B) Agree
   (C) Disagree
   (D) Strongly Disagree

7. You do not like to vary how you perform a task.
   (A) Strongly Agree
   (B) Agree
   (C) Disagree
   (D) Strongly Disagree

8. You like to help others when they are having difficulty doing a task.
   (A) Strongly Agree
   (B) Agree
   (C) Disagree
   (D) Strongly Disagree

9. You never like change in the beginning, but you adapt to it over time.
   (A) Strongly Agree
   (B) Agree
   (C) Disagree
   (D) Strongly Disagree

10. Because all jobs are stressful, you have figured out how to manage stress.
    (A) Strongly Agree
    (B) Agree
    (C) Disagree
    (D) Strongly Disagree

11. You take on new tasks at work enthusiastically.
    (A) Strongly Agree
    (B) Agree
    (C) Disagree
    (D) Strongly Disagree

12. You need quiet to work effectively.
    (A) Strongly Agree
    (B) Agree
    (C) Disagree
    (D) Strongly Disagree

13. You find details boring.
    (A) Strongly Agree
    (B) Agree
    (C) Disagree
    (D) Strongly Disagree

14. You follow through on whatever tasks you take on.
    (A) Strongly Agree
    (B) Agree
    (C) Disagree
    (D) Strongly Disagree

15. You put other people at ease.
    (A) Strongly Agree
    (B) Agree
    (C) Disagree
    (D) Strongly Disagree

16. You find change exciting.
    (A) Strongly Agree
    (B) Agree
    (C) Disagree
    (D) Strongly Disagree

17. Details are the most important part of a task.
    (A) Strongly Agree
    (B) Agree
    (C) Disagree
    (D) Strongly Disagree

18. You enjoy the feeling of a job well done.
    (A) Strongly Agree
    (B) Agree
    (C) Disagree
    (D) Strongly Disagree

19. You do not like having to ask for additional information to do a task.
    (A) Strongly Agree
    (B) Agree
    (C) Disagree
    (D) Strongly Disagree

20. You never stop until you have finished a task to the best of your ability.
    (A) Strongly Agree
    (B) Agree
    (C) Disagree
    (D) Strongly Disagree

21. You like to move around in your job.
    (A) Strongly Agree
    (B) Agree
    (C) Disagree
    (D) Strongly Disagree

22. You like helping other people solve a problem.
    (A) Strongly Agree
    (B) Agree
    (C) Disagree
    (D) Strongly Disagree

23. You like a job that involves physical activity such as lifting or moving things.
    (A) Strongly Agree
    (B) Agree
    (C) Disagree
    (D) Strongly Disagree

24. You like a job that requires performing a number of different tasks.
    (A) Strongly Agree
    (B) Agree
    (C) Disagree
    (D) Strongly Disagree

25. You are very organized in how you perform your work.
    (A) Strongly Agree
    (B) Agree
    (C) Disagree
    (D) Strongly Disagree

26. You can explain procedures easily to others.
    (A) Strongly Agree
    (B) Agree
    (C) Disagree
    (D) Strongly Disagree

practice test

**27.** The more complicated a task is, the better you like doing it.
- **(A)** Strongly Agree
- **(B)** Agree
- **(C)** Disagree
- **(D)** Strongly Disagree

**28.** You do not like having to make decisions about how to get your job done.
- **(A)** Strongly Agree
- **(B)** Agree
- **(C)** Disagree
- **(D)** Strongly Disagree

**29.** You find criticism difficult to accept.
- **(A)** Strongly Agree
- **(B)** Agree
- **(C)** Disagree
- **(D)** Strongly Disagree

**30.** You like jobs that start early in the morning.
- **(A)** Strongly Agree
- **(B)** Agree
- **(C)** Disagree
- **(D)** Strongly Disagree

**31.** You like to work in a place with a lot of other people around.
- **(A)** Strongly Agree
- **(B)** Agree
- **(C)** Disagree
- **(D)** Strongly Disagree

**32.** You are comfortable with routine.
- **(A)** Strongly Agree
- **(B)** Agree
- **(C)** Disagree
- **(D)** Strongly Disagree

**33.** You like to set your own pace at work.
- **(A)** Strongly Agree
- **(B)** Agree
- **(C)** Disagree
- **(D)** Strongly Disagree

**34.** You enjoy finding different ways to accomplish tasks.
- **(A)** Strongly Agree
- **(B)** Agree
- **(C)** Disagree
- **(D)** Strongly Disagree

**35.** A leadership role makes you uncomfortable.
- **(A)** Strongly Agree
- **(B)** Agree
- **(C)** Disagree
- **(D)** Strongly Disagree

**36.** You like to figure out why something is not working.
- **(A)** Strongly Agree
- **(B)** Agree
- **(C)** Disagree
- **(D)** Strongly Disagree

**37.** You find change challenging, but manageable.
- **(A)** Strongly Agree
- **(B)** Agree
- **(C)** Disagree
- **(D)** Strongly Disagree

**38.** You always do what you say you will.
- **(A)** Strongly Agree
- **(B)** Agree
- **(C)** Disagree
- **(D)** Strongly Disagree

**39.** You prefer to work with a small number of people.
- **(A)** Strongly Agree
- **(B)** Agree
- **(C)** Disagree
- **(D)** Strongly Disagree

**40.** Repeating tasks is boring.
- **(A)** Strongly Agree
- **(B)** Agree
- **(C)** Disagree
- **(D)** Strongly Disagree

**41.** You worry whether you did a task as well as you could have.
- **(A)** Strongly Agree
- **(B)** Agree
- **(C)** Disagree
- **(D)** Strongly Disagree

**42.** You would rather have someone else in charge.
- **(A)** Strongly Agree
- **(B)** Agree
- **(C)** Disagree
- **(D)** Strongly Disagree

43. You like to work behind the scenes to get things done.
    (A) Strongly Agree
    (B) Agree
    (C) Disagree
    (D) Strongly Disagree

44. Work-related stress does not bother you.
    (A) Strongly Agree
    (B) Agree
    (C) Disagree
    (D) Strongly Disagree

45. You could be better organized about how you manage your time.
    (A) Strongly Agree
    (B) Agree
    (C) Disagree
    (D) Strongly Disagree

46. You prefer to work alone.
    (A) Strongly Agree
    (B) Agree
    (C) Disagree
    (D) Strongly Disagree

47. You do not mind sitting for long periods of time when you work.
    (A) Strongly Agree
    (B) Agree
    (C) Disagree
    (D) Strongly Disagree

48. You like a job with a number of tasks to complete.
    (A) Strongly Agree
    (B) Agree
    (C) Disagree
    (D) Strongly Disagree

49. You do not find it easy to explain things to others.
    (A) Strongly Agree
    (B) Agree
    (C) Disagree
    (D) Strongly Disagree

50. You like interaction with large numbers of coworkers.
    (A) Strongly Agree
    (B) Agree
    (C) Disagree
    (D) Strongly Disagree

51. A job with a great deal of routine would be boring.
    (A) Strongly Agree
    (B) Agree
    (C) Disagree
    (D) Strongly Disagree

52. You do not mind asking for help when you do not know how to do something.
    (A) Strongly Agree
    (B) Agree
    (C) Disagree
    (D) Strongly Disagree

53. Job satisfaction is not important to you.
    (A) Strongly Agree
    (B) Agree
    (C) Disagree
    (D) Strongly Disagree

54. You like to move from one task to another during a workday.
    (A) Strongly Agree
    (B) Agree
    (C) Disagree
    (D) Strongly Disagree

55. You work well late in the day when others begin to fade.
    (A) Strongly Agree
    (B) Agree
    (C) Disagree
    (D) Strongly Disagree

56. You would rather work past quitting time than ask for help to finish a job.
    (A) Strongly Agree
    (B) Agree
    (C) Disagree
    (D) Strongly Disagree

57. You can pick up the pace if the amount of work increases during certain periods.
    (A) Strongly Agree
    (B) Agree
    (C) Disagree
    (D) Strongly Disagree

**58.** You leave troubleshooting problems to someone else.
- **(A)** Strongly Agree
- **(B)** Agree
- **(C)** Disagree
- **(D)** Strongly Disagree

**59.** You enjoy trying new tasks.
- **(A)** Strongly Agree
- **(B)** Agree
- **(C)** Disagree
- **(D)** Strongly Disagree

**60.** You tend to take on too many responsibilities.
- **(A)** Strongly Agree
- **(B)** Agree
- **(C)** Disagree
- **(D)** Strongly Disagree

**61.** Feeling productive and appreciated at work is important to you.
- **(A)** Strongly Agree
- **(B)** Agree
- **(C)** Disagree
- **(D)** Strongly Disagree

**62.** You find the details of a job uninteresting.
- **(A)** Strongly Agree
- **(B)** Agree
- **(C)** Disagree
- **(D)** Strongly Disagree

**63.** You like someone else to set the pace at work.
- **(A)** Strongly Agree
- **(B)** Agree
- **(C)** Disagree
- **(D)** Strongly Disagree

**64.** You like to make decisions about how you get your work done.
- **(A)** Strongly Agree
- **(B)** Agree
- **(C)** Disagree
- **(D)** Strongly Disagree

**65.** You learn from criticism.
- **(A)** Strongly Agree
- **(B)** Agree
- **(C)** Disagree
- **(D)** Strongly Disagree

**66.** You do not like having to stand for a long time when you work.
- **(A)** Strongly Agree
- **(B)** Agree
- **(C)** Disagree
- **(D)** Strongly Disagree

**67.** Doing your best is your number-one work priority.
- **(A)** Strongly Agree
- **(B)** Agree
- **(C)** Disagree
- **(D)** Strongly Disagree

**68.** You make decisions only when you have all the facts.
- **(A)** Strongly Agree
- **(B)** Agree
- **(C)** Disagree
- **(D)** Strongly Disagree

**69.** You find out as much information as you can before you begin a new task.
- **(A)** Strongly Agree
- **(B)** Agree
- **(C)** Disagree
- **(D)** Strongly Disagree

**70.** Speed results in errors.
- **(A)** Strongly Agree
- **(B)** Agree
- **(C)** Disagree
- **(D)** Strongly Disagree

**71.** You always finish what you start.
- **(A)** Strongly Agree
- **(B)** Agree
- **(C)** Disagree
- **(D)** Strongly Disagree

**72.** You prefer jobs where you do not have to interact with a number of people.
- **(A)** Strongly Agree
- **(B)** Agree
- **(C)** Disagree
- **(D)** Strongly Disagree

**73.** You become tense when working under the pressure of a deadline.
- **(A)** Strongly Agree
- **(B)** Agree
- **(C)** Disagree
- **(D)** Strongly Disagree

74. You find it difficult to stop and start tasks because of interruptions.
   (A) Strongly Agree
   (B) Agree
   (C) Disagree
   (D) Strongly Disagree

75. You do not like having to deal with angry or frustrated people.
   (A) Strongly Agree
   (B) Agree
   (C) Disagree
   (D) Strongly Disagree

76. You appreciate when a coworker puts a new person at ease.
   (A) Strongly Agree
   (B) Agree
   (C) Disagree
   (D) Strongly Disagree

77. You are very good at details.
   (A) Strongly Agree
   (B) Agree
   (C) Disagree
   (D) Strongly Disagree

78. You can always find something in the way a task is done that needs improving.
   (A) Strongly Agree
   (B) Agree
   (C) Disagree
   (D) Strongly Disagree

79. You find it difficult to ask for help when you do not know how to do something.
   (A) Strongly Agree
   (B) Agree
   (C) Disagree
   (D) Strongly Disagree

80. You find it easy to shift from one task to another.
   (A) Strongly Agree
   (B) Agree
   (C) Disagree
   (D) Strongly Disagree

81. You like being challenged in your job to find new ways of doing things.
   (A) Strongly Agree
   (B) Agree
   (C) Disagree
   (D) Strongly Disagree

82. Working at a fast pace is difficult and uncomfortable for you.
   (A) Strongly Agree
   (B) Agree
   (C) Disagree
   (D) Strongly Disagree

83. You like routine in your job.
   (A) Strongly Agree
   (B) Agree
   (C) Disagree
   (D) Strongly Disagree

84. You become bored if you have to repeat the same tasks.
   (A) Strongly Agree
   (B) Agree
   (C) Disagree
   (D) Strongly Disagree

85. You find working with a large group makes a job easier to do.
   (A) Strongly Agree
   (B) Agree
   (C) Disagree
   (D) Strongly Disagree

86. You enjoy working at difficult tasks.
   (A) Strongly Agree
   (B) Agree
   (C) Disagree
   (D) Strongly Disagree

87. You find it easy to deal with people.
   (A) Strongly Agree
   (B) Agree
   (C) Disagree
   (D) Strongly Disagree

88. You try to make the best of less than perfect situations.
   (A) Strongly Agree
   (B) Agree
   (C) Disagree
   (D) Strongly Disagree

practice test

89. When asked to do a new task, you ask very practical questions about how to do it.
    (A) Strongly Agree
    (B) Agree
    (C) Disagree
    (D) Strongly Disagree

90. You prefer doing many tasks at once rather than one after another.
    (A) Strongly Agree
    (B) Agree
    (C) Disagree
    (D) Strongly Disagree

91. You figure out how to accomplish your tasks more quickly and efficiently than others.
    (A) Strongly Agree
    (B) Agree
    (C) Disagree
    (D) Strongly Disagree

92. You adapt easily to changes in how things are done.
    (A) Strongly Agree
    (B) Agree
    (C) Disagree
    (D) Strongly Disagree

93. You are an accurate judge of how long tasks will take you.
    (A) Strongly Agree
    (B) Agree
    (C) Disagree
    (D) Strongly Disagree

94. When your ideas do not work, you can easily admit it.
    (A) Strongly Agree
    (B) Agree
    (C) Disagree
    (D) Strongly Disagree

95. You work well with people on a one-to-one basis.
    (A) Strongly Agree
    (B) Agree
    (C) Disagree
    (D) Strongly Disagree

96. You work against the clock, not against other people.
    (A) Strongly Agree
    (B) Agree
    (C) Disagree
    (D) Strongly Disagree

97. You reexamine how things are done from time to time to see whether you can make improvements.
    (A) Strongly Agree
    (B) Agree
    (C) Disagree
    (D) Strongly Disagree

98. A slow, steady pace gets the job done.
    (A) Strongly Agree
    (B) Agree
    (C) Disagree
    (D) Strongly Disagree

99. You concentrate on one task at a time even if you have several to work on at the same time.
    (A) Strongly Agree
    (B) Agree
    (C) Disagree
    (D) Strongly Disagree

100. Most things that go wrong on a job are beyond your control.
    (A) Strongly Agree
    (B) Agree
    (C) Disagree
    (D) Strongly Disagree

101. Unclear instructions are the cause of most of your problems on the job.
    (A) Strongly Agree
    (B) Agree
    (C) Disagree
    (D) Strongly Disagree

102. The biggest problem on a job is the unrealistic expectations of a supervisor.
    (A) Strongly Agree
    (B) Agree
    (C) Disagree
    (D) Strongly Disagree

## Section 2: Frequency

**Directions:** Read each item carefully. Decide which of the four responses, ranging from **Very Often** to **Rarely,** fits you best. For some items, more than one response may describe you, but choose the best description and mark only one answer on the answer sheet. It is important to answer each item, even if you are not certain which response is best for you. Try to work at a fairly rapid pace.

103. You think things through carefully before making a decision.
    (A) Very often
    (B) Often
    (C) Sometimes
    (D) Rarely

104. Whatever you start, you finish.
    (A) Very often
    (B) Often
    (C) Sometimes
    (D) Rarely

105. You find it easy to pick up a task if you are interrupted.
    (A) Very often
    (B) Often
    (C) Sometimes
    (D) Rarely

106. You put others at ease.
    (A) Very often
    (B) Often
    (C) Sometimes
    (D) Rarely

107. You put off making decisions hoping that the problem will solve itself.
    (A) Very often
    (B) Often
    (C) Sometimes
    (D) Rarely

108. You accomplish tasks more quickly than coworkers.
    (A) Very often
    (B) Often
    (C) Sometimes
    (D) Rarely

109. You ask questions in meetings if you do not understand something.
    (A) Very often
    (B) Often
    (C) Sometimes
    (D) Rarely

110. You are the person who sets the pace at work.
    (A) Very often
    (B) Often
    (C) Sometimes
    (D) Rarely

111. You find criticism helpful in improving your job performance.
    (A) Very often
    (B) Often
    (C) Sometimes
    (D) Rarely

112. Deadlines create stress for you.
    (A) Very often
    (B) Often
    (C) Sometimes
    (D) Rarely

113. You are willing to explain something several times if a person does not understand.
    (A) Very often
    (B) Often
    (C) Sometimes
    (D) Rarely

114. You consider others' points of view in making decisions.
    (A) Very often
    (B) Often
    (C) Sometimes
    (D) Rarely

**115.** You lose track of the details of a task.
- **(A)** Very often
- **(B)** Often
- **(C)** Sometimes
- **(D)** Rarely

**116.** You restate instructions to make sure that you understand what to do.
- **(A)** Very often
- **(B)** Often
- **(C)** Sometimes
- **(D)** Rarely

**117.** You carry work stress into your outside life.
- **(A)** Very often
- **(B)** Often
- **(C)** Sometimes
- **(D)** Rarely

**118.** You wait for someone else to offer suggestions about how to complete a task.
- **(A)** Very often
- **(B)** Often
- **(C)** Sometimes
- **(D)** Rarely

**119.** You become impatient with people who want to do something the same way all the time.
- **(A)** Very often
- **(B)** Often
- **(C)** Sometimes
- **(D)** Rarely

**120.** You compliment others on a job well done.
- **(A)** Very often
- **(B)** Often
- **(C)** Sometimes
- **(D)** Rarely

**121.** When shown that another way would work better, you stick with the original way.
- **(A)** Very often
- **(B)** Often
- **(C)** Sometimes
- **(D)** Rarely

**122.** You shift from task to task without slowing your work pace.
- **(A)** Very often
- **(B)** Often
- **(C)** Sometimes
- **(D)** Rarely

**123.** You become impatient with people who make small talk about family and friends during work time.
- **(A)** Very often
- **(B)** Often
- **(C)** Sometimes
- **(D)** Rarely

**124.** You take criticism personally.
- **(A)** Very often
- **(B)** Often
- **(C)** Sometimes
- **(D)** Rarely

**125.** You overpromise what you can reasonably accomplish in a given period of time.
- **(A)** Very often
- **(B)** Often
- **(C)** Sometimes
- **(D)** Rarely

**126.** You ask for help if you cannot finish a task by the deadline.
- **(A)** Very often
- **(B)** Often
- **(C)** Sometimes
- **(D)** Rarely

**127.** You lose interest in what you are doing if the task is going well.
- **(A)** Very often
- **(B)** Often
- **(C)** Sometimes
- **(D)** Rarely

**128.** You can figure out the problem when others cannot.
- **(A)** Very often
- **(B)** Often
- **(C)** Sometimes
- **(D)** Rarely

129. You become impatient with others when you are rushing to finish a task.
     - **(A)** Very often
     - **(B)** Often
     - **(C)** Sometimes
     - **(D)** Rarely

130. You become tense when dealing with angry or frustrated people.
     - **(A)** Very often
     - **(B)** Often
     - **(C)** Sometimes
     - **(D)** Rarely

131. If you speed up doing tasks, you make errors.
     - **(A)** Very often
     - **(B)** Often
     - **(C)** Sometimes
     - **(D)** Rarely

132. Without being asked, you offer criticism of coworkers' job performance.
     - **(A)** Very often
     - **(B)** Often
     - **(C)** Sometimes
     - **(D)** Rarely

133. You are the leader in a group.
     - **(A)** Very often
     - **(B)** Often
     - **(C)** Sometimes
     - **(D)** Rarely

134. You worry about your work even after you leave the job.
     - **(A)** Very often
     - **(B)** Often
     - **(C)** Sometimes
     - **(D)** Rarely

135. You become impatient if others do not understand something as quickly as you do.
     - **(A)** Very often
     - **(B)** Often
     - **(C)** Sometimes
     - **(D)** Rarely

136. You try to calm the situation if conflicts develop.
     - **(A)** Very often
     - **(B)** Often
     - **(C)** Sometimes
     - **(D)** Rarely

137. You ask for help if you cannot finish a task by the deadline.
     - **(A)** Very often
     - **(B)** Often
     - **(C)** Sometimes
     - **(D)** Rarely

138. You plan ahead so that you do not miss any details.
     - **(A)** Very often
     - **(B)** Often
     - **(C)** Sometimes
     - **(D)** Rarely

139. You change routines to fit you rather than follow the established process.
     - **(A)** Very often
     - **(B)** Often
     - **(C)** Sometimes
     - **(D)** Rarely

140. You let others try new tasks before you yourself try them.
     - **(A)** Very often
     - **(B)** Often
     - **(C)** Sometimes
     - **(D)** Rarely

141. You become sidetracked by the details of a task.
     - **(A)** Very often
     - **(B)** Often
     - **(C)** Sometimes
     - **(D)** Rarely

142. You ignore conflict when it develops.
     - **(A)** Very often
     - **(B)** Often
     - **(C)** Sometimes
     - **(D)** Rarely

143. You are the first to notice when someone is having a bad day.
     - **(A)** Very often
     - **(B)** Often
     - **(C)** Sometimes
     - **(D)** Rarely

144. You step in to help coworkers solve problems.
     - **(A)** Very often
     - **(B)** Often
     - **(C)** Sometimes
     - **(D)** Rarely

**145.** You seek out complicated tasks to do.
- **(A)** Very often
- **(B)** Often
- **(C)** Sometimes
- **(D)** Rarely

**146.** You figure out for yourself how to accomplish a task rather than follow someone else's directions.
- **(A)** Very often
- **(B)** Often
- **(C)** Sometimes
- **(D)** Rarely

**147.** You encourage others to do their best at their jobs.
- **(A)** Very often
- **(B)** Often
- **(C)** Sometimes
- **(D)** Rarely

**148.** You lose focus on what you are doing if you do the same thing for a long period of time.
- **(A)** Very often
- **(B)** Often
- **(C)** Sometimes
- **(D)** Rarely

**149.** You are the one whom others ask to explain something they do not understand.
- **(A)** Very often
- **(B)** Often
- **(C)** Sometimes
- **(D)** Rarely

**150.** You do a job exactly as your supervisor explains the process.
- **(A)** Very often
- **(B)** Often
- **(C)** Sometimes
- **(D)** Rarely

**151.** You become frustrated if you cannot perform a task.
- **(A)** Very often
- **(B)** Often
- **(C)** Sometimes
- **(D)** Rarely

**152.** Your work area is disorganized.
- **(A)** Very often
- **(B)** Often
- **(C)** Sometimes
- **(D)** Rarely

**153.** You see the practical issues involved in getting a task done.
- **(A)** Very often
- **(B)** Often
- **(C)** Sometimes
- **(D)** Rarely

**154.** You complete tasks to the best of your ability.
- **(A)** Very often
- **(B)** Often
- **(C)** Sometimes
- **(D)** Rarely

**155.** You are one of the crowd rather than the leader.
- **(A)** Very often
- **(B)** Often
- **(C)** Sometimes
- **(D)** Rarely

**156.** You take on tasks that allow you to work on your own.
- **(A)** Very often
- **(B)** Often
- **(C)** Sometimes
- **(D)** Rarely

**157.** You increase the pace of your work to outdo your coworkers.
- **(A)** Very often
- **(B)** Often
- **(C)** Sometimes
- **(D)** Rarely

**158.** You find it difficult to maintain a steady, rapid pace at tasks.
- **(A)** Very often
- **(B)** Often
- **(C)** Sometimes
- **(D)** Rarely

**159.** You become tense because of stress on the job.
- **(A)** Very often
- **(B)** Often
- **(C)** Sometimes
- **(D)** Rarely

**160.** You are the first to suggest changes in routines.
- **(A)** Very often
- **(B)** Often
- **(C)** Sometimes
- **(D)** Rarely

**161.** You get into arguments.
- **(A)** Very often
- **(B)** Often
- **(C)** Sometimes
- **(D)** Rarely

**162.** You troubleshoot problems rather than ask someone else what is wrong.
- **(A)** Very often
- **(B)** Often
- **(C)** Sometimes
- **(D)** Rarely

**163.** You accept others' suggestions about how a task can be done.
- **(A)** Very often
- **(B)** Often
- **(C)** Sometimes
- **(D)** Rarely

**164.** You set goals for yourself to accomplish certain things each day.
- **(A)** Very often
- **(B)** Often
- **(C)** Sometimes
- **(D)** Rarely

**165.** You offer help when someone is having difficulty with a task.
- **(A)** Very often
- **(B)** Often
- **(C)** Sometimes
- **(D)** Rarely

**166.** You worry whether you performed a task as well as you could have.
- **(A)** Very often
- **(B)** Often
- **(C)** Sometimes
- **(D)** Rarely

**167.** You anticipate problems that may arise in doing a task.
- **(A)** Very often
- **(B)** Often
- **(C)** Sometimes
- **(D)** Rarely

**168.** You tell others how to do their jobs without their asking.
- **(A)** Very often
- **(B)** Often
- **(C)** Sometimes
- **(D)** Rarely

**169.** You volunteer to try new ways of doing things.
- **(A)** Very often
- **(B)** Often
- **(C)** Sometimes
- **(D)** Rarely

**170.** You lose track of what you are doing if you are interrupted while you work.
- **(A)** Very often
- **(B)** Often
- **(C)** Sometimes
- **(D)** Rarely

**171.** You make decisions quickly rather than wait for complete information.
- **(A)** Very often
- **(B)** Often
- **(C)** Sometimes
- **(D)** Rarely

**172.** You confront conflict when it arises, rather than let it grow.
- **(A)** Very often
- **(B)** Often
- **(C)** Sometimes
- **(D)** Rarely

**173.** The details of a task can seem overwhelming to you at times.
- **(A)** Very often
- **(B)** Often
- **(C)** Sometimes
- **(D)** Rarely

**174.** You encourage others to try new ways of doing things.
- **(A)** Very often
- **(B)** Often
- **(C)** Sometimes
- **(D)** Rarely

practice test

**175.** You become impatient if others do not understand your explanation.
- **(A)** Very often
- **(B)** Often
- **(C)** Sometimes
- **(D)** Rarely

**176.** You are the one to whom others turn for help on the job.
- **(A)** Very often
- **(B)** Often
- **(C)** Sometimes
- **(D)** Rarely

**177.** You vary the way you accomplish tasks.
- **(A)** Very often
- **(B)** Often
- **(C)** Sometimes
- **(D)** Rarely

**178.** You are not satisfied with how you do your job.
- **(A)** Very often
- **(B)** Often
- **(C)** Sometimes
- **(D)** Rarely

**179.** You make sure that you follow through on whatever task you take on.
- **(A)** Very often
- **(B)** Often
- **(C)** Sometimes
- **(D)** Rarely

**180.** You ask for help if you do not understand how to do something.
- **(A)** Very often
- **(B)** Often
- **(C)** Sometimes
- **(D)** Rarely

**181.** You take on more responsibilities than you can handle comfortably.
- **(A)** Very often
- **(B)** Often
- **(C)** Sometimes
- **(D)** Rarely

**182.** You push to get your point of view across in a group.
- **(A)** Very often
- **(B)** Often
- **(C)** Sometimes
- **(D)** Rarely

**183.** You become angry if coworkers interrupt your work.
- **(A)** Very often
- **(B)** Often
- **(C)** Sometimes
- **(D)** Rarely

**184.** You find alternate ways of completing tasks.
- **(A)** Very often
- **(B)** Often
- **(C)** Sometimes
- **(D)** Rarely

**185.** You misjudge how long it will take to accomplish tasks.
- **(A)** Very often
- **(B)** Often
- **(C)** Sometimes
- **(D)** Rarely

**186.** You let others ask questions for you.
- **(A)** Very often
- **(B)** Often
- **(C)** Sometimes
- **(D)** Rarely

## Section 3: Experience

**Directions:** Read each item carefully. Decide which response best describes your experience. For some items, more than one response may describe you. Choose the best description and mark only that one answer on the answer sheet. It is important to answer each item, even if you are not certain which response is best for you. Also, try to work at a fairly rapid pace.

187. Where do you most like to work?
    (A) Outdoors most of the time
    (B) Outdoors all the time
    (C) Indoors most of the time
    (D) Indoors all the time
    (E) Splitting time about equally between indoor and outdoor work
    (F) Splitting time so that you work outdoors more than indoors
    (G) Splitting time so that you work indoors more than outdoors
    (H) Would not mind doing any of these

188. Most of your contact with customers has included which of the following?
    (A) Answering customers' questions
    (B) Explaining information to customers
    (C) Selling items to customers
    (D) Do not interact directly with customers
    (E) Not sure

189. Which of the following types of contact do you least like in the work environment?
    (A) Dealing with customers
    (B) Dealing with other workers
    (C) Dealing with supervisors
    (D) Would not mind any of these
    (E) Not sure

190. Which of the following patterns of work is the most difficult for you?
    (A) Working on one task at a time
    (B) Working on several tasks at once
    (C) Shifting from task to task during a workday
    (D) Being interrupted while you work
    (E) Do not mind any of these

191. With which type of job do you have the most experience?
    (A) Operating machinery
    (B) Customer contact
    (C) Lifting and moving heavy loads of up to 70 pounds
    (D) Lifting and moving lighter loads
    (E) Handling money
    (F) Clerical work
    (G) Driving and making deliveries
    (H) Have no experience

192. When is the best time of day for you to work?
    (A) Early morning
    (B) Day
    (C) Evening
    (D) Night
    (E) Would not mind working any of these
    (F) Not sure

193. What type of work do you like the least?
    (A) Walking around throughout the work day
    (B) Driving for several hours a day
    (C) Standing or sitting in place for hours
    (D) Operating machinery all day
    (E) Lifting and moving loads
    (F) Would not mind any of these
    (G) Not sure

194. Which type of work pace do you like the most?
    (A) Fast pace
    (B) Slow pace
    (C) Steady pace: fast or slow
    (D) Moderate pace
    (E) Not sure

**195.** What kind of decision making do you want most in your job?
- **(A)** Making all the decisions about how you do your work
- **(B)** Making no decisions about how you do your work
- **(C)** Making some decisions about how you do your work
- **(D)** Being asked for suggestions about how your work should be done
- **(E)** Would not mind any of these

**196.** In dealing with customers, you are best at which of the following?
- **(A)** Answering questions
- **(B)** Explaining instructions
- **(C)** Making change
- **(D)** Not sure

**197.** One of your greatest strengths working with people is which of the following?
- **(A)** Ignoring conflict
- **(B)** Calming angry or frustrated coworkers
- **(C)** Calming angry or frustrated customers
- **(D)** Confronting a situation before it turns into conflict
- **(E)** Not sure

**198.** Which of the following describes how you feel about working with numbers?
- **(A)** Not something you like to do
- **(B)** Something you can do but would rather not
- **(C)** Something you like to do
- **(D)** Not sure

**199.** Which of the following types of problem solving do you like the most?
- **(A)** Troubleshooting problems with machines
- **(B)** Helping customers with problems
- **(C)** Figuring out ways to get tasks done
- **(D)** Prioritizing your workload
- **(E)** Not sure

**200.** Which of the following is the best type of supervision for you?
- **(A)** Be able to set priorities with minimal supervision
- **(B)** Be able to set work routines with minimal supervision
- **(C)** Have supervisor set work routines
- **(D)** Have supervisor set priorities
- **(E)** Have freedom to change work routines to fit work flow as needed
- **(F)** Have freedom to change work priorities to fit work flow as needed
- **(G)** Not sure

**201.** Which of the following is the least important to you in a work environment?
- **(A)** Quiet
- **(B)** A lot of activity around you
- **(C)** A large number of coworkers
- **(D)** A small number of coworkers
- **(E)** Lack of pressure
- **(F)** Would not mind any of these
- **(G)** Not sure

**202.** Which of the following types of work do you find the most difficult to do all day?
- **(A)** Sit in one place
- **(B)** Stand in one place
- **(C)** Drive
- **(D)** Move and lift loads
- **(E)** Operate machinery
- **(F)** Deal with customers
- **(G)** Walk
- **(H)** Do not mind any of these
- **(I)** Not sure

**203.** Which of the following types of responsibility do you like the least?
- **(A)** Handling and being accountable for money
- **(B)** Explaining instructions
- **(C)** Answering questions
- **(D)** Operating machinery
- **(E)** Driving a vehicle
- **(F)** Routing shipments
- **(G)** Making work-related decisions
- **(H)** Would not mind any of these
- **(I)** Not sure

**204.** Which of the following would you like the least?

**(A)** Being out in all kinds of weather
**(B)** Taking the same route every day
**(C)** Driving in all kinds of weather
**(D)** Working on weekends
**(E)** Starting early in the morning
**(F)** Walking all day
**(G)** Carrying loads
**(H)** Would not mind any of these
**(I)** Not sure

**205.** Which of the following tasks do you like the least?

**(A)** Handling money
**(B)** Dealing with customers
**(C)** Memorizing information
**(D)** Operating machines
**(E)** Working with details
**(F)** Sorting items
**(G)** Would not mind any of these
**(H)** Not sure

**206.** What amount of responsibility do you like to have in a job?

**(A)** Little
**(B)** Moderate
**(C)** Great deal
**(D)** Does not matter
**(E)** Not sure

**207.** Most of your experience with technology has been with which of the following?

**(A)** Cash registers
**(B)** Data entry
**(C)** Applications of databases
**(D)** Word processing
**(E)** Spreadsheets
**(F)** Internet
**(G)** Calculator
**(H)** Have no experience with technology

**208.** How important is physical activity to you in a job?

**(A)** No importance
**(B)** Little importance
**(C)** Moderate importance
**(D)** Great importance
**(E)** Not sure

**209.** Most of your experience with motor vehicles has been driving which of the following?

**(A)** Cars
**(B)** Vans
**(C)** Pick-up trucks
**(D)** Small trucks
**(E)** Tractor-trailers
**(F)** Have no experience with motor vehicles

**210.** Which type of work do you like the most?

**(A)** Driving and making deliveries
**(B)** Standing or sitting in one place
**(C)** Walking around throughout the day
**(D)** Operating machinery
**(E)** Lifting and moving loads
**(F)** Would not mind any of these
**(G)** Not sure

**211.** Which of the following characteristics of a machine-based job do you like the least?

**(A)** Working under pressure
**(B)** Focusing on a machine all day
**(C)** Feeding materials through a machine
**(D)** Moving material to and from machines
**(E)** Troubleshooting machinery problems
**(F)** Machinery noise
**(G)** Lack of coworker interaction
**(H)** Would not mind any of these
**(I)** Not sure

**212.** Which type of pressure do you like the least?

**(A)** Working under a deadline
**(B)** Working under a quota system
**(C)** Competition from coworkers
**(D)** Solving a problem for an angry or frustrated customer
**(E)** Troubleshooting a machine problem
**(F)** Would not mind any of these
**(G)** Not sure

**213.** Which type of physical activity do you like the least?

(A) Stretching, reaching, bending
(B) Lifting and moving heavy loads up to 70 pounds
(C) Lifting and moving lighter loads
(D) Packing shipments
(E) Pushing a handtruck
(F) Loading goods onto trucks
(G) Would not mind any of these
(H) Not sure

**214.** Which of the following do you like the least about working with numbers?

(A) Remembering numbers
(B) Entering data with numbers and letters
(C) Comparing information that includes numbers
(D) Handling money
(E) Coding using numbers and letters
(F) Have no experience

**215.** With which of the following do you have the least experience?

(A) Operating office machines
(B) Using databases
(C) Dealing with customers
(D) Working independently
(E) Have none of this experience

**216.** You have most experience working in which of the following situations?

(A) Working independently without direct day-to-day supervision
(B) Working as part of a small work team or work group
(C) Working as one of many workers in a department
(D) Supervising others
(E) Not sure

**217.** What is the perfect size for a work group?

(A) Alone
(B) Between 2 and 10
(C) Between 11 and 25
(D) More than 25
(E) Number does not matter
(F) Not sure

**218.** Which of the following tasks could you do best under pressure?

(A) Repetitive tasks
(B) Operate machinery
(C) Enter data in a database
(D) Retrieve information from a database
(E) Deal with customers
(F) Could do all of these
(G) Not sure

**219.** Which of the following tasks related to instructions do you like the least?

(A) Reading written instructions
(B) Following written instructions
(C) Remembering oral instructions
(D) Following oral instructions
(E) Giving oral instructions to others
(F) Writing instructions for others
(G) Would not mind any of these
(H) Not sure

**220.** Which of the following would you like least about a job?

(A) Pressure to work quickly
(B) Working on weekends
(C) Working at night
(D) Standing in one place for long periods of time
(E) Bending, stretching, reaching, lifting, and moving loads
(F) Troubleshooting problems with machines
(G) Would not mind any of these
(H) Not sure

**221.** Which of the following is the most difficult type of work for you?

(A) Working with numbers
(B) Working with details
(C) Memorizing information
(D) Dealing with people
(E) Repeating the same task over and over
(F) Doing a variety of tasks
(G) Working quickly
(H) Not sure

**222.** Which of the following describes the amount of people contact that you like the least?

    **(A)** Interacting with the same people on a daily basis

    **(B)** Interacting with many people daily—customers and coworkers

    **(C)** Having long periods of time during a day when you work alone

    **(D)** Always working around and with other people

    **(E)** Would not mind any of these

    **(F)** Not sure

**223.** Which work pattern do you like the most?

    **(A)** Varying my routine often during the day

    **(B)** Following the same routine every day

    **(C)** Having an occasional change in routine during the day

    **(D)** Would not mind any of these

**224.** Which of the following is the most likely to create tension for you?

    **(A)** Deadlines

    **(B)** Amount of work to be completed within a period of time

    **(C)** Supervisor's expectations

    **(D)** Competition from coworkers

    **(E)** Angry or frustrated customers

    **(F)** Angry coworkers

    **(G)** Mechanical problems with machinery

    **(H)** None of these

**225.** Which of the following best describes your experience with machines?

    **(A)** Operate heavy machinery

    **(B)** Operate light machinery

    **(C)** Use a computer

    **(D)** Troubleshoot mechanical problems

    **(E)** Drive a truck

    **(F)** Have no experience with machines

**226.** With which type of work do you have the least experience?

    **(A)** Customer contact

    **(B)** Handling money

    **(C)** Clerical work

    **(D)** Driving and making deliveries

    **(E)** Operating machinery

    **(F)** Lifting and moving heavy loads of up to 70 pounds

    **(G)** Lifting and moving lighter loads

    **(H)** Have none of these experiences

**227.** Which is the most difficult time for you to work?

    **(A)** Early morning

    **(B)** Day

    **(C)** Evening

    **(D)** Night

**228.** Which type of work situation do you like the most?

    **(A)** Interacting only with coworkers

    **(B)** Dealing with the public

    **(C)** Interacting with coworkers and the public

    **(D)** Would not mind any of these

    **(E)** Not sure

**229.** Which of the following is the least important to you in a job?

    **(A)** Steady work pace

    **(B)** Mix of fast and slow periods

    **(C)** Steady routine

    **(D)** Variety of tasks to accomplish

    **(E)** Only a few tasks to accomplish

    **(F)** Not sure

**230.** Which of the following skills is your strongest?

    **(A)** Working with numbers

    **(B)** Working with details

    **(C)** Dealing with people

    **(D)** Doing repetitive tasks without becoming bored

    **(E)** Not sure

practice test

231. In which type of work environment would you least like to work?
     (A) Loading dock
     (B) Open area with many machines going all day
     (C) Sales counter
     (D) Outdoors in all kinds of weather
     (E) Small work area
     (F) Would not mind any of these
     (G) Not sure

232. Which of the following types of responsibility for doing your job is most important to you?
     (A) Setting your priorities
     (B) How you set up your work routine
     (C) How much you accomplish each day
     (D) How long it takes you to do tasks during the day
     (E) Does not matter
     (F) Not sure

233. Which of the following describes how you feel about handling money and making change?
     (A) Not something you like to do
     (B) One of your strengths
     (C) Something you can do but would rather not
     (D) Not sure

234. What type of physical work do you like the least?
     (A) Sitting or standing in one place all day
     (B) Driving and making deliveries
     (C) Walking
     (D) Operating machines
     (E) Lifting and moving loads
     (F) Would not mind any of these
     (G) Not sure

235. How do you prefer to get your job done?
     (A) Following a routine set by someone else
     (B) Making your own routine
     (C) Not having a regular routine in a job
     (D) Would not mind any of these

236. In how large a group do you prefer to work?
     (A) Alone
     (B) With a small group of people
     (C) With a large group of people
     (D) With a small group within a larger group
     (E) Would not mind any of these
     (F) Not sure

## ANSWER KEY AND EXPLANATIONS

### Part A: Address Checking

| | | | | |
|---|---|---|---|---|
| 1. A | 13. B | 25. B | 37. B | 49. B |
| 2. B | 14. A | 26. B | 38. C | 50. B |
| 3. C | 15. B | 27. B | 39. B | 51. B |
| 4. B | 16. B | 28. B | 40. B | 52. B |
| 5. B | 17. B | 29. A | 41. B | 53. B |
| 6. A | 18. B | 30. B | 42. B | 54. B |
| 7. D | 19. A | 31. B | 43. B | 55. B |
| 8. D | 20. B | 32. A | 44. B | 56. D |
| 9. B | 21. B | 33. B | 45. C | 57. A |
| 10. B | 22. B | 34. B | 46. B | 58. D |
| 11. B | 23. D | 35. B | 47. B | 59. B |
| 12. B | 24. A | 36. C | 48. B | 60. B |

### Part B: Forms Completion

| | | | | |
|---|---|---|---|---|
| 1. C | 7. D | 13. B | 19. C | 25. B |
| 2. C | 8. B | 14. C | 20. C | 26. C |
| 3. A | 9. C | 15. D | 21. D | 27. D |
| 4. D | 10. A | 16. B | 22. A | 28. B |
| 5. A | 11. D | 17. A | 23. D | 29. C |
| 6. B | 12. B | 18. D | 24. A | 30. B |

1. **The correct answer is (C).** Box 5 requires a date (Month/Day). Therefore, the correct answer is (C), 12 and 20.

2. **The correct answer is (C).** Box 10 is labeled Insurance Fee. Therefore, the correct answer is (C), Box 10.

3. **The correct answer is (A).** Box 6 is labeled Return Receipt Fee. Boxes 7a, 8a, and 11b all have boxes to be checked. Therefore, the correct answer is (A), Box 6.

4. **The correct answer is (D).** Box 22 is labeled Delivery Date. Therefore, the correct answer is (D), Box 22.

5. **The correct answer is (A).** Box 4 is labeled Date Accepted. Boxes 18, 21, and 24 are all labeled Employee Signature. Therefore, the correct answer is (A), Box 4.

6. **The correct answer is (B).** Box 13b is labeled lbs. and ozs. Therefore, the correct answer is (B), 3 lbs. 6 oz.

7. **The correct answer is (D).** Box 11a is labeled Military 2nd Day. Therefore, the correct answer is (D), Box 11a.

8. **The correct answer is (B).** Box 14 is labeled Int'l Alpha Country Code. Therefore, the correct answer is (B), Box 14.

9. **The correct answer is (C).** Box 15 is labeled Acceptance Emp. Initials. Therefore, the correct answer is (C), Initials.

10. **The correct answer is (A).** Box 9 is labeled Place and Country. Therefore, the correct answer is (A), Paris, France.

11. **The correct answer is (D).** Box 1f is labeled Express Mail International. Therefore, the correct answer is (D), Express Mail International.

12. **The correct answer is (B).** Box 7 is labeled Addressee Name or Firm.

Therefore, the correct answer is (B), Computer Programmers Worldwide.

13. **The correct answer is (B).** Box 1b is labeled Letter. Therefore, the correct answer is (B), Check Box 1b.

14. **The correct answer is (C).** Box 4 is labeled Article Number. Therefore, the correct answer is (C), Box 4.

15. **The correct answer is (D).** Box 3 is labeled Insured Value. Therefore, the correct answer is (D), $250.

16. **The correct answer is (B).** Box 3 is labeled Check Number. Therefore, the correct answer is (B), Box 3.

17. **The correct answer is (A).** Box 2 is labeled Date Delivered. Therefore, the correct answer is (A), 2/22/09.

18. **The correct answer is (D).** Box 6 is labeled MO Number(s). Boxes 1, 4, and 5 are require dates. Therefore, the correct answer is (D), Box 6.

19. **The correct answer is (C).** Box 7 is labeled Sent To. Therefore, the correct answer is (C), Ms. Dy Anne Going.

20. **The correct answer is (C).** Box 6 is labeled Postmark Here. Therefore, the correct answer is (C), Box 6.

21. **The correct answer is (D).** Box 9 is labeled City, State, Zip+4. Therefore, the correct answer is (D), Box 9.

22. **The correct answer is (A).** Box 5 is labeled Route Number. Therefore, the correct answer is (A), Rural Route 5.

23. **The correct answer is (D).** Box 4 is labeled Carrier. Therefore, the correct answer is (D), Box 4.

24. **The correct answer is (A).** Box 6 is completed by making a check mark. Therefore, the correct answer is (A), A check mark.

25. **The correct answer is (B).** Box 7 is labeled Resume Delivery of Mail (Date). Therefore, the correct answer is (B), 1/20/06.

26. **The correct answer is (C).** Box 2c is labeled Perishable. Therefore, the correct answer is (C), Box 2c.

27. **The correct answer is (D).** Box 7 is labeled Total Postage and Fees. Therefore, the correct answer is (D), Box 7.

28. **The correct answer is (B).** Box 8 is labeled Postmark Here. Therefore, the correct answer is (B), Box 8.

29. **The correct answer is (C).** Box 4 is labeled Restricted Delivery Fee (Domestic only: endorsement required). Therefore, the correct answer is (C), Box 4.

30. **The correct answer is (B).** Box 2a is labeled Fragile. Therefore, the correct answer is (B), Box 2a.

## Part C: Coding and Memory

### CODING SECTION: SEGMENT 1

| 1. D | 2. A | 3. C | 4. B |
|------|------|------|------|

### CODING SECTION: SEGMENT 2

| 1. C | 3. C | 5. A | 7. C | 8. A |
|------|------|------|------|------|
| 2. B | 4. D | 6. B | | |

**CODING SECTION: SEGMENT 3**

| | | | |
|---|---|---|---|
| 1. A | 9. D | 16. D | 23. D | 30. A |
| 2. B | 10. A | 17. B | 24. C | 31. D |
| 3. D | 11. D | 18. C | 25. D | 32. B |
| 4. A | 12. C | 19. D | 26. C | 33. C |
| 5. B | 13. C | 20. D | 27. A | 34. D |
| 6. C | 14. D | 21. A | 28. D | 35. A |
| 7. C | 15. B | 22. D | 29. B | 36. D |
| 8. D | | | | |

1. **The correct answer is (A).** The address 105 N. Broad Avenue falls in one of the address ranges in the same row as Delivery Route A.

2. **The correct answer is (B).** The address 52 E. Chestnut Street falls in one of the address ranges in the same row as Delivery Route B.

3. **The correct answer is (D).** The address 220 N. Brook Street does not fall into any of the address ranges for Delivery Routes A, B, or C.

4. **The correct answer is (A).** The address 195 E. 12th Street falls in one of the address ranges in the same row as Delivery Route A.

5. **The correct answer is (B).** The address 68 E. Chestnut Street falls in one of the address ranges in the same row as Delivery Route B.

6. **The correct answer is (C).** The address 28 Rural Route 2 falls in one of the address ranges in the same row as Delivery Route C.

7. **The correct answer is (C).** The address 7801 S. Broad Avenue falls in one of the address ranges in the same row as Delivery Route C.

8. **The correct answer is (D).** The address 10 Rural Route 2 does not fall into any of the address ranges for Delivery Routes A, B, or C.

9. **The correct answer is (D).** The address 42 Rural Route 2 does not fall into any of the address ranges for Delivery Routes A, B, or C.

10. **The correct answer is (A).** The address 72 E. 12th Street falls in one of the address ranges in the same row as Delivery Route A.

11. **The correct answer is (D).** The address 152 N. Brook Street does not fall into any of the address ranges for Delivery Routes A, B, or C.

12. **The correct answer is (C).** The address 9500 South Broad Avenue falls in one of the address ranges in the same row as Delivery Route C.

13. **The correct answer is (C).** The address 900 S. Chester Road falls in one of the address ranges in the same row as Delivery Route C.

14. **The correct answer is (D).** The address 1000 N. Broad Avenue does not fall into any of the address ranges for Delivery Routes A, B, or C.

15. **The correct answer is (B).** The address 401 N. Broad Avenue falls in one of the address ranges in the same row as Delivery Route B.

16. **The correct answer is (D).** The address 76 E. Chestnut Street does not fall into any of the address ranges for Delivery Routes A, B, or C.

17. **The correct answer is (B).** The address 368 N. Broad Avenue falls in one of the address ranges in the same row as Delivery Route B.

18. **The correct answer is (C).** The address 8620 S. Broad Avenue falls in one of the address ranges in the same row as Delivery Route C.

19. **The correct answer is (D).** The address 1201 S. Clement Street does not

fall into any of the address ranges for Delivery Routes A, B, or C.

20. **The correct answer is (D).** The address 14 Rural Route 2 does not fall into any of the address ranges for Delivery Routes A, B, or C.

21. **The correct address is (A).** The address 15 E. Chestnut Street falls in one of the address ranges in the same row as Delivery Route A.

22. **The correct answer is (D).** The address 1250 E. 12th Street does not fall into any of the address ranges for Delivery Routes A, B, or C.

23. **The correct answer is (D).** The address 59 W. Chestnut Street does not fall into any of the address ranges for Delivery Routes A, B, or C.

24. **The correct address is (C).** The address 28 Rural Route 2 falls in one of the address ranges in the same row as Delivery Route C.

25. **The correct answer is (D).** The address 1400 S. Broad Avenue does not fall into any of the address ranges for Delivery Routes A, B, or C.

26. **The correct answer is (C).** The address 305 S. Chester Road falls in one of the address ranges in the same row as Delivery Route C.

27. **The correct answer is (A).** The address 178 N. Broad Avenue falls in one of the address ranges in the same row as Delivery Route A.

28. **The correct answer is (D).** The address 15101 N. Broad Avenue does not fall into any of the address ranges for Delivery Routes A, B, or C.

29. **The correct answer is (B).** The address 59 E. Chestnut Street falls in one of the address ranges in the same row as Delivery Route B.

30. **The correct answer is (A).** The address 99 E. 12th Street falls in one of the address ranges in the same row as Delivery Route A.

31. **The correct answer is (D).** The address 7000 S. Brook Avenue does not fall into any of the address ranges for Delivery Routes A, B, or C.

32. **The correct answer is (B).** The address 249 N. Broad Avenue falls in one of the address ranges in the same row as Delivery Route B.

33. **The correct answer is (C).** The address 30 Rural Route 2 falls in one of the address ranges in the same row as Delivery Route C.

34. **The correct answer is (D).** The address 1049 S. Chester Road does not fall into any of the address ranges for Delivery Routes A, B, or C.

35. **The correct answer is (A).** The address 19 E. Chestnut Street falls in one of the address ranges in the same row as Delivery Route A.

36. **The correct answer is (D).** The address 1000 S. Broad Avenue does not fall into any of the address ranges for Delivery Routes A, B, or C.

## MEMORY SECTION: SEGMENT 2

| | | | | |
|---|---|---|---|---|
| 1. D | 3. B | 5. A | 7. C | 8. A |
| 2. C | 4. D | 6. B | | |

**MEMORY SECTION: SEGMENT 4**

| | | | |
|---|---|---|---|
| 1. A | 9. D | 16. C | 23. A | 30. D |
| 2. C | 10. D | 17. D | 24. A | 31. D |
| 3. B | 11. A | 18. D | 25. D | 32. C |
| 4. D | 12. B | 19. B | 26. B | 33. D |
| 5. D | 13. D | 20. A | 27. C | 34. D |
| 6. C | 14. C | 21. A | 28. B | 35. B |
| 7. A | 15. D | 22. D | 29. D | 36. C |
| 8. D | | | | |

1. **The correct answer is (A).** The address 250 E. 12th Street falls in one of the address ranges in the same row as Delivery Route A.

2. **The correct answer is (C).** The address 12501 S. Broad Avenue falls in one of the address ranges in the same row as Delivery Route C.

3. **The correct answer is (B).** The address 205 N. Broad Avenue falls in one of the address ranges in the same row as Delivery Route B.

4. **The correct answer is (D).** The address 601 N. Broad Avenue does not fall into any of the address ranges for Delivery Routes A, B, or C.

5. **The correct answer is (D).** The address 20 Rural Route 10 does not fall into any of the address ranges for Delivery Routes A, B, or C.

6. **The correct answer is (C).** The address 30 Rural Route 2 falls in one of the address ranges in the same row as Delivery Route C.

7. **The correct answer is (A).** The address 51 E. 12th Street falls in one of the address ranges in the same row as Delivery Route (A).

8. **The correct answer is (D).** The address 25 E. 12th Street does not fall into any of the address ranges for Delivery Routes A, B, or C.

9. **The correct answer is (D).** The address 36 Belmont Lane does not fall into any of the address ranges for Delivery Routes A, B, or C.

10. **The correct answer is (D).** The address 300 E. 12th Street does not fall into any of the address ranges for Delivery Routes A, B, or C.

11. **The correct answer is (A).** The address 137 N. Broad Avenue falls in one of the address ranges in the same row as Delivery Route A.

12. **The correct answer is (B).** The address 301 N. Broad Avenue falls in one of the address ranges in the same row as Delivery Route B.

13. **The correct answer is (D).** The address 400 E. 12th Street does not fall into any of the address ranges for Delivery Routes A, B, or C.

14. **The correct answer is (C).** The address 900 S. Chester Road falls in one of the address ranges in the same row as Delivery Route C.

15. **The correct answer is (D).** The address 13040 S. Broad Street does not fall in any of the address ranges for Delivery Routes A, B, or C.

16. **The correct answer is (C).** The address 406 S. Chester Road falls in one of the address ranges in the same row as Delivery Route C.

17. **The correct answer is (D).** The address 6700 S. Broad Avenue does not fall into any of the address ranges for Delivery Routes A, B, or C.

18. **The correct answer is (D).** The address 48 E. 14th Street does not fall into any of the address ranges for Delivery Routes A, B, or C.

19. **The correct answer is (B).** The address 51 E. Chestnut Street falls in one of the address ranges in the same row as Delivery Route B.

answers practice test 1

20. **The correct answer is (A).** The address 15 E. Chestnut Street falls in one of the address ranges in the same row as Delivery Route A.

21. **The correct answer is (A).** The address 115 E. 12th Street falls in one of the address ranges in the same row as Delivery Route A.

22. **The correct answer is (D).** The address 1000 S. Brook Street does not fall into any of the address ranges for Delivery Routes A, B, or C.

23. **The correct answer is (A).** The address 210 E. 12th Street falls in one of the address ranges in the same row as Delivery Route A.

24. **The correct answer is (A).** The address 105 N. Broad Avenue falls in one of the address ranges in the same row as Delivery Route A.

25. **The correct answer is (D).** The address 15 Rural Route 2 does not fall into any of the address ranges for Delivery Routes A, B, or C.

26. **The correct answer is (B).** The address 68 E. Chestnut Street falls in one of the address ranges in the same row as Delivery Route B.

27. **The correct answer is (C).** The address 28 Rural Route 2 falls in one of the address ranges in the same row as Delivery Route C.

28. **The correct answer is (B).** The address 325 N. Broad Avenue falls in one of the address ranges in the same row as Delivery Route B.

29. **The correct answer is (D).** The address 1000 E. Chestnut Street does not fall into any of the address ranges for Delivery Routes A, B, or C.

30. **The correct answer is (D).** The address 14 North Broad Avenue does not fall into any of the address ranges for Delivery Routes A, B, or C.

31. **The correct answer is (D).** The address 117 S. 12th Street does not fall in any of the address ranges for Delivery Routes A, B, or C.

32. **The correct answer is (C).** The address 717 S. Chester Road falls in one of the address ranges in the same row as Delivery Route C.

33. **The correct answer is (D).** The address 14 N. Broad Avenue does not fall into any of the address ranges for Delivery Routes A, B, or C.

34. **The correct answer is (D).** The address 25 Belmont Lane does not fall into any of the address ranges for Delivery Routes A, B, or C.

35. **The correct answer is (B).** The address 67 E. Chestnut Street falls in one of the address ranges in the same row as Delivery Route B.

36. **The correct answer is (C).** The address 608 S. Chester Road falls in one of the address ranges in the same row as Delivery Route C.

## Part D: Personal Characteristics and Experience Inventory

*Answers will vary according to individual characteristics and experiences. There are no "correct" answers for this part of the exam.*

# PRACTICE TEST 2: EXAMS 473/473-C AND 460

## Part A: Address Checking

| | | | | |
|---|---|---|---|---|
| 1. Ⓐ Ⓑ Ⓒ Ⓓ | 13. Ⓐ Ⓑ Ⓒ Ⓓ | 25. Ⓐ Ⓑ Ⓒ Ⓓ | 37. Ⓐ Ⓑ Ⓒ Ⓓ | 49. Ⓐ Ⓑ Ⓒ Ⓓ |
| 2. Ⓐ Ⓑ Ⓒ Ⓓ | 14. Ⓐ Ⓑ Ⓒ Ⓓ | 26. Ⓐ Ⓑ Ⓒ Ⓓ | 38. Ⓐ Ⓑ Ⓒ Ⓓ | 50. Ⓐ Ⓑ Ⓒ Ⓓ |
| 3. Ⓐ Ⓑ Ⓒ Ⓓ | 15. Ⓐ Ⓑ Ⓒ Ⓓ | 27. Ⓐ Ⓑ Ⓒ Ⓓ | 39. Ⓐ Ⓑ Ⓒ Ⓓ | 51. Ⓐ Ⓑ Ⓒ Ⓓ |
| 4. Ⓐ Ⓑ Ⓒ Ⓓ | 16. Ⓐ Ⓑ Ⓒ Ⓓ | 28. Ⓐ Ⓑ Ⓒ Ⓓ | 40. Ⓐ Ⓑ Ⓒ Ⓓ | 52. Ⓐ Ⓑ Ⓒ Ⓓ |
| 5. Ⓐ Ⓑ Ⓒ Ⓓ | 17. Ⓐ Ⓑ Ⓒ Ⓓ | 29. Ⓐ Ⓑ Ⓒ Ⓓ | 41. Ⓐ Ⓑ Ⓒ Ⓓ | 53. Ⓐ Ⓑ Ⓒ Ⓓ |
| 6. Ⓐ Ⓑ Ⓒ Ⓓ | 18. Ⓐ Ⓑ Ⓒ Ⓓ | 30. Ⓐ Ⓑ Ⓒ Ⓓ | 42. Ⓐ Ⓑ Ⓒ Ⓓ | 54. Ⓐ Ⓑ Ⓒ Ⓓ |
| 7. Ⓐ Ⓑ Ⓒ Ⓓ | 19. Ⓐ Ⓑ Ⓒ Ⓓ | 31. Ⓐ Ⓑ Ⓒ Ⓓ | 43. Ⓐ Ⓑ Ⓒ Ⓓ | 55. Ⓐ Ⓑ Ⓒ Ⓓ |
| 8. Ⓐ Ⓑ Ⓒ Ⓓ | 20. Ⓐ Ⓑ Ⓒ Ⓓ | 32. Ⓐ Ⓑ Ⓒ Ⓓ | 44. Ⓐ Ⓑ Ⓒ Ⓓ | 56. Ⓐ Ⓑ Ⓒ Ⓓ |
| 9. Ⓐ Ⓑ Ⓒ Ⓓ | 21. Ⓐ Ⓑ Ⓒ Ⓓ | 33. Ⓐ Ⓑ Ⓒ Ⓓ | 45. Ⓐ Ⓑ Ⓒ Ⓓ | 57. Ⓐ Ⓑ Ⓒ Ⓓ |
| 10. Ⓐ Ⓑ Ⓒ Ⓓ | 22. Ⓐ Ⓑ Ⓒ Ⓓ | 34. Ⓐ Ⓑ Ⓒ Ⓓ | 46. Ⓐ Ⓑ Ⓒ Ⓓ | 58. Ⓐ Ⓑ Ⓒ Ⓓ |
| 11. Ⓐ Ⓑ Ⓒ Ⓓ | 23. Ⓐ Ⓑ Ⓒ Ⓓ | 35. Ⓐ Ⓑ Ⓒ Ⓓ | 47. Ⓐ Ⓑ Ⓒ Ⓓ | 59. Ⓐ Ⓑ Ⓒ Ⓓ |
| 12. Ⓐ Ⓑ Ⓒ Ⓓ | 24. Ⓐ Ⓑ Ⓒ Ⓓ | 36. Ⓐ Ⓑ Ⓒ Ⓓ | 48. Ⓐ Ⓑ Ⓒ Ⓓ | 60. Ⓐ Ⓑ Ⓒ Ⓓ |

## Part B: Forms Completion

| | | | | |
|---|---|---|---|---|
| 1. Ⓐ Ⓑ Ⓒ Ⓓ | 7. Ⓐ Ⓑ Ⓒ Ⓓ | 13. Ⓐ Ⓑ Ⓒ Ⓓ | 19. Ⓐ Ⓑ Ⓒ Ⓓ | 25. Ⓐ Ⓑ Ⓒ Ⓓ |
| 2. Ⓐ Ⓑ Ⓒ Ⓓ | 8. Ⓐ Ⓑ Ⓒ Ⓓ | 14. Ⓐ Ⓑ Ⓒ Ⓓ | 20. Ⓐ Ⓑ Ⓒ Ⓓ | 26. Ⓐ Ⓑ Ⓒ Ⓓ |
| 3. Ⓐ Ⓑ Ⓒ Ⓓ | 9. Ⓐ Ⓑ Ⓒ Ⓓ | 15. Ⓐ Ⓑ Ⓒ Ⓓ | 21. Ⓐ Ⓑ Ⓒ Ⓓ | 27. Ⓐ Ⓑ Ⓒ Ⓓ |
| 4. Ⓐ Ⓑ Ⓒ Ⓓ | 10. Ⓐ Ⓑ Ⓒ Ⓓ | 16. Ⓐ Ⓑ Ⓒ Ⓓ | 22. Ⓐ Ⓑ Ⓒ Ⓓ | 28. Ⓐ Ⓑ Ⓒ Ⓓ |
| 5. Ⓐ Ⓑ Ⓒ Ⓓ | 11. Ⓐ Ⓑ Ⓒ Ⓓ | 17. Ⓐ Ⓑ Ⓒ Ⓓ | 23. Ⓐ Ⓑ Ⓒ Ⓓ | 29. Ⓐ Ⓑ Ⓒ Ⓓ |
| 6. Ⓐ Ⓑ Ⓒ Ⓓ | 12. Ⓐ Ⓑ Ⓒ Ⓓ | 18. Ⓐ Ⓑ Ⓒ Ⓓ | 24. Ⓐ Ⓑ Ⓒ Ⓓ | 30. Ⓐ Ⓑ Ⓒ Ⓓ |

## Part C: Coding and Memory

### CODING SECTION: SEGMENT 3

| | | | | |
|---|---|---|---|---|
| 1. Ⓐ Ⓑ Ⓒ Ⓓ | 9. Ⓐ Ⓑ Ⓒ Ⓓ | 16. Ⓐ Ⓑ Ⓒ Ⓓ | 23. Ⓐ Ⓑ Ⓒ Ⓓ | 30. Ⓐ Ⓑ Ⓒ Ⓓ |
| 2. Ⓐ Ⓑ Ⓒ Ⓓ | 10. Ⓐ Ⓑ Ⓒ Ⓓ | 17. Ⓐ Ⓑ Ⓒ Ⓓ | 24. Ⓐ Ⓑ Ⓒ Ⓓ | 31. Ⓐ Ⓑ Ⓒ Ⓓ |
| 3. Ⓐ Ⓑ Ⓒ Ⓓ | 11. Ⓐ Ⓑ Ⓒ Ⓓ | 18. Ⓐ Ⓑ Ⓒ Ⓓ | 25. Ⓐ Ⓑ Ⓒ Ⓓ | 32. Ⓐ Ⓑ Ⓒ Ⓓ |
| 4. Ⓐ Ⓑ Ⓒ Ⓓ | 12. Ⓐ Ⓑ Ⓒ Ⓓ | 19. Ⓐ Ⓑ Ⓒ Ⓓ | 26. Ⓐ Ⓑ Ⓒ Ⓓ | 33. Ⓐ Ⓑ Ⓒ Ⓓ |
| 5. Ⓐ Ⓑ Ⓒ Ⓓ | 13. Ⓐ Ⓑ Ⓒ Ⓓ | 20. Ⓐ Ⓑ Ⓒ Ⓓ | 27. Ⓐ Ⓑ Ⓒ Ⓓ | 34. Ⓐ Ⓑ Ⓒ Ⓓ |
| 6. Ⓐ Ⓑ Ⓒ Ⓓ | 14. Ⓐ Ⓑ Ⓒ Ⓓ | 21. Ⓐ Ⓑ Ⓒ Ⓓ | 28. Ⓐ Ⓑ Ⓒ Ⓓ | 35. Ⓐ Ⓑ Ⓒ Ⓓ |
| 7. Ⓐ Ⓑ Ⓒ Ⓓ | 15. Ⓐ Ⓑ Ⓒ Ⓓ | 22. Ⓐ Ⓑ Ⓒ Ⓓ | 29. Ⓐ Ⓑ Ⓒ Ⓓ | 36. Ⓐ Ⓑ Ⓒ Ⓓ |
| 8. Ⓐ Ⓑ Ⓒ Ⓓ | | | | |

### MEMORY SECTION: SEGMENT 4

| | | | | |
|---|---|---|---|---|
| 1. Ⓐ Ⓑ Ⓒ Ⓓ | 9. Ⓐ Ⓑ Ⓒ Ⓓ | 16. Ⓐ Ⓑ Ⓒ Ⓓ | 23. Ⓐ Ⓑ Ⓒ Ⓓ | 30. Ⓐ Ⓑ Ⓒ Ⓓ |
| 2. Ⓐ Ⓑ Ⓒ Ⓓ | 10. Ⓐ Ⓑ Ⓒ Ⓓ | 17. Ⓐ Ⓑ Ⓒ Ⓓ | 24. Ⓐ Ⓑ Ⓒ Ⓓ | 31. Ⓐ Ⓑ Ⓒ Ⓓ |
| 3. Ⓐ Ⓑ Ⓒ Ⓓ | 11. Ⓐ Ⓑ Ⓒ Ⓓ | 18. Ⓐ Ⓑ Ⓒ Ⓓ | 25. Ⓐ Ⓑ Ⓒ Ⓓ | 32. Ⓐ Ⓑ Ⓒ Ⓓ |
| 4. Ⓐ Ⓑ Ⓒ Ⓓ | 12. Ⓐ Ⓑ Ⓒ Ⓓ | 19. Ⓐ Ⓑ Ⓒ Ⓓ | 26. Ⓐ Ⓑ Ⓒ Ⓓ | 33. Ⓐ Ⓑ Ⓒ Ⓓ |
| 5. Ⓐ Ⓑ Ⓒ Ⓓ | 13. Ⓐ Ⓑ Ⓒ Ⓓ | 20. Ⓐ Ⓑ Ⓒ Ⓓ | 27. Ⓐ Ⓑ Ⓒ Ⓓ | 34. Ⓐ Ⓑ Ⓒ Ⓓ |
| 6. Ⓐ Ⓑ Ⓒ Ⓓ | 14. Ⓐ Ⓑ Ⓒ Ⓓ | 21. Ⓐ Ⓑ Ⓒ Ⓓ | 28. Ⓐ Ⓑ Ⓒ Ⓓ | 35. Ⓐ Ⓑ Ⓒ Ⓓ |
| 7. Ⓐ Ⓑ Ⓒ Ⓓ | 15. Ⓐ Ⓑ Ⓒ Ⓓ | 22. Ⓐ Ⓑ Ⓒ Ⓓ | 29. Ⓐ Ⓑ Ⓒ Ⓓ | 36. Ⓐ Ⓑ Ⓒ Ⓓ |
| 8. Ⓐ Ⓑ Ⓒ Ⓓ | | | | |

answer sheet

# Practice Test 2: Exams 473/473-C and 460

**NOTE:** Practice Tests 1–5 are a combination of the types of questions test-takers will see on Exam 473 and Exam 460.

Exam 473 consists of four parts:

A. Address Checking

B. Forms Completion

C. Coding and Memory

D. Personal Characteristics and Experience Inventory

Exam 460 consists of four parts:

A. Address Checking

B. Memory for Addresses

C. Number Series

D. Following Oral Instructions

If you are practicing to take Exam 460, you may want to follow these tips:

- Skip Part B (Forms Completion) of Practice Tests 1 through 5. This material will not be included on your actual exam; it is only on Exam 473.

- Skip Part D (Personal Characteristics and Experience Inventory) of Practice Test 1. This material will not be included on your actual exam; it is only on Exam 473.

- To practice for Part D of Exam 460 (Following Oral Instructions), take Practice Test 7 in this book.

## PART A: ADDRESS CHECKING

**60 QUESTIONS • 11 MINUTES**

**Directions:** Compare the **List to be Checked** with the **Correct List.** Decide if there are **(A) NO ERRORS,** an error in the **(B) ADDRESS ONLY,** an error in the **(C) ZIP CODE ONLY,** or an error in **(D) BOTH** the address and ZIP Code. Record your answers on the answer sheet.

| | Correct List | | List to be Checked | |
|---|---|---|---|---|
| | *Address* | *ZIP Code* | *Address* | *ZIP Code* |
| 1. | 2929 W. Zator Pl. Covington, GA | 30014-6601 | 2929 W. Zator Pl. Covington, GA | 30014-6601 |
| 2. | 371 Smalls Parkway Archer, NE | 68816 | 371 Smalls Parkway Archer, NE | 68818 |
| 3. | 8617 South Drive Vallonia, IN | 47281 | 8671 South Drive Vallonia, IN | 47281 |
| 4. | 2300 Lemar Ter. Northumberland, PA | 17857 | 2300 Lemar Ter. Northcumberland, PA | 17857 |
| 5. | 473 Runwalt Court Brookline, MA | 02446 | 437 Runwalt Court Brookline, MA | 02246 |
| 6. | 3417 Cobalt Circle Berlin, Wisconsin | 54923 | 3417 Cobalt Circle Berlin, Wisconsin | 54923 |
| 7. | 9201 S. Lee Road Brainerd, MN | 56401 | 9201 S. Lee Road Brainard, MN | 56401 |
| 8. | 122 E. Marion Street Seattle, WA | 98114 | 122 E. Marion Street Seattle, WA | 98814 |
| 9. | 2708 Lyons Circle Saint George, SC | 29477 | 2708 Lyons Circle Saint George, SC | 29477 |
| 10. | 722 N. Albert Place Corning, Iowa | 50841 | 722 N. Alberta Place Corning, Iowa | 58841 |
| 11. | 2743 E. Charger Place Windber, PA | 15963 | 2743 E. Charger Place Windber, PA | 15963 |
| 12. | 2500 S. Finders Way Orange, CT | 06477-2432 | 2500 S. Finders Way Orange, CT | 06447-2432 |

**Directions:** Compare the **List to be Checked** with the **Correct List.** Decide if there are **(A) NO ERRORS,** an error in the **(B) ADDRESS ONLY,** an error in the **(C) ZIP CODE ONLY,** or an error in **(D) BOTH** the address and ZIP Code. Record your answers on the answer sheet.

| | List to be Checked | | Correct List | |
|---|---|---|---|---|
| 13. | 1760 Lester Dr<br>Reno, NV | 89502 | 1760 Lester Dr<br>Reno, NE | 89502 |
| 14. | 960 S. Lakes Street<br>Corpus Christi, TX | 78401-2825 | 9600 S. Lake Street<br>Corpus Christi, TX | 78401-2025 |
| 15. | 2705 S. Bond Road<br>Hardaway, AL | 36039 | 2750 S. Bond Road<br>Hardaway, AL | 36039 |
| 16. | 720 Bloomfield Road<br>Wichita, KS | 67226 | 720 Bloomfield Road<br>Wichita, KS | 67266 |
| 17. | 7201 W. Tibbs Ave.<br>Boulevard, CA | 91905 | 7201 W. Tibbs Ave.<br>Boulevard, CA | 91905 |
| 18. | 3346 Thomas Parkway<br>Ridgeville, SC | 29472 | 3364 Thomas Parkway<br>Ridgeville, SC | 29772 |
| 19. | Post Office Box 1014<br>Jackson, TN | 38301 | Post Office Box 1014<br>Jackson, TN | 38301 |
| 20. | 4468 S. Crest Ct.<br>Missoula, MT | 59802-4207 | 4468 S. Crest Ct.<br>Missoula, MN | 59802-4207 |
| 21. | 306 Eleanor Lane<br>Stanley, Wisconsin | 54768 | 306 Eleanor Lane<br>Stanley, Wisconsin | 54678 |
| 22. | 7213 Huffington Drive<br>Driscoll, ND | 58532 | 7213 Huffington Drive<br>Driscoll, ND | 58532 |
| 23. | 16000 North Drive<br>Lake Oswego, OR | 97034 | 16000 Norton Drive<br>Lake Oswego, OR | 97034 |
| 24. | 5519 Fantasia Avenue<br>Carey, ID | 83320 | 5519 Fantasia Avenue<br>Carey, IA | 88320 |
| 25. | 2377 E. Carriage Road<br>Miami, FL | 33178 | 2377 E. Carriage Road<br>Miami, FL | 33178 |
| 26. | 2313 N. Sevel Place<br>Lonoke, AR | 72086 | 2313 N. Sevel Place<br>Lonoke, AK | 72806 |
| 27. | 811 Juniper Court<br>Billings, MT | 59101 | 811 Juniper Court<br>Billings, MT | 59001 |

**Directions:** Compare the **List to be Checked** with the **Correct List.** Decide if there are **(A) NO ERRORS,** an error in the **(B) ADDRESS ONLY,** an error in the **(C) ZIP CODE ONLY,** or an error in **(D) BOTH** the address and ZIP Code. Record your answers on the answer sheet.

| # | Correct List | | List to be Checked | |
|---|---|---|---|---|
| 28. | 300 Fillmore Pl.<br>Castle Rock, Colorado | 80104-2107 | 303 Fillmore Pl.<br>Castle Rock, Colorado | 80104-2107 |
| 29. | 420 Junction Rd<br>Indore, WV | 25111 | 420 Junction Rd<br>Indore, WV | 25111 |
| 30. | 76 N. 21st St, Apt. B<br>Pocatello, ID | 83204 | 76 N. 21st St, Apt. B<br>Pocadello, ID | 83204 |
| 31. | 2900 E. Bristol Road<br>Miami, FL | 33176 | 2900 E. Bristle Road<br>Miami, FL | 33176 |
| 32. | 9806 Ellis Court<br>Casper, WY | 82604 | 9806 Ellis Court<br>Caspar, WY | 82644 |
| 33. | 659 Danzinger Ave<br>Coulee City, WA | 99115 | 655 Danzinger Ave<br>Coulie City, WA | 99115 |
| 34. | 10 Shasta Boulevard<br>Shelbyville, TN | 37160 | 10 Shasta Boulevard<br>Shelbyville, TN | 31760 |
| 35. | 2006 Urban Place<br>Wellington, KS | 67152 | 2006 Urban Place<br>Wellington, KS | 67152 |
| 36. | 4730 Ridley Trail<br>Pacific Junction, IA | 51561 | 4730 Ridley Trail<br>Pacific Junction, IA | 51651 |
| 37. | 1722 Prairie Dr.<br>Fayetteville, NC | 28301-5537 | 1772 Prairie Dr.<br>Fayetteville, NC | 23801-5537 |
| 38. | 1100 Russett Avenue<br>Mondovi, WI | 54755 | 1100 Russek Avenue<br>Mondovi, WI | 54755 |
| 39. | 1300 S. Center Road<br>North Canton, OH | 44720 | 1300 S. Center Road<br>North Canton, OH | 44720 |
| 40. | 23 Udall Court<br>Helix, OR | 97835 | 230 Udall Court<br>Helix, OR | 98735 |
| 41. | 540 Hampton Parkway<br>Saginaw, MI | 48609 | 540 Hampton Parkway<br>Saginaw, MI | 48609 |
| 42. | 375 E. 12th Ave, #102<br>Junction City, CA | 96048 | 375 E. 12th Ave, #102<br>Junction City, CA | 96408 |

**Directions:** Compare the **List to be Checked** with the **Correct List.** Decide if there are **(A) NO ERRORS,** an error in the **(B) ADDRESS ONLY,** an error in the **(C) ZIP CODE ONLY,** or an error in **(D) BOTH** the address and ZIP Code. Record your answers on the answer sheet.

**43.** 681 Henry Boulevard
Wray, Georgia          31798

681 Henry Boulevard
Wray, Georgia          31708

**44.** 40 East Spring Drive
Millinocket, ME          04462

40 East Spring Drive
Millinocket, MN          04662

**45.** P.O. Box 5350
Newtown, PA          18940-2026

P.O. Box 5355
Newtown, PA          18940-2026

**46.** 7800 Element Trail
Farmington, MN          55024

7600 Elemental Trail
Farmington, MN          55004

**47.** 976 Kitteridge Avenue
Beggs, OK          74421

976 Kitteridge Avenue
Beggs, OK          74421

**48.** 8910 Linvale Road
Austin, NV          89310

8910 Linvale Road
Austin, NV          89310

**49.** 605 Harvard Place
Milton, MA          02186

605 Halvard Place
Milton, MA          02186

**50.** 466 Robin St.
Albuquerque, NM          87105

466 Robin St.
Albequerque, NM          87015

**51.** 13 Harriet Road
Sanbornton, NH          03269

13 Harriet Road
Sanborn, NH          03269

**52.** 3907 E. Simpson Drive
Perris, CA          92570-1917

3907 E. Sampson Drive
Perris, CA          92570-1971

**53.** 2200 Turner Avenue
Noblesville, IN          46060

2200 Turner Avenue
Noblesville, IN          46066

**54.** 55 Vidalia Blvd
Turner, OR          97392

55 Vidalia Blvd
Turner, OR          97392

**55.** 700 Senta Drive
Rochester, NY          14624

700 Sentor Drive
Rochester, NY          14624

**56.** 880 S. Rider Court
Bismarck, ND          58504

880 S. Rider Court
Bismarck, ND          58554

**57.** 83 Ulysses Place
Berea, Kentucky          40403

83 Ulysses Place
Berea, Kentucky          40403

**Directions:** Compare the **List to be Checked** with the **Correct List.** Decide if there are **(A) NO ERRORS,** an error in the **(B) ADDRESS ONLY,** an error in the **(C) ZIP CODE ONLY,** or an error in **(D) BOTH** the address and ZIP Code. Record your answers on the answer sheet.

**58.** 257 Addison Pkwy
Pekin, IL                     61554-4188         207 Addison Pkwy
Pekin, IL                     61544-4188

**59.** 39 Tiffany Drive
Pearland, TX                  77581              39 Tiffany Drive
Pearland, TX                  77551

**60.** 640 Morrison Road
Globe, Arizona                85501              640 Morrison Road
Globe, Arizona                85501

## PART B: FORMS COMPLETION

### 30 QUESTIONS • 15 MINUTES

**Directions:** Read each form and answer the questions based on the information provided. Mark your answers on the answer sheet.

---

**DELIVERY EMPLOYEE - Remove Copies 1 & 2 at Time of Delivery**

Date Returned

2nd Notice

1st Notice

UNITED STATES POSTAL SERVICE®

Collect the amount shown below, if customer pays by **CHECK** made payable to the mailer.

Check Amount $

Collect the amount shown below if customer pays in **CASH** *(Includes MO fee or fees).*

Cash Amount $

M457452877

**COD**

☐ Registered Mail   ☐ Express Mail® Service   ☐ Form 3849-D Requested

Date of Mailing   ☐ Remit COD Charges to Sender via Express Mail   EMCA No.

From:

To:

| Delivered By | Date Delivered | Check Number |
| 1 | 2 | 3 |
| Date Payment Sent to Mailer | Date Form 3849-D Sent | MO Number(s) |
| 4 | 5 | 6 |

PS Form **3816**, February 2002

Copy 1 - Delivery Unit

1. DO NOT allow the recipient *(addressee or agent)* to examine the contents before payment.
2. DO NOT deliver this article until payment is collected.
◆ **Follow proper scanning procedures for COD delivery and clearance.**

3. If payment is by check, enter check number above.
4. Have customer sign Form 3849.

---

1. Which of the following would be a correct entry for Box 2 of the above form?
   - **(A)** 17.50
   - **(B)** 7/14/08
   - **(C)** Ms. Ellen Landow
   - **(D)** 30068

2. Where on the above form would you enter the date that the package was delivered?
   - **(A)** Box 1
   - **(B)** Box 2
   - **(C)** Box 4
   - **(D)** Box 6

3. The entry #4270 could be entered correctly in which of the following boxes on the form?
   - **(A)** 1
   - **(B)** 2
   - **(C)** 3
   - **(D)** 4

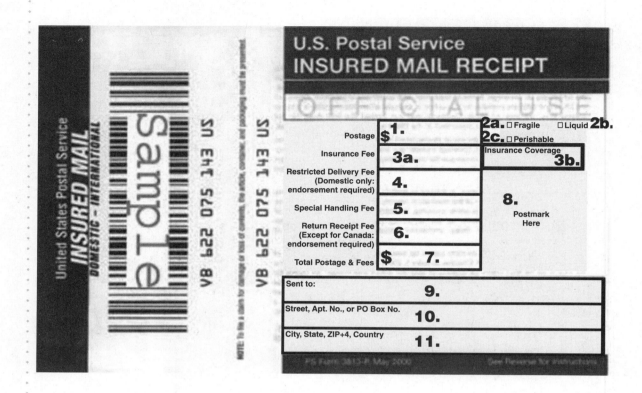

4. A ZIP Code could be entered in which of the following boxes on the above form?

**(A)** Box 5
**(B)** Box 6
**(C)** Box 10
**(D)** Box 11

5. Where on this form would you enter a special handling fee?

**(A)** Box 5
**(B)** Box 7
**(C)** Box 9
**(D)** Box 10

6. Where on this form would you note that an item is fragile?

**(A)** Box 1
**(B)** Box 2a
**(C)** Box 2b
**(D)** Box 3a

7. If the item were being mailed to Canada, which box on this form could NOT be completed?

**(A)** Box 3a
**(B)** Box 3b
**(C)** Box 4
**(D)** Box 6

8. What would be an appropriate entry for Box 9 on the form?

**(A)** A check mark
**(B)** 1742 E. Lansing Parkway
**(C)** Ms. Lee DiMarco
**(D)** $22.75

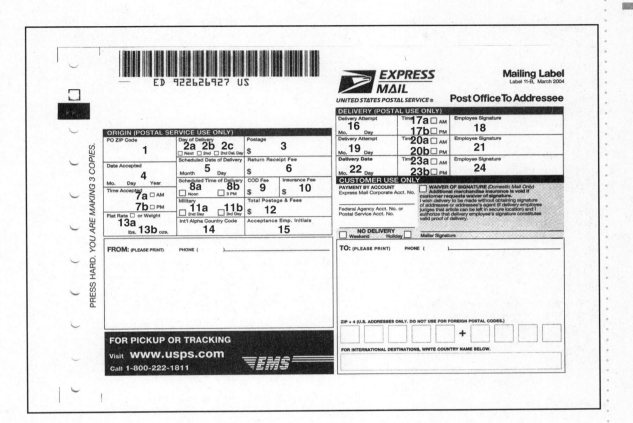

9. A check mark would be the correct entry for each of the following boxes on the above form EXCEPT

(A) Box 17a
(B) Box 20b
(C) Box 23a
(D) Box 24

10. Which of these would be an appropriate entry for Box 1?

(A) 30068
(B) $24.75
(C) May 15
(D) JK

11. Where on this form would you enter a COD fee?

(A) Box 3
(B) Box 6
(C) Box 9
(D) Box 15

12. Where on this form would you indicate the date of a delivery attempt?

(A) Box 17a
(B) Box 17b
(C) Box 19
(D) Box 20a

13. All of the following boxes on this form indicate that dates are needed EXCEPT

(A) Box 1
(B) Box 4
(C) Box 5
(D) Box 16

14. Which box would you check to show a scheduled delivery time of 3 PM?

(A) Box 8a
(B) Box 8b
(C) Box 17b
(D) Box 23b

**15.** The postage cost is entered in which box on this form?
- **(A)** Box 3
- **(B)** Box 6
- **(C)** Box 10
- **(D)** Box 15

**16.** In which box on this form would you indicate the package weight in pounds?
- **(A)** Box 2a
- **(B)** Box 6
- **(C)** Box 11b
- **(D)** Box 13a

**17.** Which of these would be an appropriate entry for Box 16 of the form?
- **(A)** Sentry Security
- **(B)** 14
- **(C)** $32.00
- **(D)** June 5

---

**Authorization to Hold Mail**

NOTE: *Complete and give to your letter carrier or mail to the post office that delivers your mail.*

➡ We can hold your mail for a minimum of **3**, but not for more than **30 days.**

**Postmaster: Please hold mail for:**

Name(s)

Address *(Number, street, apt./suite no., city, state, ZIP + 4)*

☐ **A.** Please deliver all accumulated mail and resume normal delivery on the ending date shown below.

☐ **B.** I will pick up all accumulated mail when I return and understand that mail delivery will not resume until I do.

| Beginning Date | Ending Date *(May only be changed by the customer in writing)* | Customer Signature |
|---|---|---|

**For Post Office Use Only**

| Date Received | **1.** | | |
|---|---|---|---|
| Clerk | **2.** | Bin Number | **3.** |
| Carrier | **4.** | Route Number | **5.** |

*(Complete this section only if customer selected option B)*

| **6.** ☐ Accumulated mail has been picked up. | Resume Delivery of Mail *(Date)* **7.** | By **8.** |
|---|---|---|

PS Form **8076,** April 2001

---

**18.** Which of these would be an appropriate entry for Box 1 of the above form?
- **(A)** 75 E. Lansing Place
- **(B)** 3/21/08
- **(C)** A check mark
- **(D)** $2.55

**19.** Which of these would be an appropriate entry for Box 4 of the above form?
- **(A)** 02334
- **(B)** $9.05
- **(C)** 7/9/08
- **(D)** James Ellis

**20.** Where on this form would you enter the date to resume mail delivery?

(A) Box 1
(B) Box 3
(C) Box 7
(D) Box 8

**21.** Where on this form would you enter a bin number?

(A) Box 3
(B) Box 4
(C) Box 5
(D) Box 6

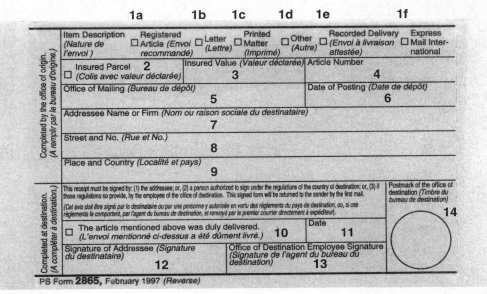

**22.** Where on the above form would you indicate that the item is Printed Matter?

(A) Box 1a
(B) Box 1c
(C) Box 10
(D) Box 14

**23.** How would you indicate on this form that the piece of mail is insured?

(A) Check Box 1e
(B) Check Box 1f
(C) Check Box 2
(D) Write the word in Box 4

**24.** Which of these would be an appropriate entry for Box 8 of this form?

(A) 724 S. Rawlings Drive
(B) Rome, Italy
(C) Mr. Arlen Hutchinson
(D) $470

**25.** Where on the form would you enter the Addressee Name?

(A) Box 3
(B) Box 4
(C) Box 5
(D) Box 7

**26.** Which of these would be a correct entry for Box 13 of this form?

(A) A check mark
(B) A signature
(C) 12/2/08
(D) 543

7000 0520 0017 2917 7637

PLACE STICKER AT TOP OF ENVELOPE TO THE RIGHT OF RETURN ADDRESS. FOLD AT DOTTED LINE

CERTIFIED MAIL™

7000 0520 0017 2917 7637

7000 0520 0017 2917 7637

U.S. Postal Service™
CERTIFIED MAIL™ RECEIPT
*(Domestic Mail Only; No Insurance Coverage Provided)*

For delivery information visit our website at www.usps.com®

OFFICIAL USE

| | | |
|---|---|---|
| Postage | $ 1 | 6 Postmark Here |
| Certified Fee | 2 | |
| Return Receipt Fee (Endorsement Required) | 3 | |
| Restricted Delivery Fee (Endorsement Required) | 4 | |
| Total Postage & Fees | $ 5 | |

| | |
|---|---|
| *Sent To:* | 7 |
| *Street, Apt. No.; or PO Box No.* | 8 |
| *City, State, ZIP+ 4* | 9 |

PS Form 3800, June 2002 See Reverse for Instructions

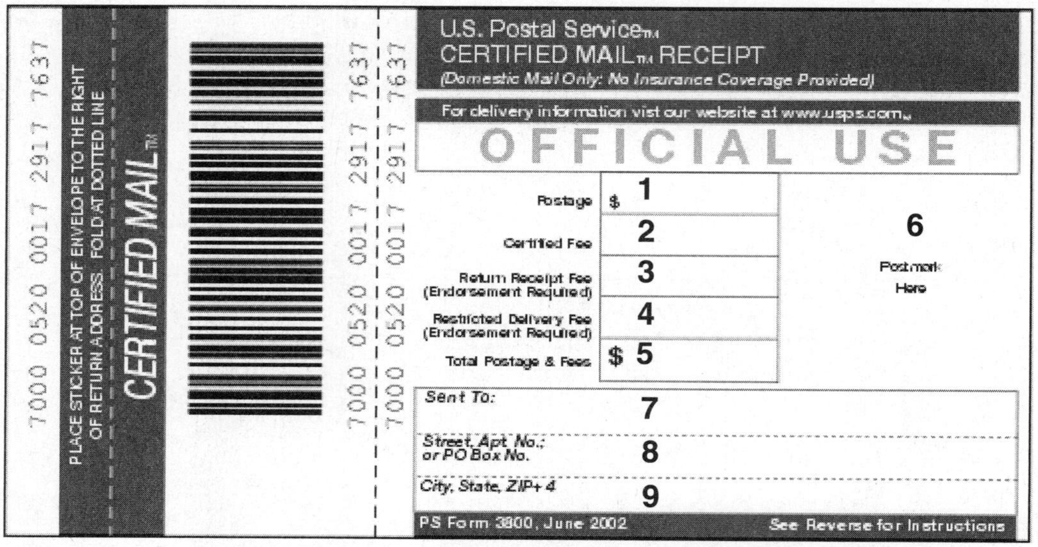

**27.** Which of these would be an appropriate entry for Box 8 of the above form?

**(A)** 89903
**(B)** 4417 Middledale Drive
**(C)** Ms. Karen Adler
**(D)** A signature

**28.** Where on this form would you indicate a certified fee?

**(A)** Box 2
**(B)** Box 4
**(C)** Box 5
**(D)** Box 6

**29.** Which of the following would be a correct entry for Box 1 of the form?

**(A)** A check mark
**(B)** 10/6/08
**(C)** A postmark
**(D)** 27.50

**30.** Where on this form would you indicate that the item is being sent to Acme Industries?

**(A)** Box 5
**(B)** Box 6
**(C)** Box 7
**(D)** Box 9

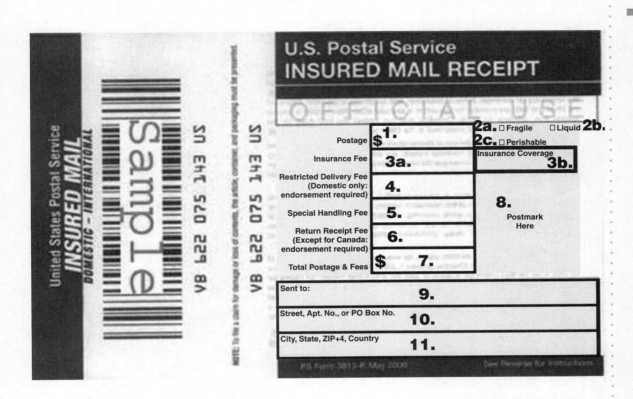

26. Where would you check that the item is perishable?
    (A) Box 2a
    (B) Box 2b
    (C) Box 2c
    (D) Box 3b

27. Where would you enter the total postage and fees?
    (A) Box 1
    (B) Box 3a
    (C) Box 5
    (D) Box 7

28. What would be the correct entry for Box 8?
    (A) A check mark
    (B) A postmark
    (C) $2.50
    (D) 12456

29. If the item was being mailed to a foreign country, which box could NOT be completed?
    (A) Box 1
    (B) Box 3b
    (C) Box 4
    (D) Box 5

30. You could enter fees in all of the following boxes EXCEPT
    (A) Box 1
    (B) Box 2a
    (C) Box 3a
    (D) Box 4

# PART C: CODING AND MEMORY

## Coding Section: Segment 1

**4 QUESTIONS • 2 MINUTES**

**Directions:** Segment 1 is *not* scored and does not count toward your total exam score. It is a practice exercise to help you with the Coding Section under a time constraint similar to the one used in the scored Coding Section. Use the coding guide below to match each address to a delivery route. Mark your answers on the answer section at the bottom of this page.

### CODING GUIDE

| ADDRESS RANGE | DELIVERY ROUTE |
|---|:---:|
| 300–499 N. Ridge Avenue<br>30–170 W. 74th Street<br>20–35 W. Wicker Street | A |
| 500–900 N. Ridge Avenue<br>36–90 W. Wicker Street | B |
| 30–45 Country Road 17<br>8000–17000 S. Ridge Avenue<br>400–1300 S. Wickell Street | C |
| All mail that doesn't fall into one of the address ranges listed above. | D |

| Address | Delivery Route | | | |
|---|:---:|:---:|:---:|:---:|
| **1.** 201 N. Ridge Avenue | A | B | C | D |
| **2.** 37 Country Road 17 | A | B | C | D |
| **3.** 84 W. Wicker Street | A | B | C | D |
| **4.** 413 S. Wickell Street | A | B | C | D |

## Sample Answer Sheet

**1.** Ⓐ Ⓑ Ⓒ Ⓓ          **3.** Ⓐ Ⓑ Ⓒ Ⓓ

**2.** Ⓐ Ⓑ Ⓒ Ⓓ          **4.** Ⓐ Ⓑ Ⓒ Ⓓ

## Coding Section: Segment 2

**8 QUESTIONS • 1.5 MINUTES (90 SECONDS)**

**Directions:** Segment 2 is *not* scored and does not count toward your total exam score. It is a practice exercise to help you with the Coding Section under a time constraint similar to the one used in the scored Coding Section. Use the coding guide below to match each address to a delivery route. Mark your answers on the answer section at the bottom of this page.

### CODING GUIDE

| ADDRESS RANGE | DELIVERY ROUTE |
| --- | --- |
| 300–499 N. Ridge Avenue<br>30–170 W. 74th Street<br>20–35 W. Wicker Street | A |
| 500–900 N. Ridge Avenue<br>36–90 W. Wicker Street | B |
| 30–45 Country Road 17<br>8000–17000 S. Ridge Avenue<br>400–1300 S. Wickell Street | C |
| All mail that doesn't fall into one of the address ranges listed above. | D |

| Address | Delivery Route | | | |
| --- | --- | --- | --- | --- |
| 1.  104 W. 74th Street | A | B | C | D |
| 2.  1390 S. Wickell Street | A | B | C | D |
| 3.  613 N. Ridge Avenue | A | B | C | D |
| 4.  15040 S. Ridge Avenue | A | B | C | D |
| 5.  60 W. Wicker Street | A | B | C | D |
| 6.  405 N. Wickell Street | A | B | C | D |
| 7.  333 N. Ridge Avenue | A | B | C | D |
| 8.  38 Country Road 17 | A | B | C | D |

## Sample Answer Sheet

1. Ⓐ Ⓑ Ⓒ Ⓓ     4. Ⓐ Ⓑ Ⓒ Ⓓ     7. Ⓐ Ⓑ Ⓒ Ⓓ

2. Ⓐ Ⓑ Ⓒ Ⓓ     5. Ⓐ Ⓑ Ⓒ Ⓓ     8. Ⓐ Ⓑ Ⓒ Ⓓ

3. Ⓐ Ⓑ Ⓒ Ⓓ     6. Ⓐ Ⓑ Ⓒ Ⓓ

## Coding Section: Segment 3

**36 QUESTIONS • 6 MINUTES**

**Directions:** Work through items 1 through 36, assigning a code to each item based on the Coding Guide below. Mark your answers on the answer sheet. Work quickly and accurately.

### CODING GUIDE

| ADDRESS RANGE | DELIVERY ROUTE |
|---|---|
| 300–499 N. Ridge Avenue<br>30–170 W. 74th Street<br>20–35 W. Wicker Street | A |
| 500–900 N. Ridge Avenue<br>36–90 W. Wicker Street | B |
| 30–45 Country Road 17<br>8000–17000 S. Ridge Avenue<br>400–1300 S. Wickell Street | C |
| All mail that doesn't fall into one of the address ranges listed above. | D |

| | Address | Delivery Route | | | |
|---|---|---|---|---|---|
| **1.** | 307 N. Ridge Avenue | A | B | C | D |
| **2.** | 47 W. Wicker Street | A | B | C | D |
| **3.** | 8800 S. Rider Street | A | B | C | D |
| **4.** | 1107 S. Wickell Street | A | B | C | D |
| **5.** | 825 N. Ridge Avenue | A | B | C | D |
| **6.** | 169 W. 74th Street | A | B | C | D |
| **7.** | 21 Country Road 17 | A | B | C | D |
| **8.** | 55 Country Road 17 | A | B | C | D |
| **9.** | 610 S. Wickell Street | A | B | C | D |
| **10.** | 401 S. Rider Street | A | B | C | D |
| **11.** | 30 W. Wicker Street | A | B | C | D |
| **12.** | 384 N. Ridge Avenue | A | B | C | D |
| **13.** | 649 N. Ridge Avenue | A | B | C | D |
| **14.** | 38 Country Road 17 | A | B | C | D |
| **15.** | 1400 S. Wickell Street | A | B | C | D |
| **16.** | 1299 S. Wickell Street | A | B | C | D |

## CODING GUIDE

| ADDRESS RANGE | DELIVERY ROUTE |
|---|:---:|
| 300–499 N. Ridge Avenue<br>30–170 W. 74th Street<br>20–35 W. Wicker Street | A |
| 500–900 N. Ridge Avenue<br>36–90 W. Wicker Street | B |
| 30–45 Country Road 17<br>8000–17000 S. Ridge Avenue<br>400–1300 S. Wickell Street | C |
| All mail that doesn't fall into one of the address ranges listed above. | D |

| | | | | | |
|---|---|:---:|:---:|:---:|:---:|
| 17. | 52 W. 74th Street | A | B | C | D |
| 18. | 838 N. Ridge Avenue | A | B | C | D |
| 19. | 350 W. Wicker Street | A | B | C | D |
| 20. | 100 W. 74th Street | A | B | C | D |
| 21. | 61 W. Wicker Street | A | B | C | D |
| 22. | 9020 S. Ridge Avenue | A | B | C | D |
| 23. | 21 W. Wicker Street | A | B | C | D |
| 24. | 1100 N. Ridge Avenue | A | B | C | D |
| 25. | 42 Country Road 17 | A | B | C | D |
| 26. | 700 N. Ridge Avenue | A | B | C | D |
| 27. | 10035 S. Ridge Avenue | A | B | C | D |
| 28. | 49 Country Road 17 | A | B | C | D |
| 29. | 930 S. Wickell Street | A | B | C | D |
| 30. | 74 W. Wicker Street | A | B | C | D |
| 31. | 800 S. Wickell Street | A | B | C | D |
| 32. | 33 W. Wicker Street | A | B | C | D |
| 33. | 822 N. Ridge Avenue | A | B | C | D |
| 34. | 180 W. 74th Street | A | B | C | D |
| 35. | 417 N. Ridge Avenue | A | B | C | D |
| 36. | 59 W. Wicker Street | A | B | C | D |

## Memory Section: Segment 1

**3 MINUTES**

**Directions:** Take 3 minutes to memorize the Coding Guide on page 184.
- You may NOT write down any addresses during the memorization period.

## Memory Section: Segment 2

**8 QUESTIONS • 1.5 MINUTES (90 SECONDS)**

**Directions:** Segment 2 is *not* scored and does not count toward your total exam score. It is an exercise to help you practice coding addresses from memory under a time constraint similar to the one used in the scored Memory Section of the actual exam. You will *not* see the Coding Guide during this segment of the exam. Based on your memory of the Coding Guide, match each address shown on the next page to a delivery route. Mark your answers on the answer section at the bottom of the this page.

• You may NOT look at the codes when answering the items.

| Address | Delivery Route | | | |
|---|---|---|---|---|
| 1.  408 N. Ridge Avenue | A | B | C | D |
| 2.  195 W. 74th Street | A | B | C | D |
| 3.  697 N. Ridge Avenue | A | B | C | D |
| 4.  41 Country Road 17 | A | B | C | D |
| 5.  78 W. Wicker Street | A | B | C | D |
| 6.  1900 S. Wickell Street | A | B | C | D |
| 7.  24 W. Wicker Street | A | B | C | D |
| 8.  300 S. Wickell Street | A | B | C | D |

## Sample Answer Sheet

1. Ⓐ Ⓑ Ⓒ Ⓓ      4. Ⓐ Ⓑ Ⓒ Ⓓ      7. Ⓐ Ⓑ Ⓒ Ⓓ

2. Ⓐ Ⓑ Ⓒ Ⓓ      5. Ⓐ Ⓑ Ⓒ Ⓓ      8. Ⓐ Ⓑ Ⓒ Ⓓ

3. Ⓐ Ⓑ Ⓒ Ⓓ      6. Ⓐ Ⓑ Ⓒ Ⓓ

practice test

## Memory Section: Segment 3

**5 MINUTES**

**Directions:** Take 5 minutes to memorize the Coding Guide on page 184.
- You may NOT write down any addresses during the memorization period.

## Memory Section: Segment 4

**36 QUESTIONS • 7 MINUTES**

**Directions:** This is the actual *scored* Memory Section of the exam. Take 3 minutes to memorize the Coding Guide on page 184. Work through items 1 through 36, assigning a code based on your memory of the Coding Guide. Mark your answers on the answer sheet. Work quickly and accurately.

- You may NOT write down any addresses during the memorization period.
- You may NOT look at the codes when answering the items.

| | Address | Delivery Route | | | |
|---|---|---|---|---|---|
| 1. | 16000 S. Ridge Avenue | A | B | C | D |
| 2. | 29 W. Wicker Street | A | B | C | D |
| 3. | 85 W. Wicker Street | A | B | C | D |
| 4. | 900 N. Ridge Avenue | A | B | C | D |
| 5. | 30 Country Road 7 | A | B | C | D |
| 6. | 40 Country Road 17 | A | B | C | D |
| 7. | 410 N. Ridge Avenue | A | B | C | D |
| 8. | 16 Ralston Lane | A | B | C | D |
| 9. | 30 W. 74th Street | A | B | C | D |
| 10. | 19 W. 74th Street | A | B | C | D |
| 11. | 30 Country Road 17 | A | B | C | D |
| 12. | 760 N. Ridge Avenue | A | B | C | D |
| 13. | 94 W. 74th Street | A | B | C | D |
| 14. | 905 N. Ridge Avenue | A | B | C | D |
| 15. | 10000 S. Ridge Avenue | A | B | C | D |
| 16. | 70 W. 74th Street | A | B | C | D |
| 17. | 1010 S. Wickell Street | A | B | C | D |
| 18. | 23000 N. Ridge Avenue | A | B | C | D |
| 19. | 10 W. 74th Street | A | B | C | D |
| 20. | 580 N. Ridge Avenue | A | B | C | D |
| 21. | 420 N. Ridge Avenue | A | B | C | D |
| 22. | 1750 S. Wickell Street | A | B | C | D |
| 23. | 36 Country Road 17 | A | B | C | D |
| 24. | 88 W. Wicker Street | A | B | C | D |

| 25. | 100 N. Ridge Avenue | A | B | C | D |
|---|---|---|---|---|---|
| 26. | 67 W. Wicker Street | A | B | C | D |
| 27. | 9600 S. Ridge Avenue | A | B | C | D |
| 28. | 28 W. Wicker Street | A | B | C | D |
| 29. | 540 S. Wickell Street | A | B | C | D |
| 30. | 40 W. Wicker Street | A | B | C | D |
| 31. | 70 Ralston Lane | A | B | C | D |
| 32. | 590 N. Ridge Avenue | A | B | C | D |
| 33. | 125 W. 74th Street | A | B | C | D |
| 34. | 16900 S. Ridge Avenue | A | B | C | D |
| 35. | 816 N. Ridge Avenue | A | B | C | D |
| 36. | 370 N. Ridge Avenue | A | B | C | D |

## ANSWER KEY AND EXPLANATIONS

### Part A: Address Checking

| | | | | |
|---|---|---|---|---|
| 1. A | 13. B | 25. A | 37. D | 49. B |
| 2. C | 14. D | 26. D | 38. B | 50. D |
| 3. B | 15. B | 27. C | 39. A | 51. B |
| 4. B | 16. C | 28. B | 40. D | 52. D |
| 5. D | 17. A | 29. A | 41. A | 53. C |
| 6. A | 18. D | 30. B | 42. C | 54. A |
| 7. B | 19. A | 31. B | 43. C | 55. B |
| 8. C | 20. B | 32. D | 44. D | 56. C |
| 9. A | 21. C | 33. B | 45. B | 57. A |
| 10. D | 22. A | 34. C | 46. D | 58. D |
| 11. A | 23. B | 35. A | 47. A | 59. C |
| 12. C | 24. D | 36. C | 48. A | 60. A |

### Part B: Forms Completion

| | | | | |
|---|---|---|---|---|
| 1. B | 7. D | 13. A | 19. D | 25. D |
| 2. B | 8. C | 14. B | 20. C | 26. B |
| 3. C | 9. D | 15. A | 21. A | 27. B |
| 4. D | 10. A | 16. D | 22. B | 28. A |
| 5. A | 11. C | 17. D | 23. C | 29. D |
| 6. B | 12. C | 18. B | 24. A | 30. C |

1. **The correct answer is (B).** Box 2 requires a date. Therefore, the correct answer is (B), 7/14/08.

2. **The correct answer is (B).** Box 2 is labeled "Date Delivered." Therefore, the correct answer is (B), Box 2.

3. **The correct answer is (C).** Box 3 requires a check number. Therefore, the correct answer is (C), Box 3.

4. **The correct answer is (D).** Box 11 requires the City, State, ZIP+4, and Country. Therefore, the correct answer is (D), Box 11.

5. **The correct answer is (A).** Box 5 is labeled "Special Handling Fee." Therefore, the correct answer is (A), Box 5.

6. **The correct answer is (B).** Box 2a is marked "Fragile." Therefore, the correct answer is (B), Box 2a.

7. **The correct answer is (D).** Box 6 is labeled "Return Receipt Fee (Except for Canada: endorsement required)." Therefore, the correct answer is (D), Box 6.

8. **The correct answer is (C).** Box 9 requires the name of the individual to whom the item is sent. Therefore, the appropriate answer is (C), Ms. Lee Di-Marco.

9. **The correct answer is (D).** Box 24 requires a signature. Therefore, the correct answer is (D), Box 24.

10. **The correct answer is (A).** Box 1 requires a ZIP Code. Therefore, the correct answer is (A), 30068.

11. **The correct answer is (C).** Box 9 is labeled COD Fee. Therefore, the correct answer is (C), Box 9.

12. **The correct answer is (C).** Box 19 is labeled "Delivery Attempt," and it requires a month and a day. Therefore, the correct answer is (C), Box 19.

13. **The correct answer is (A).** Box 1 requires a ZIP Code. Therefore, the correct answer is (A), Box 1.

14. **The correct answer is (B).** Box 8b is labeled "Scheduled Time of Delivery, 3 PM." Therefore, the correct answer is (B), Box 8b.

15. **The correct answer is (A).** Box 3 is labeled "Postage." Therefore, the correct answer is (A), Box 3.

16. **The correct answer is (D).** Box 13a requires the package weight in pounds (lbs). Therefore, the correct answer is (D), Box 13a.

17. **The correct answer is (D).** Box 16 requires the month and day of a delivery attempt. Therefore, the correct answer is (D), June 5.

18. **The correct answer is (B).** Box 1 requires a date to be entered. Therefore, the correct answer is (B), 3/21/08.

19. **The correct answer is (D).** Box 4 requires the name of the mail carrier. Therefore, the appropriate answer is (D), James Ellis.

20. **The correct answer is (C).** Box 7 is labeled "Resume Delivery of Mail (Date)." Therefore, the correct answer is (C), Box 7.

21. **The correct answer is (A).** Box 3 is labeled "Bin Number." Therefore, the correct answer is (A), Box 3.

22. **The correct answer is (B).** Box 1c is labeled "Printed Matter." Therefore, the correct answer is (B), Box 1c.

23. **The correct answer is (C).** Box 2 is labeled "Insured Parcel." Therefore, the correct answer is (C), Check Box 2.

24. **The correct answer is (A).** Box 8 requires a street and number. Therefore, the appropriate answer is (A), 724 S. Rawlings Drive.

25. **The correct answer is (D).** Box 7 is labeled "Addressee Name." Therefore, the correct answer is (D), Box 7.

26. **The correct answer is (B).** Box 13 requires a signature. Therefore, the correct answer is (B), a signature.

27. **The correct answer is (B).** Box 8 requires a street address, apartment number, or PO Box number. Therefore, the appropriate answer is (B), 4417 Middledale Drive.

28. **The correct answer is (A).** Box 2 is labeled "Certified Fee." Therefore, the correct answer is (A), Box 2.

29. **The correct answer is (D).** Box 1 is labeled "Postage." Therefore, the correct answer is (D), $27.50.

30. **The correct answer is (C).** Box 7 is labeled "Sent To." Therefore, the correct answer is (C), Box 7.

## Part C: Coding and Memory

**CODING SECTION: SEGMENT 1**

| 1. D | 2. C | 3. B | 4. C |
|------|------|------|------|

**CODING SECTION: SEGMENT 2**

| 1. A | 3. B | 5. B | 7. A | 8. C |
|------|------|------|------|------|
| 2. D | 4. C | 6. D | | |

**CODING SECTION: SEGMENT 3**

| | | | | |
|---|---|---|---|---|
| 1. A | 9. C | 16. C | 23. A | 30. B |
| 2. B | 10. D | 17. A | 24. D | 31. C |
| 3. D | 11. A | 18. B | 25. C | 32. A |
| 4. C | 12. A | 19. D | 26. B | 33. B |
| 5. B | 13. B | 20. A | 27. C | 34. D |
| 6. A | 14. C | 21. B | 28. D | 35. A |
| 7. D | 15. D | 22. C | 29. C | 36. B |
| 8. D | | | | |

1. **The correct answer is (A).** The address 307 N. Ridge Avenue falls in one of the address ranges in the same row as Delivery Route A.

2. **The correct answer is (B).** The address 47 W. Wicker Street falls in one of the address ranges in the same row as Delivery Route B.

3. **The correct answer is (D).** The address 8800 S. Rider Street does not fall into any of the address ranges for Delivery Routes A, B, or C.

4. **The correct answer is (C).** The address 1107 S. Wickell Street falls in one of the address ranges in the same row as Delivery Route C.

5. **The correct answer is (B).** The address 825 N. Ridge Avenue falls in one of the address ranges in the same row as Delivery Route B.

6. **The correct answer is (A).** The address 169 W. 74th Street falls in one of the address ranges in the same row as Delivery Route A.

7. **The correct answer is (D).** The address 21 Country Road 17 does not fall into any of the address ranges for Delivery Routes A, B, or C.

8. **The correct answer is (D).** The address 55 Country Road 17 does not fall into any of the address ranges for Delivery Routes A, B, or C.

9. **The correct answer is (C).** The address 610 S. Wickell Street falls in one of the address ranges in the same row as Delivery Route C.

10. **The correct answer is (D).** The address 401 S. Rider Street does not fall into any of the address ranges for Delivery Routes A, B, or C.

11. **The correct answer is (A).** The address 30 W. Wicker Street falls in one of the address ranges in the same row as Delivery Route A.

12. **The correct answer is (A).** The address 384 N. Ridge Avenue falls in one of the address ranges in the same row as Delivery Route A.

13. **The correct answer is (B).** The address 649 N. Ridge Avenue falls in one of the address ranges in the same row as Delivery Route B.

14. **The correct answer is (C).** The address 38 Country Road 17 falls in one of the address ranges in the same row as Delivery Route C.

15. **The correct answer is (D).** The address 1400 S. Wickell Street does not fall into any of the address ranges for Delivery Routes A, B, or C.

16. **The correct answer is (C).** The address 1299 S. Wickell Street falls in one of the address ranges in the same row as Delivery Route C.

17. **The correct answer is (A).** The address 52 W. 74th Street falls in one of the address ranges in the same row as Delivery Route A.

18. **The correct answer is (B).** The address 838 N. Ridge Avenue falls in one of the address ranges in the same row as Delivery Route B.

19. **The correct answer is (D).** The address 350 W. Wicker Street does not fall into any of the address ranges for Delivery Routes A, B, or C.

20. **The correct answer is (A).** The address 100 W. 74th Street falls in one of the address ranges in the same row as Delivery Route A.

21. **The correct answer is (B).** The address 61 W. Wicker Street falls in one of the address ranges in the same row as Delivery Route B.

22. **The correct answer is (C).** The address 9020 S. Ridge Avenue falls in one of the address ranges in the same row as Delivery Route C.

23. **The correct answer is (A).** The address 21 W. Wicker Street falls in one of the address ranges in the same row as Delivery Route A.

24. **The correct answer is (D).** The address 1100 N. Ridge Avenue does not fall into any of the address ranges for Delivery Routes A, B, or C.

25. **The correct answer is (C).** The address 42 Country Road 17 falls in one of the address ranges in the same row as Delivery Route C.

26. **The correct answer is (B).** The address 700 N. Ridge Avenue falls in one of the address ranges in the same row as Delivery Route B.

27. **The correct answer is (C).** The address 10035 S. Ridge Avenue falls in one of the address ranges in the same row as Delivery Route C.

28. **The correct answer is (D).** The address 49 Country Road 17 does not fall into any of the address ranges for Delivery Routes A, B, or C.

29. **The correct answer is (C).** The address 930 S. Wickell Street falls in one of the address ranges in the same row as Delivery Route C.

30. **The correct answer is (B).** The address 74 W. Wicker Street falls in one of the address ranges in the same row as Delivery Route B.

31. **The correct answer is (C).** The address 800 S. Wickell Street falls in one of the address ranges in the same row as Delivery Route C.

32. **The correct answer is (A).** The address 33 W. Wicker Street falls in one of the address ranges in the same row as Delivery Route A.

33. **The correct answer is (B).** The address 822 N. Ridge Avenue falls in one of the address ranges in the same row as Delivery Route B.

34. **The correct answer is (D).** The address 180 W. 74th Street does not fall into any of the address ranges for Delivery Routes A, B, or C.

35. **The correct answer is (A).** The address 417 N. Ridge Avenue falls in one of the address ranges in the same row as Delivery Route A.

36. **The correct answer is (B).** The address 59 W. Wicker Street falls in one of the address ranges in the same row as Delivery Route B.

## MEMORY SECTION: SEGMENT 2

1. A
2. D
3. B
4. C
5. B
6. D
7. A
8. D

**MEMORY SECTION: SEGMENT 4**

| | | | | |
|---|---|---|---|---|
| 1. C | 9. A | 16. A | 23. C | 30. B |
| 2. A | 10. D | 17. C | 24. B | 31. D |
| 3. B | 11. C | 18. D | 25. D | 32. B |
| 4. B | 12. B | 19. D | 26. B | 33. A |
| 5. D | 13. A | 20. B | 27. C | 34. C |
| 6. C | 14. D | 21. A | 28. A | 35. B |
| 7. A | 15. C | 22. D | 29. C | 36. A |
| 8. D | | | | |

1. **The correct answer is (C).** The address 16000 S. Ridge Avenue falls in one of the address ranges in the same row as Delivery Route C.

2. **The correct answer is (A).** The address 29 W. Wicker Street falls in one of the address ranges in the same row as Delivery Route A.

3. **The correct answer is (B).** The address 85 W. Wicker Street falls in one of the address ranges in the same row as Delivery Route B.

4. **The correct answer is (B).** The address 900 N. Ridge Avenue falls in one of the address ranges in the same row as Delivery Route B.

5. **The correct answer is (D).** The address 30 Country Road 7 does not fall into any of the address ranges for Delivery Routes A, B, or C.

6. **The correct answer is (C).** The address 40 Country Road 17 falls in one of the address ranges in the same row as Delivery Route C.

7. **The correct answer is (A).** The address 410 N. Ridge Avenue falls in one of the address ranges in the same row as Delivery Route A.

8. **The correct answer is (D).** The address 16 Ralston Lane does not fall into any of the address ranges for Delivery Routes A, B, or C.

9. **The correct answer is (A).** The address 30 W. 74th Street falls in one of the address ranges in the same row as Delivery Route A.

10. **The correct answer is (D).** The address 19 W. 74th Street does not fall into any of the address ranges for Delivery Routes A, B, or C.

11. **The correct answer is (C).** The address 30 Country Road 17 falls in one of the address ranges in the same row as Delivery Route C.

12. **The correct answer is (B).** The address 760 N. Ridge Avenue falls in one of the address ranges in the same row as Delivery Route B.

13. **The correct answer is (A).** The address 94 W. 74th Street falls in one of the address ranges in the same row as Delivery Route A.

14. **The correct answer is (D).** The address 905 N. Ridge Avenue does not fall into any of the address ranges for Delivery Routes A, B, or C.

15. **The correct answer is (C).** The address 10000 S. Ridge Avenue falls in one of the address ranges in the same row as Delivery Route C.

16. **The correct answer is (A).** The address 70 W. 74th Street falls in one of the address ranges in the same row as Delivery Route A.

17. **The correct answer is (C).** The address 1010 S. Wickell Street falls in one of the address ranges in the same row as Delivery Route C.

18. **The correct answer is (D).** The address 23000 N. Ridge Avenue does not fall into any of the address ranges for Delivery Routes A, B, or C.

19. **The correct answer is (D).** The address 10 W. 74th Street does not fall into any of the address ranges for Delivery Routes A, B, or C.

20. **The correct answer is (B).** The address 580 N. Ridge Avenue falls in one of the address ranges in the same row as Delivery Route B.

21. **The correct answer is (A).** The address 420 N. Ridge Avenue falls in one of the address ranges in the same row as Delivery Route A.

22. **The correct answer is (D).** The address 1750 S. Wickell Street does not fall into any of the address ranges for Delivery Routes A, B, or C.

23. **The correct answer is (C).** The address 36 Country Road 17 falls in one of the address ranges in the same row as Delivery Route C.

24. **The correct answer is (B).** The address 88 W. Wicker Street falls in one of the address ranges in the same row as Delivery Route B.

25. **The correct answer is (D).** The address 100 N. Ridge Avenue does not fall into any of the address ranges for Delivery Routes A, B, or C.

26. **The correct answer is (B).** The address 67 W. Wicker Street falls in one of the address ranges in the same row as Delivery Route B.

27. **The correct answer is (C).** The address 9600 S. Ridge Avenue falls in one of the address ranges in the same row as Delivery Route C.

28. **The correct answer is (A).** The address 28 W. Wicker Street falls in one of the address ranges in the same row as Delivery Route A.

29. **The correct answer is (C).** The address 540 S. Wickell Street falls in one of the address ranges in the same row as Delivery Route C.

30. **The correct answer is (B).** The address 40 W. Wicker Street falls in one of the address ranges in the same row as Delivery Route B.

31. **The correct answer is (D).** The address 70 Ralston Lane does not fall into any of the address ranges for Delivery Routes A, B, or C.

32. **The correct answer is (B).** The address 590 N. Ridge Avenue falls in one of the address ranges in the same row as Delivery Route B.

33. **The correct answer is (A).** The address 125 W. 74th Street falls in one of the address ranges in the same row as Delivery Route A.

34. **The correct answer is (C).** The address 16900 S. Ridge Avenue falls in one of the address ranges in the same row as Delivery Route C.

35. **The correct answer is (B).** The address 816 N. Ridge Avenue falls in one of the address ranges in the same row as Delivery Route B.

36. **The correct answer is (A).** The address 370 N. Ridge Avenue falls in one of the address ranges in the same row as Delivery Route A.

# PRACTICE TEST 3: EXAMS 473/473-C AND 460

## Part A: Address Checking

| | | | | |
|---|---|---|---|---|
| 1. Ⓐ Ⓑ Ⓒ Ⓓ | 13. Ⓐ Ⓑ Ⓒ Ⓓ | 25. Ⓐ Ⓑ Ⓒ Ⓓ | 37. Ⓐ Ⓑ Ⓒ Ⓓ | 49. Ⓐ Ⓑ Ⓒ Ⓓ |
| 2. Ⓐ Ⓑ Ⓒ Ⓓ | 14. Ⓐ Ⓑ Ⓒ Ⓓ | 26. Ⓐ Ⓑ Ⓒ Ⓓ | 38. Ⓐ Ⓑ Ⓒ Ⓓ | 50. Ⓐ Ⓑ Ⓒ Ⓓ |
| 3. Ⓐ Ⓑ Ⓒ Ⓓ | 15. Ⓐ Ⓑ Ⓒ Ⓓ | 27. Ⓐ Ⓑ Ⓒ Ⓓ | 39. Ⓐ Ⓑ Ⓒ Ⓓ | 51. Ⓐ Ⓑ Ⓒ Ⓓ |
| 4. Ⓐ Ⓑ Ⓒ Ⓓ | 16. Ⓐ Ⓑ Ⓒ Ⓓ | 28. Ⓐ Ⓑ Ⓒ Ⓓ | 40. Ⓐ Ⓑ Ⓒ Ⓓ | 52. Ⓐ Ⓑ Ⓒ Ⓓ |
| 5. Ⓐ Ⓑ Ⓒ Ⓓ | 17. Ⓐ Ⓑ Ⓒ Ⓓ | 29. Ⓐ Ⓑ Ⓒ Ⓓ | 41. Ⓐ Ⓑ Ⓒ Ⓓ | 53. Ⓐ Ⓑ Ⓒ Ⓓ |
| 6. Ⓐ Ⓑ Ⓒ Ⓓ | 18. Ⓐ Ⓑ Ⓒ Ⓓ | 30. Ⓐ Ⓑ Ⓒ Ⓓ | 42. Ⓐ Ⓑ Ⓒ Ⓓ | 54. Ⓐ Ⓑ Ⓒ Ⓓ |
| 7. Ⓐ Ⓑ Ⓒ Ⓓ | 19. Ⓐ Ⓑ Ⓒ Ⓓ | 31. Ⓐ Ⓑ Ⓒ Ⓓ | 43. Ⓐ Ⓑ Ⓒ Ⓓ | 55. Ⓐ Ⓑ Ⓒ Ⓓ |
| 8. Ⓐ Ⓑ Ⓒ Ⓓ | 20. Ⓐ Ⓑ Ⓒ Ⓓ | 32. Ⓐ Ⓑ Ⓒ Ⓓ | 44. Ⓐ Ⓑ Ⓒ Ⓓ | 56. Ⓐ Ⓑ Ⓒ Ⓓ |
| 9. Ⓐ Ⓑ Ⓒ Ⓓ | 21. Ⓐ Ⓑ Ⓒ Ⓓ | 33. Ⓐ Ⓑ Ⓒ Ⓓ | 45. Ⓐ Ⓑ Ⓒ Ⓓ | 57. Ⓐ Ⓑ Ⓒ Ⓓ |
| 10. Ⓐ Ⓑ Ⓒ Ⓓ | 22. Ⓐ Ⓑ Ⓒ Ⓓ | 34. Ⓐ Ⓑ Ⓒ Ⓓ | 46. Ⓐ Ⓑ Ⓒ Ⓓ | 58. Ⓐ Ⓑ Ⓒ Ⓓ |
| 11. Ⓐ Ⓑ Ⓒ Ⓓ | 23. Ⓐ Ⓑ Ⓒ Ⓓ | 35. Ⓐ Ⓑ Ⓒ Ⓓ | 47. Ⓐ Ⓑ Ⓒ Ⓓ | 59. Ⓐ Ⓑ Ⓒ Ⓓ |
| 12. Ⓐ Ⓑ Ⓒ Ⓓ | 24. Ⓐ Ⓑ Ⓒ Ⓓ | 36. Ⓐ Ⓑ Ⓒ Ⓓ | 48. Ⓐ Ⓑ Ⓒ Ⓓ | 60. Ⓐ Ⓑ Ⓒ Ⓓ |

## Part B: Forms Completion

| | | | | |
|---|---|---|---|---|
| 1. Ⓐ Ⓑ Ⓒ Ⓓ | 7. Ⓐ Ⓑ Ⓒ Ⓓ | 13. Ⓐ Ⓑ Ⓒ Ⓓ | 19. Ⓐ Ⓑ Ⓒ Ⓓ | 25. Ⓐ Ⓑ Ⓒ Ⓓ |
| 2. Ⓐ Ⓑ Ⓒ Ⓓ | 8. Ⓐ Ⓑ Ⓒ Ⓓ | 14. Ⓐ Ⓑ Ⓒ Ⓓ | 20. Ⓐ Ⓑ Ⓒ Ⓓ | 26. Ⓐ Ⓑ Ⓒ Ⓓ |
| 3. Ⓐ Ⓑ Ⓒ Ⓓ | 9. Ⓐ Ⓑ Ⓒ Ⓓ | 15. Ⓐ Ⓑ Ⓒ Ⓓ | 21. Ⓐ Ⓑ Ⓒ Ⓓ | 27. Ⓐ Ⓑ Ⓒ Ⓓ |
| 4. Ⓐ Ⓑ Ⓒ Ⓓ | 10. Ⓐ Ⓑ Ⓒ Ⓓ | 16. Ⓐ Ⓑ Ⓒ Ⓓ | 22. Ⓐ Ⓑ Ⓒ Ⓓ | 28. Ⓐ Ⓑ Ⓒ Ⓓ |
| 5. Ⓐ Ⓑ Ⓒ Ⓓ | 11. Ⓐ Ⓑ Ⓒ Ⓓ | 17. Ⓐ Ⓑ Ⓒ Ⓓ | 23. Ⓐ Ⓑ Ⓒ Ⓓ | 29. Ⓐ Ⓑ Ⓒ Ⓓ |
| 6. Ⓐ Ⓑ Ⓒ Ⓓ | 12. Ⓐ Ⓑ Ⓒ Ⓓ | 18. Ⓐ Ⓑ Ⓒ Ⓓ | 24. Ⓐ Ⓑ Ⓒ Ⓓ | 30. Ⓐ Ⓑ Ⓒ Ⓓ |

## Part C: Coding and Memory

### CODING SECTION: SEGMENT 3

| | | | | |
|---|---|---|---|---|
| 1. Ⓐ Ⓑ Ⓒ Ⓓ | 9. Ⓐ Ⓑ Ⓒ Ⓓ | 16. Ⓐ Ⓑ Ⓒ Ⓓ | 23. Ⓐ Ⓑ Ⓒ Ⓓ | 30. Ⓐ Ⓑ Ⓒ Ⓓ |
| 2. Ⓐ Ⓑ Ⓒ Ⓓ | 10. Ⓐ Ⓑ Ⓒ Ⓓ | 17. Ⓐ Ⓑ Ⓒ Ⓓ | 24. Ⓐ Ⓑ Ⓒ Ⓓ | 31. Ⓐ Ⓑ Ⓒ Ⓓ |
| 3. Ⓐ Ⓑ Ⓒ Ⓓ | 11. Ⓐ Ⓑ Ⓒ Ⓓ | 18. Ⓐ Ⓑ Ⓒ Ⓓ | 25. Ⓐ Ⓑ Ⓒ Ⓓ | 32. Ⓐ Ⓑ Ⓒ Ⓓ |
| 4. Ⓐ Ⓑ Ⓒ Ⓓ | 12. Ⓐ Ⓑ Ⓒ Ⓓ | 19. Ⓐ Ⓑ Ⓒ Ⓓ | 26. Ⓐ Ⓑ Ⓒ Ⓓ | 33. Ⓐ Ⓑ Ⓒ Ⓓ |
| 5. Ⓐ Ⓑ Ⓒ Ⓓ | 13. Ⓐ Ⓑ Ⓒ Ⓓ | 20. Ⓐ Ⓑ Ⓒ Ⓓ | 27. Ⓐ Ⓑ Ⓒ Ⓓ | 34. Ⓐ Ⓑ Ⓒ Ⓓ |
| 6. Ⓐ Ⓑ Ⓒ Ⓓ | 14. Ⓐ Ⓑ Ⓒ Ⓓ | 21. Ⓐ Ⓑ Ⓒ Ⓓ | 28. Ⓐ Ⓑ Ⓒ Ⓓ | 35. Ⓐ Ⓑ Ⓒ Ⓓ |
| 7. Ⓐ Ⓑ Ⓒ Ⓓ | 15. Ⓐ Ⓑ Ⓒ Ⓓ | 22. Ⓐ Ⓑ Ⓒ Ⓓ | 29. Ⓐ Ⓑ Ⓒ Ⓓ | 36. Ⓐ Ⓑ Ⓒ Ⓓ |
| 8. Ⓐ Ⓑ Ⓒ Ⓓ | | | | |

### MEMORY SECTION: SEGMENT 4

| | | | | |
|---|---|---|---|---|
| 1. Ⓐ Ⓑ Ⓒ Ⓓ | 9. Ⓐ Ⓑ Ⓒ Ⓓ | 16. Ⓐ Ⓑ Ⓒ Ⓓ | 23. Ⓐ Ⓑ Ⓒ Ⓓ | 30. Ⓐ Ⓑ Ⓒ Ⓓ |
| 2. Ⓐ Ⓑ Ⓒ Ⓓ | 10. Ⓐ Ⓑ Ⓒ Ⓓ | 17. Ⓐ Ⓑ Ⓒ Ⓓ | 24. Ⓐ Ⓑ Ⓒ Ⓓ | 31. Ⓐ Ⓑ Ⓒ Ⓓ |
| 3. Ⓐ Ⓑ Ⓒ Ⓓ | 11. Ⓐ Ⓑ Ⓒ Ⓓ | 18. Ⓐ Ⓑ Ⓒ Ⓓ | 25. Ⓐ Ⓑ Ⓒ Ⓓ | 32. Ⓐ Ⓑ Ⓒ Ⓓ |
| 4. Ⓐ Ⓑ Ⓒ Ⓓ | 12. Ⓐ Ⓑ Ⓒ Ⓓ | 19. Ⓐ Ⓑ Ⓒ Ⓓ | 26. Ⓐ Ⓑ Ⓒ Ⓓ | 33. Ⓐ Ⓑ Ⓒ Ⓓ |
| 5. Ⓐ Ⓑ Ⓒ Ⓓ | 13. Ⓐ Ⓑ Ⓒ Ⓓ | 20. Ⓐ Ⓑ Ⓒ Ⓓ | 27. Ⓐ Ⓑ Ⓒ Ⓓ | 34. Ⓐ Ⓑ Ⓒ Ⓓ |
| 6. Ⓐ Ⓑ Ⓒ Ⓓ | 14. Ⓐ Ⓑ Ⓒ Ⓓ | 21. Ⓐ Ⓑ Ⓒ Ⓓ | 28. Ⓐ Ⓑ Ⓒ Ⓓ | 35. Ⓐ Ⓑ Ⓒ Ⓓ |
| 7. Ⓐ Ⓑ Ⓒ Ⓓ | 15. Ⓐ Ⓑ Ⓒ Ⓓ | 22. Ⓐ Ⓑ Ⓒ Ⓓ | 29. Ⓐ Ⓑ Ⓒ Ⓓ | 36. Ⓐ Ⓑ Ⓒ Ⓓ |
| 8. Ⓐ Ⓑ Ⓒ Ⓓ | | | | |

**answer sheet**

# Practice Test 3: Exams 473/473-C and 460

**NOTE:** Practice Tests 1–5 are a combination of the types of questions test-takers will see on Exam 473 and Exam 460.

Exam 473 consists of four parts:

A. Address Checking

B. Forms Completion

C. Coding and Memory

D. Personal Characteristics and Experience Inventory

Exam 460 consists of four parts:

A. Address Checking

B. Memory for Addresses

C. Number Series

D. Following Oral Instructions

If you are practicing to take Exam 460, you may want to follow these tips:

- Skip Part B (Forms Completion) of Practice Tests 1 through 5. This material will not be included on your actual exam; it is only on Exam 473.

- Skip Part D (Personal Characteristics and Experience Inventory) of Practice Test 1. This material will not be included on your actual exam; it is only on Exam 473.

- To practice for Part D of Exam 460 (Following Oral Instructions), take Practice Test 7 in this book.

practice test 3

## PART A: ADDRESS CHECKING

**60 QUESTIONS • 11 MINUTES**

> **Directions:** Compare the **List to be Checked** with the **Correct List.** Decide if there are **(A) NO ERRORS,** an error in the **(B) ADDRESS ONLY,** an error in the **(C) ZIP CODE ONLY,** or an error in **(D) BOTH** the address and ZIP Code. Record your answers on the answer sheet.

| | Correct List | | List to be Checked | |
|---|---|---|---|---|
| | *Address* | *ZIP Code* | *Address* | *ZIP Code* |
| **1.** | 728 Bartholomew Ave<br>Farmington, MN | 55024 | 728 Bartholomew Ave<br>Farmington, MN | 55024 |
| **2.** | 16 Dupont Highway<br>Caspar, WY | 82604 | 16 Dupont Highway<br>Caspar, WY | 82644 |
| **3.** | 2014 Everley Drive<br>Billings, MT | 59105-3232 | 2014 Everley Drive<br>Billings, MN | 59105-3233 |
| **4.** | 900 Listing Circle<br>Barre, Vermont | 05641 | 900 Lesting Circle<br>Barre, Vermont | 05641 |
| **5.** | 1617 Bates Terrace<br>Rayville, Louisiana | 71269 | 1617 Bates Terrace<br>Rayetville, Louisiana | 71669 |
| **6.** | 830 Kerry Parkway<br>Denver, CO | 80218-3501 | 830 Kerry Parkway<br>Denver, CO | 80218-3501 |
| **7.** | 2730 Tungsten Street<br>Spanish Fork, UT | 84660 | 2730 Tungsten Street<br>Spanish Fork, UT | 84060 |
| **8.** | 60 Dumont Street<br>Crittenden, Kentucky | 41030 | 60 Dumont Street<br>Crittenden, Kentucky | 41030 |
| **9.** | 491 Rider Ct, Apt 4<br>Mosinee, WI | 54455 | 491 Rider Ct, Apt 4<br>Mosinee, WY | 54455 |
| **10.** | 3307 Adams Road<br>Lindsborg, KS | 67456 | 3337 Adams Road<br>Lindsborg, KS | 67546 |
| **11.** | 6520 E. Abilene Place<br>Houston, TX | 77087 | 6520 E. Abilene Place<br>Houston, TX | 78087 |
| **12.** | 1705 Lyons Blvd.<br>St. Martinville, LA | 70582 | 1705 Lyons Blvd.<br>St. Martinville, LA | 70582 |

**Directions:** Compare the **List to be Checked** with the **Correct List.** Decide if there are **(A) NO ERRORS,** an error in the **(B) ADDRESS ONLY,** an error in the **(C) ZIP CODE ONLY,** or an error in **(D) BOTH** the address and ZIP Code. Record your answers on the answer sheet.

| | | | |
|---|---|---|---|
| 13. 8300 Domino Drive<br>Hanover, NH | 03755-2098 | 8330 Domino Drive<br>Hanover, NY | 03775-2098 |
| 14. 768 First Street<br>Ashland, MO | 65010 | 786 First Street<br>Ashland, MO | 65010 |
| 15. 2295 Sylvan Court<br>Wedgefield, SC | 29168 | 2295 Sylvan Court<br>Wedgefield, SC | 29168 |
| 16. 800 Pinkerton Pl.<br>Reno, Nevada | 89502-1427 | 800 Pinkerton Pl.<br>Reno, Nevada | 85902-1427 |
| 17. 5050 Michael Drive<br>Montgomery, AL | 36117 | 5050 Micheal Drive<br>Montgomery, AL | 36117 |
| 18. 2712 Inglenook St.<br>Hutchins, TX | 75141 | 2702 Inglenook St.<br>Hutchins, TX | 75441 |
| 19. Post Office Box 1345<br>Louisville, KY | 40243-1345 | Post Office Box 1345<br>Louisville, KY | 40243-1340 |
| 20. 3007 Toulouse Way<br>La Verne, CA | 91750 | 3077 Toulouse Way<br>La Verne, CA | 91750 |
| 21. 671 Ellington Trail<br>Las Cruces, NM | 88011 | 671 Ellingson Trail<br>Las Cruces, NM | 88011 |
| 22. 900 S. Bridge Lane<br>Prineville, OR | 97754 | 900 S. Bridge Lane<br>Prineville, OR | 97754 |
| 23. 1612 Pines Avenue<br>Berkeley, CA | 94704-1480 | 1612 Pines Avenue<br>Berkeley, CA | 97404-1480 |
| 24. PO Box 28840<br>Alexandria, VA | 22309-1841 | PO Box 28840<br>Alexandria, VA | 22309-1841 |
| 25. 1306 Leslie Street<br>Creston, WA | 99117 | 1360 Leslie Street<br>Creston, WA | 99177 |
| 26. 47 Hughes Ter.<br>Maricopa, AZ | 85239 | 47 Hughes Ter.<br>Maricopa, AR | 85239 |
| 27. 1800 Palace Dr.<br>Steele, ND | 58482 | 1800 Palace Dr.<br>Steele, ND | 58428 |

**Directions:** Compare the **List to be Checked** with the **Correct List.** Decide if there are **(A) NO ERRORS,** an error in the **(B) ADDRESS ONLY,** an error in the **(C) ZIP CODE ONLY,** or an error in **(D) BOTH** the address and ZIP Code. Record your answers on the answer sheet.

**28.** 5900 W. Eden Lane
Dixon, KY                    42409

5900 W. Edith Lane
Dixon, KY                    42490

**29.** 295 Opal Street
Clay, West Virginia          25043

295 Opal Court
Clay, West Virginia          25043

**30.** 13 E. 8th Avenue
Bucyrus, OH                  44820

13 E. 8th Avenue
Bucyrus, OH                  44820

**31.** 101 Prentice Road
Boise, ID          83702-7360

101 Prentice Road
Boise, ID          83702-7630

**32.** 484 Strong Circle
Grand Island, NE             68801

4848 Strong Circle
Grand Island, NE             68801

**33.** 770 Sebastian Drive
Richmond, VA                 23231

7706 Sebastian Court
Richmond, VA                 23001

**34.** 399 Cloud Court
Sykesville, Maryland         21784

399 Cloud Court
Sykesville, Maryland         21704

**35.** 1604 E. Funnel Way
Minneapolis, MN              55406

1604 E. Funnel Way
Minneapolis, MN              55406

**36.** 7780 Newland Ave.
Greenville, NC               27858

7780 Newland Ave.
Greenville, NC               28758

**37.** 1515 Alston Highway
Grass Range, MT              59032

1555 Alston Highway
Grass Range, MT              59302

**38.** 2745 S. Paulina Dr.
Alvarado, TX                 76009

2745 S. Paulina Dr.
Alvarado, TX                 76009

**39.** 5609 Flint Trail
Tampa, FL          33607-3600

5609 Flint Trail
Tampa, FL          33607-3660

**40.** 633 Archer Court
Savannah, GA                 31410

630 Archer Court
Savannah, GA                 31410

**41.** 200 Thunder Parkway
Encampment, WY               82325

200 Thunder Parkway
Encampment, WY               82335

**42.** 486 Lindale Lane
Happy Jack, AZ               86024

486 Lindale Lane
Happy Jack, AK               86624

**Directions:** Compare the **List to be Checked** with the **Correct List.** Decide if there are **(A) NO ERRORS,** an error in the **(B) ADDRESS ONLY,** an error in the **(C) ZIP CODE ONLY,** or an error in **(D) BOTH** the address and ZIP Code. Record your answers on the answer sheet.

| | | | | |
|---|---|---|---|---|
| **43.** | 37 Skyline Circle<br>Portland, OR | 97214-3346 | 37 Skyline Circle<br>Portland, OR | 97214-3346 |
| **44.** | 1216 E. Calvary St.<br>Loveland, CO | 80538 | 1216 E. Calvary St.<br>Longmont, CO | 80548 |
| **45.** | 450 Piston Parkway<br>Friendship, ME | 04547 | 450 Piston Parkway<br>Friendship, ME | 04547 |
| **46.** | 69 Bleeker Court<br>Grants Pass, Oregon | 97526 | 609 Bleeker Court<br>Grants Pass, Oregon | 97256 |
| **47.** | 2875 N. Frontage Road<br>Riverview, FL | 33579 | 2875 N. Frontage Road<br>Riverpoint, FL | 33579 |
| **48.** | 949 Willow Avenue<br>Detroit, MI | 48212-1529 | 909 Willow Drive<br>Detroit, MI | 48222-1529 |
| **49.** | 325 Range Trail, #2<br>Torreon, NM | 87061 | 325 Range Trail, #2<br>Torreon, NM | 87061 |
| **50.** | 1600 W. Frye Ter.<br>Fort Gordon, GA | 30905-3097 | 1600 E. Frye Ter.<br>Fort Gordon, GA | 30905-3097 |
| **51.** | 2980 Degas Street<br>Bellevue, Iowa | 52031 | 2980 Degas Street<br>Bellevue, Iowa | 52013 |
| **52.** | 737 S. Briggs Lane<br>Dexter, NM | 88230 | 737 S. Briggs Lane<br>Dickson, NM | 88830 |
| **53.** | 439 Youngfield Pkwy<br>Nashville, TN | 37213-1105 | 493 Youngfield Pkwy<br>Nashville, TN | 37213-1105 |
| **54.** | 55 Steele Street<br>Watseka, IL | 60970 | 55 Steele Street<br>Watseka, IL | 60979 |
| **55.** | 866 Overton Place<br>Brooklyn, New York | 11234 | 866 Overton Place<br>Brooklyn, New York | 11234 |
| **56.** | 2007 Fortune Drive<br>Seattle, WA | 98104-2550 | 2007 Fortuna Drive<br>Seattle, WA | 98104-2550 |
| **57.** | 34 W. Eaton Highway<br>Indianapolis, IN | 46220-1712 | 34 E. Eaton Highway<br>Indianapolis, IN | 46220-1722 |

**Directions:** Compare the **List to be Checked** with the **Correct List.** Decide if there are **(A) NO ERRORS,** an error in the **(B) ADDRESS ONLY,** an error in the **(C) ZIP CODE ONLY,** or an error in **(D) BOTH** the address and ZIP Code. Record your answers on the answer sheet.

**58.** 9756 20th Street
Austin, NV　　　　　　　89310

9756 20th Street
Austin, NV　　　　　　　89310

**59.** 440 Division Blvd
Santa Ana, CA　　　　92707-1537

440 Division Blvd
Santa Ana, CA　　　　97207-1537

**60.** 780 N. Sutter Avenue
Choctaw, OK　　　　　　73020

780 N. Sutton Avenue
Choctaw, OK　　　　　　73020

## PART B: FORMS COMPLETION

**30 QUESTIONS • 15 MINUTES**

**Directions:** Read each form and answer the questions based on the information provided. Mark your answers on the answer sheet.

---

**Authorization to Hold Mail**

NOTE: *Complete and give to your letter carrier or mail to the post office that delivers your mail.*

We can hold your mail for a minimum of **3**, but not for more than **30 days.**

Postmaster: Please hold mail for:

Name(s)

**1.**

Address *(Number, street, apt./suite no., city, state, ZIP + 4)*

**2.**

Beginning Date

**3.**

Ending Date *(May only be changed by the customer in writing)*

**4.**

**5a.** ☐ A. Please deliver all accumulated mail and resume normal delivery on the ending date shown below.

**5b.** ☐ B. I will pick up all accumulated mail when I return and understand that mail delivery will not resume until I do.

Customer Signature

**6.**

**For Post Office Use Only**

Date Received

Clerk

Bin Number

Carrier

Route Number

*(Complete this section only if customer selected option B)*

☐ Accumulated mail has been picked up.

Resume Delivery of Mail *(Date)*

By

PS Form **8076**, April 2001

---

1. Where on the above form would the beginning date of the authorization be entered?
   - **(A)** Box 3
   - **(B)** Box 4
   - **(C)** Box 5b
   - **(D)** Box 6

2. Which of these would be an appropriate entry for Box 1 on this form?
   - **(A)** $25.00
   - **(B)** A check mark
   - **(C)** Marshall Saltzman
   - **(D)** 7/30/08

3. Which of these would be an appropriate entry for Box 5a on this form?
   - **(A)** A check mark
   - **(B)** 02288
   - **(C)** $7.05
   - **(D)** Cheyenne, WY

4. Where on this form would you find a customer's signature?
   - **(A)** Box 1
   - **(B)** Box 2
   - **(C)** Box 4
   - **(D)** Box 6

**UNITED STATES POSTAL SERVICE**®

**Certificate Of Mailing**

To pay fee, affix stamps or meter postage here.

This Certificate of Mailing provides evidence that mail has been presented to USPS® for mailing. This form may be used for domestic and international mail.

From:

**1.**

**3.**

To:

**2.**

Postmark Here

**4.**

PS Form **3817**, April 2007  PSN 7530-02-000-9065

5. Where on the above form would the postmark be stamped?
   - **(A)** Box 1
   - **(B)** Box 2
   - **(C)** Box 3
   - **(D)** Box 4

6. If an item were being mailed to a P.O. Box, where on the form would the box number be indicated?
   - **(A)** Box 1
   - **(B)** Box 2
   - **(C)** Box 3
   - **(D)** Box 4

7. Where on the form would meter postage be placed?
   - **(A)** Box 1
   - **(B)** Box 2
   - **(C)** Box 3
   - **(D)** Box 4

8. Where on this form would the sender's mailing address be entered?
   - **(A)** Box 1
   - **(B)** Box 2
   - **(C)** Box 3
   - **(D)** Box 4

United States Postal Service
**Pickup Service Statement**
**Express Mail, Global Express Guaranteed, Priority Mail, or Parcel Post**

**1. Customer Information**

Customer Name **1.**

Company Name **2.**

Address 1 **3.**

Address 2 **4.**

City **5.**

State **6.** ZIP + 4 **7.**

**2. Product Information**

*Quantity*

Express Mail

Global Express Guaranteed

Priority Mail

Parcel Post
*(Domestic or international)*

Estimated total weight
of all packages
*(In pounds)*

**3. Payment Method**

**8a.** ☐ Check made payable to "Postmaster"

**8b.** ☐ Express Mail Corporate Account No. or Federal Agency No.:

**8c.** ☐ Merchandise Return Label

☐ Postage Due Account

☐ Stamps or Metered Postage *(Affix at right)*

**4. Affix Stamps or Meter Strip Here** *(If applicable)*

**10.**

5. Customer Signature **9.**

6. USPS Signature **11.**

7. Date & Time of Pickup **12.**

PS Form **5541**, October 2001

1 - Finance     2 - Customer

9. What would be the most appropriate entry for Box 7 on the above form?
   (A) $39.00
   (B) 02818-9033
   (C) 5/27/07
   (D) A check mark

10. Which of these would be the appropriate entry for Box 2 on the form?
    (A) 42 E. Winter Place
    (B) White Printing Company
    (C) New York, NY
    (D) Suite 1004

11. A check mark would be the appropriate entry for each of the following boxes on this form EXCEPT
    (A) Box 8a
    (B) Box 8b
    (C) Box 8c
    (D) Box 9

12. Where on the form would you enter the date and time of pickup?
    (A) Box 9
    (B) Box 10
    (C) Box 11
    (D) Box 12

13. Which of these would be an appropriate entry for Box 6 on the above form?
    (A) Mrs. Ellen Harkness
    (B) Tampa
    (C) Indiana
    (D) 24 Wisconsin Way

14. Where on the form would a postal service employee sign?
    (A) Box 1
    (B) Box 2
    (C) Box 9
    (D) Box 11

15. Where on the form would you indicate the customer's street address?
    (A) Box 3
    (B) Box 5
    (C) Box 6
    (D) Box 7

16. Which box would you check on the form to show that a customer paid by check?
    (A) 8a
    (B) 8b
    (C) 8c
    (D) 10

17. Where would stamps be affixed on this form?
    (A) Box 7
    (B) Box 9
    (C) Box 10
    (D) Box 11

18. Which of the following would be an appropriate entry for Box 8c on the form?
    (A) Mr. Alonzo Jackson
    (B) A check mark
    (C) 04429
    (D) #124

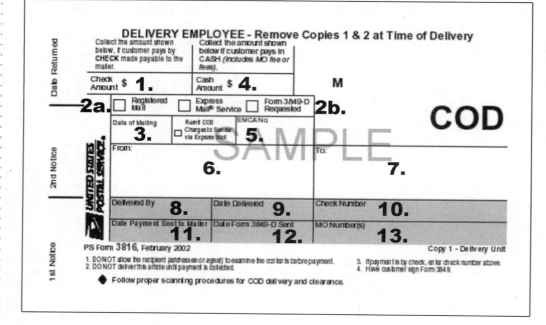

19. Where on the above form would a check amount be entered?
    (A) Box 1
    (B) Box 2
    (C) Box 3
    (D) Box 4

20. Each of the following boxes on the form must be completed by a postal employee EXCEPT
    (A) Box 6
    (B) Box 8
    (C) Box 10
    (D) Box 12

21. The entry 4/17/08 would be an appropriate entry for which of the following boxes on the form?
    (A) 4
    (B) 5
    (C) 8
    (D) 9

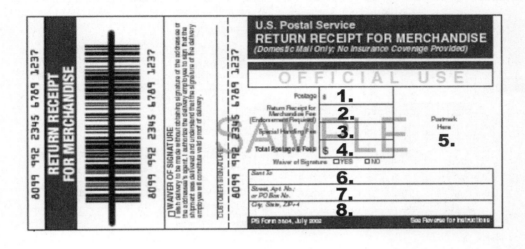

**22.** Where on the above form would you indicate the total postage and fees?

**(A)** Box 1
**(B)** Box 2
**(C)** Box 3
**(D)** Box 4

**23.** Where on the form would you indicate the recipient's name?

**(A)** Box 1
**(B)** Box 3
**(C)** Box 6
**(D)** Box 8

**24.** Which of these would be an appropriate entry for Box 5 on the form?

**(A)** A postmark
**(B)** 25.00
**(C)** A check mark
**(D)** 66058

**25.** Which of these would be an appropriate entry for Box 3 on the form?

**(A)** A signature
**(B)** $14.75
**(C)** P.O. Box 2700
**(D)** Hal Anderson

**26.** Which of these would be an appropriate entry for Box 24 on the above form?

(A) A signature

(B) 17.00

(C) A check mark

(D) August 8

**27.** A check mark would be an appropriate entry for each of the following boxes on the form EXCEPT

(A) Box 2a

(B) Box 11a

(C) Box 14

(D) Box 17b

**28.** Where on this form would you enter the return receipt fee?

(A) Box 3

(B) Box 6

(C) Box 9

(D) Box 10

**29.** Which of these would be a correct entry for Box 9 on the form?

(A) A signature

(B) 21.00

(C) CE

(D) #224

**30.** Where on the form would you indicate a package's weight in pounds and ounces?

(A) Box 4

(B) Box 5

(C) Box 13b

(D) Box 15

## PART C: CODING AND MEMORY

### Coding Section: Segment 1

**4 QUESTIONS • 2 MINUTES**

**Directions:** Segment 1 is *not* scored and does not count toward your total exam score. It is a practice exercise to help you with the Coding Section under a time constraint similar to the one used in the scored Coding Section. Use the coding guide below to match each address to a delivery route. Mark your answers on the answer section at the bottom of this page.

### CODING GUIDE

| ADDRESS RANGE | DELIVERY ROUTE |
|---|---|
| 700–1200 S. Sewell Road<br>60–240 E. 31st Street<br>10–54 E. Broder Avenue | A |
| 200–699 S. Sewell Road<br>55–80 E. Broder Avenue | B |
| 20–65 Highway 98<br>14000–19000 N. Sewell Road<br>500–1700 N. Brodie Avenue | C |
| All mail that doesn't fall into one of the address ranges listed above. | D |

| Address | Delivery Route | | | |
|---|---|---|---|---|
| 1. 750 S. Sewell Road | A | B | C | D |
| 2. 23 E. 31st Street | A | B | C | D |
| 3. 31 Highway 98 | A | B | C | D |
| 4. 650 S. Sewell Road | A | B | C | D |

## Sample Answer Sheet

1. Ⓐ Ⓑ Ⓒ Ⓓ     3. Ⓐ Ⓑ Ⓒ Ⓓ

2. Ⓐ Ⓑ Ⓒ Ⓓ     4. Ⓐ Ⓑ Ⓒ Ⓓ

## Coding Section: Segment 2

**8 QUESTIONS • 1.5 MINUTES (90 SECONDS)**

**Directions:** Segment 2 is *not* scored and does not count toward your total exam score. It is a practice exercise to help you with the Coding Section under a time constraint similar to the one used in the scored Coding Section. Use the coding guide below to match each address to a delivery route. Mark your answers on the answer section at the bottom of this page.

### CODING GUIDE

| ADDRESS RANGE | DELIVERY ROUTE |
|---|:---:|
| 700–1200 S. Sewell Road<br>60–240 E. 31st Street<br>10–54 E. Broder Avenue | A |
| 200–699 S. Sewell Road<br>55–80 E. Broder Avenue | B |
| 20–65 Highway 98<br>14000–19000 N. Sewell Road<br>500–1700 N. Brodie Avenue | C |
| All mail that doesn't fall into one of the address ranges listed above. | D |

| Address | Delivery Route | | | |
|---|:---:|:---:|:---:|:---:|
| 1.  80 E. Broder Avenue | A | B | C | D |
| 2.  17600 N. Sewell Road | A | B | C | D |
| 3.  100 S. Sewell Road | A | B | C | D |
| 4.  229 E. 31st Street | A | B | C | D |
| 5.  27000 N. Sewell Road | A | B | C | D |
| 6.  63 E. Broder Avenue | A | B | C | D |
| 7.  43 Highway 98 | A | B | C | D |
| 8.  340 S. Sewell Road | A | B | C | D |

## Sample Answer Sheet

1. Ⓐ Ⓑ Ⓒ Ⓓ        4. Ⓐ Ⓑ Ⓒ Ⓓ        7. Ⓐ Ⓑ Ⓒ Ⓓ
2. Ⓐ Ⓑ Ⓒ Ⓓ        5. Ⓐ Ⓑ Ⓒ Ⓓ        8. Ⓐ Ⓑ Ⓒ Ⓓ
3. Ⓐ Ⓑ Ⓒ Ⓓ        6. Ⓐ Ⓑ Ⓒ Ⓓ

## Coding Section: Segment 3

**36 QUESTIONS • 6 MINUTES**

**Directions:** Work through items 1 through 36, assigning a code to each item based on the Coding Guide below. Mark your answers on the answer sheet. Work quickly and accurately.

### CODING GUIDE

| ADDRESS RANGE | DELIVERY ROUTE |
|---|---|
| 700–1200 S. Sewell Road<br>60–240 E. 31st Street<br>10–54 E. Broder Avenue | A |
| 200–699 S. Sewell Road<br>55–80 E. Broder Avenue | B |
| 20–65 Highway 98<br>14000–19000 N. Sewell Road<br>500–1700 N. Brodie Avenue | C |
| All mail that doesn't fall into one of the address ranges listed above. | D |

| | Address | Delivery Route | | | |
|---|---|---|---|---|---|
| 1. | 200 E. 31st Street | A | B | C | D |
| 2. | 2000 N. Brodie Avenue | A | B | C | D |
| 3. | 18018 N. Sewell Road | A | B | C | D |
| 4. | 590 S. Sewell Road | A | B | C | D |
| 5. | 1100 S. Sewell Road | A | B | C | D |
| 6. | 530 N. Brodie Avenue | A | B | C | D |
| 7. | 50 Highway 98 | A | B | C | D |
| 8. | 42 E. Broder Avenue | A | B | C | D |
| 9. | 27 E. Broder Avenue | A | B | C | D |
| 10. | 640 N. Brodie Avenue | A | B | C | D |
| 11. | 3060 S. Sewell Road | A | B | C | D |
| 12. | 56 E. Broder Avenue | A | B | C | D |
| 13. | 900 N. Brodie Avenue | A | B | C | D |
| 14. | 59 E. 31st Street | A | B | C | D |
| 15. | 62 E. 31st Street | A | B | C | D |
| 16. | 407 S. Sewell Road | A | B | C | D |

## CODING GUIDE

| ADDRESS RANGE | DELIVERY ROUTE |
|---|---|
| 700–1200 S. Sewell Road<br>60–240 E. 31st Street<br>10–54 E. Broder Avenue | A |
| 200–699 S. Sewell Road<br>55–80 E. Broder Avenue | B |
| 20–65 Highway 98<br>14000–19000 N. Sewell Road<br>500–1700 N. Brodie Avenue | C |
| All mail that doesn't fall into one of the address ranges listed above. | D |

| | | | | | |
|---|---|---|---|---|---|
| **17.** | 7 E. Broder Avenue | A | B | C | D |
| **18.** | 39 Highway 98 | A | B | C | D |
| **19.** | 75 E. Broder Avenue | A | B | C | D |
| **20.** | 40 E. Broder Avenue | A | B | C | D |
| **21.** | 1250 S. Sewell Road | A | B | C | D |
| **22.** | 58 E. Broder Avenue | A | B | C | D |
| **23.** | 14200 N. Sewell Road | A | B | C | D |
| **24.** | 807 S. Sewell Road | A | B | C | D |
| **25.** | 222 S. Sewell Road | A | B | C | D |
| **26.** | 660 S. Sewell Road | A | B | C | D |
| **27.** | 450 N. Brodie Avenue | A | B | C | D |
| **28.** | 66 E. Broder Avenue | A | B | C | D |
| **29.** | 93 E. 31st Street | A | B | C | D |
| **30.** | 95 E. Broder Avenue | A | B | C | D |
| **31.** | 16 Highway 98 | A | B | C | D |
| **32.** | 15000 N. Sewell Road | A | B | C | D |
| **33.** | 1010 S. Sewell Road | A | B | C | D |
| **34.** | 600 N. Brodie Avenue | A | B | C | D |
| **35.** | 277 S. Sewell Road | A | B | C | D |
| **36.** | 95 S. Sewell Road | A | B | C | D |

## Memory Section: Segment 1

**3 MINUTES**

**Directions:** Take 3 minutes to memorize the Coding Guide on page 213.
- You may NOT write down any addresses during the memorization period.

## Memory Section: Segment 2

**8 QUESTIONS • 1.5 MINUTES (90 SECONDS)**

**Directions:** Segment 2 is *not* scored and does not count toward your total exam score. It is an exercise to help you practice coding addresses from memory under a time constraint similar to the one used in the scored Memory Section of the actual exam. You will *not* see the Coding Guide during this segment of the exam. Based on your memory of the Coding Guide, match each address shown on the next page to a delivery route. Mark your answers on the answer section at the bottom of this page.

• You may NOT look at the codes when answering the items.

| Address | Delivery Route | | | |
|---|---|---|---|---|
| 1.  1313 N. Brodie Avenue | A | B | C | D |
| 2.  62 E. Broder Avenue | A | B | C | D |
| 3.  990 S. Sewell Road | A | B | C | D |
| 4.  361 E. 31st Street | A | B | C | D |
| 5.  18999 N. Sewell Road | A | B | C | D |
| 6.  12 E. Broder Avenue | A | B | C | D |
| 7.  313 S. Sewell Road | A | B | C | D |
| 8.  1890 N. Brodie Avenue | A | B | C | D |

## Sample Answer Sheet

1. Ⓐ Ⓑ Ⓒ Ⓓ    4. Ⓐ Ⓑ Ⓒ Ⓓ    7. Ⓐ Ⓑ Ⓒ Ⓓ

2. Ⓐ Ⓑ Ⓒ Ⓓ    5. Ⓐ Ⓑ Ⓒ Ⓓ    8. Ⓐ Ⓑ Ⓒ Ⓓ

3. Ⓐ Ⓑ Ⓒ Ⓓ    6. Ⓐ Ⓑ Ⓒ Ⓓ

## Memory Section: Segment 3

**5 MINUTES**

**Directions:** Take 5 minutes to memorize the Coding Guide on page 213.
- You may NOT write down any addresses during the memorization period.

practice test

## Memory Section: Segment 4

**36 QUESTIONS • 7 MINUTES**

**Directions:** This is the actual *scored* Memory Section of the exam. Take 3 minutes to memorize the Coding Guide on page 123. Work through items 1 through 36, assigning a code based on your memory of the Coding Guide. Mark your answers on the answer sheet. Work quickly and accurately.

- You may NOT write down any addresses during the memorization period.
- You may NOT look at the codes when answering the items.

| Address | Delivery Route | | | |
|---|---|---|---|---|
| 1.   140 E. Broder Avenue | A | B | C | D |
| 2.   77 E. Broder Avenue | A | B | C | D |
| 3.   18700 N. Sewell Road | A | B | C | D |
| 4.   13000 N. Sewell Road | A | B | C | D |
| 5.   33 E. Broder Avenue | A | B | C | D |
| 6.   21 Highway 98 | A | B | C | D |
| 7.   500 S. Sewell Road | A | B | C | D |
| 8.   1674 S. Sewell Road | A | B | C | D |
| 9.   1145 S. Sewell Road | A | B | C | D |
| 10.   17400 N. Sewell Road | A | B | C | D |
| 11.   72 E. Broder Avenue | A | B | C | D |
| 12.   2 E. Broder Avenue | A | B | C | D |
| 13.   21 E. Broder Avenue | A | B | C | D |
| 14.   29 Highway 98 | A | B | C | D |
| 15.   100 Highway 98 | A | B | C | D |
| 16.   372 S. Sewell Road | A | B | C | D |
| 17.   185 E. 31st Street | A | B | C | D |
| 18.   16000 N. Sewell Road | A | B | C | D |
| 19.   69 E. Broder Avenue | A | B | C | D |
| 20.   1750 N. Brodie Avenue | A | B | C | D |
| 21.   74 E. 31st Street | A | B | C | D |
| 22.   57 Highway 98 | A | B | C | D |
| 23.   634 S. Sewell Road | A | B | C | D |
| 24.   1000 N. Sewell Road | A | B | C | D |

| 25. | 270 E. 31st Street | A | B | C | D |
|-----|--------------------|---|---|---|---|
| 26. | 1121 N. Brodie Avenue | A | B | C | D |
| 27. | 1199 S. Sewell Road | **A** | B | C | D |
| 28. | 60 E. Broder Avenue | A | B | C | D |
| 29. | 100 E. 31st Street | A | B | C | D |
| 30. | 250 S. Sewell Road | A | B | C | D |
| 31. | 800 N. Brodie Avenue | A | B | C | D |
| 32. | 930 S. Sewell Road | A | B | C | D |
| 33. | 26500 N. Sewell Road | A | B | C | D |
| 34. | 65 E. Broder Avenue | A | B | C | D |
| 35. | 1560 N. Brodie Avenue | A | B | C | D |
| 36. | 54 E. Broder Avenue | A | B | C | D |

practice test

# ANSWER KEY AND EXPLANATIONS

## Part A: Address Checking

| | | | | |
|---|---|---|---|---|
| 1. A | 13. D | 25. D | 37. D | 49. A |
| 2. C | 14. B | 26. B | 38. A | 50. B |
| 3. D | 15. A | 27. C | 39. C | 51. C |
| 4. B | 16. C | 28. D | 40. B | 52. D |
| 5. D | 17. B | 29. B | 41. C | 53. B |
| 6. A | 18. D | 30. A | 42. D | 54. C |
| 7. C | 19. C | 31. C | 43. A | 55. A |
| 8. A | 20. B | 32. B | 44. D | 56. B |
| 9. B | 21. B | 33. D | 45. A | 57. D |
| 10. D | 22. A | 34. C | 46. D | 58. A |
| 11. C | 23. C | 35. A | 47. B | 59. C |
| 12. A | 24. A | 36. C | 48. D | 60. B |

## Part B: Forms Completion

| | | | | |
|---|---|---|---|---|
| 1. A | 7. C | 13. C | 19. A | 25. B |
| 2. C | 8. A | 14. D | 20. A | 26. A |
| 3. A | 9. B | 15. A | 21. D | 27. C |
| 4. D | 10. B | 16. A | 22. D | 28. B |
| 5. D | 11. D | 17. C | 23. C | 29. B |
| 6. B | 12. D | 18. B | 24. A | 30. C |

1. **The correct answer is (A).** Box 3 is labeled "Beginning Date." Therefore, the correct answer is (A), Box 3.

2. **The correct answer is (C).** Box 1 requires a name. Therefore, the appropriate answer is (C), Marshall Saltzman.

3. **The correct answer is (A).** Box 5a requires a check mark. Therefore, the correct answer is (A), a check mark.

4. **The correct answer is (D).** Box 6 is labeled "Customer Signature." Therefore, the correct answer is (D), Box 6.

5. **The correct answer is (D).** Box 4 is labeled "Postmark Here." Therefore, the correct answer is (D), Box 4.

6. **The correct answer is (B).** Box 2 requires the recipient's name and address. Therefore, the correct answer is (B), Box 2.

7. **The correct answer is (C).** Box 3 is labeled "Affix Stamps or Meter Postage Here." Therefore, the correct answer is (C), Box 3.

8. **The correct answer is (A).** Box 1 requires the sender's name and address. Therefore, the correct answer is (A), Box 1.

9. **The correct answer is (B).** Box 7 is labeled "ZIP + 4." Therefore, the correct answer is (B), 02818-9033.

10. **The correct answer is (B).** Box 2 requires a company name. Therefore, the correct answer is (B), White Printing Company.

11. **The correct answer is (D).** Box 9 is labeled "Customer Signature." Therefore, the correct answer is (D), Box 9.

12. **The correct answer is (D).** Box 12 is labeled "Date & Time of Pickup." Therefore, the correct answer is (D), Box 12.

13. **The correct answer is (C).** Box 6 is labeled "State." Therefore, the correct answer is (C), Indiana.

14. **The correct answer is (D).** Box 11 is labeled "USPS Signature." Therefore, the correct answer is (D), Box 11.

15. **The correct answer is (A).** Box 3 requires the customer's street address. Therefore, the correct answer is (A), Box 3.

16. **The correct answer is (A).** Box 8a is labeled "Check Made Payable to 'Postmaster.'" Therefore, the correct answer is (A), Box 8a.

17. **The correct answer is (C).** Box 10 is labeled "Affix Stamps or Meter Strip Here." Therefore, the correct answer is (C), Box 10.

18. **The correct answer is (B).** Box 8c requires a check mark. Therefore, the correct answer is (B), a check mark.

19. **The correct answer is (A).** Box 1 is labeled "Check Amount." Therefore, the correct answer is (A), Box 1.

20. **The correct answer is (A).** Box 6 requires the sender's name and address, so this box could be completed by a customer. Therefore, the correct answer is (A), Box 6.

21. **The correct answer is (D).** Box 9 requires the date of delivery. Therefore, the correct answer is (D), Box 9.

22. **The correct answer is (D).** Box 4 is labeled "Total Postage & Fees." Therefore, the correct answer is (D), Box 4.

23. **The correct answer is (C).** Box 6 requires the recipient's name. Therefore, the correct answer is (C), Box 6.

24. **The correct answer is (A).** Box 5 is labeled "Postmark Here." Therefore, the correct answer is (A), a postmark.

25. **The correct answer is (B).** Box 3 requires entering the amount of any special handling fees. Therefore, the correct answer is (B), $14.75.

26. **The correct answer is (A).** Box 24 is labeled "Employee Signature." Therefore, the correct answer is (A), a signature.

27. **The correct answer is (C).** Box 14 requires an alphabetical country code. Therefore, the correct answer is (C), Box 14.

28. **The correct answer is (B).** Box 6 is labeled "Return Receipt Fee." Therefore, the correct answer is (B), Box 6.

29. **The correct answer is (B).** Box 9 is labeled "COD Fee." Therefore, the appropriate answer is (B), 21.00.

30. **The correct answer is (C).** Box 13b requires the package weight in pounds (lbs) and ounces (ozs). Therefore, the correct answer is (C), Box 13b.

## Part C: Coding and Memory

### CODING SECTION: SEGMENT 1

| 1. A | 2. D | 3. C | 4. B |
|---|---|---|---|

### CODING SECTION: SEGMENT 2

| 1. B | 3. D | 5. D | 7. C | 8. B |
|---|---|---|---|---|
| 2. C | 4. A | 6. B | | |

## CODING SECTION: SEGMENT 3

| | | | | |
|---|---|---|---|---|
| 1. A | 9. A | 16. B | 23. C | 30. D |
| 2. D | 10. C | 17. D | 24. A | 31. D |
| 3. C | 11. D | 18. C | 25. B | 32. C |
| 4. B | 12. B | 19. B | 26. B | 33. A |
| 5. A | 13. C | 20. A | 27. D | 34. C |
| 6. C | 14. D | 21. D | 28. B | 35. B |
| 7. C | 15. A | 22. B | 29. A | 36. D |
| 8. A | | | | |

1. **The correct answer is (A).** The address 200 E. 31st Street falls in one of the address ranges in the same row as Delivery Route A.

2. **The correct answer is (D).** The address 2000 N. Brodie Avenue does not fall into any of the address ranges for Delivery Routes A, B, or C.

3. **The correct answer is (C).** The address 18018 N. Sewell Road falls in one of the address ranges in the same row as Delivery Route C.

4. **The correct answer is (B).** The address 590 S. Sewell Road falls in one of the address ranges in the same row as Delivery Route B.

5. **The correct answer is (A).** The address 1100 S. Sewell Road falls in one of the address ranges in the same row as Delivery Route A.

6. **The correct answer is (C).** The address 530 N. Brodie Avenue falls in one of the address ranges in the same row as Delivery Route C.

7. **The correct answer is (C).** The address 50 Highway 98 falls in one of the address ranges in the same row as Delivery Route C.

8. **The correct answer is (A).** The address 42 E. Broder Avenue falls in one of the address ranges in the same row as Delivery Route A.

9. **The correct answer is (A).** The address 27 E. Broder Avenue falls in one of the address ranges in the same row as Delivery Route A.

10. **The correct answer is (C).** The address 640 N. Brodie Avenue falls in one of the address ranges in the same row as Delivery Route C.

11. **The correct answer is (D).** The address 3060 S. Sewell Road does not fall into any of the address ranges for Delivery Routes A, B, or C.

12. **The correct answer is (B).** The address 56 E. Broder Avenue falls in one of the address ranges in the same row as Delivery Route B.

13. **The correct answer is (C).** The address 900 N. Brodie Avenue falls in one of the address ranges in the same row as Delivery Route C.

14. **The correct answer is (D).** The address 59 E. 31st Street does not fall into any of the address ranges for Delivery Routes A, B, or C.

15. **The correct answer is (A).** The address 62 E. 31st Street falls in one of the address ranges in the same row as Delivery Route A.

16. **The correct answer is (B).** The address 407 S. Sewell Road falls in one of the address ranges in the same row as Delivery Route B.

17. **The correct answer is (D).** The address 7 E. Broder Avenue does not fall into any of the address ranges for Delivery Routes A, B, or C.

18. **The correct answer is (C).** The address 39 Highway 98 falls in one of the address ranges in the same row as Delivery Route C.

19. **The correct answer is (B).** The address 75 E. Broder Avenue falls in one of the address ranges in the same row as Delivery Route B.

20. **The correct answer is (A).** The address 40 E. Broder Avenue falls in one of the address ranges in the same row as Delivery Route A.

21. **The correct answer is (D).** The address 1250 S. Sewell Road does not fall into any of the address ranges for Delivery Routes A, B, or C.

22. **The correct answer is (B).** The address 58 E. Broder Avenue falls in one of the address ranges in the same row as Delivery Route B.

23. **The correct answer is (C).** The address 14200 N. Sewell Road falls in one of the address ranges in the same row as Delivery Route C.

24. **The correct answer is (A).** The address 807 S. Sewell Road falls in one of the address ranges in the same row as Delivery Route A.

25. **The correct answer is (B).** The address 222 S. Sewell Road falls in one of the address ranges in the same row as Delivery Route B.

26. **The correct answer is (B).** The address 660 S. Sewell Road falls in one of the address ranges in the same row as Delivery Route B.

27. **The correct answer is (D).** The address 450 N. Brodie Avenue does not fall into any of the address ranges for Delivery Routes A, B, or C.

28. **The correct answer is (B).** The address 66 E. Broder Avenue falls in one of the address ranges in the same row as Delivery Route B.

29. **The correct answer is (A).** The address 93 E. 31st Street falls in one of the address ranges in the same row as Delivery Route A.

30. **The correct answer is (D).** The address 95 E. Broder Avenue does not fall into any of the address ranges for Delivery Routes A, B, or C.

31. **The correct answer is (D).** The address 16 Highway 98 does not fall into any of the address ranges for Delivery Routes A, B, or C.

32. **The correct answer is (C).** The address 15000 N. Sewell Road falls in one of the address ranges in the same row as Delivery Route C.

33. **The correct answer is (A).** The address 1010 S. Sewell Road falls in one of the address ranges in the same row as Delivery Route A.

34. **The correct answer is (C).** The address 600 N. Brodie Avenue falls in one of the address ranges in the same row as Delivery Route C.

35. **The correct answer is (B).** The address 277 S. Sewell Road falls in one of the address ranges in the same row as Delivery Route B.

36. **The correct answer is (D).** The address 95 S. Sewell Road does not fall into any of the address ranges for Delivery Routes A, B, or C.

## MEMORY SECTION: SEGMENT 2

| | | | | |
|---|---|---|---|---|
| 1. C | 3. A | 5. C | 7. B | 8. D |
| 2. B | 4. D | 6. A | | |

**MEMORY SECTION: SEGMENT 4**

| | | | | |
|---|---|---|---|---|
| 1. D | 9. A | 16. B | 23. B | 30. B |
| 2. B | 10. C | 17. A | 24. D | 31. C |
| 3. C | 11. B | 18. C | 25. D | 32. A |
| 4. D | 12. D | 19. B | 26. C | 33. D |
| 5. A | 13. A | 20. D | 27. A | 34. B |
| 6. C | 14. C | 21. A | 28. B | 35. C |
| 7. B | 15. D | 22. C | 29. A | 36. A |
| 8. D | | | | |

1. **The correct answer is (D).** The address 140 E. Broder Avenue does not fall into any of the address ranges for Delivery Routes A, B, or C.

2. **The correct answer is (B).** The address 77 E. Broder Avenue falls in one of the address ranges in the same row as Delivery Route B.

3. **The correct answer is (C).** The address 18700 N. Sewell Road falls in one of the address ranges in the same row as Delivery Route C.

4. **The correct answer is (D).** The address 13000 N. Sewell Road does not fall into any of the address ranges for Delivery Routes A, B, or C.

5. **The correct answer is (A).** The address 33 E. Broder Avenue falls in one of the address ranges in the same row as Delivery Route A.

6. **The correct answer is (C).** The address 21 Highway 98 falls in one of the address ranges in the same row as Delivery Route C.

7. **The correct answer is (B).** The address 500 S. Sewell Road falls in one of the address ranges in the same row as Delivery Route B.

8. **The correct answer is (D).** The address 1674 S. Sewell Road does not fall into any of the address ranges for Delivery Routes A, B, or C.

9. **The correct answer is (A).** The address 1145 S. Sewell Road falls in one of the address ranges in the same row as Delivery Route A.

10. **The correct answer is (C).** The address 17400 N. Sewell Road falls in one of the address ranges in the same row as Delivery Route C.

11. **The correct answer is (B).** The address 72 E. Broder Avenue falls in one of the address ranges in the same row as Delivery Route B.

12. **The correct answer is (D).** The address 2 E. Broder Avenue does not fall into any of the address ranges for Delivery Routes A, B, or C.

13. **The correct answer is (A).** The address 21 E. Broder Avenue falls in one of the address ranges in the same row as Delivery Route A.

14. **The correct answer is (C).** The address 29 Highway 98 falls in one of the address ranges in the same row as Delivery Route C.

15. **The correct answer is (D).** The address 100 Highway 98 does not fall into any of the address ranges for Delivery Routes A, B, or C.

16. **The correct answer is (B).** The address 372 S. Sewell Road falls in one of the address ranges in the same row as Delivery Route B.

17. **The correct answer is (A).** The address 185 E. 31st Street falls in one of the address ranges in the same row as Delivery Route A.

18. **The correct answer is (C).** The address 16000 N. Sewell Road falls in one of the address ranges in the same row as Delivery Route C.

19. **The correct answer is (B).** The address 69 E. Broder Avenue falls in one of the address ranges in the same row as Delivery Route B.

20. **The correct answer is (D).** The address 1750 N. Brodie Avenue does not fall into any of the address ranges for Delivery Routes A, B, or C.

21. **The correct answer is (A).** The address 74 E. 31st Street falls in one of the address ranges in the same row as Delivery Route A.

22. **The correct answer is (C).** The address 57 Highway 98 falls in one of the address ranges in the same row as Delivery Route C.

23. **The correct answer is (B).** The address 634 S. Sewell Road falls in one of the address ranges in the same row as Delivery Route B.

24. **The correct answer is (D).** The address 1000 N. Sewell Road does not fall into any of the address ranges for Delivery Routes A, B, or C.

25. **The correct answer is (D).** The address 270 E. 31st Street does not fall into any of the address ranges for Delivery Routes A, B, or C.

26. **The correct answer is (C).** The address 1121 N. Brodie Avenue falls in one of the address ranges in the same row as Delivery Route C.

27. **The correct answer is (A).** The address 1199 S. Sewell Road falls in one of the address ranges in the same row as Delivery Route A.

28. **The correct answer is (B).** The address 60 E. Broder Avenue falls in one of the address ranges in the same row as Delivery Route B.

29. **The correct answer is (A).** The address 100 E. 31st Street falls in one of the address ranges in the same row as Delivery Route A.

30. **The correct answer is (B).** The address 250 S. Sewell Road falls in one of the address ranges in the same row as Delivery Route B.

31. **The correct answer is (C).** The address 800 N. Brodie Avenue falls in one of the address ranges in the same row as Delivery Route C.

32. **The correct answer is (A).** The address 930 S. Sewell Road falls in one of the address ranges in the same row as Delivery Route A.

33. **The correct answer is (D).** The address 26500 N. Sewell Road does not fall into any of the address ranges for Delivery Routes A, B, or C.

34. **The correct answer is (B).** The address 65 E. Broder Avenue falls in one of the address ranges in the same row as Delivery Route B.

35. **The correct answer is (C).** The address 1560 N. Brodie Avenue falls in one of the address ranges in the same row as Delivery Route C.

36. **The correct answer is (A).** The address 54 E. Broder Avenue falls in one of the address ranges in the same row as Delivery Route A.

answers practice test 3

# PRACTICE TEST 4: EXAMS 473/473-C AND 460

## Part A: Address Checking

1. Ⓐ Ⓑ Ⓒ Ⓓ
2. Ⓐ Ⓑ Ⓒ Ⓓ
3. Ⓐ Ⓑ Ⓒ Ⓓ
4. Ⓐ Ⓑ Ⓒ Ⓓ
5. Ⓐ Ⓑ Ⓒ Ⓓ
6. Ⓐ Ⓑ Ⓒ Ⓓ
7. Ⓐ Ⓑ Ⓒ Ⓓ
8. Ⓐ Ⓑ Ⓒ Ⓓ
9. Ⓐ Ⓑ Ⓒ Ⓓ
10. Ⓐ Ⓑ Ⓒ Ⓓ
11. Ⓐ Ⓑ Ⓒ Ⓓ
12. Ⓐ Ⓑ Ⓒ Ⓓ

13. Ⓐ Ⓑ Ⓒ Ⓓ
14. Ⓐ Ⓑ Ⓒ Ⓓ
15. Ⓐ Ⓑ Ⓒ Ⓓ
16. Ⓐ Ⓑ Ⓒ Ⓓ
17. Ⓐ Ⓑ Ⓒ Ⓓ
18. Ⓐ Ⓑ Ⓒ Ⓓ
19. Ⓐ Ⓑ Ⓒ Ⓓ
20. Ⓐ Ⓑ Ⓒ Ⓓ
21. Ⓐ Ⓑ Ⓒ Ⓓ
22. Ⓐ Ⓑ Ⓒ Ⓓ
23. Ⓐ Ⓑ Ⓒ Ⓓ
24. Ⓐ Ⓑ Ⓒ Ⓓ

25. Ⓐ Ⓑ Ⓒ Ⓓ
26. Ⓐ Ⓑ Ⓒ Ⓓ
27. Ⓐ Ⓑ Ⓒ Ⓓ
28. Ⓐ Ⓑ Ⓒ Ⓓ
29. Ⓐ Ⓑ Ⓒ Ⓓ
30. Ⓐ Ⓑ Ⓒ Ⓓ
31. Ⓐ Ⓑ Ⓒ Ⓓ
32. Ⓐ Ⓑ Ⓒ Ⓓ
33. Ⓐ Ⓑ Ⓒ Ⓓ
34. Ⓐ Ⓑ Ⓒ Ⓓ
35. Ⓐ Ⓑ Ⓒ Ⓓ
36. Ⓐ Ⓑ Ⓒ Ⓓ

37. Ⓐ Ⓑ Ⓒ Ⓓ
38. Ⓐ Ⓑ Ⓒ Ⓓ
39. Ⓐ Ⓑ Ⓒ Ⓓ
40. Ⓐ Ⓑ Ⓒ Ⓓ
41. Ⓐ Ⓑ Ⓒ Ⓓ
42. Ⓐ Ⓑ Ⓒ Ⓓ
43. Ⓐ Ⓑ Ⓒ Ⓓ
44. Ⓐ Ⓑ Ⓒ Ⓓ
45. Ⓐ Ⓑ Ⓒ Ⓓ
46. Ⓐ Ⓑ Ⓒ Ⓓ
47. Ⓐ Ⓑ Ⓒ Ⓓ
48. Ⓐ Ⓑ Ⓒ Ⓓ

49. Ⓐ Ⓑ Ⓒ Ⓓ
50. Ⓐ Ⓑ Ⓒ Ⓓ
51. Ⓐ Ⓑ Ⓒ Ⓓ
52. Ⓐ Ⓑ Ⓒ Ⓓ
53. Ⓐ Ⓑ Ⓒ Ⓓ
54. Ⓐ Ⓑ Ⓒ Ⓓ
55. Ⓐ Ⓑ Ⓒ Ⓓ
56. Ⓐ Ⓑ Ⓒ Ⓓ
57. Ⓐ Ⓑ Ⓒ Ⓓ
58. Ⓐ Ⓑ Ⓒ Ⓓ
59. Ⓐ Ⓑ Ⓒ Ⓓ
60. Ⓐ Ⓑ Ⓒ Ⓓ

## Part B: Forms Completion

1. Ⓐ Ⓑ Ⓒ Ⓓ
2. Ⓐ Ⓑ Ⓒ Ⓓ
3. Ⓐ Ⓑ Ⓒ Ⓓ
4. Ⓐ Ⓑ Ⓒ Ⓓ
5. Ⓐ Ⓑ Ⓒ Ⓓ
6. Ⓐ Ⓑ Ⓒ Ⓓ

7. Ⓐ Ⓑ Ⓒ Ⓓ
8. Ⓐ Ⓑ Ⓒ Ⓓ
9. Ⓐ Ⓑ Ⓒ Ⓓ
10. Ⓐ Ⓑ Ⓒ Ⓓ
11. Ⓐ Ⓑ Ⓒ Ⓓ
12. Ⓐ Ⓑ Ⓒ Ⓓ

13. Ⓐ Ⓑ Ⓒ Ⓓ
14. Ⓐ Ⓑ Ⓒ Ⓓ
15. Ⓐ Ⓑ Ⓒ Ⓓ
16. Ⓐ Ⓑ Ⓒ Ⓓ
17. Ⓐ Ⓑ Ⓒ Ⓓ
18. Ⓐ Ⓑ Ⓒ Ⓓ

19. Ⓐ Ⓑ Ⓒ Ⓓ
20. Ⓐ Ⓑ Ⓒ Ⓓ
21. Ⓐ Ⓑ Ⓒ Ⓓ
22. Ⓐ Ⓑ Ⓒ Ⓓ
23. Ⓐ Ⓑ Ⓒ Ⓓ
24. Ⓐ Ⓑ Ⓒ Ⓓ

25. Ⓐ Ⓑ Ⓒ Ⓓ
26. Ⓐ Ⓑ Ⓒ Ⓓ
27. Ⓐ Ⓑ Ⓒ Ⓓ
28. Ⓐ Ⓑ Ⓒ Ⓓ
29. Ⓐ Ⓑ Ⓒ Ⓓ
30. Ⓐ Ⓑ Ⓒ Ⓓ

## Part C: Coding and Memory

### CODING SECTION: SEGMENT 3

1. Ⓐ Ⓑ Ⓒ Ⓓ
2. Ⓐ Ⓑ Ⓒ Ⓓ
3. Ⓐ Ⓑ Ⓒ Ⓓ
4. Ⓐ Ⓑ Ⓒ Ⓓ
5. Ⓐ Ⓑ Ⓒ Ⓓ
6. Ⓐ Ⓑ Ⓒ Ⓓ
7. Ⓐ Ⓑ Ⓒ Ⓓ
8. Ⓐ Ⓑ Ⓒ Ⓓ

9. Ⓐ Ⓑ Ⓒ Ⓓ
10. Ⓐ Ⓑ Ⓒ Ⓓ
11. Ⓐ Ⓑ Ⓒ Ⓓ
12. Ⓐ Ⓑ Ⓒ Ⓓ
13. Ⓐ Ⓑ Ⓒ Ⓓ
14. Ⓐ Ⓑ Ⓒ Ⓓ
15. Ⓐ Ⓑ Ⓒ Ⓓ

16. Ⓐ Ⓑ Ⓒ Ⓓ
17. Ⓐ Ⓑ Ⓒ Ⓓ
18. Ⓐ Ⓑ Ⓒ Ⓓ
19. Ⓐ Ⓑ Ⓒ Ⓓ
20. Ⓐ Ⓑ Ⓒ Ⓓ
21. Ⓐ Ⓑ Ⓒ Ⓓ
22. Ⓐ Ⓑ Ⓒ Ⓓ

23. Ⓐ Ⓑ Ⓒ Ⓓ
24. Ⓐ Ⓑ Ⓒ Ⓓ
25. Ⓐ Ⓑ Ⓒ Ⓓ
26. Ⓐ Ⓑ Ⓒ Ⓓ
27. Ⓐ Ⓑ Ⓒ Ⓓ
28. Ⓐ Ⓑ Ⓒ Ⓓ
29. Ⓐ Ⓑ Ⓒ Ⓓ

30. Ⓐ Ⓑ Ⓒ Ⓓ
31. Ⓐ Ⓑ Ⓒ Ⓓ
32. Ⓐ Ⓑ Ⓒ Ⓓ
33. Ⓐ Ⓑ Ⓒ Ⓓ
34. Ⓐ Ⓑ Ⓒ Ⓓ
35. Ⓐ Ⓑ Ⓒ Ⓓ
36. Ⓐ Ⓑ Ⓒ Ⓓ

### MEMORY SECTION: SEGMENT 4

1. Ⓐ Ⓑ Ⓒ Ⓓ
2. Ⓐ Ⓑ Ⓒ Ⓓ
3. Ⓐ Ⓑ Ⓒ Ⓓ
4. Ⓐ Ⓑ Ⓒ Ⓓ
5. Ⓐ Ⓑ Ⓒ Ⓓ
6. Ⓐ Ⓑ Ⓒ Ⓓ
7. Ⓐ Ⓑ Ⓒ Ⓓ
8. Ⓐ Ⓑ Ⓒ Ⓓ

9. Ⓐ Ⓑ Ⓒ Ⓓ
10. Ⓐ Ⓑ Ⓒ Ⓓ
11. Ⓐ Ⓑ Ⓒ Ⓓ
12. Ⓐ Ⓑ Ⓒ Ⓓ
13. Ⓐ Ⓑ Ⓒ Ⓓ
14. Ⓐ Ⓑ Ⓒ Ⓓ
15. Ⓐ Ⓑ Ⓒ Ⓓ

16. Ⓐ Ⓑ Ⓒ Ⓓ
17. Ⓐ Ⓑ Ⓒ Ⓓ
18. Ⓐ Ⓑ Ⓒ Ⓓ
19. Ⓐ Ⓑ Ⓒ Ⓓ
20. Ⓐ Ⓑ Ⓒ Ⓓ
21. Ⓐ Ⓑ Ⓒ Ⓓ
22. Ⓐ Ⓑ Ⓒ Ⓓ

23. Ⓐ Ⓑ Ⓒ Ⓓ
24. Ⓐ Ⓑ Ⓒ Ⓓ
25. Ⓐ Ⓑ Ⓒ Ⓓ
26. Ⓐ Ⓑ Ⓒ Ⓓ
27. Ⓐ Ⓑ Ⓒ Ⓓ
28. Ⓐ Ⓑ Ⓒ Ⓓ
29. Ⓐ Ⓑ Ⓒ Ⓓ

30. Ⓐ Ⓑ Ⓒ Ⓓ
31. Ⓐ Ⓑ Ⓒ Ⓓ
32. Ⓐ Ⓑ Ⓒ Ⓓ
33. Ⓐ Ⓑ Ⓒ Ⓓ
34. Ⓐ Ⓑ Ⓒ Ⓓ
35. Ⓐ Ⓑ Ⓒ Ⓓ
36. Ⓐ Ⓑ Ⓒ Ⓓ

answer sheet

# Practice Test 4: Exams 473/473-C and 460

**NOTE:** Practice Tests 1–5 are a combination of the types of questions test-takers will see on Exam 473 and Exam 460.

Exam 473 consists of four parts:

A. Address Checking

B. Forms Completion

C. Coding and Memory

D. Personal Characteristics and Experience Inventory

Exam 460 consists of four parts:

A. Address Checking

B. Memory for Addresses

C. Number Series

D. Following Oral Instructions

If you are practicing to take Exam 460, you may want to follow these tips:

- Skip Part B (Forms Completion) of Practice Tests 1 through 5. This material will not be included on your actual exam; it is only on Exam 473.

- Skip Part D (Personal Characteristics and Experience Inventory) of Practice Test 1. This material will not be included on your actual exam; it is only on Exam 473.

- To practice for Part D of Exam 460 (Following Oral Instructions), take Practice Test 7 in this book.

## PART A: ADDRESS CHECKING

**60 QUESTIONS • 11 MINUTES**

**Directions:** Compare the **List to be Checked** with the **Correct List.** Decide if there are **(A) NO ERRORS,** an error in the **(B) ADDRESS ONLY,** an error in the **(C) ZIP CODE ONLY,** or an error in **(D) BOTH** the address and ZIP Code. Record your answers on the answer sheet.

| | Correct List | | | List to be Checked | |
| --- | --- | --- | --- | --- | --- |
| | *Address* | *ZIP Code* | | *Address* | *ZIP Code* |
| **1.** | 700 E. Riesling Circle<br>St. Paul, MN | 55102-1002 | | 700 N. Riesling Circle<br>St. Paul, MN | 55102-1002 |
| **2.** | 2400 Lampett Court<br>Pickett, WI | 54964 | | 2400 Lampett Court<br>Pickett, WI | 59464 |
| **3.** | 72 W. 20th St., Apt. A<br>Prole, Iowa | 50229 | | 72 W. 20th St., Apt. 4<br>Prole, Iowa | 50299 |
| **4.** | 9205 Wendington Way<br>Betterton, MD | 21610 | | 9205 Wendington Way<br>Betterton, MD | 21610 |
| **5.** | 2500 First Avenue<br>East Chicago, IN | 46312 | | 2500 First Avenue<br>Chicago, IL | 46312 |
| **6.** | 379 Main Street<br>White Castle, LA | 70788 | | 379 Main Street<br>White Castle, LA | 70888 |
| **7.** | 800 Washington Drive<br>Bayard, NE | 69334 | | 800 Washington Drive<br>Bayard, NC | 69934 |
| **8.** | 765 Boston Highway<br>Smithton, IL | 62285 | | 765 Boston Highway<br>Smithton, IL | 62285 |
| **9.** | 2040 South Street<br>West Falls, NY | 14170 | | 2040 South Street<br>West Falls, NY | 14170 |
| **10.** | 55 Winding Hills Trail<br>New Portland, ME | 04961 | | 55 Windy Hills Trail<br>New Portland, ME | 04691 |
| **11.** | 602 Napa Ridge Ter.<br>Christmas Valley, OR | 97641 | | 602 Napa Ridge Ter.<br>Christmas Valley, OR | 97461 |
| **12.** | 3417 Oneida Lane<br>Middleburg, PA | 17842 | | 3417 Oneida Lane<br>Middleburg, PA | 17822 |

**Directions:** Compare the **List to be Checked** with the **Correct List.** Decide if there are **(A) NO ERRORS,** an error in the **(B) ADDRESS ONLY,** an error in the **(C) ZIP CODE ONLY,** or an error in **(D) BOTH** the address and ZIP Code. Record your answers on the answer sheet.

| | | | | |
|---|---|---|---|---|
| **13.** | 40 Country Road 11<br>Gillette, WY | 82718 | 40 Country Road 11<br>Gillette, WY | 82718 |
| **14.** | 830 University Blvd.<br>Dover, NH | 03820-3860 | 803 University Blvd.<br>Dover, NH | 03820-3800 |
| **15.** | 2701 E. Prescott Ave.<br>North Canton, Ohio | 44720 | 2710 E. Prescott Ave.<br>North Central, Ohio | 44720 |
| **16.** | 10 N. Lake Street<br>Tunnel Hill, Georgia | 30755 | 10 N. Lake Street<br>Tunnel Hill, Georgia | 30775 |
| **17.** | 1 Alexandra Way<br>Oroville, CA | 95965 | 10 Alexandra Way<br>Oroville, CA | 95665 |
| **18.** | 8600 Forest Court<br>Slaton, TX | 79364 | 8600 Forest Court<br>Slaton, TX | 79364 |
| **19.** | 909 Liberty Highway<br>Calhoun City, MS | 38916 | 909 Liberty Highway<br>Calhoun City, MS | 39816 |
| **20.** | 6213 Sherman Street<br>Williams, AZ | 86046 | 6213 Sherman Street<br>Williams, AZ | 86046 |
| **21.** | 17 El Greco Pl.<br>Reddick, FL | 32686 | 17 El Grano Pl.<br>Reddick, FL | 32686 |
| **22.** | 904 Walnut Peaks Dr.<br>Lexington, KY | 40507-1333 | 904 Walnut Peaks Dr.<br>Lexington, KY | 40507-1333 |
| **23.** | 1408 E. Cassandra Rd.<br>Gabbs, NV | 89409 | 1408 E. Cassandra Rd.<br>Gabbs, ND | 89449 |
| **24.** | 1904 Chase Dr, #102<br>Mountainair, NM | 87036 | 1904 Chase Dr, #102<br>Mountainair, NM | 87006 |
| **25.** | 299 Melody Lane<br>Broken Arrow, OK | 74012 | 299 S. Melody Ave.<br>Broken Arrow, OK | 74012 |
| **26.** | 500 Princeton Avenue<br>Spiritwood, ND | 58481 | 500 Princeton Avenue<br>Spiritwood, ND | 58441 |
| **27.** | 6050 River Trail<br>Green River, WY | 82935 | 6050 River Trail<br>Green River, WY | 82935 |

practice test

**Directions:** Compare the **List to be Checked** with the **Correct List.** Decide if there are **(A) NO ERRORS,** an error in the **(B) ADDRESS ONLY,** an error in the **(C) ZIP CODE ONLY,** or an error in **(D) BOTH** the address and ZIP Code. Record your answers on the answer sheet.

| | | |
|---|---|---|
| **28.** 3700 S. Mexico Blvd.<br>Somerset, CO | 81434 | 3700 S. Mexico Blvd.<br>Somerville, CO | 84134 |
| **29.** 12 Country Route 9<br>Santa Fe, NM | 87506 | 12 Country Route 9<br>Santa Fe, ND | 87506 |
| **30.** 400 W. 18th Street<br>Chapel Hill, TN | 37034 | 400 W. 18th Street<br>Chapel Hill, TN | 37304 |
| **31.** 9111 Greenview Lane<br>Vale, NC | 28168 | 9111 Green Valley Lane<br>Vale, NC | 28178 |
| **32.** 61 N. Hilldale Pkwy<br>Charleston, SC | 29407-6138 | 61 N. Hilldale Pkwy<br>Charleston, SC | 29407-8138 |
| **33.** 760 Eliza Street<br>West Monroe, LA | 71292 | 760 Eliza Street<br>West Monroe, LA | 71292 |
| **34.** 307 Downing Road<br>Dawson, ND | 58428 | 407 Downing Road<br>Dawson, ND | 58428 |
| **35.** 440 North Terrace<br>Billings, MT | 59101 | 440 North Trail<br>Billings, MT | 58101 |
| **36.** 800 Brookdale Blvd.<br>Dixon, MO | 65459 | 800 Brookdale Blvd.<br>Dixon, MI | 65459 |
| **37.** 50 Ross Court<br>Brecksville, OH | 44141 | 50 Reston Court<br>Brecksville, OH | 74141 |
| **38.** 427 Briggs Circle<br>Westport, MA | 02790 | 427 Briggs Circle<br>Westport, MA | 02790 |
| **39.** 755 Armitage Lane<br>Ebensburg, PA | 15931 | 755 Hermitage Lane<br>Ebensburg, PA | 15931 |
| **40.** 99 Obelisk Avenue<br>Drakesboro, KY | 42337 | 99 Obelisk Avenue<br>Drakesboro, KY | 42327 |
| **41.** 32 Lisa Circle<br>Noble, IL | 62868 | 32 Lisa Circle<br>Nobleton, IL | 62868 |
| **42.** P.O. Box 7060<br>Madison, WI | 53703-3359 | P.O. Box 7060<br>Maddox, WI | 53730-3359 |

**Directions:** Compare the **List to be Checked** with the **Correct List.** Decide if there are **(A) NO ERRORS,** an error in the **(B) ADDRESS ONLY,** an error in the **(C) ZIP CODE ONLY,** or an error in **(D) BOTH** the address and ZIP Code. Record your answers on the answer sheet.

| | List to be Checked | | Correct List | |
|---|---|---|---|---|
| 43. | 400 Baton Court<br>North Freedom, WI | 53951 | 400 Baton Court<br>North Freedom, WI | 53951 |
| 44. | 2069 Caspar Street<br>Sedro Wooley, WA | 98284 | 2069 Caspar Street<br>Sedro Wooley, WI | 92884 |
| 45. | 5570 Van Deer Way<br>Luther, OK | 73054 | 5770 Van Deer Way<br>Luther, OK | 73054 |
| 46. | 3000 Lighthouse Road<br>Ashby, NE | 69333 | 3000 Lighthouse Road<br>Ashby, NE | 69933 |
| 47. | 8299 E. Sterling Ave.<br>Del Valle, Texas | 78617 | 8299 E. Sterling Ave.<br>Del Valle, Texas | 78617 |
| 48. | 459 Ivy Lane<br>Exeter, CA | 93221 | 459 Ivy Circle<br>Exeter, CA | 93321 |
| 49. | 71 Curry Court<br>Midland, MI | 48642 | 71 Curry Circle<br>Midland, MI | 48642 |
| 50. | 160 Pagosa Parkway<br>Honolulu, HI | 96813 | 1600 Pagosa Parkway<br>Honolulu, HI | 86813 |
| 51. | Post Office Box 1200<br>Newark, New Jersey | 07105-3542 | Post Office Box 1200<br>Newark, New Jersey | 07105-3542 |
| 52. | 994 Davis Drive<br>Lawton, IA | 51030 | 994 Davis Drive<br>Lawton, IA | 50130 |
| 53. | 36 S. 22nd Street<br>Bemidji, MN | 56601 | 36 N. 22nd Street<br>Bemidji, MN | 56601 |
| 54. | 4800 Court Place<br>Charlestown, RI | 02813 | 4800 Court Place<br>Charlesville, RI | 02803 |
| 55. | 282 Whistleton Rd.<br>Paramount, CA | 90723 | 282 Whistleton Rd.<br>Paramount, CA | 90723 |
| 56. | 68 Barry Lane<br>Sandy Hook, CT | 06482 | 608 Barry Lane<br>Sandy Hook, CO | 06482 |
| 57. | 7700 Vineyard Circle<br>Sumner, Nebraska | 68878 | 7700 Vineyard Circle<br>Sumner, Nebraska | 68778 |

**Directions:** Compare the **List to be Checked** with the **Correct List.** Decide if there are **(A) NO ERRORS,** an error in the **(B) ADDRESS ONLY,** an error in the **(C) ZIP CODE ONLY,** or an error in **(D) BOTH** the address and ZIP Code. Record your answers on the answer sheet.

**58.** 300 Shipman Way
Ellensburg, WA      98926      300 Shipman Way
Ellensburg, WA      98926

**59.** 5990 Fillmore Street
Birmingham, AL      35242      599 Fillmore Road
Birmingham, AL      35242

**60.** 1100 Monroe Avenue
Iowa City, IA      52240-3987      1100 Monroe Avenue
Iowa City, IA      52440-3987

## PART B: FORMS COMPLETION

**30 QUESTIONS • 15 MINUTES**

**Directions:** Read each form and answer the questions based on the information provided. Mark your answers on the answer sheet.

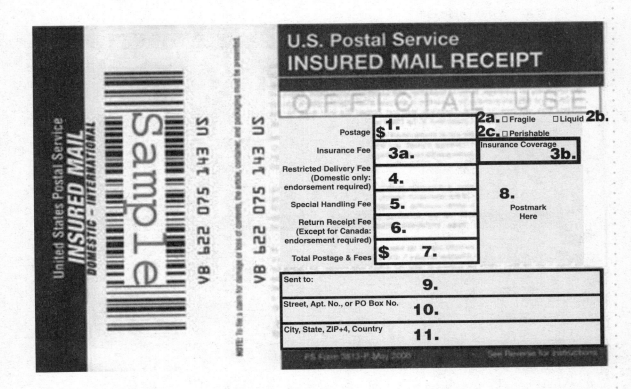

1. Which of the following boxes on the above form requires an endorsement?
   - **(A)** Box 3a
   - **(B)** Box 3b
   - **(C)** Box 5
   - **(D)** Box 6

2. Where on this form would you enter a restricted delivery fee?
   - **(A)** Box 4
   - **(B)** Box 6
   - **(C)** Box 8
   - **(D)** Box 9

3. You could place a check mark in all of the following boxes on this form EXCEPT
   - **(A)** Box 2a
   - **(B)** Box 2b
   - **(C)** Box 2c
   - **(D)** Box 3b

4. A postmark could be placed in which of the following boxes on this form?
   - **(A)** Box 6
   - **(B)** Box 7
   - **(C)** Box 8
   - **(D)** Box 10

5. What would be an appropriate entry for Box 3a of this form?
  (A) $15.00
  (B) 3/2/08
  (C) #127
  (D) 17 S. Sutton Terrace

**United States Postal Service**
**Pickup Service Statement**
**Express Mail, Global Express Guaranteed, Priority Mail, or Parcel Post**

**1. Customer Information**

| | |
|---|---|
| Customer Name | **1.** |
| Company Name | **2.** |
| Address 1 | **3.** |
| Address 2 | **4.** |
| City | **5.** |
| State | **6.** ZIP + 4 **7.** |

**2. Product Information**

| | Quantity |
|---|---|
| Express Mail | |
| Global Express Guaranteed | |
| Priority Mail | |
| Parcel Post (Domestic or International) | |
| Estimated total weight of all packages (In pounds) | |

**3. Payment Method**

**8a.** ☐ Check made payable to "Postmaster"
**8b.** ☐ Express Mail Corporate Account No. or Federal Agency No.:
**8c.** ☐ Merchandise Return Label
☐ Postage Due Account
☐ Stamps or Metered Postage (Affix at right)

**4. Affix Stamps or Meter Strip Here** (If applicable)

**10.**

5. Customer Signature **9.**
6. USPS Signature **11.**
7. Date & Time of Pickup **12.**

PS Form **5541**, October 2001          1 - Finance   2 - Customer

6. Where on the above form would you enter a customer's name?
  (A) Box 1
  (B) Box 4
  (C) Box 11
  (D) Box 12

7. Which of these would be an appropriate entry for Box 5 on the form?
  (A) West Virginia
  (B) Cincinnati
  (C) 52334
  (D) #1575

8. Where on this form would you enter an Express Mail Corporate Account Number?
  (A) Box 8a
  (B) Box 8b
  (C) Box 8c
  (D) Box 9

9. Which of the following boxes must be completed by a postal employee?
  (A) 1
  (B) 2
  (C) 9
  (D) 11

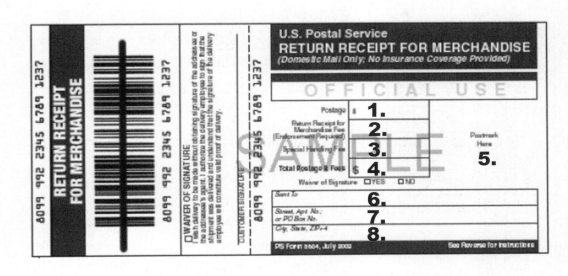

**10.** Where on the above form would you enter the postage amount?

   **(A)** Box 1

   **(B)** Box 2

   **(C)** Box 3

   **(D)** Box 5

**11.** Which of the following would be an appropriate entry for Box 4 on the form?

   **(A)** A check mark

   **(B)** #2484

   **(C)** 29.50

   **(D)** A signature

**12.** The entry "Mr. Jacob Salieri" could be entered correctly in which of the following boxes on this form?

   **(A)** 3

   **(B)** 4

   **(C)** 5

   **(D)** 6

**13.** Where on the form would you indicate the P.O. Box number of the addressee?

   **(A)** Box 3

   **(B)** Box 6

   **(C)** Box 7

   **(D)** Box 8

**U.S. Postal Service™**
**CERTIFIED MAIL™ RECEIPT**
*(Domestic Mail Only; No Insurance Coverage Provided)*

For delivery information vist our website at www.usps.com™

**OFFICIAL USE**

| | |
|---|---|
| Postage | $ **1** |
| Certified Fee | **2** |
| Return Receipt Fee (Endorsement Required) | **3** |
| Restricted Delivery Fee (Endorsement Required) | **4** |
| Total Postage & Fees | $ **5** |

**6**

Postmark Here

Sent To: **7**

Street, Apt No.; or PO Box No. **8**

City, State, ZIP+ 4 **9**

PS Form 3800, June 2002    See Reverse for Instructions

7000 0520 0017 2917 7637

CERTIFIED MAIL™

PLACE STICKER AT TOP OF ENVELOPE TO THE RIGHT OF RETURN ADDRESS  FOLD AT DOTTED LINE

14. Where on the above form would you indicate that the item is being sent to 47 Norwich Drive?
   (A) Box 4
   (B) Box 5
   (C) Box 7
   (D) Box 8

15. Which of these would be an appropriate entry for Box 9 on the form?
   (A) $17.43
   (B) Portland, OR 97214-3320
   (C) #2884
   (D) 35 W. Potomac Ave.

16. Which of these would be a correct entry for Box 2 on the form?
   (A) $18.00
   (B) A signature
   (C) A check mark
   (D) A postmark

17. A fee amount would be the correct entry for each of the following boxes on this form EXCEPT
   (A) Box 1
   (B) Box 2
   (C) Box 5
   (D) Box 7

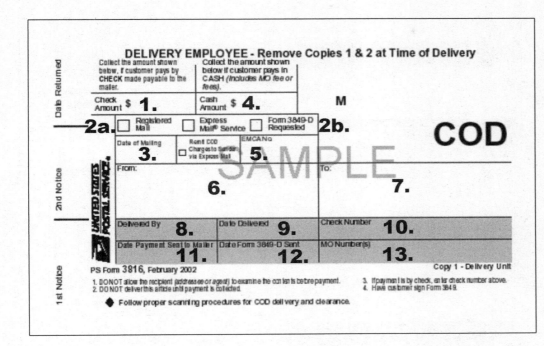

practice test

**18.** Which of these would be an appropriate entry for Box 12 on the above form?

(A) 2 lbs. 3 ozs.

(B) 9/3/08

(C) 130 Westview Lane

(D) Mr. Robert Salazar

**19.** Which of the following would be an appropriate entry for Box 4 on the above form?

(A) 3/19/08

(B) A check mark

(C) 22.80

(D) 27–083

**20.** Where on this form should the sender's name and address be entered?

(A) Box 1

(B) Box 2a

(C) Box 2b

(D) Box 6

**21.** Which of these would be an appropriate entry for Box 2b on this form?

(A) A signature

(B) #423

(C) A check mark

(D) 77024

**22.** Where on the form would you indicate who delivered the item?

(A) Box 6

(B) Box 7

(C) Box 8

(D) Box 9

**23.** Which of these would be an appropriate entry for Box 18 on the above form?

(A) A signature
(B) A check mark
(C) 27.04
(D) September 9

**24.** A signature would be an appropriate entry for each of the following boxes on the form EXCEPT

(A) Box 16
(B) Box 18
(C) Box 21
(D) Box 24

**25.** Where on this form would you indicate the time the item was accepted?

(A) Box 2a
(B) Box 7a
(C) Box 11b
(D) Box 16

**26.** Which of these would be an appropriate entry for Box 15 on this form?

(A) #9003
(B) A check mark
(C) R.F.
(D) 247 Plaines Highway

**27.** Which box would you check on this form to indicate next-day delivery?

(A) Box 2a
(B) Box 8a
(C) Box 17a
(D) Box 23b

**28.** The PO Zip Code is entered in which box on this form?

(A) Box 1
(B) Box 4
(C) Box 9
(D) Box 12

**29.** Which box on the form would you check to show third–day military delivery?

  **(A)** 8b
  **(B)** 11b
  **(C)** 13a
  **(D)** 20b

**30.** Which of these would be an appropriate entry for Box 6?

  **(A)** A signature
  **(B)** 88034
  **(C)** 17.00
  **(D)** J.K.

# PART C: CODING AND MEMORY

## Coding Section: Segment 1

**4 QUESTIONS • 2 MINUTES**

**Directions:** Segment 1 is *not* scored and does not count toward your total exam score. It is a practice exercise to help you with the Coding Section under a time constraint similar to the one used in the scored Coding Section. Use the coding guide below to match each address to a delivery route. Mark your answers on the answer section at the bottom of this page.

### CODING GUIDE

| ADDRESS RANGE | DELIVERY ROUTE |
|---|---|
| 200–1900 W. Lansing Parkway<br>1300–6000 E. Archway Drive | A |
| 25000–50000 E. Lansing Parkway<br>80–150 2nd Avenue<br>30–60 S. Archer Drive | B |
| 40–180 Country Route 12<br>51000–85000 E. Lansing Parkway<br>10–29 S. Archer Drive | C |
| All mail that doesn't fall into one of the address ranges listed above. | D |

| | Address | Delivery Route | | | |
|---|---|---|---|---|---|
| **1.** | 25500 E. Lansing Parkway | A | B | C | D |
| **2.** | 40 Country Route 12 | A | B | C | D |
| **3.** | 199 W. Lansing Parkway | A | B | C | D |
| **4.** | 6000 E. Archway Drive | A | B | C | D |

## Sample Answer Sheet

**1.** Ⓐ Ⓑ Ⓒ Ⓓ      **3.** Ⓐ Ⓑ Ⓒ Ⓓ

**2.** Ⓐ Ⓑ Ⓒ Ⓓ      **4.** Ⓐ Ⓑ Ⓒ Ⓓ

## Coding Section: Segment 2

**8 QUESTIONS • 1.5 MINUTES (90 SECONDS)**

**Directions:** Segment 2 is *not* scored and does not count toward your total exam score. It is a practice exercise to help you with the Coding Section under a time constraint similar to the one used in the scored Coding Section. Use the coding guide below to match each address to a delivery route. Mark your answers on the answer section at the bottom of this page.

### CODING GUIDE

| ADDRESS RANGE | DELIVERY ROUTE |
|---|---|
| 200–1900 W. Lansing Parkway<br>1300–6000 E. Archway Drive | A |
| 25000–50000 E. Lansing Parkway<br>80–150 2nd Avenue<br>30–60 S. Archer Drive | B |
| 40–180 Country Route 12<br>51000–85000 E. Lansing Parkway<br>10–29 S. Archer Drive | C |
| All mail that doesn't fall into one of the address ranges listed above. | D |

| Address | Delivery Route | | | |
|---|---|---|---|---|
| 1.  18 S. Archer Drive | A | B | C | D |
| 2.  1790 E. Archway Drive | A | B | C | D |
| 3.  1200 E. Archway Drive | A | B | C | D |
| 4.  87 2nd Avenue | A | B | C | D |
| 5.  490 W. Lansing Parkway | A | B | C | D |
| 6.  70400 E. Lansing Parkway | A | B | C | D |
| 7.  60 2nd Avenue | A | B | C | D |
| 8.  32 S. Archer Drive | A | B | C | D |

## Sample Answer Sheet

1. Ⓐ Ⓑ Ⓒ Ⓓ     4. Ⓐ Ⓑ Ⓒ Ⓓ     7. Ⓐ Ⓑ Ⓒ Ⓓ

2. Ⓐ Ⓑ Ⓒ Ⓓ     5. Ⓐ Ⓑ Ⓒ Ⓓ     8. Ⓐ Ⓑ Ⓒ Ⓓ

3. Ⓐ Ⓑ Ⓒ Ⓓ     6. Ⓐ Ⓑ Ⓒ Ⓓ

## Coding Section: Segment 3

**36 QUESTIONS • 6 MINUTES**

**Directions:** This is the actual *scored* Coding Section of the exam. Work through items 1 through 36, assigning a code to each item based on the Coding Guide below. Mark your answers on the answer sheet. Work quickly and accurately.

### CODING GUIDE

| ADDRESS RANGE | DELIVERY ROUTE |
|---|:---:|
| 200–1900 W. Lansing Parkway<br>1300–6000 E. Archway Drive | A |
| 25000–50000 E. Lansing Parkway<br>80–150 2nd Avenue<br>30–60 S. Archer Drive | B |
| 40–180 Country Route 12<br>51000–85000 E. Lansing Parkway<br>10–29 S. Archer Drive | C |
| All mail that doesn't fall into one of the address ranges listed above. | D |

| | Address | Delivery Route | | | |
|---|---|:---:|:---:|:---:|:---:|
| 1. | 49000 E. Lansing Parkway | A | B | C | D |
| 2. | 2000 W. Lansing Parkway | A | B | C | D |
| 3. | 69000 E. Lansing Parkway | A | B | C | D |
| 4. | 4600 E. Archway Drive | A | B | C | D |
| 5. | 93 2nd Avenue | A | B | C | D |
| 6. | 14 S. Archer Drive | A | B | C | D |
| 7. | 577 W. Lansing Parkway | A | B | C | D |
| 8. | 17 Country Route 12 | A | B | C | D |
| 9. | 79 2nd Avenue | A | B | C | D |
| 10. | 2780 E. Archway Drive | A | B | C | D |
| 11. | 153 Country Route 12 | A | B | C | D |
| 12. | 43000 E. Lansing Parkway | A | B | C | D |
| 13. | 6050 E. Archway Drive | A | B | C | D |
| 14. | 1623 W. Lansing Parkway | A | B | C | D |
| 15. | 47 Country Route 12 | A | B | C | D |
| 16. | 40 S. Archer Drive | A | B | C | D |

## CODING GUIDE

| ADDRESS RANGE | DELIVERY ROUTE |
|---|---|
| 200–1900 W. Lansing Parkway<br>1300–6000 E. Archway Drive | A |
| 25000–50000 E. Lansing Parkway<br>80–150 2nd Avenue<br>30–60 S. Archer Drive | B |
| 40–180 Country Route 12<br>51000–85000 E. Lansing Parkway<br>10–29 S. Archer Drive | C |
| All mail that doesn't fall into one of the address ranges listed above. | D |

| | | | | | |
|---|---|---|---|---|---|
| **17.** | 57000 E. Lansing Parkway | A | B | C | D |
| **18.** | 16000 E. Lansing Parkway | A | B | C | D |
| **19.** | 111 2nd Avenue | A | B | C | D |
| **20.** | 11 S. Archer Drive | A | B | C | D |
| **21.** | 97000 E. Lansing Parkway | A | B | C | D |
| **22.** | 4000 E. Archway Drive | A | B | C | D |
| **23.** | 37 S. Archer Drive | A | B | C | D |
| **24.** | 7 S. Archer Drive | A | B | C | D |
| **25.** | 997 W. Lansing Parkway | A | B | C | D |
| **26.** | 59 Country Route 12 | A | B | C | D |
| **27.** | 2600 W. Lansing Parkway | A | B | C | D |
| **28.** | 37000 E. Lansing Parkway | A | B | C | D |
| **29.** | 1860 W. Lansing Parkway | A | B | C | D |
| **30.** | 84999 E. Lansing Parkway | A | B | C | D |
| **31.** | 27 W. Lansing Parkway | A | B | C | D |
| **32.** | 1044 W. Lansing Parkway | A | B | C | D |
| **33.** | 2100 E. Archway Drive | A | B | C | D |
| **34.** | 70 Country Route 12 | A | B | C | D |
| **35.** | 150 2nd Avenue | A | B | C | D |
| **36.** | 185 Country Route 12 | A | B | C | D |

## Memory Section: Segment 1

**3 MINUTES**

> **Directions:** Take 3 minutes to memorize the Coding Guide on page 241.
> - You may NOT write down any addresses during the memorization period.

practice test

## Memory Section: Segment 2

**8 QUESTIONS • 1.5 MINUTES (90 SECONDS)**

**Directions:** Segment 2 is *not* scored and does not count toward your total exam score. It is an exercise to help you practice coding addresses from memory under a time constraint similar to the one used in the scored Memory Section of the actual exam. You will *not* see the Coding Guide during this segment of the exam. Based on your memory of the Coding Guide, match each address to a delivery route. Mark your answers on the answer section at the bottom of this page.

| Address | Delivery Route | | | |
|---|---|---|---|---|
| 1. 44000 E. Lansing Parkway | A | B | C | D |
| 2. 2500 E. Lansing Parkway | A | B | C | D |
| 3. 75000 E. Lansing Parkway | A | B | C | D |
| 4. 20 S. Archer Drive | A | B | C | D |
| 5. 200 W. Lansing Parkway | A | B | C | D |
| 6. 48 S. Archer Drive | A | B | C | D |
| 7. 220 Country Route 12 | A | B | C | D |
| 8. 1432 W. Lansing Parkway | A | B | C | D |

## Sample Answer Sheet

1. Ⓐ Ⓑ Ⓒ Ⓓ      4. Ⓐ Ⓑ Ⓒ Ⓓ      7. Ⓐ Ⓑ Ⓒ Ⓓ
2. Ⓐ Ⓑ Ⓒ Ⓓ      5. Ⓐ Ⓑ Ⓒ Ⓓ      8. Ⓐ Ⓑ Ⓒ Ⓓ
3. Ⓐ Ⓑ Ⓒ Ⓓ      6. Ⓐ Ⓑ Ⓒ Ⓓ

## Memory Section: Segment 3

**5 MINUTES**

**Directions:** Take 5 minutes to memorize the Coding Guide on page 241.
- You may NOT write down any addresses during the memorization period.

practice test

## Memory Section: Segment 4

**36 QUESTIONS • 7 MINUTES**

**Directions:** This is the actual *scored* Memory Section of the exam. Take 3 minutes to memorize the Coding Guide on page 241. Work through items 1 through 36, assigning a code based on your memory of the Coding Guide. Mark your answers on the answer sheet. Work quickly and accurately.

- You may NOT write down any addresses during the memorization period.
- You may NOT look at the codes when answering the items.

| Address | | Delivery Route | | | |
|---|---|---|---|---|---|
| 1. | 35000 E. Lansing Parkway | A | B | C | D |
| 2. | 84 2nd Avenue | A | B | C | D |
| 3. | 5900 E. Archway Drive | A | B | C | D |
| 4. | 140 Country Route 12 | A | B | C | D |
| 5. | 127000 E. Archway Drive | A | B | C | D |
| 6. | 1360 W. Lansing Parkway | A | B | C | D |
| 7. | 29 S. Archer Drive | A | B | C | D |
| 8. | 170 2nd Avenue | A | B | C | D |
| 9. | 3360 E. Archway Drive | A | B | C | D |
| 10. | 750 W. Lansing Parkway | A | B | C | D |
| 11. | 170 2nd Avenue | A | B | C | D |
| 12. | 59 S. Archer Drive | A | B | C | D |
| 13. | 64000 E. Lansing Parkway | A | B | C | D |
| 14. | 126 2nd Avenue | A | B | C | D |
| 15. | 5500 E. Archway Drive | A | B | C | D |
| 16. | 95 S. Archer Drive | A | B | C | D |
| 17. | 55 S. Archer Drive | A | B | C | D |
| 18. | 175 Country Route 12 | A | B | C | D |
| 19. | 26 S. Archer Drive | A | B | C | D |
| 20. | 1100 E. Archway Drive | A | B | C | D |
| 21. | 304 W. Lansing Parkway | A | B | C | D |
| 22. | 100 2nd Avenue | A | B | C | D |
| 23. | 52000 E. Lansing Parkway | A | B | C | D |
| 24. | 2340 E. Archway Drive | A | B | C | D |

| 25. | 128 Country Route 12 | A | B | C | D |
|-----|----------------------|---|---|---|---|
| 26. | 8500 E. Lansing Parkway | A | B | C | D |
| 27. | 250 2nd Avenue | A | B | C | D |
| 28. | 25250 E. Lansing Parkway | A | B | C | D |
| 29. | 70 S. Archer Drive | A | B | C | D |
| 30. | 1270 W. Lansing Parkway | A | B | C | D |
| 31. | 27 S. Archer Drive | A | B | C | D |
| 32. | 1450 E. Archway Drive | A | B | C | D |
| 33. | 30 Country Route 12 | A | B | C | D |
| 34. | 58080 E. Lansing Parkway | A | B | C | D |
| 35. | 39 S. Archer Drive | A | B | C | D |
| 36. | 138 2nd Avenue | A | B | C | D |

practice test

# ANSWER KEY AND EXPLANATIONS

## Part A: Address Checking

| | | | | |
|---|---|---|---|---|
| 1. B | 13. A | 25. B | 37. D | 49. B |
| 2. C | 14. D | 26. C | 38. A | 50. D |
| 3. D | 15. B | 27. A | 39. B | 51. A |
| 4. A | 16. C | 28. D | 40. C | 52. C |
| 5. B | 17. D | 29. B | 41. B | 53. B |
| 6. C | 18. A | 30. C | 42. D | 54. D |
| 7. D | 19. C | 31. D | 43. A | 55. A |
| 8. A | 20. A | 32. C | 44. D | 56. B |
| 9. A | 21. B | 33. A | 45. B | 57. C |
| 10. D | 22. A | 34. B | 46. C | 58. A |
| 11. C | 23. D | 35. D | 47. A | 59. B |
| 12. C | 24. C | 36. B | 48. D | 60. C |

## Part B: Forms Completion

| | | | | |
|---|---|---|---|---|
| 1. D | 7. B | 13. C | 19. C | 25. B |
| 2. A | 8. B | 14. D | 20. D | 26. C |
| 3. D | 9. D | 15. B | 21. C | 27. A |
| 4. C | 10. A | 16. A | 22. C | 28. A |
| 5. A | 11. C | 17. D | 23. A | 29. B |
| 6. A | 12. D | 18. B | 24. A | 30. C |

1. **The correct answer is (D).** Box 6 requires an endorsement. Therefore, the correct answer is (D), Box 6.

2. **The correct answer is (A).** Box 4 is labeled "Restricted Delivery Fee." Therefore, the correct answer is (A), Box 4.

3. **The correct answer is (D).** Box 3b does not contain a check box. Therefore, the correct answer is (D), Box 3b.

4. **The correct answer is (C).** Box 8 is labeled "Postmark Here." Therefore, the correct answer is (C), Box 8.

5. **The correct answer is (A).** Box 3a is labeled "Insurance Fee." Therefore, the correct answer is (A), $15.00.

6. **The correct answer is (A).** Box 1 is marked "Customer Name." Therefore, the correct answer is (A), Box 1.

7. **The correct answer is (B).** Box 5 requires a city. Therefore, the correct answer is (B), Cincinnati.

8. **The correct answer is (B).** Box 8b contains a blank for the Express Mail Corporate Account Number or the Federal Agency Number. Therefore, the correct answer is (B), Box 8b.

9. **The correct answer is (D).** Box 11 is labeled "USPS Signature." Therefore, the correct answer is (D), Box 11.

10. **The correct answer is (A).** Box 1 is labeled "Postage." Therefore, the correct answer is (A), Box 1.

11. **The correct answer is (C).** Box 4 is labeled "Total Postage & Fees." Therefore, the correct answer is (C), 29.50.

12. **The correct answer is (D).** Box 6 requires the recipient's name. Therefore, the correct answer is (D), 6.

13. **The correct answer is (C).** Box 7 is labeled "Street, Apt. No.; or PO Box No." Therefore, the correct answer is (C), Box 7.

14. **The correct answer is (D).** Box 8 is labeled "Street, Apt. No.; or PO Box No." Therefore, the correct answer is (D), Box 8.

15. **The correct answer is (B).** Box 9 is labeled "City, State, ZIP + 4." Therefore, the correct answer is (B), Portland, OR 97214–3320.

16. **The correct answer is (A).** Box 2 requires a Certified Fee amount. Therefore, the correct answer is (A), $18.00.

17. **The correct answer is (D).** Box 7 requires the name of the addressee. Therefore, the correct answer is (D), Box 7.

18. **The correct answer is (B).** Box 12 requires the date that Form 3849-D was sent. Therefore, the correct answer is (B), 9/3/08.

19. **The correct answer is (C).** Box 4 is labeled "Cash Amount." Therefore, the correct answer is (C), 22.80.

20. **The correct answer is (D).** Box 6 requires the sender's name and address. Therefore, the correct answer is (D), Box 6.

21. **The correct answer is (C).** Box 2b requires a check mark. Therefore, the correct answer is (C), A check mark.

22. **The correct answer is (C).** Box 8 is labeled "Delivered By." Therefore, the correct answer is (C), Box 8.

23. **The correct answer is (A).** Box 18 requires an employee signature. Therefore, the correct answer is (A), A signature.

24. **The correct answer is (A).** Box 16 requires a month and a day. Therefore, the correct answer is (A), Box 16.

25. **The correct answer is (B).** Box 7a is labeled "Time Accepted AM." Therefore, the correct answer is (B), Box 7a.

26. **The correct answer is (C).** Box 15 requires employee initials. Therefore, the correct answer is (C), R.F.

27. **The correct answer is (A).** Box 2a is marked "Next Day Delivery." Therefore, the correct answer is (A), Box 2a.

28. **The correct answer is (A).** Box 1 is labeled "PO ZIP Code." Therefore, the correct answer is (A), Box 1.

29. **The correct answer is (B).** Box 11b is labeled "Military 3rd Day." Therefore, the correct answer is (B), Box 11b.

30. **The correct answer is (C).** Box 6 requires the return receipt fee. Therefore, the correct answer is (C), 17.00.

## Part C: Coding and Memory

### CODING SECTION: SEGMENT 1

1. B    2. C    3. D    4. A

### CODING SECTION: SEGMENT 2

1. C    3. D    5. A    7. D    8. B
2. A    4. B    6. C

## CODING SECTION: SEGMENT 3

| | | | | | | | | | |
|---|---|---|---|---|---|---|---|---|---|
| 1. B | | 9. D | | 16. B | | 23. B | | 30. C | |
| 2. D | | 10. A | | 17. C | | 24. D | | 31. D | |
| 3. C | | 11. C | | 18. D | | 25. A | | 32. A | |
| 4. A | | 12. B | | 19. B | | 26. C | | 33. A | |
| 5. B | | 13. D | | 20. C | | 27. D | | 34. C | |
| 6. C | | 14. A | | 21. D | | 28. B | | 35. B | |
| 7. A | | 15. C | | 22. A | | 29. A | | 36. D | |
| 8. D | | | | | | | | | |

1. **The correct answer is (B).** The address 49000 E. Lansing Parkway falls in one of the address ranges in the same row as Delivery Route B.

2. **The correct answer is (D).** The address 2000 W. Lansing Parkway does not fall into any of the address ranges for Delivery Routes A, B, or C.

3. **The correct answer is (C).** The address 69000 E. Lansing Parkway falls in one of the address ranges in the same row as Delivery Route C.

4. **The correct answer is (A).** The address 4600 E. Archway Drive falls in one of the address ranges in the same row as Delivery Route A.

5. **The correct answer is (B).** The address 93 2nd Avenue falls in one of the address ranges in the same row as Delivery Route B.

6. **The correct answer is (C).** The address 14 S. Archer Drive falls in one of the address ranges in the same row as Delivery Route C.

7. **The correct answer is (A).** The address 577 W. Lansing Parkway falls in one of the address ranges in the same row as Delivery Route A.

8. **The correct answer is (D).** The address 17 Country Route 12 does not fall into any of the address ranges for Delivery Routes A, B, or C.

9. **The correct answer is (D).** The address 79 2nd Avenue does not fall into any of the address ranges for Delivery Routes A, B, or C

10. **The correct answer is (A).** The address 2780 E. Archway Drive falls in one of the address ranges in the same row as Delivery Route A.

11. **The correct answer is (C).** The address 153 Country Route 12 falls in one of the address ranges in the same row as Delivery Route C.

12. **The correct answer is (B).** The address 43000 E. Lansing Parkway falls in one of the address ranges in the same row as Delivery Route B.

13. **The correct answer is (D).** The address 6050 E. Archway Drive does not fall into any of the address ranges for Delivery Routes A, B, or C.

14. **The correct answer is (A).** The address 1623 W. Lansing Parkway falls in one of the address ranges in the same row as Delivery Route A.

15. **The correct answer is (C).** The address 47 Country Route 12 falls in one of the address ranges in the same row as Delivery Route C.

16. **The correct answer is (B).** The address 40 S. Archer Drive falls in one of the address ranges in the same row as Delivery Route B.

17. **The correct answer is (C).** The address 57000 E. Lansing Parkway falls in one of the address ranges in the same row as Delivery Route C.

18. **The correct answer is (D).** The address 16000 E. Lansing Parkway does not fall into any of the address ranges for Delivery Routes A, B, or C.

19. **The correct answer is (B).** The address 111 2nd Avenue falls in one of the address ranges in the same row as Delivery Route B.

20. **The correct answer is (C).** The address 11 S. Archer Drive falls in one of the address ranges in the same row as Delivery Route C.

21. **The correct answer is (D).** The address 97000 E. Lansing Parkway does not fall into any of the address ranges for Delivery Routes A, B, or C.

22. **The correct answer is (A).** The address 4000 E. Archway Drive falls in one of the address ranges in the same row as Delivery Route A.

23. **The correct answer is (B).** The address 37 S. Archer Drive falls in one of the address ranges in the same row as Delivery Route B.

24. **The correct answer is (D).** The address 7 S. Archer Drive does not fall into any of the address ranges for Delivery Routes A, B, or C

25. **The correct answer is (A).** The address 997 W. Lansing Parkway falls in one of the address ranges in the same row as Delivery Route A.

26. **The correct answer is (C).** The address 59 Country Route 12 falls in one of the address ranges in the same row as Delivery Route C.

27. **The correct answer is (D).** The address 2600 W. Lansing Parkway does not fall into any of the address ranges for Delivery Routes A, B, or C.

28. **The correct answer is (B).** The address 37000 E. Lansing Parkway falls in one of the address ranges in the same row as Delivery Route B.

29. **The correct answer is (A).** The address 1860 W. Lansing Parkway falls in one of the address ranges in the same row as Delivery Route A.

30. **The correct answer is (C).** The address 84999 E. Lansing Parkway falls in one of the address ranges in the same row as Delivery Route C.

31. **The correct answer is (D).** The address 27 W. Lansing Parkway does not fall into any of the address ranges for Delivery Routes A, B, or C.

32. **The correct answer is (A).** The address 1044 W. Lansing Parkway falls in one of the address ranges in the same row as Delivery Route A.

33. **The correct answer is (A).** The address 2100 E. Archway Drive falls in one of the address ranges in the same row as Delivery Route A.

34. **The correct answer is (C).** The address 70 Country Route 12 falls in one of the address ranges in the same row as Delivery Route C.

35. **The correct answer is (B).** The address 150 2nd Avenue falls in one of the address ranges in the same row as Delivery Route B.

36. **The correct answer is (D).** The address 185 Country Route 12 does not fall into any of the address ranges for Delivery Routes A, B, or C.

## MEMORY SECTION: SEGMENT 2

| | | | | |
|---|---|---|---|---|
| 1. B | 3. C | 5. A | 7. D | 8. A |
| 2. D | 4. C | 6. B | | |

## MEMORY SECTION: SEGMENT 4

| | | | | |
|---|---|---|---|---|
| 1. B | 9. A | 16. D | 23. C | 30. A |
| 2. B | 10. A | 17. B | 24. A | 31. C |
| 3. A | 11. D | 18. C | 25. C | 32. A |
| 4. C | 12. B | 19. C | 26. D | 33. D |
| 5. D | 13. C | 20. D | 27. D | 34. C |
| 6. A | 14. B | 21. A | 28. B | 35. B |
| 7. C | 15. A | 22. B | 29. D | 36. B |
| 8. D | | | | |

1. **The correct answer is (B).** The address 35000 E. Lansing Parkway falls in one of the address ranges in the same row as Delivery Route B.

2. **The correct answer is (B).** The address 84 2nd Avenue falls in one of the address ranges in the same row as Delivery Route B.

3. **The correct answer is (A).** The address 5900 E. Archway Drive falls in one of the address ranges in the same row as Delivery Route A.

4. **The correct answer is (C).** The address 140 Country Route 12 falls in one of the address ranges in the same row as Delivery Route C.

5. **The correct answer is (D).** The address 127000 E. Archway Drive does not fall into any of the address ranges for Delivery Routes A, B, or C.

6. **The correct answer is (A).** The address 1360 W. Lansing Parkway falls in one of the address ranges in the same row as Delivery Route A.

7. **The correct answer is (C).** The address 29 S. Archer Drive falls in one of the address ranges in the same row as Delivery Route C.

8. **The correct answer is (D).** The address 170 2nd Avenue does not fall into any of the address ranges for Delivery Routes A, B, or C.

9. **The correct answer is (A).** The address 3360 E. Archway Drive falls in one of the address ranges in the same row as Delivery Route A.

10. **The correct answer is (A).** The address 750 W. Lansing Parkway falls in one of the address ranges in the same row as Delivery Route A.

11. **The correct answer is (D).** The address 170 2nd Avenue does not fall into any of the address ranges for Delivery Routes A, B, or C.

12. **The correct answer is (B).** The address 59 S. Archer Drive falls in one of the address ranges in the same row as Delivery Route B.

13. **The correct answer is (C).** The address 64000 E. Lansing Parkway falls in one of the address ranges in the same row as Delivery Route C.

14. **The correct answer is (B).** The address 126 2nd Avenue falls in one of the address ranges in the same row as Delivery Route B.

15. **The correct answer is (A).** The address 5500 E. Archway Drive falls in one of the address ranges in the same row as Delivery Route A.

16. **The correct answer is (D).** The address 95 S. Archer Drive does not fall into any of the address ranges for Delivery Routes A, B, or C.

17. **The correct answer is (B).** The address 55 S. Archer Drive falls in one of the address ranges in the same row as Delivery Route B.

18. **The correct answer is (C).** The address 175 Country Route 12 falls in one of the address ranges in the same row as Delivery Route C.

19. **The correct answer is (C).** The address 26 S. Archer Drive falls in one of the address ranges in the same row as Delivery Route C.

20. **The correct answer is (D).** The address 1100 E. Archway Drive does not fall into any of the address ranges for Delivery Routes A, B, or C.

21. **The correct answer is (A).** The address 304 W. Lansing Parkway falls in one of the address ranges in the same row as Delivery Route A.

22. **The correct answer is (B).** The address 100 2nd Avenue falls in one of the address ranges in the same row as Delivery Route B.

23. **The correct answer is (C).** The address 52000 E. Lansing Parkway falls in one of the address ranges in the same row as Delivery Route C.

24. **The correct answer is (A).** The address 2340 E. Archway Drive falls in one of the address ranges in the same row as Delivery Route A.

25. **The correct answer is (C).** The address 128 Country Route 12 falls in one of the address ranges in the same row as Delivery Route C.

26. **The correct answer is (D).** The address 8500 E. Lansing Parkway does not fall into any of the address ranges for Delivery Routes A, B, or C.

27. **The correct answer is (D).** The address 250 2nd Avenue does not fall into any of the address ranges for Delivery Routes A, B, or C.

28. **The correct answer is (B).** The address 25250 E. Lansing Parkway falls in one of the address ranges in the same row as Delivery Route B.

29. **The correct answer is (D).** The address 70 S. Archer Drive does not fall into any of the address ranges for Delivery Routes A, B, or C.

30. **The correct answer is (A).** The address 1270 W. Lansing Parkway falls in one of the address ranges in the same row as Delivery Route A.

31. **The correct answer is (C).** The address 27 S. Archer Drive falls in one of the address ranges in the same row as Delivery Route C.

32. **The correct answer is (A).** The address 1450 E. Archway Drive falls in one of the address ranges in the same row as Delivery Route A.

33. **The correct answer is (D).** The address 30 Country Route 12 does not fall into any of the address ranges for Delivery Routes A, B, or C.

34. **The correct answer is (C).** The address 58080 E. Lansing Parkway falls in one of the address ranges in the same row as Delivery Route C.

35. **The correct answer is (B).** The address 39 S. Archer Drive falls in one of the address ranges in the same row as Delivery Route B.

36. **The correct answer is (B).** The address 138 2nd Avenue falls in one of the address ranges in the same row as Delivery Route B.

**answers practice test 4**

# PRACTICE TEST 5: EXAMS 473/473-C AND 460

## Part A: Address Checking

| | | | | |
|---|---|---|---|---|
| 1. Ⓐ Ⓑ Ⓒ Ⓓ | 13. Ⓐ Ⓑ Ⓒ Ⓓ | 25. Ⓐ Ⓑ Ⓒ Ⓓ | 37. Ⓐ Ⓑ Ⓒ Ⓓ | 49. Ⓐ Ⓑ Ⓒ Ⓓ |
| 2. Ⓐ Ⓑ Ⓒ Ⓓ | 14. Ⓐ Ⓑ Ⓒ Ⓓ | 26. Ⓐ Ⓑ Ⓒ Ⓓ | 38. Ⓐ Ⓑ Ⓒ Ⓓ | 50. Ⓐ Ⓑ Ⓒ Ⓓ |
| 3. Ⓐ Ⓑ Ⓒ Ⓓ | 15. Ⓐ Ⓑ Ⓒ Ⓓ | 27. Ⓐ Ⓑ Ⓒ Ⓓ | 39. Ⓐ Ⓑ Ⓒ Ⓓ | 51. Ⓐ Ⓑ Ⓒ Ⓓ |
| 4. Ⓐ Ⓑ Ⓒ Ⓓ | 16. Ⓐ Ⓑ Ⓒ Ⓓ | 28. Ⓐ Ⓑ Ⓒ Ⓓ | 40. Ⓐ Ⓑ Ⓒ Ⓓ | 52. Ⓐ Ⓑ Ⓒ Ⓓ |
| 5. Ⓐ Ⓑ Ⓒ Ⓓ | 17. Ⓐ Ⓑ Ⓒ Ⓓ | 29. Ⓐ Ⓑ Ⓒ Ⓓ | 41. Ⓐ Ⓑ Ⓒ Ⓓ | 53. Ⓐ Ⓑ Ⓒ Ⓓ |
| 6. Ⓐ Ⓑ Ⓒ Ⓓ | 18. Ⓐ Ⓑ Ⓒ Ⓓ | 30. Ⓐ Ⓑ Ⓒ Ⓓ | 42. Ⓐ Ⓑ Ⓒ Ⓓ | 54. Ⓐ Ⓑ Ⓒ Ⓓ |
| 7. Ⓐ Ⓑ Ⓒ Ⓓ | 19. Ⓐ Ⓑ Ⓒ Ⓓ | 31. Ⓐ Ⓑ Ⓒ Ⓓ | 43. Ⓐ Ⓑ Ⓒ Ⓓ | 55. Ⓐ Ⓑ Ⓒ Ⓓ |
| 8. Ⓐ Ⓑ Ⓒ Ⓓ | 20. Ⓐ Ⓑ Ⓒ Ⓓ | 32. Ⓐ Ⓑ Ⓒ Ⓓ | 44. Ⓐ Ⓑ Ⓒ Ⓓ | 56. Ⓐ Ⓑ Ⓒ Ⓓ |
| 9. Ⓐ Ⓑ Ⓒ Ⓓ | 21. Ⓐ Ⓑ Ⓒ Ⓓ | 33. Ⓐ Ⓑ Ⓒ Ⓓ | 45. Ⓐ Ⓑ Ⓒ Ⓓ | 57. Ⓐ Ⓑ Ⓒ Ⓓ |
| 10. Ⓐ Ⓑ Ⓒ Ⓓ | 22. Ⓐ Ⓑ Ⓒ Ⓓ | 34. Ⓐ Ⓑ Ⓒ Ⓓ | 46. Ⓐ Ⓑ Ⓒ Ⓓ | 58. Ⓐ Ⓑ Ⓒ Ⓓ |
| 11. Ⓐ Ⓑ Ⓒ Ⓓ | 23. Ⓐ Ⓑ Ⓒ Ⓓ | 35. Ⓐ Ⓑ Ⓒ Ⓓ | 47. Ⓐ Ⓑ Ⓒ Ⓓ | 59. Ⓐ Ⓑ Ⓒ Ⓓ |
| 12. Ⓐ Ⓑ Ⓒ Ⓓ | 24. Ⓐ Ⓑ Ⓒ Ⓓ | 36. Ⓐ Ⓑ Ⓒ Ⓓ | 48. Ⓐ Ⓑ Ⓒ Ⓓ | 60. Ⓐ Ⓑ Ⓒ Ⓓ |

## Part B: Forms Completion

| | | | | |
|---|---|---|---|---|
| 1. Ⓐ Ⓑ Ⓒ Ⓓ | 7. Ⓐ Ⓑ Ⓒ Ⓓ | 13. Ⓐ Ⓑ Ⓒ Ⓓ | 19. Ⓐ Ⓑ Ⓒ Ⓓ | 25. Ⓐ Ⓑ Ⓒ Ⓓ |
| 2. Ⓐ Ⓑ Ⓒ Ⓓ | 8. Ⓐ Ⓑ Ⓒ Ⓓ | 14. Ⓐ Ⓑ Ⓒ Ⓓ | 20. Ⓐ Ⓑ Ⓒ Ⓓ | 26. Ⓐ Ⓑ Ⓒ Ⓓ |
| 3. Ⓐ Ⓑ Ⓒ Ⓓ | 9. Ⓐ Ⓑ Ⓒ Ⓓ | 15. Ⓐ Ⓑ Ⓒ Ⓓ | 21. Ⓐ Ⓑ Ⓒ Ⓓ | 27. Ⓐ Ⓑ Ⓒ Ⓓ |
| 4. Ⓐ Ⓑ Ⓒ Ⓓ | 10. Ⓐ Ⓑ Ⓒ Ⓓ | 16. Ⓐ Ⓑ Ⓒ Ⓓ | 22. Ⓐ Ⓑ Ⓒ Ⓓ | 28. Ⓐ Ⓑ Ⓒ Ⓓ |
| 5. Ⓐ Ⓑ Ⓒ Ⓓ | 11. Ⓐ Ⓑ Ⓒ Ⓓ | 17. Ⓐ Ⓑ Ⓒ Ⓓ | 23. Ⓐ Ⓑ Ⓒ Ⓓ | 29. Ⓐ Ⓑ Ⓒ Ⓓ |
| 6. Ⓐ Ⓑ Ⓒ Ⓓ | 12. Ⓐ Ⓑ Ⓒ Ⓓ | 18. Ⓐ Ⓑ Ⓒ Ⓓ | 24. Ⓐ Ⓑ Ⓒ Ⓓ | 30. Ⓐ Ⓑ Ⓒ Ⓓ |

## Part C: Coding and Memory

### CODING SECTION: SEGMENT 3

| | | | | |
|---|---|---|---|---|
| 1. Ⓐ Ⓑ Ⓒ Ⓓ | 9. Ⓐ Ⓑ Ⓒ Ⓓ | 16. Ⓐ Ⓑ Ⓒ Ⓓ | 23. Ⓐ Ⓑ Ⓒ Ⓓ | 30. Ⓐ Ⓑ Ⓒ Ⓓ |
| 2. Ⓐ Ⓑ Ⓒ Ⓓ | 10. Ⓐ Ⓑ Ⓒ Ⓓ | 17. Ⓐ Ⓑ Ⓒ Ⓓ | 24. Ⓐ Ⓑ Ⓒ Ⓓ | 31. Ⓐ Ⓑ Ⓒ Ⓓ |
| 3. Ⓐ Ⓑ Ⓒ Ⓓ | 11. Ⓐ Ⓑ Ⓒ Ⓓ | 18. Ⓐ Ⓑ Ⓒ Ⓓ | 25. Ⓐ Ⓑ Ⓒ Ⓓ | 32. Ⓐ Ⓑ Ⓒ Ⓓ |
| 4. Ⓐ Ⓑ Ⓒ Ⓓ | 12. Ⓐ Ⓑ Ⓒ Ⓓ | 19. Ⓐ Ⓑ Ⓒ Ⓓ | 26. Ⓐ Ⓑ Ⓒ Ⓓ | 33. Ⓐ Ⓑ Ⓒ Ⓓ |
| 5. Ⓐ Ⓑ Ⓒ Ⓓ | 13. Ⓐ Ⓑ Ⓒ Ⓓ | 20. Ⓐ Ⓑ Ⓒ Ⓓ | 27. Ⓐ Ⓑ Ⓒ Ⓓ | 34. Ⓐ Ⓑ Ⓒ Ⓓ |
| 6. Ⓐ Ⓑ Ⓒ Ⓓ | 14. Ⓐ Ⓑ Ⓒ Ⓓ | 21. Ⓐ Ⓑ Ⓒ Ⓓ | 28. Ⓐ Ⓑ Ⓒ Ⓓ | 35. Ⓐ Ⓑ Ⓒ Ⓓ |
| 7. Ⓐ Ⓑ Ⓒ Ⓓ | 15. Ⓐ Ⓑ Ⓒ Ⓓ | 22. Ⓐ Ⓑ Ⓒ Ⓓ | 29. Ⓐ Ⓑ Ⓒ Ⓓ | 36. Ⓐ Ⓑ Ⓒ Ⓓ |
| 8. Ⓐ Ⓑ Ⓒ Ⓓ | | | | |

### MEMORY SECTION: SEGMENT 4

| | | | | |
|---|---|---|---|---|
| 1. Ⓐ Ⓑ Ⓒ Ⓓ | 9. Ⓐ Ⓑ Ⓒ Ⓓ | 16. Ⓐ Ⓑ Ⓒ Ⓓ | 23. Ⓐ Ⓑ Ⓒ Ⓓ | 30. Ⓐ Ⓑ Ⓒ Ⓓ |
| 2. Ⓐ Ⓑ Ⓒ Ⓓ | 10. Ⓐ Ⓑ Ⓒ Ⓓ | 17. Ⓐ Ⓑ Ⓒ Ⓓ | 24. Ⓐ Ⓑ Ⓒ Ⓓ | 31. Ⓐ Ⓑ Ⓒ Ⓓ |
| 3. Ⓐ Ⓑ Ⓒ Ⓓ | 11. Ⓐ Ⓑ Ⓒ Ⓓ | 18. Ⓐ Ⓑ Ⓒ Ⓓ | 25. Ⓐ Ⓑ Ⓒ Ⓓ | 32. Ⓐ Ⓑ Ⓒ Ⓓ |
| 4. Ⓐ Ⓑ Ⓒ Ⓓ | 12. Ⓐ Ⓑ Ⓒ Ⓓ | 19. Ⓐ Ⓑ Ⓒ Ⓓ | 26. Ⓐ Ⓑ Ⓒ Ⓓ | 33. Ⓐ Ⓑ Ⓒ Ⓓ |
| 5. Ⓐ Ⓑ Ⓒ Ⓓ | 13. Ⓐ Ⓑ Ⓒ Ⓓ | 20. Ⓐ Ⓑ Ⓒ Ⓓ | 27. Ⓐ Ⓑ Ⓒ Ⓓ | 34. Ⓐ Ⓑ Ⓒ Ⓓ |
| 6. Ⓐ Ⓑ Ⓒ Ⓓ | 14. Ⓐ Ⓑ Ⓒ Ⓓ | 21. Ⓐ Ⓑ Ⓒ Ⓓ | 28. Ⓐ Ⓑ Ⓒ Ⓓ | 35. Ⓐ Ⓑ Ⓒ Ⓓ |
| 7. Ⓐ Ⓑ Ⓒ Ⓓ | 15. Ⓐ Ⓑ Ⓒ Ⓓ | 22. Ⓐ Ⓑ Ⓒ Ⓓ | 29. Ⓐ Ⓑ Ⓒ Ⓓ | 36. Ⓐ Ⓑ Ⓒ Ⓓ |
| 8. Ⓐ Ⓑ Ⓒ Ⓓ | | | | |

*answer sheet*

# Practice Test 5: Exams 473/473-C and 460

**NOTE:** Practice Tests 1–5 are a combination of the types of questions test-takers will see on Exam 473 and Exam 460.

Exam 473 consists of four parts:

A.  Address Checking
B.  Forms Completion
C.  Coding and Memory
D.  Personal Characteristics and Experience Inventory

Exam 460 consists of four parts:

A.  Address Checking
B.  Memory for Addresses
C.  Number Series
D.  Following Oral Instructions

If you are practicing to take Exam 460, you may want to follow these tips:

* Skip Part B (Forms Completion) of Practice Tests 1 through 5. This material will not be included on your actual exam; it is only on Exam 473.

* Skip Part D (Personal Characteristics and Experience Inventory) of Practice Test 1. This material will not be included on your actual exam; it is only on Exam 473.

* To practice for Part D of Exam 460 (Following Oral Instructions), take Practice Test 7 in this book.

practice test 5

## PART A: ADDRESS CHECKING

**60 QUESTIONS • 11 MINUTES**

**Directions:** Compare the **List to be Checked** with the **Correct List.** Decide if there are **(A) NO ERRORS,** an error in the **(B) ADDRESS ONLY,** an error in the **(C) ZIP CODE ONLY,** or an error in **(D) BOTH** the address and ZIP Code. Record your answers on the answer sheet.

| Correct List | | List to be Checked | |
|---|---|---|---|
| *Address* | *ZIP Code* | *Address* | *ZIP Code* |
| **1.** 580 Stockton Drive<br>Stanford, KY | 40484 | 580 Stockton Drive<br>Stanford, KY | 40884 |
| **2.** 4300 11th Avenue<br>Shreveport, LA | 71107-1838 | 4300 11th Avenue<br>Shreveport, LA | 71107-1838 |
| **3.** 76 S. Chesterfield Ct.<br>Glade Hill, VA | 24092 | 76 N. Chesterfield Ct.<br>Glade Hill, VA | 24092 |
| **4.** 231 E. Bristol Blvd.<br>Nixa, MO | 65714 | 231 N. Bristol Blvd.<br>Nixa, MO | 67514 |
| **5.** 5592 Somerset Road<br>Denton, TX | 76210 | 5592 Somerset Road<br>Denton, TX | 72610 |
| **6.** 770 Ashton Place<br>Wallula, WA | 99363 | 770 Ashton Place<br>Wallula, WA | 99363 |
| **7.** 2504 Fitzsimmons Ter<br>Saint Louis, MI | 48880 | 2540 Fitzsimmons Ter<br>Saint Louis, MI | 48880 |
| **8.** 1919 Old Alabama Dr.<br>Little Rock, AR | 72201-1531 | 1919 Old Alabama Dr.<br>Little Rock, AL | 72221-1531 |
| **9.** 576 Wilmington Lane<br>Cottage Grove, OR | 97424 | 576 Wilmington Lane<br>Cottage Grove, OR | 97224 |
| **10.** 330 Beach Bluffs Hwy<br>Myersville, MD | 21773 | 330 Beach Bluffs Hwy<br>Meyersville, MD | 21733 |
| **11.** 8765 14th Street<br>Petersham, MA | 01366 | 8765 14th Street<br>Petersham, MS | 01366 |
| **12.** 622 S. Brigham Pkwy.<br>Chicago, Illinois | 60605 | 622 S. Brigham Pkwy.<br>Chicago, Illinois | 60605 |

**Directions:** Compare the **List to be Checked** with the **Correct List.** Decide if there are **(A) NO ERRORS,** an error in the **(B) ADDRESS ONLY,** an error in the **(C) ZIP CODE ONLY,** or an error in **(D) BOTH** the address and ZIP Code. Record your answers on the answer sheet.

| | | | | |
|---|---|---|---|---|
| **13.** 21 Aztec Circle<br>Bellingham, WA | 98225-2841 | 21 Aztec Circle<br>Bellingham, WA | 98225-2481 | |
| **14.** 3400 Silver Thorne Ct.<br>Pacific Junction, IA | 51561 | 3400 Silverton Ct.<br>Pacific Junction, IA | 51561 | |
| **15.** 88 E. Landreth Place<br>Ruso, ND | 58778 | 88 E. Landreth Place<br>Ruso, ND | 58778 | |
| **16.** 513 Eagle Heights Dr<br>Castleford, ID | 83321 | 513 Eagle Cliffs Dr<br>Castleford, ID | 80321 | |
| **17.** 400 Bluebird Terrace<br>Forest Lakes, AZ | 85931 | 400 Bluebird Terrace<br>Forest Lakes, AZ | 85933 | |
| **18.** P.O. Box 225<br>Farmington, NM | 87401-6276 | P.O. Box 225<br>Farmington, NM | 87410-6276 | |
| **19.** 850 Chippewa Trail<br>Huntington, VT | 05462 | 850 Chippewa Trail<br>Huntington, VT | 05462 | |
| **20.** 2903 Huntington Drive<br>Coatesville, PA | 19320 | 2930 Huntington Drive<br>Coatesville, PA | 19322 | |
| **21.** 6000 Stardust Lane<br>Dos Palos, CA | 93620 | 6000 Stardust Lane<br>Los Palos, CA | 93620 | |
| **22.** 1070 N. Cable Lane<br>Garryowen, MT | 59031 | 1070 N. Cable Lane<br>Garryowen, MT | 59331 | |
| **23.** 344 Eliza Boulevard<br>Homer, Alaska | 99603-7847 | 344 Eliza Boulevard<br>Homer, Alaska | 99603-7847 | |
| **24.** 7022 W. Crane Rd.<br>Utica, Ohio | 43080 | 7022 W. Crane Rd.<br>Utica, Iowa | 43080 | |
| **25.** 940 Pirate's Cove Trail<br>Memphis, TN | 38118 | 940 Pirate's Cove Trail<br>Memphis, TN | 31818 | |
| **26.** 86 Lexington Parkway<br>Los Angeles, CA | 90029-3000 | 68 Lexington Parkway<br>Los Angeles, CA | 90029-3000 | |
| **27.** 5025 Hickory Avenue<br>Price, UT | 84501 | 5025 Hickory Avenue<br>Price, UT | 84501 | |

**Directions:** Compare the **List to be Checked** with the **Correct List.** Decide if there are **(A) NO ERRORS,** an error in the **(B) ADDRESS ONLY,** an error in the **(C) ZIP CODE ONLY,** or an error in **(D) BOTH** the address and ZIP Code. Record your answers on the answer sheet.

| | | | | |
|---|---|---|---|---|
| **28.** 30 Preston Terrace<br>Eustis, FL | 32736 | 30 Preston Terrace<br>Euclid, FL | 32376 | |
| **29.** 4757 S. Turnbull Road<br>Weir, MS | 39772 | 4755 S. Turnbull Road<br>Weir, MS | 39722 | |
| **30.** 636 McAllister Street<br>Graham, Texas | 76450 | 630 McAllister Street<br>Graham, Texas | 76450 | |
| **31.** 7200 N. Salisbury Pl.<br>Hartford, CT | 06106-1896 | 7200 N. Salisbury Pl.<br>Hartland, CT | 06166-1896 | |
| **32.** 3530 Englewood Drive<br>Wayzata, MN | 55391 | 3530 Englewood Drive<br>Wayzata, MN | 55391 | |
| **33.** 264 Bella Vista Lane<br>Riverton, WY | 82501 | 264 Bella Vista Lane<br>Riverton, WY | 85501 | |
| **34.** 19 Country Route 1<br>Santa Rosa, NM | 88435 | 19 Country Route 1<br>Santa Rosa, NM | 88435 | |
| **35.** 855 Missouri Trail<br>Roland, AR | 72135 | 855 Missouri Terrace<br>Roland, AR | 72135 | |
| **36.** 431 Oak Street<br>Boulder, CO | 80303 | 413 Oak Street<br>Boulder, CO | 80313 | |
| **37.** 2995 Pearl Court<br>Whitman, NE | 69366 | 2955 Pearl Court<br>Whitman, ND | 69366 | |
| **38.** 6488 Greenview Ave.<br>Cochran, GA | 31014 | 6488 Greenvalley Ave.<br>Cochran, GA | 31104 | |
| **39.** Post Office Box 17<br>Union, Iowa | 50258 | Post Office Box 17<br>Union, Iowa | 50258 | |
| **40.** 404 E. 7th Street<br>Alexander, KS | 67513 | 404 E. 7th Street<br>Alexander, KS | 67503 | |
| **41.** 42 Bright St., Apt. C<br>Cimarron, CO | 81220 | 42 Bright St., Apt. C<br>Cinnamon, CO | 81220 | |
| **42.** 111 Kensington Pkwy<br>Bangor, Maine | 04401-6353 | 110 Kensington Pkwy<br>Bangor, Maine | 04401-6355 | |

**Directions:** Compare the **List to be Checked** with the **Correct List.** Decide if there are **(A) NO ERRORS,** an error in the **(B) ADDRESS ONLY,** an error in the **(C) ZIP CODE ONLY,** or an error in **(D) BOTH** the address and ZIP Code. Record your answers on the answer sheet.

43. 23 Dillon Boulevard
Arvin, CA                        93203

23 Dillon Boulevard
Arvin, CA                        93203

44. 700 Highway 16
Congress, AZ                     85332

700 Highway 160
Congress, AZ                     85332

45. 59 E. Monroe Drive
Stockett, MT                     59480

59 E. Monroe Drive
Stockett, MT                     59880

46. 2000 Prince Court
West Falls, NY                   14170

2000 Prince Court
West Falls, NY                   14170

47. 10 Westminster Lane
Twentynine Palms, CA             92277

10 Westminster Lane
Twentynine Palms, CA             97227

48. 3212 E. Military Hwy.
Midland, TX                      79706

3212 S. Military Hwy.
Midland, TX                      79776

49. 1400 Penelope Road
Tulsa, OK                        74103

1400 Penelope Road
Tulsa, OH                        74103

50. 566 Crestone Circle
Lumberton, MS                    39455

506 Crestone Circle
Lumberton, MS                    39455

51. 878 Phillips Way
Madison, WI          53703-3359

878 Phillips Way
Madison, WI          53703-3359

52. 4905 Coleston Avenue
Philadelphia, PA                 19146

4905 Coleton Avenue
Philadelphia, PA                 19046

53. 2200 Lake Street
Lawrenceville, NJ    08648-1697

2200 Lake Street
Lawrenceville, NJ    08688-1697

54. 133 Willow Court
Scottsbluff, NE                  69361

133 Willow Court
Scottsbluff, NE                  69361

55. 70 Rural Route 5
Clendenin, WV                    25045

70 Rural Route 5
Clendanon, WV                    25405

56. 1662 Valencia Blvd
Provo, Utah          84606-6597

1662 Valencia Blvd
Provo, Utah          84606-6957

57. 200 Rhode Island Lane
Cambridge, MA                    02138

202 Rhode Island Lane
Cambridge, MA                    02338

**practice test**

**Directions:** Compare the **List to be Checked** with the **Correct List.** Decide if there are **(A) NO ERRORS,** an error in the **(B) ADDRESS ONLY,** an error in the **(C) ZIP CODE ONLY,** or an error in **(D) BOTH** the address and ZIP Code. Record your answers on the answer sheet.

**58.** 381 Griffin Way
Brodhead, WI      53520      381 Griffith Way
Broadhead, WI      53520

**59.** 55 Jason Highway
Chaseley, ND      58423      55 Jason Highway
Chaseley, ND      58823

**60.** 4077 Adams Drive
Ely, NV      89301      4077 Adams Drive
Ely, NV      89301

## PART B: FORMS COMPLETION

**30 QUESTIONS • 15 MINUTES**

**Directions:** Read each form and answer the questions based on the information provided. Mark your answers on the answer sheet.

PS Form **2865**, February 1997 *(Reverse)*

1. Where on the above form would you enter the date an item was delivered?
   - **(A)** Box 6
   - **(B)** Box 9
   - **(C)** Box 11
   - **(D)** Box 13

2. How would you indicate the insured value of the item on this form?
   - **(A)** Check Box 1e
   - **(B)** Write the value in Box 3
   - **(C)** Check Box 4
   - **(D)** Write the value in Box 5

3. Which of these would be an appropriate entry for Box 10 on this form?
   - **(A)** #755
   - **(B)** A signature
   - **(C)** C.R.
   - **(D)** A check mark

4. Which of the following would be an appropriate entry for Box 6 on the form?
   - **(A)** A check mark
   - **(B)** 89044
   - **(C)** Indianapolis
   - **(D)** 4/3/08

5. Where on the above form would you indicate that the item ships via Express Mail International?
   - **(A)** Box 1a
   - **(B)** Box 1e
   - **(C)** Box 1f
   - **(D)** Box 2

**6.** A check mark would be the correct entry for each of the following boxes EXCEPT

- **(A)** Box 1a
- **(B)** Box 2
- **(C)** Box 4
- **(D)** Box 10

**7.** Which of these boxes on the above form would be completed at the post office of origin?

- **(A)** Box 2
- **(B)** Box 10
- **(C)** Box 12
- **(D)** Box 14

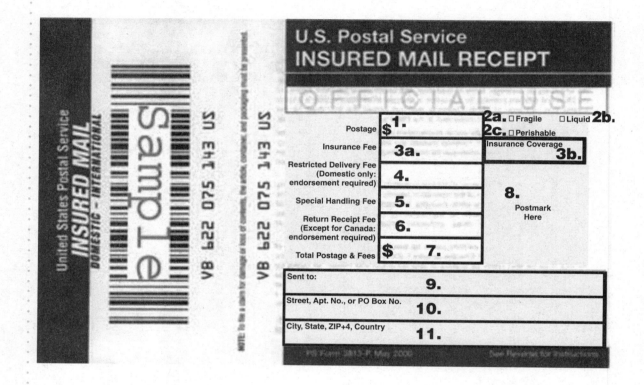

**8.** Where on the above form would you enter an insurance fee?

- **(A)** Box 2c
- **(B)** Box 3a
- **(C)** Box 3b
- **(D)** Box 4

**9.** Where on the above form would you note that the item contains a liquid?

- **(A)** Box 1
- **(B)** Box 2a
- **(C)** Box 2b
- **(D)** Box 2c

**10.** What would be the most appropriate entry for Box 6 on this form?

- **(A)** $29.00
- **(B)** A postmark
- **(C)** A check mark
- **(D)** #700

**11.** The entry "Mr. Allen Richardson" would be appropriate for which of the following boxes on the form?

- **(A)** Box 8
- **(B)** Box 9
- **(C)** Box 10
- **(D)** Box 11

12. Which of the following would be an appropriate entry for Box 2a on this form?
   (A) A check mark
   (B) $17.80
   (C) A signature
   (D) 44055

**Authorization to Hold Mail**

NOTE: Complete and give to your letter carrier or mail to the post office that delivers your mail.

➤ We can hold your mail for a minimum of **3**, but not for more than **30 days**.

Postmaster: Please hold mail for:

Name(s)

**1.**

**5a.** ☐ A. Please deliver all accumulated mail and resume normal delivery on the ending date shown below.

Address (Number, street, apt./suite no., city, state, ZIP + 4)

**2.**

**5b.** ☐ B. I will pick up all accumulated mail when I return and understand that mail delivery will not resume until I do.

| Beginning Date **3.** | Ending Date (May only be changed by the customer in writing) **4.** | Customer Signature **6.** |
|---|---|---|

**For Post Office Use Only**

Date Received

| Clerk | Bin Number |
|---|---|
| Carrier | Route Number |

(Complete this section only if customer selected option B)

| ☐ Accumulated mail has been picked up. | Resume Delivery of Mail (Date) | By |
|---|---|---|

PS Form **8076**, April 2001

13. Which of these would be an appropriate entry for Box 14 on the above form?
   (A) #2900
   (B) Wilhelmina Hutchins, M.D.
   (C) A signature
   (D) 17.35

14. Which of the following boxes on this form must be completed by a postal employee?
   (A) Box 1
   (B) Box 4
   (C) Box 6
   (D) Box 7

15. Which of these would be the most appropriate answer for Box 8 on this form?
   (A) Ronald Jackson
   (B) A signature
   (C) A check mark
   (D) 170 N. Brookdale Drive

16. Where on the above form would you enter the date the authorization form was received?
   (A) Box 3
   (B) Box 4
   (C) Box 7
   (D) Box 10

17. Where on this form would a customer's signature be entered?

    (A) Box 6
    (B) Box 8
    (C) Box 13
    (D) Box 14

18. If a customer checks box 5a, which of the following boxes on this form must NOT be completed?

    (A) Box 1
    (B) Box 2
    (C) Box 3
    (D) Box 12

19. The entry "Country Route 17" would be appropriate for which of the following boxes on this form?

    (A) Box 11
    (B) Box 12
    (C) Box 13
    (D) Box 14

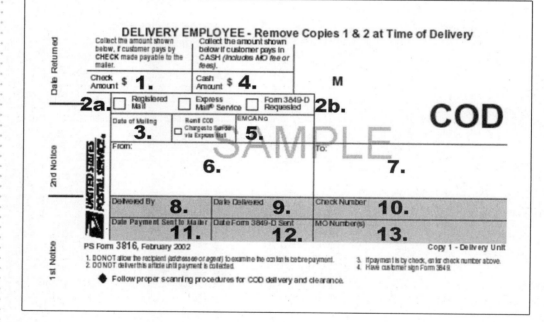

20. Where on the above form would you enter a cash amount?

    (A) Box 1
    (B) Box 4
    (C) Box 5
    (D) Box 8

21. Which of the following would be an appropriate entry for Box 11 on the form?

    (A) Windsor, PA
    (B) 6/12/08
    (C) A postmark
    (D) 35.00

22. A check mark would be the proper entry for which of the following boxes on this form?

    (A) 2a
    (B) 3
    (C) 5
    (D) 7

23. Where on the form would you enter the recipient's name and address?

    (A) Box 6
    (B) Box 7
    (C) Box 10
    (D) Box 13

**UNITED STATES POSTAL SERVICE®**

**Certificate Of Mailing**

To pay fee, affix stamps or meter postage here.

This Certificate of Mailing provides evidence that mail has been presented to USPS® for mailing. This form may be used for domestic and international mail.

From:

**1.**

**3.**

To:

Postmark Here

**2.**

**4.**

PS Form **3817**, April 2007 PSN 7530-02-000-9065

---

**24.** Which of the following would be an appropriate entry for Box 4 on the above form?

(A) 24.95
(B) 90022
(C) A signature
(D) A postmark

**25.** Where on the form would you indicate the recipient's name and address?

(A) Box 1
(B) Box 2
(C) Box 3
(D) Box 4

**26.** Which of the following could be properly entered in Box 3 on the above form?

(A) A mailing address
(B) A postmark
(C) A signature
(D) A postage stamp

**27.** An item is being mailed from Boise, Idaho. Where on the form would this information be entered?

(A) Box 1
(B) Box 2
(C) Box 3
(D) Box 4

practice test

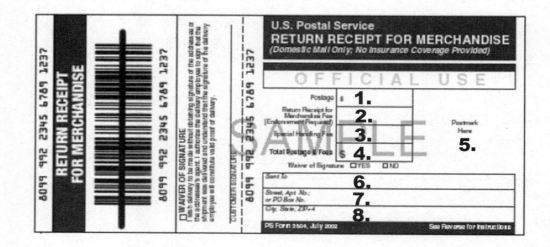

**28.** Where on the above form would you enter a special handling fee?

**(A)** Box 1

**(B)** Box 3

**(C)** Box 4

**(D)** Box 5

**29.** A ZIP Code is required in which of the following boxes on this form?

**(A)** Box 5

**(B)** Box 6

**(C)** Box 7

**(D)** Box 8

**30.** How would you indicate on this form the postage cost for an item?

**(A)** Write the amount in Box 1

**(B)** Check Box 3

**(C)** Write the amount in Box 5

**(D)** Check Box 8

# PART C: CODING AND MEMORY

## Coding Section: Segment 1

**4 QUESTIONS • 2 MINUTES**

**Directions:** Segment 1 is *not* scored and does not count toward your total exam score. It is a practice exercise to help you with the Coding Section under a time constraint similar to the one used in the scored Coding Section. Use the coding guide below to match each address to a delivery route. Mark your answers on the answer section at the bottom of this page.

### CODING GUIDE

| ADDRESS RANGE | DELIVERY ROUTE |
|---|:---:|
| 20000–40000 W. Harbor Road<br>300–700 E. Rolante Street | A |
| 851–1300 E. Harbor Road<br>11–40 N. Roland Street<br>1200–1400 N. 21st Avenue | B |
| 600–850 E. Harbor Road<br>41–70 N. Roland Street<br>75–100 Highway 347 | C |
| All mail that doesn't fall into one of the address ranges listed above. | D |

| Address | Delivery Route | | | |
|---|:---:|:---:|:---:|:---:|
| 1.   727 E. Harbor Road | A | B | C | D |
| 2.   1100 E. Harbor Road | A | B | C | D |
| 3.   34 Highway 347 | A | B | C | D |
| 4.   39000 W. Harbor Road | A | B | C | D |

## Sample Answer Sheet

1. Ⓐ Ⓑ Ⓒ Ⓓ     3. Ⓐ Ⓑ Ⓒ Ⓓ

2. Ⓐ Ⓑ Ⓒ Ⓓ     4. Ⓐ Ⓑ Ⓒ Ⓓ

## Coding Section: Segment 2

**8 QUESTIONS • 1.5 MINUTES (90 SECONDS)**

**Directions:** Segment 2 is *not* scored and does not count toward your total exam score. It is a practice exercise to help you with the Coding Section under a time constraint similar to the one used in the scored Coding Section. Use the coding guide below to match each address to a delivery route. Mark your answers on the answer section at the bottom of this page.

### CODING GUIDE

| ADDRESS RANGE | DELIVERY ROUTE |
|---|---|
| 20000–40000 W. Harbor Road<br>300–700 E. Rolante Street | A |
| 851–1300 E. Harbor Road<br>11–40 N. Roland Street<br>1200–1400 N. 21st Avenue | B |
| 600–850 E. Harbor Road<br>41–70 N. Roland Street<br>75–100 Highway 347 | C |
| All mail that doesn't fall into one of the address ranges listed above. | D |

| Address | Delivery Route | | | |
|---|---|---|---|---|
| 1.   4100 W. Harbor Road | A | B | C | D |
| 2.   877 E. Harbor Road | A | B | C | D |
| 3.   61 N. Roland Street | A | B | C | D |
| 4.   110 N. Roland Street | A | B | C | D |
| 5.   84 Highway 347 | A | B | C | D |
| 6.   24600 W. Harbor Road | A | B | C | D |
| 7.   301 E. Rolante Street | A | B | C | D |
| 8.   20 N. Roland Street | A | B | C | D |

## Sample Answer Sheet

1. Ⓐ Ⓑ Ⓒ Ⓓ     4. Ⓐ Ⓑ Ⓒ Ⓓ     7. Ⓐ Ⓑ Ⓒ Ⓓ

2. Ⓐ Ⓑ Ⓒ Ⓓ     5. Ⓐ Ⓑ Ⓒ Ⓓ     8. Ⓐ Ⓑ Ⓒ Ⓓ

3. Ⓐ Ⓑ Ⓒ Ⓓ     6. Ⓐ Ⓑ Ⓒ Ⓓ

## Coding Section: Segment 3

**36 QUESTIONS • 6 MINUTES**

**Directions:** This is the actual *scored* Coding Section of the exam. Work through items 1 through 36, assigning a code to each item based on the Coding Guide below. Mark your answers on the answer sheet. Work quickly and accurately.

### CODING GUIDE

| ADDRESS RANGE | DELIVERY ROUTE |
|---|:---:|
| 20000–40000 W. Harbor Road<br>300–700 E. Rolante Street | A |
| 851–1300 E. Harbor Road<br>11–40 N. Roland Street<br>1200–1400 N. 21st Avenue | B |
| 600–850 E. Harbor Road<br>41–70 N. Roland Street<br>75–100 Highway 347 | C |
| All mail that doesn't fall into one of the address ranges listed above. | D |

| | Address | Delivery Route | | | |
|---|---|:---:|:---:|:---:|:---:|
| 1. | 615 E. Harbor Road | A | B | C | D |
| 2. | 11 N. Roland Street | A | B | C | D |
| 3. | 1600 W. Harbor Road | A | B | C | D |
| 4. | 30800 W. Harbor Road | A | B | C | D |
| 5. | 487 E. Rolante Street | A | B | C | D |
| 6. | 76 Highway 347 | A | B | C | D |
| 7. | 863 E. Harbor Road | A | B | C | D |
| 8. | 1390 N. 21st Avenue | A | B | C | D |
| 9. | 30000 W. Harbor Road | A | B | C | D |
| 10. | 53 N. Roland Street | A | B | C | D |
| 11. | 17 N. Roland Street | A | B | C | D |
| 12. | 170 Highway 347 | A | B | C | D |
| 13. | 20500 W. Harbor Road | A | B | C | D |
| 14. | 700 N. Roland Street | A | B | C | D |
| 15. | 698 E. Harbor Road | A | B | C | D |

## CODING GUIDE

| ADDRESS RANGE | DELIVERY ROUTE |
|---|---|
| 20000–40000 W. Harbor Road<br>300–700 E. Rolante Street | A |
| 851–1300 E. Harbor Road<br>11–40 N. Roland Street<br>1200–1400 N. 21st Avenue | B |
| 600–850 E. Harbor Road<br>41–70 N. Roland Street<br>75–100 Highway 347 | C |
| All mail that doesn't fall into one of the address ranges listed above. | D |

| | | | | | |
|---|---|---|---|---|---|
| 16. | 449 E. Rolante Street | A | B | C | D |
| 17. | 1600 N. 21st Avenue | A | B | C | D |
| 18. | 1360 N. 21st Avenue | A | B | C | D |
| 19. | 97 Highway 347 | A | B | C | D |
| 20. | 37000 W. Harbor Road | A | B | C | D |
| 21. | 56 N. Roland Street | A | B | C | D |
| 22. | 35 N. Roland Street | A | B | C | D |
| 23. | 367 E. Rolante Street | A | B | C | D |
| 24. | 1228 N. 21st Avenue | A | B | C | D |
| 25. | 844 E. Harbor Road | A | B | C | D |
| 26. | 2300 E. Harbor Road | A | B | C | D |
| 27. | 49 N. Roland Street | A | B | C | D |
| 28. | 25500 W. Harbor Road | A | B | C | D |
| 29. | 560 E. Harbor Road | A | B | C | D |
| 30. | 37000 W. Harbor Road | A | B | C | D |
| 31. | 91 Highway 347 | A | B | C | D |
| 32. | 1062 E. Harbor Road | A | B | C | D |
| 33. | 730 E. Rolante Street | A | B | C | D |
| 34. | 605 E. Rolante Street | A | B | C | D |
| 35. | 22 N. Roland Street | A | B | C | D |
| 36. | 705 E. Harbor Road | A | B | C | D |

## Memory Section: Segment 1

**3 MINUTES**

**Directions:** Take 3 minutes to memorize the Coding Guide on page 271.
- You may NOT write down any addresses during the memorization period.

## Memory Section: Segment 2

**8 QUESTIONS • 1.5 MINUTES (90 SECONDS)**

**Directions:** Segment 2 is *not* scored and does not count toward your total exam score. It is an exercise to help you practice coding addresses from memory under a time constraint similar to the one used in the scored Memory Section of the actual exam. You will *not* see the Coding Guide during this segment of the exam. Based on your memory of the Coding Guide, match each address to a delivery route. Mark your answers on the answer section at the bottom of this page.

| Address | Delivery Route | | | |
|---|---|---|---|---|
| 1. 88 Highway 347 | A | B | C | D |
| 2. 32000 W. Harbor Road | A | B | C | D |
| 3. 1078 E. Harbor Road | A | B | C | D |
| 4. 1250 N. 21st Avenue | A | B | C | D |
| 5. 67 N. Roland Street | A | B | C | D |
| 6. 474 E. Rolante Street | A | B | C | D |
| 7. 105 Highway 347 | A | B | C | D |
| 8. 29 N. Roland Street | A | B | C | D |

## Sample Answer Sheet

1. Ⓐ Ⓑ Ⓒ Ⓓ     4. Ⓐ Ⓑ Ⓒ Ⓓ     7. Ⓐ Ⓑ Ⓒ Ⓓ

2. Ⓐ Ⓑ Ⓒ Ⓓ     5. Ⓐ Ⓑ Ⓒ Ⓓ     8. Ⓐ Ⓑ Ⓒ Ⓓ

3. Ⓐ Ⓑ Ⓒ Ⓓ     6. Ⓐ Ⓑ Ⓒ Ⓓ

## Memory Section: Segment 3

**5 MINUTES**

**Directions:** Take 5 minutes to memorize the Coding Guide on page 271.
- You may NOT write down any addresses during the memorization period.

practice test

## Memory Section: Segment 4

**36 QUESTIONS • 7 MINUTES**

**Directions:** This is the actual *scored* Memory Section of the exam. Take 3 minutes to memorize the Coding Guide on page 271. Work through items 1 through 36, assigning a code based on your memory of the Coding Guide. Mark your answers on the answer sheet. Work quickly and accurately.

- You may NOT write down any addresses during the memorization period.
- You may NOT look at the codes when answering the items.

| Address | Delivery Route | | | |
|---|---|---|---|---|
| 1.  1210 N. 21st Avenue | A | B | C | D |
| 2.  33 N. Roland Street | A | B | C | D |
| 3.  63000 W. Harbor Road | A | B | C | D |
| 4.  13 Highway 347 | A | B | C | D |
| 5.  402 E. Rolante Street | A | B | C | D |
| 6.  550 E. Rolante Street | A | B | C | D |
| 7.  1384 N. 21st Avenue | A | B | C | D |
| 8.  41 N. Roland Street | A | B | C | D |
| 9.  120 N. 21st Avenue | A | B | C | D |
| 10.  36700 W. Harbor Road | A | B | C | D |
| 11.  749 E. Harbor Road | A | B | C | D |
| 12.  80 Highway 347 | A | B | C | D |
| 13.  510 E. Rolante Street | A | B | C | D |
| 14.  20 E. Rolante Street | A | B | C | D |
| 15.  64 N. Roland Street | A | B | C | D |
| 16.  1183 E. Harbor Road | A | B | C | D |
| 17.  500 E. Rolante Street | A | B | C | D |
| 18.  633 E. Harbor Road | A | B | C | D |
| 19.  40 N. Roland Street | A | B | C | D |
| 20.  45 N. Roland Street | A | B | C | D |
| 21.  28600 W. Harbor Road | A | B | C | D |
| 22.  6000 E. Harbor Road | A | B | C | D |
| 23.  99 Highway 347 | A | B | C | D |
| 24.  100 N. Roland Street | A | B | C | D |

| 25. | 313 E. Rolante Street | A | B | C | D |
|---|---|---|---|---|---|
| 26. | 1450 N. 21st Avenue | A | B | C | D |
| 27. | 850 E. Harbor Road | A | B | C | D |
| 28. | 1255 E. Harbor Road | A | B | C | D |
| 29. | 1345 N. 21st Avenue | A | B | C | D |
| 30. | 21000 W. Harbor Road | A | B | C | D |
| 31. | 79 Highway 347 | A | B | C | D |
| 32. | 950 E. Rolante Street | A | B | C | D |
| 33. | 699 E. Rolante Street | A | B | C | D |
| 34. | 45000 W. Harbor Road | A | B | C | D |
| 35. | 1290 E. Harbor Road | A | B | C | D |
| 36. | 23000 W. Harbor Road | A | B | C | D |

practice test

# ANSWER KEY AND EXPLANATIONS

## Part A: Address Checking

| | | | | |
|---|---|---|---|---|
| 1. C | 13. C | 25. C | 37. B | 49. B |
| 2. A | 14. B | 26. B | 38. D | 50. B |
| 3. B | 15. A | 27. A | 39. A | 51. A |
| 4. D | 16. D | 28. D | 40. C | 52. D |
| 5. C | 17. C | 29. D | 41. B | 53. C |
| 6. A | 18. C | 30. B | 42. D | 54. A |
| 7. B | 19. A | 31. D | 43. A | 55. D |
| 8. D | 20. D | 32. A | 44. B | 56. C |
| 9. C | 21. B | 33. C | 45. C | 57. D |
| 10. D | 22. C | 34. A | 46. A | 58. B |
| 11. B | 23. A | 35. B | 47. C | 59. C |
| 12. A | 24. B | 36. D | 48. D | 60. A |

## Part B: Forms Completion

| | | | | |
|---|---|---|---|---|
| 1. C | 7. A | 13. C | 19. A | 25. B |
| 2. B | 8. B | 14. D | 20. B | 26. D |
| 3. D | 9. C | 15. A | 21. B | 27. A |
| 4. D | 10. A | 16. C | 22. A | 28. B |
| 5. C | 11. B | 17. A | 23. B | 29. D |
| 6. C | 12. A | 18. D | 24. D | 30. A |

1. **The correct answer is (C).** Box 11 requires the date that the item was delivered. Therefore, the correct answer is (C), Box 11.

2. **The correct answer is (B).** Box 3 is labeled "Insured Value." Therefore, the correct answer is (B), Box 3.

3. **The correct answer is (D).** Box 10 requires a check mark. Therefore, the correct answer is (D), a check mark.

4. **The correct answer is (D).** Box 6 requires a date. Therefore, the correct answer is (D), 4/3/08.

5. **The correct answer is (C).** Box 1f is labeled "Express Mail International." Therefore, the correct answer is (C), Box 1f.

6. **The correct answer is (C).** Box 4 requires an article number. Therefore, the correct answer is (C), Box 4.

7. **The correct answer is (A).** Box 2 lies within the section of the form labeled "Completed by the Office of Origin." Therefore, the correct answer is (A), Box 2.

8. **The correct answer is (B).** Box 3a is labeled "Insurance Fee." Therefore, the correct answer is (B), Box 3a.

9. **The correct answer is (C).** Box 2b is labeled "Liquid." Therefore, the correct answer is (C), Box 2b.

10. **The correct answer is (A).** Box 6 requires a fee. Therefore, the correct answer is (A), $29.00.

11. **The correct answer is (B).** Box 9 requires the recipient's name. Therefore, the correct answer is (B), Box 9.

12. **The correct answer is (A).** Box 2a requires a check mark. Therefore, the correct answer is (A), Box 2a.

13. **The correct answer is (C).** Box 14 requires a signature. Therefore, the correct answer is (C), A signature.

14. **The correct answer is (D).** Box 7 is under the section labeled "For Post Office Use Only." Therefore, the correct answer is (D), Box 7.

15. **The correct answer is (A).** Box 8 requires the name of the postal clerk. Therefore, the correct answer is (A), Ronald Jackson.

16. **The correct answer is (C).** Box 7 is labeled "Date Received." Therefore, the correct answer is (C), Box 7.

17. **The correct answer is (A).** Box 6 is labeled "Customer Signature." Therefore, the correct answer is (A), Box 6. (D) is incorrect because Box 14 requires the signature of a postal employee.

18. **The correct answer is (D).** Box 12 is to be completed only if the customer checks box 5b. Therefore, the correct answer is (D), Box 12.

19. **The correct answer is (A).** Box 11 is labeled "Route Number." Therefore, the correct answer is (A), Box 11.

20. **The correct answer is (B).** Box 4 is labeled "Cash Amount." Therefore, the correct answer is (B), Box 4.

21. **The correct answer is (B).** Box 11 requires a date. Therefore, the correct answer is (B), 6/12/08.

22. **The correct answer is (A).** Box 2a requires a check mark. Therefore, the correct answer is (A), Box 2a.

23. **The correct answer is (B).** Box 7 is labeled "To" and requires the recipient's name and address. Therefore, the correct answer is (B), Box 7.

24. **The correct answer is (D).** Box 4 requires a postmark. Therefore, the correct answer is (D), A postmark.

25. **The correct answer is (B).** Box 2 requires the recipient's name and address. Therefore, the correct answer is (B), Box 2.

26. **The correct answer is (D).** Postage stamps can be affixed at Box 3. Therefore, the correct answer is (D), A postage stamp.

27. **The correct answer is (A).** Box 1 requires the sender's name and address. Therefore, the correct answer is (A), Box 1.

28. **The correct answer is (B).** Box 3 is labeled "Special Handling Fees." Therefore, the correct answer is (B), Box 3.

29. **The correct answer is (D).** Box 8 is labeled "City, State, ZIP + 4." Therefore, the correct answer is (D), Box 8.

30. **The correct answer is (A).** Box 1 is labeled "Postage." Therefore, the correct answer is (A), Write the amount in Box 1.

## Part C: Coding and Memory

**CODING SECTION: SEGMENT 1**

| | | | |
|---|---|---|---|
| 1. C | 2. B | 3. D | 4. A |

**CODING SECTION: SEGMENT 2**

| | | | | |
|---|---|---|---|---|
| 1. D | 3. C | 5. C | 7. A | 8. B |
| 2. B | 4. D | 6. A | | |

**CODING SECTION: SEGMENT 3**

| | | | | |
|---|---|---|---|---|
| 1. C | 9. A | 16. A | 23. A | 30. A |
| 2. B | 10. C | 17. D | 24. B | 31. C |
| 3. D | 11. B | 18. B | 25. C | 32. B |
| 4. A | 12. D | 19. C | 26. D | 33. D |
| 5. A | 13. A | 20. A | 27. C | 34. A |
| 6. C | 14. D | 21. C | 28. A | 35. B |
| 7. B | 15. C | 22. B | 29. D | 36. C |
| 8. B | | | | |

1. **The correct answer is (C).** The address 615 E. Harbor Road falls in one of the address ranges in the same row as Delivery Route C.

2. **The correct answer is (B).** The address 11 N. Roland Street falls in one of the address ranges in the same row as Delivery Route B.

3. **The correct answer is (D).** The address 1600 W. Harbor Road does not fall into any of the address ranges for Delivery Routes A, B, or C.

4. **The correct answer is (A).** The address 30800 W. Harbor Road falls in one of the address ranges in the same row as Delivery Route A.

5. **The correct answer is (A).** The address 487 E. Rolante Street falls in one of the address ranges in the same row as Delivery Route A.

6. **The correct answer is (C).** The address 76 Highway 347 falls in one of the address ranges in the same row as Delivery Route C.

7. **The correct answer is (B).** The address 863 E. Harbor Road falls in one of the address ranges in the same row as Delivery Route B.

8. **The correct answer is (B).** The address 1390 N. 21st Avenue falls in one of the address ranges in the same row as Delivery Route B.

9. **The correct answer is (A).** The address 30000 W. Harbor Road falls in one of the address ranges in the same row as Delivery Route A.

10. **The correct answer is (C).** The address 53 N. Roland Street falls in one of the address ranges in the same row as Delivery Route C.

11. **The correct answer is (B).** The address 17 N. Roland Street falls in one of the address ranges in the same row as Delivery Route B.

12. **The correct answer is (D).** The address 170 Highway 347 does not fall into any of the address ranges for Delivery Routes A, B, or C.

13. **The correct answer is (A).** The address 20500 W. Harbor Road falls in one of the address ranges in the same row as Delivery Route A.

14. **The correct answer is (D).** The address 700 N. Roland Street does not fall into any of the address ranges for Delivery Routes A, B, or C.

15. **The correct answer is (C).** The address 698 E. Harbor Road falls in one of the address ranges in the same row as Delivery Route C.

16. **The correct answer is (A).** The address 449 E. Rolante Street falls in one of the address ranges in the same row as Delivery Route A.

17. **The correct answer is (D).** The address 1600 N. 21st Avenue does not fall into any of the address ranges for Delivery Routes A, B, or C.

18. **The correct answer is (B).** The address 1360 N. 21st Avenue falls in one of the address ranges in the same row as Delivery Route B.

19. **The correct answer is (C).** The address 97 Highway 347 falls in one of the address ranges in the same row as Delivery Route C.

20. **The correct answer is (A).** The address 37000 W. Harbor Road falls in one of the address ranges in the same row as Delivery Route A.

21. **The correct answer is (C).** The address 56 N. Roland Street falls in one of the address ranges in the same row as Delivery Route C.

22. **The correct answer is (B).** The address 35 N. Roland Street falls in one of the address ranges in the same row as Delivery Route B.

23. **The correct answer is (A).** The address 367 E. Rolante Street falls in one of the address ranges in the same row as Delivery Route A.

24. **The correct answer is (B).** The address 1228 N. 21st Avenue falls in one of the address ranges in the same row as Delivery Route B.

25. **The correct answer is (C).** The address 844 E. Harbor Road falls in one of the address ranges in the same row as Delivery Route C.

26. **The correct answer is (D).** The address 2300 E. Harbor Road does not fall into any of the address ranges for Delivery Routes A, B, or C

27. **The correct answer is (C).** The address 49 N. Roland Street falls in one of the address ranges in the same row as Delivery Route C.

28. **The correct answer is (A).** The address 25500 W. Harbor Road falls in one of the address ranges in the same row as Delivery Route A.

29. **The correct answer is (D).** The address 560 E. Harbor Road does not fall into any of the address ranges for Delivery Routes A, B, or C

30. **The correct answer is (A).** The address 37000 W. Harbor Road falls in one of the address ranges in the same row as Delivery Route A.

31. **The correct answer is (C).** The address 91 Highway 347 falls in one of the address ranges in the same row as Delivery Route C.

32. **The correct answer is (B).** The address 1062 E. Harbor Road falls in one of the address ranges in the same row as Delivery Route B.

33. **The correct answer is (D).** The address 730 E. Rolante Street does not fall into any of the address ranges for Delivery Routes A, B, or C.

34. **The correct answer is (A).** The address 605 E. Rolante Street falls in one of the address ranges in the same row as Delivery Route A.

35. **The correct answer is (B).** The address 22 N. Roland Street falls in one of the address ranges in the same row as Delivery Route B.

36. **The correct answer is (C).** The address 705 E. Harbor Road falls in one of the address ranges in the same row as Delivery Route C.

answers practice test 5

**MEMORY SECTION: SEGMENT 2**

| | | | | |
|---|---|---|---|---|
| 1. C | 3. B | 5. C | 7. D | 8. B |
| 2. A | 4. B | 6. A | | |

**MEMORY SECTION: SEGMENT 4**

| | | | | |
|---|---|---|---|---|
| 1. B | 9. D | 16. B | 23. C | 30. A |
| 2. B | 10. A | 17. A | 24. D | 31. C |
| 3. D | 11. C | 18. C | 25. A | 32. D |
| 4. D | 12. C | 19. B | 26. D | 33. A |
| 5. A | 13. A | 20. C | 27. C | 34. D |
| 6. A | 14. D | 21. A | 28. B | 35. B |
| 7. B | 15. C | 22. D | 29. B | 36. A |
| 8. C | | | | |

1. **The correct answer is (B).** The address 1210 N. 21st Avenue falls in one of the address ranges in the same row as Delivery Route B.

2. **The correct answer is (B).** The address 33 N. Roland Street falls in one of the address ranges in the same row as Delivery Route B.

3. **The correct answer is (D).** The address 63000 W. Harbor Road does not fall into any of the address ranges for Delivery Routes A, B, or C.

4. **The correct answer is (D).** The address 13 Highway 347 does not fall into any of the address ranges for Delivery Routes A, B, or C.

5. **The correct answer is (A).** The address 402 E. Rolante Street falls in one of the address ranges in the same row as Delivery Route A.

6. **The correct answer is (A).** The address 550 E. Rolante Street falls in one of the address ranges in the same row as Delivery Route A.

7. **The correct answer is (B).** The address 1384 N. 21st Avenue falls in one of the address ranges in the same row as Delivery Route B.

8. **The correct answer is (C).** The address 41 N. Roland Street falls in one of the address ranges in the same row as Delivery Route C.

9. **The correct answer is (D).** The address 120 N. 21st Avenue does not fall into any of the address ranges for Delivery Routes A, B, or C.

10. **The correct answer is (A).** The address 36700 W. Harbor Road falls in one of the address ranges in the same row as Delivery Route A.

11. **The correct answer is (C).** The address 749 E. Harbor Road falls in one of the address ranges in the same row as Delivery Route C.

12. **The correct answer is (C).** The address 80 Highway 347 falls in one of the address ranges in the same row as Delivery Route C.

13. **The correct answer is (A).** The address 510 E. Rolante Street falls in one of the address ranges in the same row as Delivery Route A.

14. **The correct answer is (D).** The address 20 E. Rolante Street does not fall into any of the address ranges for Delivery Routes A, B, or C.

15. **The correct answer is (C).** The address 64 N. Roland Street falls in one of the address ranges in the same row as Delivery Route C.

16. **The correct answer is (B).** The address 1183 E. Harbor Road falls in one of the address ranges in the same row as Delivery Route B.

17. **The correct answer is (A).** The address 500 E. Rolante Street falls in one of the address ranges in the same row as Delivery Route A.

18. **The correct answer is (C).** The address 633 E. Harbor Road falls in one of the address ranges in the same row as Delivery Route C.

19. **The correct answer is (B).** The address 40 N. Roland Street falls in one of the address ranges in the same row as Delivery Route B.

20. **The correct answer is (C).** The address 45 N. Roland Street falls in one of the address ranges in the same row as Delivery Route C.

21. **The correct answer is (A).** The address 28600 W. Harbor Road falls in one of the address ranges in the same row as Delivery Route A.

22. **The correct answer is (D).** The address 6000 E. Harbor Road does not fall into any of the address ranges for Delivery Routes A, B, or C.

23. **The correct answer is (C).** The address 99 Highway 347 falls in one of the address ranges in the same row as Delivery Route C.

24. **The correct answer is (D).** The address 100 N. Roland Street does not fall into any of the address ranges for Delivery Routes A, B, or C.

25. **The correct answer is (A).** The address 313 E. Rolante Street falls in one of the address ranges in the same row as Delivery Route A.

26. **The correct answer is (D).** The address 1450 N. 21st Avenue does not fall into any of the address ranges for Delivery Routes A, B, or C.

27. **The correct answer is (C).** The address 850 E. Harbor Road falls in one of the address ranges in the same row as Delivery Route C.

28. **The correct answer is (B).** The address 1255 E. Harbor Road falls in one of the address ranges in the same row as Delivery Route B.

29. **The correct answer is (B).** The address 1345 N. 21st Avenue falls in one of the address ranges in the same row as Delivery Route B.

30. **The correct answer is (A).** The address 21000 W. Harbor Road falls in one of the address ranges in the same row as Delivery Route A.

31. **The correct answer is (C).** The address 79 Highway 347 falls in one of the address ranges in the same row as Delivery Route C.

32. **The correct answer is (D).** The address 950 E. Rolante Street does not fall into any of the address ranges for Delivery Routes A, B, or C.

33. **The correct answer is (A).** The address 699 E. Rolante Street falls in one of the address ranges in the same row as Delivery Route A.

34. **The correct answer is (D).** The address 45000 W. Harbor Road does not fall into any of the address ranges for Delivery Routes A, B, or C.

35. **The correct answer is (B).** The address 1290 E. Harbor Road falls in one of the address ranges in the same row as Delivery Route B.

36. **The correct answer is (A).** The address 23000 W. Harbor Road falls in one of the address ranges in the same row as Delivery Route A.

answers practice test 5

## PRACTICE TEST 6: EXAM 710

### Part A: Clerical Ability

1. Ⓐ Ⓑ Ⓒ Ⓓ Ⓔ
2. Ⓐ Ⓑ Ⓒ Ⓓ Ⓔ
3. Ⓐ Ⓑ Ⓒ Ⓓ Ⓔ
4. Ⓐ Ⓑ Ⓒ Ⓓ Ⓔ
5. Ⓐ Ⓑ Ⓒ Ⓓ Ⓔ
6. Ⓐ Ⓑ Ⓒ Ⓓ Ⓔ
7. Ⓐ Ⓑ Ⓒ Ⓓ Ⓔ
8. Ⓐ Ⓑ Ⓒ Ⓓ Ⓔ
9. Ⓐ Ⓑ Ⓒ Ⓓ Ⓔ
10. Ⓐ Ⓑ Ⓒ Ⓓ Ⓔ
11. Ⓐ Ⓑ Ⓒ Ⓓ Ⓔ
12. Ⓐ Ⓑ Ⓒ Ⓓ Ⓔ
13. Ⓐ Ⓑ Ⓒ Ⓓ Ⓔ
14. Ⓐ Ⓑ Ⓒ Ⓓ Ⓔ
15. Ⓐ Ⓑ Ⓒ Ⓓ Ⓔ
16. Ⓐ Ⓑ Ⓒ Ⓓ Ⓔ
17. Ⓐ Ⓑ Ⓒ Ⓓ Ⓔ
18. Ⓐ Ⓑ Ⓒ Ⓓ Ⓔ
19. Ⓐ Ⓑ Ⓒ Ⓓ Ⓔ
20. Ⓐ Ⓑ Ⓒ Ⓓ Ⓔ
21. Ⓐ Ⓑ Ⓒ Ⓓ Ⓔ
22. Ⓐ Ⓑ Ⓒ Ⓓ Ⓔ

23. Ⓐ Ⓑ Ⓒ Ⓓ Ⓔ
24. Ⓐ Ⓑ Ⓒ Ⓓ Ⓔ
25. Ⓐ Ⓑ Ⓒ Ⓓ Ⓔ
26. Ⓐ Ⓑ Ⓒ Ⓓ Ⓔ
27. Ⓐ Ⓑ Ⓒ Ⓓ Ⓔ
28. Ⓐ Ⓑ Ⓒ Ⓓ Ⓔ
29. Ⓐ Ⓑ Ⓒ Ⓓ Ⓔ
30. Ⓐ Ⓑ Ⓒ Ⓓ Ⓔ
31. Ⓐ Ⓑ Ⓒ Ⓓ Ⓔ
32. Ⓐ Ⓑ Ⓒ Ⓓ Ⓔ
33. Ⓐ Ⓑ Ⓒ Ⓓ Ⓔ
34. Ⓐ Ⓑ Ⓒ Ⓓ Ⓔ
35. Ⓐ Ⓑ Ⓒ Ⓓ Ⓔ
36. Ⓐ Ⓑ Ⓒ Ⓓ Ⓔ
37. Ⓐ Ⓑ Ⓒ Ⓓ Ⓔ
38. Ⓐ Ⓑ Ⓒ Ⓓ Ⓔ
39. Ⓐ Ⓑ Ⓒ Ⓓ Ⓔ
40. Ⓐ Ⓑ Ⓒ Ⓓ Ⓔ
41. Ⓐ Ⓑ Ⓒ Ⓓ Ⓔ
42. Ⓐ Ⓑ Ⓒ Ⓓ Ⓔ
43. Ⓐ Ⓑ Ⓒ Ⓓ Ⓔ

44. Ⓐ Ⓑ Ⓒ Ⓓ Ⓔ
45. Ⓐ Ⓑ Ⓒ Ⓓ Ⓔ
46. Ⓐ Ⓑ Ⓒ Ⓓ Ⓔ
47. Ⓐ Ⓑ Ⓒ Ⓓ Ⓔ
48. Ⓐ Ⓑ Ⓒ Ⓓ Ⓔ
49. Ⓐ Ⓑ Ⓒ Ⓓ Ⓔ
50. Ⓐ Ⓑ Ⓒ Ⓓ Ⓔ
51. Ⓐ Ⓑ Ⓒ Ⓓ Ⓔ
52. Ⓐ Ⓑ Ⓒ Ⓓ Ⓔ
53. Ⓐ Ⓑ Ⓒ Ⓓ Ⓔ
54. Ⓐ Ⓑ Ⓒ Ⓓ Ⓔ
55. Ⓐ Ⓑ Ⓒ Ⓓ Ⓔ
56. Ⓐ Ⓑ Ⓒ Ⓓ Ⓔ
57. Ⓐ Ⓑ Ⓒ Ⓓ Ⓔ
58. Ⓐ Ⓑ Ⓒ Ⓓ Ⓔ
59. Ⓐ Ⓑ Ⓒ Ⓓ Ⓔ
60. Ⓐ Ⓑ Ⓒ Ⓓ Ⓔ
61. Ⓐ Ⓑ Ⓒ Ⓓ Ⓔ
62. Ⓐ Ⓑ Ⓒ Ⓓ Ⓔ
63. Ⓐ Ⓑ Ⓒ Ⓓ Ⓔ
64. Ⓐ Ⓑ Ⓒ Ⓓ Ⓔ

65. Ⓐ Ⓑ Ⓒ Ⓓ Ⓔ
66. Ⓐ Ⓑ Ⓒ Ⓓ Ⓔ
67. Ⓐ Ⓑ Ⓒ Ⓓ Ⓔ
68. Ⓐ Ⓑ Ⓒ Ⓓ Ⓔ
69. Ⓐ Ⓑ Ⓒ Ⓓ Ⓔ
70. Ⓐ Ⓑ Ⓒ Ⓓ Ⓔ
71. Ⓐ Ⓑ Ⓒ Ⓓ Ⓔ
72. Ⓐ Ⓑ Ⓒ Ⓓ Ⓔ
73. Ⓐ Ⓑ Ⓒ Ⓓ Ⓔ
74. Ⓐ Ⓑ Ⓒ Ⓓ Ⓔ
75. Ⓐ Ⓑ Ⓒ Ⓓ Ⓔ
76. Ⓐ Ⓑ Ⓒ Ⓓ Ⓔ
77. Ⓐ Ⓑ Ⓒ Ⓓ Ⓔ
78. Ⓐ Ⓑ Ⓒ Ⓓ Ⓔ
79. Ⓐ Ⓑ Ⓒ Ⓓ Ⓔ
80. Ⓐ Ⓑ Ⓒ Ⓓ Ⓔ
81. Ⓐ Ⓑ Ⓒ Ⓓ Ⓔ
82. Ⓐ Ⓑ Ⓒ Ⓓ Ⓔ
83. Ⓐ Ⓑ Ⓒ Ⓓ Ⓔ
84. Ⓐ Ⓑ Ⓒ Ⓓ Ⓔ
85. Ⓐ Ⓑ Ⓒ Ⓓ Ⓔ

**answer sheet**

## Part B: Verbal Ability

1. Ⓐ Ⓑ Ⓒ Ⓓ Ⓔ
2. Ⓐ Ⓑ Ⓒ Ⓓ Ⓔ
3. Ⓐ Ⓑ Ⓒ Ⓓ Ⓔ
4. Ⓐ Ⓑ Ⓒ Ⓓ Ⓔ
5. Ⓐ Ⓑ Ⓒ Ⓓ Ⓔ
6. Ⓐ Ⓑ Ⓒ Ⓓ Ⓔ
7. Ⓐ Ⓑ Ⓒ Ⓓ Ⓔ
8. Ⓐ Ⓑ Ⓒ Ⓓ Ⓔ
9. Ⓐ Ⓑ Ⓒ Ⓓ Ⓔ
10. Ⓐ Ⓑ Ⓒ Ⓓ Ⓔ
11. Ⓐ Ⓑ Ⓒ Ⓓ Ⓔ

12. Ⓐ Ⓑ Ⓒ Ⓓ Ⓔ
13. Ⓐ Ⓑ Ⓒ Ⓓ Ⓔ
14. Ⓐ Ⓑ Ⓒ Ⓓ Ⓔ
15. Ⓐ Ⓑ Ⓒ Ⓓ Ⓔ
16. Ⓐ Ⓑ Ⓒ Ⓓ Ⓔ
17. Ⓐ Ⓑ Ⓒ Ⓓ Ⓔ
18. Ⓐ Ⓑ Ⓒ Ⓓ Ⓔ
19. Ⓐ Ⓑ Ⓒ Ⓓ Ⓔ
20. Ⓐ Ⓑ Ⓒ Ⓓ Ⓔ
21. Ⓐ Ⓑ Ⓒ Ⓓ Ⓔ
22. Ⓐ Ⓑ Ⓒ Ⓓ Ⓔ

23. Ⓐ Ⓑ Ⓒ Ⓓ Ⓔ
24. Ⓐ Ⓑ Ⓒ Ⓓ Ⓔ
25. Ⓐ Ⓑ Ⓒ Ⓓ Ⓔ
26. Ⓐ Ⓑ Ⓒ Ⓓ Ⓔ
27. Ⓐ Ⓑ Ⓒ Ⓓ Ⓔ
28. Ⓐ Ⓑ Ⓒ Ⓓ Ⓔ
29. Ⓐ Ⓑ Ⓒ Ⓓ Ⓔ
30. Ⓐ Ⓑ Ⓒ Ⓓ Ⓔ
31. Ⓐ Ⓑ Ⓒ Ⓓ Ⓔ
32. Ⓐ Ⓑ Ⓒ Ⓓ Ⓔ
33. Ⓐ Ⓑ Ⓒ Ⓓ Ⓔ

34. Ⓐ Ⓑ Ⓒ Ⓓ Ⓔ
35. Ⓐ Ⓑ Ⓒ Ⓓ Ⓔ
36. Ⓐ Ⓑ Ⓒ Ⓓ Ⓔ
37. Ⓐ Ⓑ Ⓒ Ⓓ Ⓔ
38. Ⓐ Ⓑ Ⓒ Ⓓ Ⓔ
39. Ⓐ Ⓑ Ⓒ Ⓓ Ⓔ
40. Ⓐ Ⓑ Ⓒ Ⓓ Ⓔ
41. Ⓐ Ⓑ Ⓒ Ⓓ Ⓔ
42. Ⓐ Ⓑ Ⓒ Ⓓ Ⓔ
43. Ⓐ Ⓑ Ⓒ Ⓓ Ⓔ
44. Ⓐ Ⓑ Ⓒ Ⓓ Ⓔ

45. Ⓐ Ⓑ Ⓒ Ⓓ Ⓔ
46. Ⓐ Ⓑ Ⓒ Ⓓ Ⓔ
47. Ⓐ Ⓑ Ⓒ Ⓓ Ⓔ
48. Ⓐ Ⓑ Ⓒ Ⓓ Ⓔ
49. Ⓐ Ⓑ Ⓒ Ⓓ Ⓔ
50. Ⓐ Ⓑ Ⓒ Ⓓ Ⓔ
51. Ⓐ Ⓑ Ⓒ Ⓓ Ⓔ
52. Ⓐ Ⓑ Ⓒ Ⓓ Ⓔ
53. Ⓐ Ⓑ Ⓒ Ⓓ Ⓔ
54. Ⓐ Ⓑ Ⓒ Ⓓ Ⓔ
55. Ⓐ Ⓑ Ⓒ Ⓓ Ⓔ

# Practice Test 6:
# Exam 710

## PART A: CLERICAL ABILITY

### Sequencing

**20 QUESTIONS • 3 MINUTES**

**Directions:** For each question there is a name, number, or code in a box at the left and four other names, numbers, or codes in alphabetical or numerical order at the right. Find the correct space for the boxed name or number so that it will be in alphabetical and/or numerical order with the others and mark the letter of that space on your answer sheet.

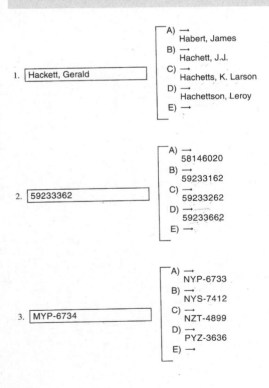

1. Hackett, Gerald

A) →
   Habert, James
B) →
   Hachett, J.J.
C) →
   Hachetts, K. Larson
D) →
   Hachettson, Leroy
E) →

2. 59233362

A) →
   58146020
B) →
   59233162
C) →
   59233262
D) →
   59233662
E) →

3. MYP-6734

A) →
   NYP-6733
B) →
   NYS-7412
C) →
   NZT-4899
D) →
   PYZ-3636
E) →

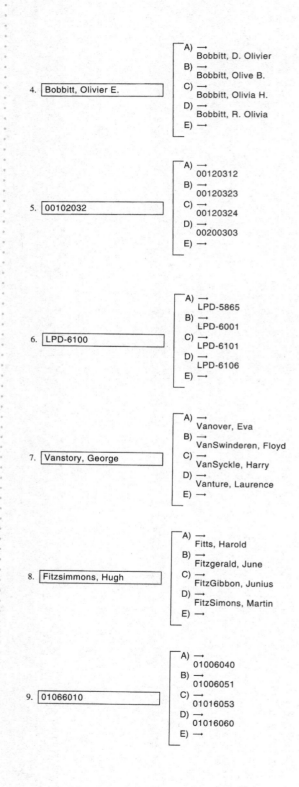

4. Bobbitt, Olivier E.

A) →
    Bobbitt, D. Olivier
B) →
    Bobbitt, Olive B.
C) →
    Bobbitt, Olivia H.
D) →
    Bobbitt, R. Olivia
E) →

5. 00102032

A) →
    00120312
B) →
    00120323
C) →
    00120324
D) →
    00200303
E) →

6. LPD-6100

A) →
    LPD-5865
B) →
    LPD-6001
C) →
    LPD-6101
D) →
    LPD-6106
E) →

7. Vanstory, George

A) →
    Vanover, Eva
B) →
    VanSwinderen, Floyd
C) →
    VanSyckle, Harry
D) →
    Vanture, Laurence
E) →

8. Fitzsimmons, Hugh

A) →
    Fitts, Harold
B) →
    Fitzgerald, June
C) →
    FitzGibbon, Junius
D) →
    FitzSimons, Martin
E) →

9. 01066010

A) →
    01006040
B) →
    01006051
C) →
    01016053
D) →
    01016060
E) →

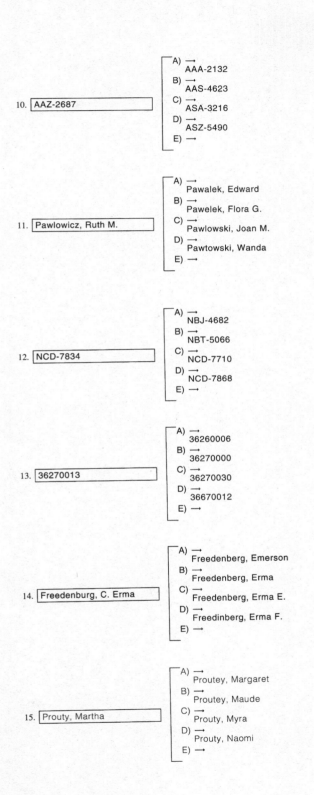

10. AAZ-2687

    A) →
       AAA-2132
    B) →
       AAS-4623
    C) →
       ASA-3216
    D) →
       ASZ-5490
    E) →

11. Pawlowicz, Ruth M.

    A) →
       Pawalek, Edward
    B) →
       Pawelek, Flora G.
    C) →
       Pawlowski, Joan M.
    D) →
       Pawtowski, Wanda
    E) →

12. NCD-7834

    A) →
       NBJ-4682
    B) →
       NBT-5066
    C) →
       NCD-7710
    D) →
       NCD-7868
    E) →

13. 36270013

    A) →
       36260006
    B) →
       36270000
    C) →
       36270030
    D) →
       36670012
    E) →

14. Freedenburg, C. Erma

    A) →
       Freedenberg, Emerson
    B) →
       Freedenberg, Erma
    C) →
       Freedenberg, Erma E.
    D) →
       Freedinberg, Erma F.
    E) →

15. Prouty, Martha

    A) →
       Proutey, Margaret
    B) →
       Proutey, Maude
    C) →
       Prouty, Myra
    D) →
       Prouty, Naomi
    E) →

practice test

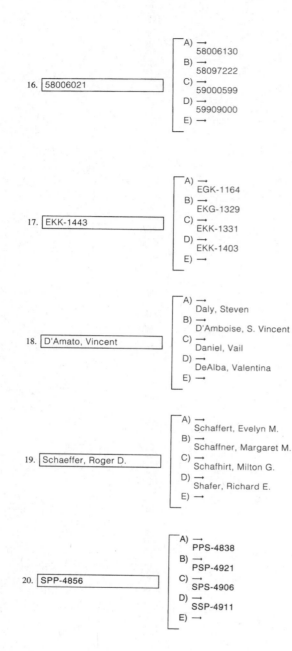

16. 58006021
- A) → 58006130
- B) → 58097222
- C) → 59000599
- D) → 59909000
- E) →

17. EKK-1443
- A) → EGK-1164
- B) → EKG-1329
- C) → EKK-1331
- D) → EKK-1403
- E) →

18. D'Amato, Vincent
- A) → Daly, Steven
- B) → D'Amboise, S. Vincent
- C) → Daniel, Vail
- D) → DeAlba, Valentina
- E) →

19. Schaeffer, Roger D.
- A) → Schaffert, Evelyn M.
- B) → Schaffner, Margaret M.
- C) → Schafhirt, Milton G.
- D) → Shafer, Richard E.
- E) →

20. SPP-4856
- A) → PPS-4838
- B) → PSP-4921
- C) → SPS-4906
- D) → SSP-4911
- E) →

## Comparisons

**30 QUESTIONS • 5 MINUTES**

**Directions:** In each line across the page there are three names, addresses, or codes that are very much alike. Compare the three and decide which ones are EXACTLY alike. On your answer sheet, mark:

**(A)** if **ALL THREE** names, addresses, or codes are exactly **ALIKE**
**(B)** if only the **FIRST** and **SECOND** names, addresses, or codes are exactly **ALIKE**
**(C)** if only the **FIRST** and **THIRD** names, addresses, or codes are exactly **ALIKE**
**(D)** if only the **SECOND** and **THIRD** names, addresses, or codes are exactly **ALIKE**
**(E)** if **ALL THREE** names, addresses, or codes are **DIFFERENT**

| | | | |
|---|---|---|---|
| **21.** | Drusilla S. Ridgeley | Drusilla S. Ridgeley | Drusilla S. Ridgeley |
| **22.** | Andrei I. Toumantzev | Andrei I. Tourmantzev | Andrei I. Toumantzov |
| **23.** | 6-78912-e3e42 | 6-78912-3e3e42 | 6-78912-e3e42 |
| **24.** | 86529 Dunwoodie Drive | 86529 Dunwoodie Drive | 85629 Dunwoodie Drive |
| **25.** | 1592514 | 1592574 | 1592574 |
| **26.** | Ella Burk Newham | Ella Burk Newnham | Elena Burk Newnham |
| **27.** | 5416R-1952TZ-op | 5416R-1952TZ-op | 5416R-1952TZ-op |
| **28.** | 60646 West Touhy Avenue | 60646 West Touhy Avenue | 60646 West Touhey Avenue |
| **29.** | Mardikian & Moore, Inc. | Mardikian and Moore, Inc. | Mardikian & Moore, Inc. |
| **30.** | 9670243 | 9670423 | 9670423 |
| **31.** | Eduardo Ingles | Eduardo Inglese | Eduardo Inglese |
| **32.** | Roger T. DeAngelis | Roger T. D'Angelis | Roger T. DeAngeles |
| **33.** | 7692138 | 7692138 | 7692138 |
| **34.** | 2695 East 3435 South | 2695 East 3435 South | 2695 East 3435 South |
| **35.** | 63qs5-95YT3-001 | 63qs5-95YT3-001 | 63qs5-95YT3-001 |
| **36.** | 2789350 | 2789350 | 2798350 |
| **37.** | Helmut V. Lochner | Helmut V. Lockner | Helmut W. Lochner |
| **38.** | 2454803 | 2548403 | 2454803 |
| **39.** | Lemberger, WA 28094-9182 | Lemberger, VA 28094-9182 | Lemberger, VA 28094-9182 |
| **40.** | 4168-GNP-78852 | 4168-GNP-78852 | 4168-GNP-78852 |
| **41.** | Yoshihito Saito | Yoshihito Saito | Yoshihito Saito |
| **42.** | 5927681 | 5927861 | 5927681 |
| **43.** | O'Reilly Bay, LA 56212 | O'Reillys Bay, LA 56212 | O'Reilly Bay, LA 56212 |
| **44.** | Francis Ransdell | Frances Ramsdell | Francis Ramsdell |
| **45.** | 5634-OotV5a-16867 | 5634-Ootv5a-16867 | 5634-Ootv5a-16867 |
| **46.** | Dolores Mollicone | Dolores Mollicone | Doloras Mollicone |
| **47.** | David C. Routzon | David E. Routzon | David C. Routzron |
| **48.** | 8932 Shimabui Hwy. | 8932 Shimabui Hwy. | 8932 Shimabui Hwy. |
| **49.** | 6177396 | 6177936 | 6177396 |
| **50.** | A8987-B73245 | A8987-B73245 | A8987-B73245 |

## Spelling

### 20 QUESTIONS • 3 MINUTES

**Directions:** Find the correct spelling of the word and darken the appropriate space on your answer sheet. If none of the spellings is correct, darken choice (D).

51. **(A)** anticipate
    **(B)** antisipate
    **(C)** anticapate
    **(D)** none of these

52. **(A)** similiar
    **(B)** simmilar
    **(C)** similar
    **(D)** none of these

53. **(A)** sufficiantly
    **(B)** suficeintly
    **(C)** sufficiently
    **(D)** none of these

54. **(A)** intelligence
    **(B)** inteligence
    **(C)** intellegence
    **(D)** none of these

55. **(A)** referance
    **(B)** referrence
    **(C)** referense
    **(D)** none of these

56. **(A)** conscious
    **(B)** consious
    **(C)** conscius
    **(D)** none of these

57. **(A)** paralell
    **(B)** parellel
    **(C)** parellell
    **(D)** none of these

58. **(A)** abundence
    **(B)** abundance
    **(C)** abundants
    **(D)** none of these

59. **(A)** corregated
    **(B)** corrigated
    **(C)** corrugated
    **(D)** none of these

60. **(A)** accumalation
    **(B)** accumulation
    **(C)** accumullation
    **(D)** none of these

61. **(A)** resonance
    **(B)** resonence
    **(C)** resonnance
    **(D)** none of these

62. **(A)** benaficial
    **(B)** benefitial
    **(C)** beneficial
    **(D)** none of these

63. **(A)** spesifically
    **(B)** specificially
    **(C)** specifically
    **(D)** none of these

64. **(A)** elemanate
    **(B)** elimenate
    **(C)** elliminate
    **(D)** none of these

65. **(A)** collosal
    **(B)** colosal
    **(C)** collossal
    **(D)** none of these

66. **(A)** auxillary
    **(B)** auxilliary
    **(C)** auxiliary
    **(D)** none of these

67. **(A)** inimitable
    **(B)** inimitible
    **(C)** inimatable
    **(D)** none of these

68. **(A)** disapearance
    **(B)** dissapearance
    **(C)** disappearence
    **(D)** none of these

69. **(A)** appelate
    **(B)** appellate
    **(C)** apellate
    **(D)** none of these

70. **(A)** esential
    **(B)** essential
    **(C)** essencial
    **(D)** none of these

## Computations

**15 QUESTIONS • 8 MINUTES**

**Directions:** Perform the computation as indicated in the question and find the answer among the list of alternative responses. If the correct answer is not given among the choices, mark (E).

**71.**
$$\begin{array}{r} 83 \\ -\ 56 \\ \hline \end{array}$$

(A) 23
(B) 29
(C) 33
(D) 37
(E) none of these

**72.**
$$\begin{array}{r} 15 \\ +\ 17 \\ \hline \end{array}$$

(A) 22
(B) 32
(C) 39
(D) 42
(E) none of these

**73.**
$$\begin{array}{r} 32 \\ \times\ 7 \\ \hline \end{array}$$

(A) 224
(B) 234
(C) 324
(D) 334
(E) none of these

**74.**
$$\begin{array}{r} 39 \\ \times\ 2 \\ \hline \end{array}$$

(A) 77
(B) 78
(C) 79
(D) 81
(E) none of these

**75.**
$$\begin{array}{r} 43 \\ -\ 15 \\ \hline \end{array}$$

(A) 23
(B) 32
(C) 33
(D) 35
(E) none of these

**76.**
$$\begin{array}{r} 50 \\ +\ 49 \\ \hline \end{array}$$

(A) 89
(B) 90
(C) 99
(D) 109
(E) none of these

practice test

**77.** 6)366

 **(A)** 11
 **(B)** 31
 **(C)** 36
 **(D)** 66
 **(E)** none of these

**78.** 38
× 3

 **(A)** 111
 **(B)** 113
 **(C)** 115
 **(D)** 117
 **(E)** none of these

**79.** 19
+ 21

 **(A)** 20
 **(B)** 30
 **(C)** 40
 **(D)** 50
 **(E)** none of these

**80.** 13
− 6

 **(A)** 5
 **(B)** 7
 **(C)** 9
 **(D)** 11
 **(E)** none of these

**81.** 6)180

 **(A)** 29
 **(B)** 31
 **(C)** 33
 **(D)** 39
 **(E)** none of these

**82.** 10
× 1

 **(A)** 0
 **(B)** 1
 **(C)** 10
 **(D)** 100
 **(E)** none of these

**83.** 7)287

 **(A)** 21
 **(B)** 27
 **(C)** 31
 **(D)** 37
 **(E)** none of these

**84.** 12
+ 11

 **(A)** 21
 **(B)** 22
 **(C)** 23
 **(D)** 24
 **(E)** none of these

**85.** 85
− 64

 **(A)** 19
 **(B)** 21
 **(C)** 29
 **(D)** 31
 **(E)** none of these

## PART B: VERBAL ABILITY

**55 QUESTIONS • 50 MINUTES**

**Directions:** Questions 1–20 test your ability to follow instructions. Each question directs you to mark a specific number and letter combination on your answer sheet. The questions require your total concentration because the answers that you are instructed to mark are, for the most part, NOT in numerical sequence (i.e., you would not use Number 1 on your answer sheet to answer Question 1; Number 2 for Question 2; etc.). Instead, you must mark the number and space specifically designated in each test question.

1. Look at the letters below. Draw a circle around the letter that comes first in the alphabet. Now, on your answer sheet, find Number 12 and darken the space for the letter you just circled.

    E G D Z B F

2. Draw a line under the odd number below that is more than 5 but less than 10. Find this number on your answer sheet and darken choice (E).

    8 10 5 6 11 9

3. Divide the number 16 by 4 and write your answer on the line below. Now find this number on your answer sheet and darken choice (A).

    _____

4. Write the letter C on the line next to the left-hand number below. Now, on your answer sheet, darken the space for the number-letter combination you see.

    5_____ 19_____ 7_____

5. If in any week Wednesday comes before Tuesday, write the number 15 on the line below. If not, write the number 18. Now, on your answer sheet, darken choice (A) for the number you just wrote.

    _____

6. Count the number of Bs in the line below and write that number at the end of the line. Now, on your answer sheet, darken choice (D) for the number you wrote.

    A D A E B D C A_____

7. Write the letter B on the line with the highest number. Now, on your answer sheet, darken the number-letter combination that appears on that line.

    16_____ 9_____ 20_____ 11_____

8. If the product of 6 × 4 is greater than the product of 8 × 3, write the letter E on the line below. If not, write the letter C. Now, on your answer sheet find number 8 and darken the space for the letter you just wrote.

    _____

9. Write the number 2 in the larger circle below. Now, on your answer sheet, darken the space for the number-letter combination in that circle.

10. Write the letter D on the line next to the number that is the sum of 7 + 4 + 4. Now, on your answer sheet, darken the space for that number-letter combination.

     13_____ 14_____ 15_____ 16_____ 17_____

11. If 5 × 5 equals 25 and 5 + 5 equals 10, write the number 17 on the line below. If not, write the number 10. Now, on your answer sheet, darken choice (E) for the number you just wrote.

     _____

12. Circle the second letter below. On the line beside that letter write the number that represents the number of days in a week. Now, on your answer sheet, darken the space for that number-letter combination.

     _____C _____D _____B _____E

13. If a triangle has more angles than a rectangle, write the number 13 in the circle below. If not, write the number 14 in the square. Now, on your answer sheet, darken the space for the number-letter combination in the figure that you just wrote in.

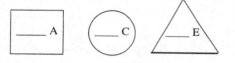

14. Count the number of Bs below and write that number at the end of the line. Subtract 2 from that number. Now, on your answer sheet, darken choice (E) for the number that represents 2 less than the number of Bs in the line.

     B E A D E C C B B B A E B D_____

15. The numbers below represent morning pick-up times from neighborhood letter boxes. Draw a line under the number that represents the latest pick-up time. Now, on your answer sheet, darken choice (D) for the number that is the same as the "minutes" of the time that you underlined.

     9:19 10:16 10:10

16. If a person who is 6 feet tall is taller than a person who is 5 feet tall and if a pillow is softer than a rock, darken choice 11(A) on your answer sheet. If not, darken choice 6(B).

17. Write the fourth letter of the alphabet on the line next to the third number below. Now, on your answer sheet, darken that number-letter combination.

     10_____ 19_____ 13_____ 4_____

18. Write the letter B in the box containing the next to smallest number. On your answer sheet, darken the space for that number-letter combination.

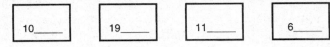

19. Directly below you will see three boxes and three words. Write the third letter of the first word on the line in the second box. Now, on your answer sheet, darken the space for that number-letter combination.

   BAD   DRAB   ALE

20. Count the number of points on the figure below. If there are five or more points, darken choice 6(E) on your answer sheet. If there are fewer than five points, darken choice 6(A).

★

**Directions:** Each question from 21–40 consists of a sentence written in four different ways. Choose the sentence that is most appropriate with respect to grammar, usage, and punctuation, so as to be suitable for a business letter or report and darken its letter on your answer sheet. Answer each question in the answer space with the corresponding number.

21. **(A)** Double parking is when you park your car alongside one that is already having been parked.
    **(B)** When one double parks, you park your car alongside one that is already parked.
    **(C)** Double parking is parking alongside a car already parked.
    **(D)** To double park is alongside a car already parked.

22. **(A)** This is entirely among you and he.
    **(B)** This is completely among him and you.
    **(C)** This is between you and him.
    **(D)** This is between he and you.

23. **(A)** As I said, "neither of them are guilty."
    **(B)** As I said, "neither of them are guilty".
    **(C)** As I said, "neither of them is guilty."
    **(D)** As I said, neither of them is guilty.

24. **(A)** I think that they will promote whoever has the best record.
    **(B)** The firm would have liked to have promoted all employees with good records.
    **(C)** Such of them that have the best records have excellent prospects of promotion.
    **(D)** I feel sure they will give the promotion to whomever has the best record.

**25. (A)** The receptionist must answer courteously the questions of all them callers.
 **(B)** The receptionist must answer courteously the questions what are asked by the callers.
 **(C)** There would have been no trouble if the receptionist had have always answered courteously.
 **(D)** The receptionist should answer courteously the questions of all callers.

**26. (A)** Since the report lacked the needed information, it was of no use to them.
 **(B)** This report was useless to them because there were no needed information in it.
 **(C)** Since the report did not contain the needed information, it was not real useful to them.
 **(D)** Being that the report lacked the needed information, they could not use it.

**27. (A)** The company had hardly declared the dividend till the notices were prepared for mailing.
 **(B)** They had no sooner declared the dividend when they sent the notices to the stockholders.
 **(C)** No sooner had the dividend been declared than the notices were prepared for mailing.
 **(D)** Scarcely had the dividend been declared than the notices were sent out.

**28. (A)** The supervisors reprimanded the typists, whom she believed had made careless errors.
 **(B)** The typists would have corrected the errors had they of known that the supervisor would see the report.
 **(C)** The errors in the typed reports were so numerous that they could hardly be overlooked.
 **(D)** Many errors were found in the reports which they typed and could not disregard them.

**29. (A)** "Are you absolutely certain, she asked, that you are right?"
 **(B)** "Are you absolutely certain," she asked, "that you are right?"
 **(C)** "Are you absolutely certain," she asked, "That you are right"?
 **(D)** "Are you absolutely certain", she asked, "That you are right?"

**30. (A)** He goes only to church on Christmas and Easter.
 **(B)** He only goes to church on Christmas and Easter.
 **(C)** He goes to only church on Christmas and Easter.
 **(D)** He goes to church only on Christmas and Easter.

**31. (A)** Most all these statements have been supported by persons who are reliable and can be depended upon.
 **(B)** The persons which have guaranteed these statements are reliable.
 **(C)** Reliable persons guarantee the facts with regards to the truth of these statements.
 **(D)** These statements can be depended on, for their truth has been guaranteed by reliable persons.

**32. (A)** The success of the book pleased both the publisher and authors.
 **(B)** Both the publisher and they was pleased with the success of the book.
 **(C)** Neither they or their publisher was disappointed with the success of the book.
 **(D)** Their publisher was as pleased as they with the success of the book.

33. **(A)** In reviewing the typists' work reports, the job analyst found records of unusual typing speeds.

**(B)** It says in the job analyst's report that some employees type with great speed.

**(C)** The job analyst found that, in reviewing the typists' work reports, that some unusual typing speeds had been made.

**(D)** In the reports of typists' speeds, the job analyst found some records that are kind of unusual.

34. **(A)** Every carrier should always have something to throw; not something to throw at the dog but something what will divert its attention.

**(B)** Every carrier should have something to throw—not something to throw at the dog but something to divert its attention.

**(C)** Every carrier should always carry something to throw not something to throw at the dog but something that will divert it's attention.

**(D)** Every carrier should always carry something to throw, not something to throw at the dog, but, something that will divert its' attention.

35. **(A)** Brown's & Company employees have recently received increases in salary.

**(B)** Brown & Company recently increased the salaries of all its employees.

**(C)** Recently Brown & Company has increased their employees' salaries.

**(D)** Brown & Company have recently increased the salaries of all its employees.

36. **(A)** If properly addressed, the letter will reach my mother and I.

**(B)** The letter had been addressed to myself and my mother.

**(C)** I believe the letter was addressed to either my mother or I.

**(D)** My mother's name, as well as mine, was on the letter.

37. **(A)** One of us have to make the reply before tomorrow.

**(B)** Making the reply before tomorrow will have to be done by one of us.

**(C)** One of us has to reply before tomorrow.

**(D)** Anyone has to reply before tomorrow.

38. **(A)** You have got to get rid of some of these people if you expect to have the quality of the work improve.

**(B)** The quality of the work would improve if they would leave fewer people do it.

**(C)** I believe it would be desirable to have fewer persons doing this work.

**(D)** If you had planned on employing fewer people than this to do the work, this situation would not have arose.

39. **(A)** The paper we use for this purpose must be light, glossy, and stand hard usage as well.

**(B)** Only a light and a glossy, but durable, paper must be used for this purpose.

**(C)** For this purpose, we want a paper that is light, glossy, but that will stand hard wear.

**(D)** For this purpose, paper that is light, glossy, and durable is essential.

40. **(A)** This letter, together with the reports, are to be sent to the postmaster.
   **(B)** The reports, together with this letter, is to be sent to the postmaster.
   **(C)** The reports and this letter is to be sent to the postmaster.
   **(D)** This letter, together with the reports, is to be sent to the postmaster.

---

**Directions:** Questions 41–48 each consist of a sentence containing a word in boldface type. Choose the best meaning for the word in boldface type and darken its letter on your answer sheet. Answer each question in the answer space with the corresponding number.

---

41. Please consult your office **manual** to learn the proper operation of our copying machine. **Manual** means most nearly
   **(A)** labor
   **(B)** handbook
   **(C)** typewriter
   **(D)** handle

42. There is a specified punishment for each **infraction** of the rules. **Infraction** means most nearly
   **(A)** violation
   **(B)** use
   **(C)** interpretation
   **(D)** part

43. The order was **rescinded** within the week. **Rescinded** means most nearly
   **(A)** revised
   **(B)** canceled
   **(C)** misinterpreted
   **(D)** confirmed

44. If you have a question, please raise your hand to **summon** the test proctor. **Summon** means most nearly
   **(A)** ticket
   **(B)** fine
   **(C)** give
   **(D)** call

45. We dared not prosecute the terrorist for fear of **reprisal**. **Reprisal** means most nearly
   **(A)** retaliation
   **(B)** advantage
   **(C)** warning
   **(D)** denial

46. The increased use of dictation machines has severely **reduced** the need for office stenographers. **Reduced** means most nearly
   **(A)** enlarged
   **(B)** cut out
   **(C)** lessened
   **(D)** expanded

47. Frequent use of marijuana may **impair** your judgment. **Impair** means most nearly
   **(A)** weaken
   **(B)** conceal
   **(C)** improve
   **(D)** expose

48. It is altogether **fitting** that the parent discipline the child. **Fitting** means most nearly
   **(A)** illegal
   **(B)** bad practice
   **(C)** appropriate
   **(D)** required

**Directions:** For questions 49–55, read each paragraph and answer the question that follows it by darkening the letter of the correct answer on your answer sheet. Answer each question in the answer space with the corresponding number.

49. A survey to determine the subjects that have helped students most in their jobs shows that typewriting leads all other subjects in the business group. It also leads among the subjects college students consider most valuable and would take again if they were to return to high school.

The paragraph best supports the statement that

(A) the ability to type is an asset in business and in school

(B) students who return to night school take typing

(C) students with a knowledge of typing do superior work in college

(D) success in business is assured those who can type

50. Telegrams should be clear, concise, and brief. Omit all unnecessary words. The parts of speech most often used in telegrams are nouns, verbs, adjectives, and adverbs. If possible, do not use pronouns, prepositions, articles, and copulative verbs. Use simple sentences, rather than complex and compound.

The paragraph best supports the statement that in writing telegrams one should always use

(A) common and simple words

(B) only nouns, verbs, adjectives, and adverbs

(C) incomplete sentences

(D) only words essential to the meaning

51. Since the government can spend only what it obtains from the people, and this amount is ultimately limited by their capacity and willingness to pay taxes, it is very important that people be given full information about the work of the government.

The paragraph best supports the statement that

(A) governmental employees should be trained not only in their own work, but also in how to perform the duties of other employees in their agency

(B) taxation by the government rests upon the consent of the people

(C) the release of full information on the work of the government will increase the efficiency of governmental operations

(D) the work of the government, in recent years, has been restricted because of reduced tax collections

52. Both the high school and the college should take the responsibility for preparing the student to get a job. Since the ability to write a good application letter is one of the first steps toward this goal, every teacher should be willing to do what he can to help the student learn to write such letters.

The paragraph best supports the statement that

(A) inability to write a good letter may reduce one's job prospects

(B) the major responsibility of the school is to obtain jobs for its students

(C) success is largely a matter of the kind of work the student applies for first

(D) every teacher should teach a course in the writing of application letters

**53.** Direct lighting is the least satisfactory lighting arrangement. The desk or ceiling light with a reflector that diffuses all the rays downward is sure to cause a glare on the working surface.

The paragraph best supports the statement that direct lighting is least satisfactory as a method of lighting chiefly because

**(A)** the light is diffused causing eye strain

**(B)** the shade on the individual desk lamp is not constructed along scientific lines

**(C)** the working surface is usually obscured by the glare

**(D)** direct lighting is injurious to the eyes

**54.** "White collar" is a term used to describe one of the largest groups of workers in American industry and trade. It distinguishes those who work with the pencil and the mind from those who depend on their hands and the machine. It suggests occupations in which physical exertion and handling of materials are not primary features of the job.

The paragraph best supports the statement that "white collar" workers are

**(A)** not so strong physically as those who work with their hands

**(B)** those who supervise workers handling materials

**(C)** all whose work is entirely indoors

**(D)** not likely to use machines as much as are other groups of workers

**55.** In large organizations some standardized, simple, inexpensive method of giving employees information about company policies and rules, as well as specific instructions regarding their duties, is practically essential. This is the purpose of all office manuals of whatever type.

The paragraph best supports the statement that office manuals

**(A)** are all about the same

**(B)** should be simple enough for the average employee to understand

**(C)** are necessary to large organizations

**(D)** act as constant reminders to the employee of his or her duties

## ANSWER KEY AND EXPLANATIONS

### Part A: Clerical Ability

| | | | | |
|---|---|---|---|---|
| 1. E | 18. B | 35. A | 52. C | 69. B |
| 2. D | 19. A | 36. B | 53. C | 70. B |
| 3. A | 20. C | 37. E | 54. A | 71. E |
| 4. D | 21. A | 38. C | 55. D | 72. B |
| 5. A | 22. E | 39. D | 56. A | 73. A |
| 6. C | 23. C | 40. A | 57. D | 74. B |
| 7. B | 24. B | 41. A | 58. B | 75. E |
| 8. D | 25. D | 42. C | 59. C | 76. C |
| 9. E | 26. E | 43. C | 60. B | 77. E |
| 10. C | 27. A | 44. E | 61. A | 78. E |
| 11. C | 28. B | 45. D | 62. C | 79. C |
| 12. D | 29. C | 46. B | 63. C | 80. B |
| 13. C | 30. D | 47. E | 64. D | 81. E |
| 14. D | 31. D | 48. A | 65. D | 82. C |
| 15. C | 32. E | 49. C | 66. C | 83. E |
| 16. A | 33. A | 50. A | 67. A | 84. C |
| 17. E | 34. A | 51. A | 68. D | 85. B |

1. **The correct answer is (E).** Hachettson; Hackett

2. **The correct answer is (D).** 59233262; 59233362

3. **The correct answer is (A).** MYP; NYP

4. **The correct answer is (D).** Olivia H.; Olivier E.; R. Olivia

5. **The correct answer is (A).** 0010; 0012

6. **The correct answer is (C).** 6001; 6100; 6101

7. **The correct answer is (B).** Vanover; Vanstory; VanSwinderen

8. **The correct answer is (D).** FitzGibbon; Fitzsimmons; FitzSimons

9. **The correct answer is (E).** 01016060; 01066010

10. **The correct answer is (C).** AAS; AAZ; ASA

11. **The correct answer is (C).** Pawelek; Pawlowicz; Pawlowski

12. **The correct answer is (D).** 7710; 7834; 7868

13. **The correct answer is (C).** 36270000; 36270013; 36270030

14. **The correct answer is (D).** Freedenberg; Freedenburg; Freedinberg

15. **The correct answer is (C).** Proutey; Prouty, Martha; Prouty, Myra

16. **The correct answer is (A).** 58006021; 58006130

**17. The correct answer is (E).** EKK-14<u>03</u>; EKK-14<u>43</u>

**18. The correct answer is (B).** <u>Daly</u>; D'Amato; D'Amboise

**19. The correct answer is (A).** Sch<u>ae</u>ffer; Sch<u>a</u>ffert

**20. The correct answer is (C).** P<u>SP</u>; <u>SPP</u>; <u>SPS</u>

**21. The correct answer is (A).**

| | | |
|---|---|---|
| Drusilla S. Ridgeley | Drusilla S. Ridgeley | Drusilla S. Ridgeley |

**22. The correct answer is (E).**

| | | |
|---|---|---|
| Andrei I. Toumantzev | Andrei I. To<u>ur</u>mantzev | Andrei I. Toumant<u>zov</u> |

**23. The correct answer is (C).**

| | | |
|---|---|---|
| 6-78912-e3e42 | 6-78912-<u>3</u>e3e42 | 6-78912-e3e42 |

**24. The correct answer is (B).**

| | | |
|---|---|---|
| 86529 Dunwoodie Drive | 86529 Dunwoodie Drive | 8<u>5</u>629 Dunwoodie Drive |

**25. The correct answer is (D).**

| | | |
|---|---|---|
| 1592<u>514</u> | 1592574 | 1592574 |

**26. The correct answer is (E).**

| | | |
|---|---|---|
| Ella Burk N<u>ew</u>ham | Ella Burk Newnham | <u>Elena</u> Burk Newnham |

**27. The correct answer is (A).**

| | | |
|---|---|---|
| 5416R-1952TZ-op | 5416R-1952TZ-op | 5416R-1952TZ-op |

**28. The correct answer is (B).**

| | | |
|---|---|---|
| 60646 West Touhy Avenue | 60646 West Touhy Avenue | 60646 West Tou<u>hey</u> Avenue |

**29. The correct answer is (C).**

| | | |
|---|---|---|
| Mardikian & Moore, Inc. | Mardikian <u>and</u> Moore, Inc. | Mardikian & Moore, Inc. |

**30. The correct answer is (D).**

| | | |
|---|---|---|
| 9670<u>243</u> | 9670423 | 9670423 |

**31. The correct answer is (D).**

| | | |
|---|---|---|
| Eduardo Ingles_ | Eduardo Inglese | Eduardo Inglese |

**32. The correct answer is (E).**

| | | |
|---|---|---|
| Roger T. DeAngelis | Roger T. <u>D'</u>Angelis | Roger T. DeAng<u>e</u>les |

**33. The correct answer is (A).**

| | | |
|---|---|---|
| 7692138 | 7692138 | 7692138 |

**34. The correct answer is (A).**

| | | |
|---|---|---|
| 2695 East 3435 South | 2695 East 3435 South | 2695 East 3435 South |

**35. The correct answer is (A).**

| | | |
|---|---|---|
| 63qs5-95YT3-001 | 63qs5-95YT3-001 | 63qs5-95YT3-001 |

**36. The correct answer is (B).**

| | | |
|---|---|---|
| 2789350 | 2789350 | 27<u>9</u>8350 |

**37. The correct answer is (E).**

| | | |
|---|---|---|
| Helmut V. Lochner | Helmut V. Loc<u>k</u>ner | Helmut <u>W.</u> Lochner |

**38. The correct answer is (C).**

| | | |
|---|---|---|
| 2454803 | 2<u>548</u>403 | 2454803 |

39. **The correct answer is (D).**
Lemberger, <u>WA</u> 28094-9182      Lemberger, VA 28094-9182      Lemberger, VA 28094-9182

40. **The correct answer is (A).**
4168-GNP-78852                 4168-GNP-78852                  4168-GNP-78852

41. **The correct answer is (A).**
Yoshihito Saito               Yoshihito Saito                 Yoshihito Saito

42. **The correct answer is (C).**
5927681                        59<u>27861</u>                         5927681

43. **The correct answer is (C).**
O'Reilly Bay, LA 56212         O'Reilly<u>s</u> Bay, LA 56212        O'Reilly Bay, LA 56212

44. **The correct answer is (E).**
Francis Ran<u>s</u>dell              Franc<u>es</u> Ramsdell               Francis Ramsdell

45. **The correct answer is (D).**
5634-Oot<u>V</u>5a-16867            5634-Ootv5a-16867               5634-Ootv5a-16867

46. **The correct answer is (B).**
Dolores Mollicone              Dolores Mollicone              Dolor<u>as</u> Mollicone

47. **The correct answer is (E).**
David C. Routzon              David <u>E</u>. Routzon               David C. Routz<u>r</u>on

48. **The correct answer is (A).**
8932 Shimabui Hwy.            8932 Shimabui Hwy.              8932 Shimabui Hwy.

49. **The correct answer is (C).**
6177396                        6177<u>936</u>                         6177396

50. **The correct answer is (A).**
A8987-B73245                   A8987-B73245                   A8987-B73245

51. **The correct answer is (A).** anticipate
52. **The correct answer is (C).** similar
53. **The correct answer is (C).** sufficiently
54. **The correct answer is (A).** intelligence
55. **The correct answer is (D).** reference
56. **The correct answer is (A).** conscious
57. **The correct answer is (D).** parallel
58. **The correct answer is (B).** abundance
59. **The correct answer is (C).** corrugated
60. **The correct answer is (B).** accumulation
61. **The correct answer is (A).** resonance
62. **The correct answer is (C).** beneficial
63. **The correct answer is (C).** specifically
64. **The correct answer is (D).** eliminate
65. **The correct answer is (D).** colossal
66. **The correct answer is (C).** auxiliary
67. **The correct answer is (A).** inimitable
68. **The correct answer is (D).** disappearance
69. **The correct answer is (B).** appellate
70. **The correct answer is (B).** essential

71. The correct answer is (E).
$$\begin{array}{r} 83 \\ -\ 56 \\ \hline 27 \end{array}$$

72. The correct answer is (B).
$$\begin{array}{r} 15 \\ +\ 17 \\ \hline 32 \end{array}$$

73. The correct answer is (A).
$$\begin{array}{r} 32 \\ \times\ \ 7 \\ \hline 224 \end{array}$$

74. The correct answer is (B).
$$\begin{array}{r} 39 \\ \times\ \ 2 \\ \hline 78 \end{array}$$

75. The correct answer is (E).
$$\begin{array}{r} 43 \\ -\ 15 \\ \hline 28 \end{array}$$

76. The correct answer is (C).
$$\begin{array}{r} 50 \\ +\ 49 \\ \hline 99 \end{array}$$

77. The correct answer is (E). $6\overline{)366}$ with quotient $61$

78. The correct answer is (E).
$$\begin{array}{r} 38 \\ \times\ \ 3 \\ \hline 114 \end{array}$$

79. The correct answer is (C).
$$\begin{array}{r} 19 \\ +\ 21 \\ \hline 40 \end{array}$$

80. The correct answer is (B).
$$\begin{array}{r} 13 \\ -\ \ 6 \\ \hline 7 \end{array}$$

81. The correct answer is (E). $6\overline{)180}$ with quotient $30$

82. The correct answer is (C).
$$\begin{array}{r} 10 \\ \times\ \ 1 \\ \hline 10 \end{array}$$

83. The correct answer is (E). $7\overline{)287}$ with quotient $41$

84. The correct answer is (C).
$$\begin{array}{r} 12 \\ +\ 11 \\ \hline 23 \end{array}$$

85. The correct answer is (B).
$$\begin{array}{r} 85 \\ -\ 64 \\ \hline 21 \end{array}$$

## Part B: Verbal Ability

| | | | | |
|---|---|---|---|---|
| 1. D | 12. B | 23. D | 34. B | 45. A |
| 2. C | 13. D | 24. A | 35. B | 46. C |
| 3. E | 14. A | 25. D | 36. D | 47. A |
| 4. A | 15. D | 26. A | 37. C | 48. C |
| 5. C | 16. D | 27. C | 38. C | 49. A |
| 6. E | 17. E | 28. C | 39. D | 50. D |
| 7. D | 18. A | 29. B | 40. D | 51. B |
| 8. C | 19. D | 30. D | 41. B | 52. A |
| 9. E | 20. B | 31. D | 42. A | 53. C |
| 10. B | 21. C | 32. A | 43. B | 54. D |
| 11. A | 22. C | 33. A | 44. D | 55. C |

21. **The correct answer is (C).** Sentence (C) is the best expression of the idea. Sentence (A) has two grammatical errors: the use of *when* to introduce a definition and the unacceptable verb form *is already having been parked.* Sentence (B) incorrectly shifts subjects from *one* to *you.* Sentence (D) does not make sense.

22. **The correct answer is (C).** Choice (B) is incorrect because only two persons are involved in this statement. *Between* is used when there are only two, *among* is reserved for three or more. Choice (A) makes a similar error. In addition, both (A) and (D) use the pronoun *he.* The object of a preposition, in this case *between,* must be in the objective case, hence *him.*

23. **The correct answer is (D).** Punctuation aside, both (A) and (B) incorrectly place the verb in the plural, *are. Neither* is a singular indefinite pronoun. It means *not one and not the other* and requires a singular verb. The choice between (C) and (D) is more difficult, but basically this is a simple statement and not a direct quote.

24. **The correct answer is (A).** *Whoever* is the subject of the phrase *whoever has the best record.* Hence (A) is the correct answer and (D) is wrong. Both (B) and (C) are wordy and awkward.

25. **The correct answer is (D).** All the other choices contain obvious errors.

26. **The correct answer is (A).** Choice (B) uses the plural verb *were* with the singular subject *report.* (C) and (D) are colloquial and incorrect even for informal speech. They have no place in business writing.

27. **The correct answer is (C).** Choices (A) and (B) use adverbs incorrectly; choice (D) is awkward and unidiomatic.

28. **The correct answer is (C).** Choices (B) and (D) are obviously incorrect. In (A), the pronoun *who* should be the subject of the phrase *who had made careless errors.*

29. **The correct answer is (B).** Only the quoted material should appear enclosed by quotation marks, so (A) is incorrect. Only the first word of a sentence should begin with a capital letter, so both (C) and (D) are wrong. In addition, only the quoted material itself is a question; the entire sentence is a statement. Therefore, the question mark must be placed inside the quotes.

30. **The correct answer is (D).** Choices (A) and (B) imply that he stays in church all day on Christmas and Easter and goes nowhere else. Choice (C) makes the same implication and in addition splits the infinitive awkwardly. In (D) the modifier *only* is correctly placed to tell us that the only times he goes to church are on Christmas and Easter.

**31. The correct answer is (D).** Choice (A) might state either *most* or *all* but not both; choice (B) should read *persons who;* choice (C) should read *with regard to....*

**32. The correct answer is (A).** Choice (A) is the clearest expression of the idea; choice (B) requires the plural verb *were;* choice (C) requires the correlative construction *neither ... nor;* choice (D) is awkward.

**33. The correct answer is (A).** Choices (C) and (D) are glaringly poor. Choice (B) is not incorrect, but choice (A) is far better.

**34. The correct answer is (B).** Choice (A) incorrectly uses a semicolon to separate a complete clause from a sentence fragment. In addition, (A) incorrectly uses *what* in place of *that.* Choice (C) is a run-on sentence that also misuses an apostrophe: *It's* is the contraction for *it is,* not the possessive of *it.* Choice (D) uses commas indiscriminately; it also misuses the apostrophe.

**35. The correct answer is (B).** In choice (A) the placement of the apostrophe is inappropriate; choices (C) and (D) use the plural, but there is only one company.

**36. The correct answer is (D).** Choices (A) and (C) are incorrect in use of the subject form *I* instead of the object of the preposition *me.* Choice (B) incorrectly uses the reflexive *myself.* Only I can address a letter to myself.

**37. The correct answer is (C).** Choice (A) incorrectly uses the plural verb form *have* with the singular subject *one.* Choice (B) is awkward and wordy. Choice (D) incorrectly changes the subject from *one of us* to *anyone.*

**38. The correct answer is (C).** (A) is wordy. In (B), the correct verb should be *have* in place of *leave.* In (D), the word *arose* should be *arisen.*

**39. The correct answer is (D).** The first three sentences lack parallel construction. All the words that modify *paper* must appear in the same form.

**40. The correct answer is (D).** The phrase *together with...* is extra information and not a part of the subject; therefore, both (A) and (B) represent similar errors of agreement. Choice (C) also presents disagreement in number between subject and verb, but in this case the compound subject, indicated by the use of the conjunction *and,* requires a plural verb.

**41. The correct answer is (B).** Even if you do not recognize the root *manu* meaning *hand* and relating directly to *handbook,* you should have no trouble getting this question right. If you substitute each of the choices in the sentence, you will readily see that only one makes sense.

**42. The correct answer is (A).** Within the context of the sentence, the thought of a specified punishment for *use, interpretation,* or *part* of the rules does not make too much sense. *Fraction* gives a hint of *part,* but you must also contend with the negative prefix *in.* Since it is reasonable to expect punishment for negative behavior with relation to the rules, *violation,* which is the meaning of INFRACTION, is the proper answer.

**43. The correct answer is (B).** The prefix should help you narrow your choices. The prefix *re* meaning *back* or *again* narrows the choices to (A) or (B). To RESCIND is to *take back* or to *cancel.*

**44. The correct answer is (D).** First eliminate (C) since it does not make sense in the sentence. Your experience with the word *summons* may be with relation to *tickets* and *fines,* but tickets and fines have nothing to do with asking questions while taking a test. Even if you are unfamiliar with the word SUMMON, you should be able to choose *call* as the best synonym in this context.

**45. The correct answer is (A).** REPRISAL means injury done for injury received or *retaliation.*

46. **The correct answer is (C).** To RE-DUCE is to *make smaller* or to *lessen.*

47. **The correct answer is (A).** To IM-PAIR is to *make worse,* to *injure,* or to *weaken.*

48. **The correct answer is (C).** FITTING in this context means *suitable* or *appropriate.*

49. **The correct answer is (A).** The survey showed that of all subjects typing has helped most in business. It was also considered valuable by college students in their schoolwork.

50. **The correct answer is (D).** See the second sentence.

51. **The correct answer is (B).** According to the paragraph, the government can spend only what it obtains from the people. The government obtains money from the people by taxation. If the people are unwilling to pay taxes, the government has no source of funds.

52. **The correct answer is (A).** Step one in the job application process is often the application letter. If the letter is not effective, the applicant will not move on to the next step and job prospects will be greatly lessened.

53. **The correct answer is (C).** The second sentence states that direct lighting causes glare on the working surface.

54. **The correct answer is (D).** While all the answer choices are likely to be true, the answer suggested by the paragraph is that "white collar" workers work with their pencils and their minds rather than with their hands and machines.

55. **The correct answer is (C).** All the paragraph says is that office manuals are a necessity in large organizations.

answers practice test 6

## PRACTICE TEST 7: FOLLOWING ORAL INSTRUCTIONS

| | | | |
|---|---|---|---|
| 1. Ⓐ Ⓑ Ⓒ Ⓓ Ⓔ | 23. Ⓐ Ⓑ Ⓒ Ⓓ Ⓔ | 45. Ⓐ Ⓑ Ⓒ Ⓓ Ⓔ | 67. Ⓐ Ⓑ Ⓒ Ⓓ Ⓔ |
| 2. Ⓐ Ⓑ Ⓒ Ⓓ Ⓔ | 24. Ⓐ Ⓑ Ⓒ Ⓓ Ⓔ | 46. Ⓐ Ⓑ Ⓒ Ⓓ Ⓔ | 68. Ⓐ Ⓑ Ⓒ Ⓓ Ⓔ |
| 3. Ⓐ Ⓑ Ⓒ Ⓓ Ⓔ | 25. Ⓐ Ⓑ Ⓒ Ⓓ Ⓔ | 47. Ⓐ Ⓑ Ⓒ Ⓓ Ⓔ | 69. Ⓐ Ⓑ Ⓒ Ⓓ Ⓔ |
| 4. Ⓐ Ⓑ Ⓒ Ⓓ Ⓔ | 26. Ⓐ Ⓑ Ⓒ Ⓓ Ⓔ | 48. Ⓐ Ⓑ Ⓒ Ⓓ Ⓔ | 70. Ⓐ Ⓑ Ⓒ Ⓓ Ⓔ |
| 5. Ⓐ Ⓑ Ⓒ Ⓓ Ⓔ | 27. Ⓐ Ⓑ Ⓒ Ⓓ Ⓔ | 49. Ⓐ Ⓑ Ⓒ Ⓓ Ⓔ | 71. Ⓐ Ⓑ Ⓒ Ⓓ Ⓔ |
| 6. Ⓐ Ⓑ Ⓒ Ⓓ Ⓔ | 28. Ⓐ Ⓑ Ⓒ Ⓓ Ⓔ | 50. Ⓐ Ⓑ Ⓒ Ⓓ Ⓔ | 72. Ⓐ Ⓑ Ⓒ Ⓓ Ⓔ |
| 7. Ⓐ Ⓑ Ⓒ Ⓓ Ⓔ | 29. Ⓐ Ⓑ Ⓒ Ⓓ Ⓔ | 51. Ⓐ Ⓑ Ⓒ Ⓓ Ⓔ | 73. Ⓐ Ⓑ Ⓒ Ⓓ Ⓔ |
| 8. Ⓐ Ⓑ Ⓒ Ⓓ Ⓔ | 30. Ⓐ Ⓑ Ⓒ Ⓓ Ⓔ | 52. Ⓐ Ⓑ Ⓒ Ⓓ Ⓔ | 74. Ⓐ Ⓑ Ⓒ Ⓓ Ⓔ |
| 9. Ⓐ Ⓑ Ⓒ Ⓓ Ⓔ | 31. Ⓐ Ⓑ Ⓒ Ⓓ Ⓔ | 53. Ⓐ Ⓑ Ⓒ Ⓓ Ⓔ | 75. Ⓐ Ⓑ Ⓒ Ⓓ Ⓔ |
| 10. Ⓐ Ⓑ Ⓒ Ⓓ Ⓔ | 32. Ⓐ Ⓑ Ⓒ Ⓓ Ⓔ | 54. Ⓐ Ⓑ Ⓒ Ⓓ Ⓔ | 76. Ⓐ Ⓑ Ⓒ Ⓓ Ⓔ |
| 11. Ⓐ Ⓑ Ⓒ Ⓓ Ⓔ | 33. Ⓐ Ⓑ Ⓒ Ⓓ Ⓔ | 55. Ⓐ Ⓑ Ⓒ Ⓓ Ⓔ | 77. Ⓐ Ⓑ Ⓒ Ⓓ Ⓔ |
| 12. Ⓐ Ⓑ Ⓒ Ⓓ Ⓔ | 34. Ⓐ Ⓑ Ⓒ Ⓓ Ⓔ | 56. Ⓐ Ⓑ Ⓒ Ⓓ Ⓔ | 78. Ⓐ Ⓑ Ⓒ Ⓓ Ⓔ |
| 13. Ⓐ Ⓑ Ⓒ Ⓓ Ⓔ | 35. Ⓐ Ⓑ Ⓒ Ⓓ Ⓔ | 57. Ⓐ Ⓑ Ⓒ Ⓓ Ⓔ | 79. Ⓐ Ⓑ Ⓒ Ⓓ Ⓔ |
| 14. Ⓐ Ⓑ Ⓒ Ⓓ Ⓔ | 36. Ⓐ Ⓑ Ⓒ Ⓓ Ⓔ | 58. Ⓐ Ⓑ Ⓒ Ⓓ Ⓔ | 80. Ⓐ Ⓑ Ⓒ Ⓓ Ⓔ |
| 15. Ⓐ Ⓑ Ⓒ Ⓓ Ⓔ | 37. Ⓐ Ⓑ Ⓒ Ⓓ Ⓔ | 59. Ⓐ Ⓑ Ⓒ Ⓓ Ⓔ | 81. Ⓐ Ⓑ Ⓒ Ⓓ Ⓔ |
| 16. Ⓐ Ⓑ Ⓒ Ⓓ Ⓔ | 38. Ⓐ Ⓑ Ⓒ Ⓓ Ⓔ | 60. Ⓐ Ⓑ Ⓒ Ⓓ Ⓔ | 82. Ⓐ Ⓑ Ⓒ Ⓓ Ⓔ |
| 17. Ⓐ Ⓑ Ⓒ Ⓓ Ⓔ | 39. Ⓐ Ⓑ Ⓒ Ⓓ Ⓔ | 61. Ⓐ Ⓑ Ⓒ Ⓓ Ⓔ | 83. Ⓐ Ⓑ Ⓒ Ⓓ Ⓔ |
| 18. Ⓐ Ⓑ Ⓒ Ⓓ Ⓔ | 40. Ⓐ Ⓑ Ⓒ Ⓓ Ⓔ | 62. Ⓐ Ⓑ Ⓒ Ⓓ Ⓔ | 84. Ⓐ Ⓑ Ⓒ Ⓓ Ⓔ |
| 19. Ⓐ Ⓑ Ⓒ Ⓓ Ⓔ | 41. Ⓐ Ⓑ Ⓒ Ⓓ Ⓔ | 63. Ⓐ Ⓑ Ⓒ Ⓓ Ⓔ | 85. Ⓐ Ⓑ Ⓒ Ⓓ Ⓔ |
| 20. Ⓐ Ⓑ Ⓒ Ⓓ Ⓔ | 42. Ⓐ Ⓑ Ⓒ Ⓓ Ⓔ | 64. Ⓐ Ⓑ Ⓒ Ⓓ Ⓔ | 86. Ⓐ Ⓑ Ⓒ Ⓓ Ⓔ |
| 21. Ⓐ Ⓑ Ⓒ Ⓓ Ⓔ | 43. Ⓐ Ⓑ Ⓒ Ⓓ Ⓔ | 65. Ⓐ Ⓑ Ⓒ Ⓓ Ⓔ | 87. Ⓐ Ⓑ Ⓒ Ⓓ Ⓔ |
| 22. Ⓐ Ⓑ Ⓒ Ⓓ Ⓔ | 44. Ⓐ Ⓑ Ⓒ Ⓓ Ⓔ | 66. Ⓐ Ⓑ Ⓒ Ⓓ Ⓔ | 88. Ⓐ Ⓑ Ⓒ Ⓓ Ⓔ |

answer sheet

# Practice Test 7: Following Oral Instructions

**NOTE:** Practice Test 7 is part of Postal Service Exam 460, Rural Carrier Associate. To practice for Part D of Exam 460 (Following Oral Instructions), you may want to take this test. Also see the note at the beginning of Practice Test 1 for more tips on how to prepare to take Exam 460.

Practice Test 7 is also similar to one part of each of the four Postal Service exams used to test applicants for maintenance positions:

1. Exam 916 (Custodial Maintenance)

2. Exam 931 (General Maintenance)

3. Exam 932 (Electronic Technician)

4. Exam 933 (Maintenance Mechanic)

The other sections of these four exams assess specific skills and abilities related to job tasks—for example, electrical and electronic knowledge, computer concepts, safety procedures, and mechanical skills—that cannot be reproduced in a book. If you plan to apply for a maintenance position with the USPS, you should take Practice Test 7 to gain experience in this part of your exam. Note, however, that the specific exam administered to you may differ somewhat from Practice Test 7 in number of questions, time allotted, and so on.

## 25 MINUTES

**Directions:** Give the following instructions to a friend and have him or her read them aloud to you at the rate of 80 words per minute. (The person should NOT read aloud the words in parentheses.) Do NOT read them to yourself. Your friend will need a watch with a second hand. Listen carefully and do exactly what your friend tells you to do with the worksheet and with the answer sheet. Your friend will tell you what to do with each item on the worksheet. After each set of instructions, your friend will give you time to mark your answer by darkening a circle on the answer sheet. Since B and D sound very much alike, have your friend say "B as in baker" when he or she means B, and "D as in dog" when he or she means D.

Before proceeding, tear out or copy the worksheet beginning on page 313. Then hand this book to your friend.

## Read Aloud to the Candidate

**To the Person Who Is to Read the Instructions:** The instructions should be read at the rate of 80 words per minute. Do not read aloud the material that is in parentheses. Once you have begun the test itself, do not repeat any instructions.

The next three paragraphs consist of approximately 120 words. Read these three paragraphs aloud to the candidate in about one and one-half minutes. You may practice rereading these three paragraphs as often as necessary to establish an 80-words-per-minute reading speed.

"On the job you will have to listen to directions and then do what you have been told to do. In this test, I will read instructions to you. Try to understand them as I read them; I cannot repeat them. Once we begin, you may not ask any questions until the end of the test.

"On the job, you won't have to deal with pictures, numbers, and letters like those in the test, but you will have to listen to instructions and follow them. We are using this test to see how well you can follow instructions.

"Mark your test booklet according to the instructions that I'll read to you. After each set of instructions, I'll give you time to record your answers on the separate answer sheet."

The actual test begins now.

**Look at line 1 on your worksheet.** Each number represents a length of rope. (Pause briefly.) Draw two lines under the number that represents the longest length of rope. (Pause 2 seconds.) Now, on your answer sheet, find the number under which you just drew two lines and darken B as in baker for that number. (Pause 5 seconds.)

**Look at line 1 again.** (Pause briefly.) Find the number that represents the shortest length of rope and draw one wavy line above that number. (Pause 2 seconds.) Now, on your answer sheet, darken space A for the number over which you just drew the wavy line. (Pause 5 seconds.)

**Look at line 2 on your worksheet.** The number in each carton represents the number of boxes of soap powder in the carton. (Pause briefly.) Write the letter D as in dog in the carton that is closest to empty. (Pause 2 seconds.) Now, on your answer sheet, darken the space for the number-letter combination in the carton you just wrote in. (Pause 5 seconds.)

**Look at line 3 on your worksheet.** (Pause briefly.) If Christmas is always on a Thursday, write the letter C next to the first number on line 3; if not, write the letter E next to the second number. (Pause 5 seconds.) Now, on your answer sheet, darken the space for the number next to which you just wrote a letter. (Pause 5 seconds.)

**Look at line 3 again.** (Pause briefly.) Write the second letter of the alphabet next to the lowest number on line 3. (Pause 2 seconds.) Now, on your answer sheet, darken the space for the number-letter combination you just wrote. (Pause 5 seconds.)

**Look at line 4 on your worksheet.** (Pause briefly.) Count the number of letters in the word and write the number of letters at the end of line 4. (Pause 2 seconds.) Now, on your answer sheet, darken letter C for the number you just wrote. (Pause 5 seconds.)

**Look at line 4 again.** (Pause briefly.) Draw a circle around the fifth letter in the word. (Pause 2 seconds.) Now, on your answer sheet, find number 64 and darken the space for the letter you just circled. (Pause 5 seconds.)

**Look at line 5 on your worksheet.** The numbers represent days of the month. Floors are to be washed on odd-numbered days. (Pause briefly.) Draw one line under the number of each day on which floors should be washed. (Pause 5 seconds.) Now, on your answer sheet, darken letter D as in dog for each number under which you drew a line. (Pause 10 seconds.)

**Look at line 6 on your worksheet.** (Pause briefly.) Write the letter C on the line in the bucket with the highest number. (Pause 2 seconds.) Now, on your answer sheet, darken the space for the number-letter combination in that bucket. (Pause 5 seconds.)

**Look at line 6 again.** (Pause briefly.) Write the letter B as in baker on the line in the middle bucket. (Pause 2 seconds.) Now, on your answer sheet, darken the space for the number-letter combination in that bucket. (Pause 5 seconds.)

**Look at line 7 on your worksheet.** (Pause briefly.) Count the number of times the letter A appears on line 7 and write that number at the end of the line. (Pause 2 seconds.) Add 10 to the number you just wrote. Now, on your answer sheet, find the number that represents the sum of the number you wrote plus 10 and darken space E for that number. (Pause 10 seconds.)

**Look at line 8 on your worksheet.** Each item on line 8 represents a key code. Only keys with odd-numbered codes open the restroom doors in the post office. (Pause briefly.) Draw two lines under the code for each key that will open a restroom door. (Pause 5 seconds.) Now, on your answer sheet, darken each space that represents a key that will open a restroom. (Pause 15 seconds.)

**Look at line 9 on your worksheet.** Each box contains a different kind of screw. (Pause briefly.) The box with the higher number holds wood screws, and the box with the lower number holds sheet-metal screws. (Pause 2 seconds.) Write the letter A in the box that holds sheet-metal screws. (Pause 2 seconds.) Write the letter E in the box that holds wood screws. (Pause 2 seconds.) Now, on your answer sheet, darken the spaces for the number-letter combinations in the boxes. (Pause 10 seconds.)

**Look at line 10 on your worksheet.** (Pause briefly.) If brooms are used for sweeping floors, write B as in baker in the triangle. If not, write D as in dog in the square. (Pause 2 seconds.) Now, on your answer sheet, darken the space for the number-letter combination in the figure you just wrote in. (Pause 5 seconds.)

**Look at line 10 again.** (Pause briefly.) Write the letter C in every figure that has no angles. (Pause 5 seconds.) Now, on your answer sheet, darken the number-letter combination in each figure that you just wrote in. (Pause 10 seconds.)

**Look at line 11 on your worksheet.** (Pause briefly.) The third mailbox on line 11 has a broken lock and must be reported for repair. Write the letter D as in dog on the line in the broken mailbox. (Pause 2 seconds.) Now, on your answer sheet, darken the space for the number-letter combination in the mailbox with the broken lock. (Pause 5 seconds.)

**Look at line 11 again.** (Pause briefly.) The first mailbox belongs to Mr. and Mrs. Dana. Write the second letter of the Danas' name in their mailbox. (Pause 2 seconds.) Now, on your answer sheet, darken the space for the number-letter combination in the Danas' mailbox. (Pause 5 seconds.)

**Look at line 12 on your worksheet.** (Pause briefly.) Write the number of minutes in an hour next to the fourth letter of the alphabet. (Pause 2 seconds.) Now, on your answer sheet, darken the space for the number-letter combination you just wrote. (Pause 5 seconds.)

**Look at the brooms on line 13 on your worksheet.** (Pause briefly.) Write the first letter of the word "broom" on the line under the first broom. (Pause 2 seconds.) Now, on your answer sheet, darken the space for the number-letter combination under the broom. (Pause 5 seconds.)

**Look at the brooms on line 13 again.** (Pause briefly.) Write the letter E on the line under the broom that is different from the other brooms. (Pause 2 seconds.) Now, on your answer sheet, darken the space for the number-letter combination under the broom. (Pause 5 seconds.)

## Worksheet

**Directions:** Listen carefully to each set of instructions and mark each item on this worksheet as directed. Then complete each question by marking the answer sheet as directed. For each direction you will darken the space for a number-letter combination. Should you fall behind and miss an instruction, don't panic. Let that one go and listen for the next one. If, when you start to darken a space for a number, you find that you have already darkened another space for that number, either erase the first mark and darken the space for the new combination or let the first mark stay and do not darken a space for the new combination. Write with a pencil that has a clean eraser. When you finish, you should have no more than one space darkened for each number. Correct answers are on pages 321–323.

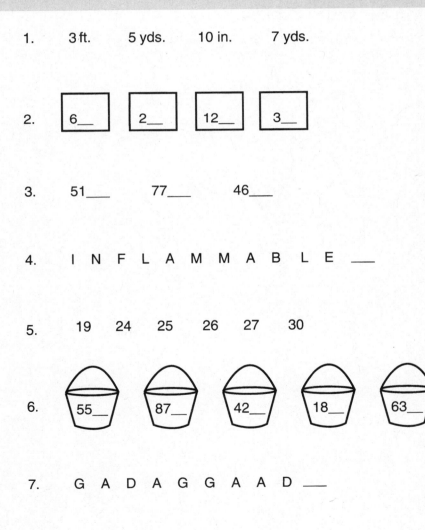

1.      3 ft.        5 yds.       10 in.        7 yds.

2.     [ 6__ ]    [ 2__ ]    [ 12__ ]    [ 3__ ]

3.      51___          77___          46___

4.     I N F L A M M A B L E  ___

5.      19   24   25   26   27   30

6.     55__    87__    42__    18__    63__

7.     G A D A G G A A D ___

8.     83A      50C      59E      37B      32C      69C

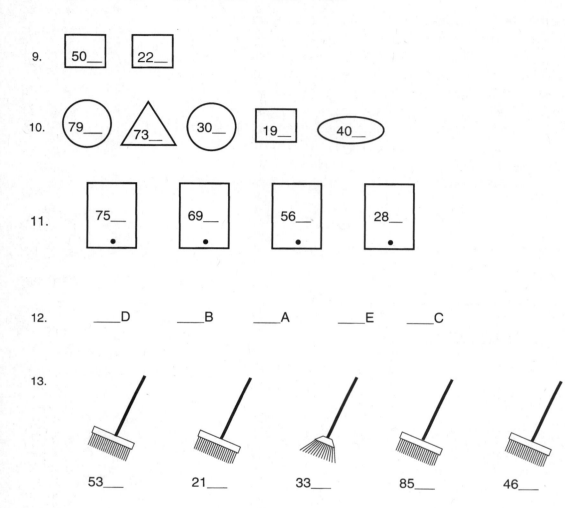

9.   [50__]   [22__]

10.   (79__)   △73__   (30__)   [19__]   ⬭40__

11.   [75__ •]   [69__ •]   [56__ •]   [28__ •]

12.   ___D       ___B       ___A       ___E       ___C

13.

53___      21___      33___      85___      46___

## ANSWER KEY

**Correctly Filled Worksheet**

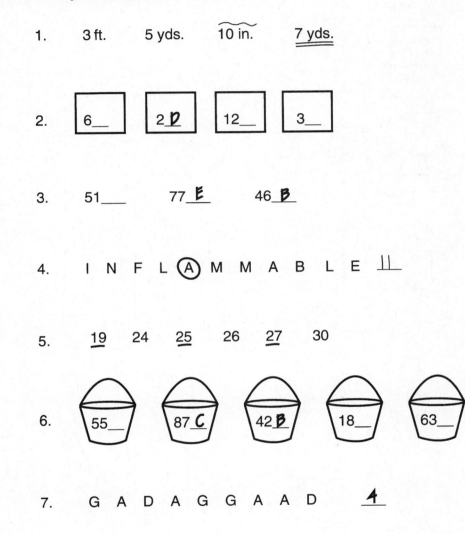

1.    3 ft.     5 yds.    10 in.    7 yds.

2.    6__    2 *D*    12__    3__

3.    51___     77 *E*     46 *B*

4.    I N F L (A) M M A B L E    II

5.    19   24   25   26   27   30

6.    55__    87 *C*    42 *B*    18__    63__

7.    G A D A G G A A D     4

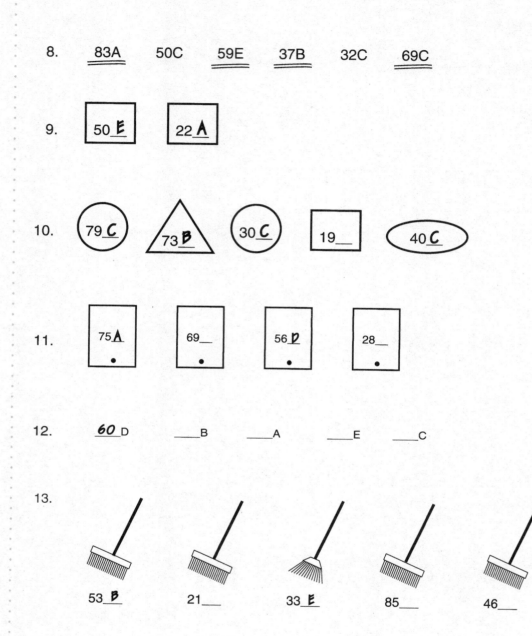

8.    <u>83A</u>      50C      <u>59E</u>      <u>37B</u>      32C      <u>69C</u>

9.    [ 50 <u>E</u> ]    [ 22 **A** ]

10.    ( 79 <u>C</u> )    △ 73 **B**    ( 30 <u>C</u> )    [ 19 ___ ]    ⬭ 40 <u>C</u>

11.    [ 75 **A** • ]    [ 69 ___ • ]    [ 56 **D** • ]    [ 28 ___ • ]

12.    **60** D      ___ B      ___ A      ___ E      ___ C

13.    53 **B**      21 ___      33 **E**      85 ___      46 ___

## Correctly Filled Answer Sheet

1. Ⓐ Ⓑ Ⓒ Ⓓ Ⓔ
2. Ⓐ Ⓑ Ⓒ ● Ⓔ
3. Ⓐ Ⓑ Ⓒ Ⓓ Ⓔ
4. Ⓐ Ⓑ Ⓒ Ⓓ Ⓔ
5. Ⓐ Ⓑ Ⓒ Ⓓ Ⓔ
6. Ⓐ Ⓑ Ⓒ Ⓓ Ⓔ
7. Ⓐ ● Ⓒ Ⓓ Ⓔ
8. Ⓐ Ⓑ Ⓒ Ⓓ Ⓔ
9. Ⓐ Ⓑ Ⓒ Ⓓ Ⓔ
10. ● Ⓑ Ⓒ Ⓓ Ⓔ
11. Ⓐ Ⓑ ● Ⓓ Ⓔ
12. Ⓐ Ⓑ Ⓒ Ⓓ Ⓔ
13. Ⓐ Ⓑ Ⓒ Ⓓ Ⓔ
14. Ⓐ Ⓑ Ⓒ Ⓓ ●
15. Ⓐ Ⓑ Ⓒ Ⓓ Ⓔ
16. Ⓐ Ⓑ Ⓒ Ⓓ Ⓔ
17. Ⓐ Ⓑ Ⓒ Ⓓ Ⓔ
18. Ⓐ Ⓑ Ⓒ Ⓓ Ⓔ
19. Ⓐ Ⓑ Ⓒ ● Ⓔ
20. Ⓐ Ⓑ Ⓒ Ⓓ Ⓔ
21. Ⓐ Ⓑ Ⓒ Ⓓ Ⓔ
22. ● Ⓑ Ⓒ Ⓓ Ⓔ

23. Ⓐ Ⓑ Ⓒ Ⓓ Ⓔ
24. Ⓐ Ⓑ Ⓒ Ⓓ Ⓔ
25. Ⓐ Ⓑ Ⓒ ● Ⓔ
26. Ⓐ Ⓑ Ⓒ Ⓓ Ⓔ
27. Ⓐ Ⓑ Ⓒ ● Ⓔ
28. Ⓐ Ⓑ Ⓒ Ⓓ Ⓔ
29. Ⓐ Ⓑ Ⓒ Ⓓ Ⓔ
30. Ⓐ Ⓑ ● Ⓓ Ⓔ
31. Ⓐ Ⓑ Ⓒ Ⓓ Ⓔ
32. Ⓐ Ⓑ Ⓒ Ⓓ Ⓔ
33. Ⓐ Ⓑ Ⓒ Ⓓ ●
34. Ⓐ Ⓑ Ⓒ Ⓓ Ⓔ
35. Ⓐ Ⓑ Ⓒ Ⓓ Ⓔ
36. Ⓐ Ⓑ Ⓒ Ⓓ Ⓔ
37. Ⓐ ● Ⓒ Ⓓ Ⓔ
38. Ⓐ Ⓑ Ⓒ Ⓓ Ⓔ
39. Ⓐ Ⓑ Ⓒ Ⓓ Ⓔ
40. Ⓐ Ⓑ ● Ⓓ Ⓔ
41. Ⓐ Ⓑ Ⓒ Ⓓ Ⓔ
42. Ⓐ ● Ⓒ Ⓓ Ⓔ
43. Ⓐ Ⓑ Ⓒ Ⓓ Ⓔ
44. Ⓐ Ⓑ Ⓒ Ⓓ Ⓔ

45. Ⓐ Ⓑ Ⓒ Ⓓ Ⓔ
46. Ⓐ ● Ⓒ Ⓓ Ⓔ
47. Ⓐ Ⓑ Ⓒ Ⓓ Ⓔ
48. Ⓐ Ⓑ Ⓒ Ⓓ Ⓔ
49. Ⓐ Ⓑ Ⓒ Ⓓ Ⓔ
50. Ⓐ Ⓑ Ⓒ Ⓓ ●
51. Ⓐ Ⓑ Ⓒ Ⓓ Ⓔ
52. Ⓐ Ⓑ Ⓒ Ⓓ Ⓔ
53. Ⓐ ● Ⓒ Ⓓ Ⓔ
54. Ⓐ Ⓑ Ⓒ Ⓓ Ⓔ
55. Ⓐ Ⓑ Ⓒ Ⓓ Ⓔ
56. Ⓐ Ⓑ Ⓒ ● Ⓔ
57. Ⓐ Ⓑ Ⓒ Ⓓ Ⓔ
58. Ⓐ Ⓑ Ⓒ Ⓓ Ⓔ
59. Ⓐ Ⓑ Ⓒ Ⓓ ●
60. Ⓐ Ⓑ Ⓒ ● Ⓔ
61. Ⓐ Ⓑ Ⓒ Ⓓ Ⓔ
62. Ⓐ Ⓑ Ⓒ Ⓓ Ⓔ
63. Ⓐ Ⓑ Ⓒ Ⓓ Ⓔ
64. ● Ⓑ Ⓒ Ⓓ Ⓔ
65. Ⓐ Ⓑ Ⓒ Ⓓ Ⓔ
66. Ⓐ Ⓑ Ⓒ Ⓓ Ⓔ

67. Ⓐ Ⓑ Ⓒ Ⓓ Ⓔ
68. Ⓐ Ⓑ Ⓒ Ⓓ Ⓔ
69. Ⓐ Ⓑ ● Ⓓ Ⓔ
70. Ⓐ Ⓑ Ⓒ Ⓓ Ⓔ
71. Ⓐ Ⓑ Ⓒ Ⓓ Ⓔ
72. Ⓐ Ⓑ Ⓒ Ⓓ Ⓔ
73. Ⓐ ● Ⓒ Ⓓ Ⓔ
74. Ⓐ Ⓑ Ⓒ Ⓓ Ⓔ
75. ● Ⓑ Ⓒ Ⓓ Ⓔ
76. Ⓐ Ⓑ Ⓒ Ⓓ Ⓔ
77. Ⓐ Ⓑ Ⓒ Ⓓ ●
78. Ⓐ Ⓑ Ⓒ Ⓓ Ⓔ
79. Ⓐ Ⓑ ● Ⓓ Ⓔ
80. Ⓐ Ⓑ Ⓒ Ⓓ Ⓔ
81. Ⓐ Ⓑ Ⓒ Ⓓ Ⓔ
82. Ⓐ Ⓑ Ⓒ Ⓓ Ⓔ
83. ● Ⓑ Ⓒ Ⓓ Ⓔ
84. Ⓐ Ⓑ Ⓒ Ⓓ Ⓔ
85. Ⓐ Ⓑ Ⓒ Ⓓ Ⓔ
86. Ⓐ Ⓑ Ⓒ Ⓓ Ⓔ
87. Ⓐ Ⓑ ● Ⓓ Ⓔ
88. Ⓐ Ⓑ Ⓒ Ⓓ Ⓔ

answers practice test 7

## PRACTICE TEST 8: EXAMS 230, 238, 240

**Part A**

1. _____

2. _____

_____

3. _____

_____

4. _____

_____

5. _____

_____

6. _____

_____

7. _____

_____

8. _____

_____

9. _____

_____

10.

answer sheet

11. _____

_____

12. _____

_____

13. _____

_____

14. _____

_____

15. _____

_____

16. _____

_____

17. _____

18. _____

19. _____

20. _____

21. _____

22. _____

### CHART A

| | Truck License Number | Kind of Service | Odometer Reading When Serviced |
|---|---|---|---|
| | 835 XYZ | tune up | 22,305 |
| 23. | | | |
| 24. | | | |

answer sheet

## CHART B

| Driver ID Number | Truck License Number | Odometer Reading |
|---|---|---|
| 8723 | 997 IUP | 88,141 |
| 25. | | |
| 26. | | |

## CHART C

| Driver ID Number | Odometer Reading When Taken Out | Odometer Reading When Returned |
|---|---|---|
| 3406 | 12,562 | 12,591 |
| 27. | | |
| 28. | | |

## CHART D

| Vehicle License Number | Kind of Service | Serviceperson ID Number |
|---|---|---|
| 592 TJD | grease job | 8452 |
| 29. | | |
| 30. | | |

## CHART E

| Truck License Number | Driver ID Number | Serviceperson ID Number |
|---|---|---|
| 042 RVB | 5842 | 4307 |
| 31. | | |
| 32. | | |

33. _____
 _____

34. _____
 _____

35. _____
 _____

36. _____

37. _____

38. _____
 _____

39. _____
 _____

40. _____
 _____

## Part B

41. Ⓐ Ⓑ Ⓒ Ⓓ Ⓔ　　49. Ⓐ Ⓑ Ⓒ Ⓓ Ⓔ　　57. Ⓐ Ⓑ Ⓒ Ⓓ Ⓔ　　65. Ⓐ Ⓑ Ⓒ Ⓓ Ⓔ　　73. Ⓐ Ⓑ Ⓒ Ⓓ Ⓔ
42. Ⓐ Ⓑ Ⓒ Ⓓ Ⓔ　　50. Ⓐ Ⓑ Ⓒ Ⓓ Ⓔ　　58. Ⓐ Ⓑ Ⓒ Ⓓ Ⓔ　　66. Ⓐ Ⓑ Ⓒ Ⓓ Ⓔ　　74. Ⓐ Ⓑ Ⓒ Ⓓ Ⓔ
43. Ⓐ Ⓑ Ⓒ Ⓓ Ⓔ　　51. Ⓐ Ⓑ Ⓒ Ⓓ Ⓔ　　59. Ⓐ Ⓑ Ⓒ Ⓓ Ⓔ　　67. Ⓐ Ⓑ Ⓒ Ⓓ Ⓔ　　75. Ⓐ Ⓑ Ⓒ Ⓓ Ⓔ
44. Ⓐ Ⓑ Ⓒ Ⓓ Ⓔ　　52. Ⓐ Ⓑ Ⓒ Ⓓ Ⓔ　　60. Ⓐ Ⓑ Ⓒ Ⓓ Ⓔ　　68. Ⓐ Ⓑ Ⓒ Ⓓ Ⓔ　　76. Ⓐ Ⓑ Ⓒ Ⓓ Ⓔ
45. Ⓐ Ⓑ Ⓒ Ⓓ Ⓔ　　53. Ⓐ Ⓑ Ⓒ Ⓓ Ⓔ　　61. Ⓐ Ⓑ Ⓒ Ⓓ Ⓔ　　69. Ⓐ Ⓑ Ⓒ Ⓓ Ⓔ　　77. Ⓐ Ⓑ Ⓒ Ⓓ Ⓔ
46. Ⓐ Ⓑ Ⓒ Ⓓ Ⓔ　　54. Ⓐ Ⓑ Ⓒ Ⓓ Ⓔ　　62. Ⓐ Ⓑ Ⓒ Ⓓ Ⓔ　　70. Ⓐ Ⓑ Ⓒ Ⓓ Ⓔ　　78. Ⓐ Ⓑ Ⓒ Ⓓ Ⓔ
47. Ⓐ Ⓑ Ⓒ Ⓓ Ⓔ　　55. Ⓐ Ⓑ Ⓒ Ⓓ Ⓔ　　63. Ⓐ Ⓑ Ⓒ Ⓓ Ⓔ　　71. Ⓐ Ⓑ Ⓒ Ⓓ Ⓔ　　79. Ⓐ Ⓑ Ⓒ Ⓓ Ⓔ
48. Ⓐ Ⓑ Ⓒ Ⓓ Ⓔ　　56. Ⓐ Ⓑ Ⓒ Ⓓ Ⓔ　　64. Ⓐ Ⓑ Ⓒ Ⓓ Ⓔ　　72. Ⓐ Ⓑ Ⓒ Ⓓ Ⓔ　　80. Ⓐ Ⓑ Ⓒ Ⓓ Ⓔ

# Practice Test 8: Exams 230, 238, 240

Practice Test 8 will help you prepare for the following Postal Service exams:

1. Exam 230 (Motor Vehicle Operator)

2. Exam 238 (Motor Vehicle Operator/Tractor-Trailer Operator)

3. Exam 240 (Tractor-Trailer Operator)

If you wish to apply for a Motor Vehicle Operator or Tractor-Trailer Operator position with the USPS, you must first complete an assessment questionnaire online or by phone. The questionnaire requires specific information about your driving history and safety record. You must receive a passing score of at least 70 on the assessment to be considered for employment. If the Postal Service determines that you are eligible, you will be contacted to continue the process for employment.

## Part A

### 40 QUESTIONS • 60 MINUTES

**Directions:** Read the questions carefully. Be sure you know what the questions are about and then answer each question. Write or draw your answers on the separate answer sheet for Part A. When you answer the questions in Part B, you may not look back at the pictures.

### Picture 1

1. How many vehicles are shown in the picture?

2. What is happening in this picture?

## Picture 2

3. What does the driver see in his rearview mirror? Be as complete as possible in your description.

## Picture 3

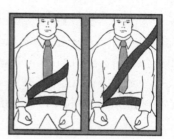

4. Describe the man on the left. Take special note of his seat belt.

5. Describe the man on the right.

## Picture 4

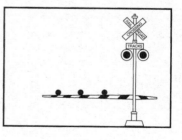

6. If you come upon the scene shown in Picture 4 as you are driving along the road, what must you do?

**Picture 5**

**7.** What are the vehicles in picture 5 doing?

**Picture 6**

**8.** How is the sign on the left related to the vehicle on the right? What does it mean?

**Question 9 is about Picture 7. Based on the picture, decide which description—A, B, C, or D—best fits the picture, and write the letter of that choice on your answer sheet.**

**Picture 7**

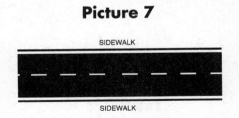

**9.** The roadway in Picture 7 is a

    **(A)** four-lane superhighway
    **(B)** no-passing zone
    **(C)** two-way street
    **(D)** single-lane street

**10.** On your answer sheet, draw arrows in the roadway indicating the direction of traffic flow.

## Picture 8

**11.** Write as complete a description as you can of the objects and activities in Picture 8.

## Picture 9

**12.** Describe the pattern of wear on this tire.

**Question 13 is about Picture 10. Based on the picture, decide which description—A, B, C, or D—best fits the picture, and write the letter of that choice on your answer sheet.**

## Picture 10

**13.** The meaning of this sign is

  **(A)** no parking
  **(B)** no truck parking
  **(C)** no trucks
  **(D)** trucks only

**Picture 11**

**14.** What should you look for when you see this sign?

**Picture 12**

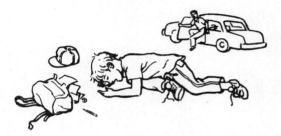

**15.** What is the boy doing?

**16.** What else is happening in Picture 12?

**Question 17 is about Picture 13. Based on the picture, decide which description—A, B, C, or D—best fits the picture, and write the letter of that choice on your answer sheet.**

**Picture 13**

**17.** The purpose of this sign is to caution you against

**(A)** a winding road
**(B)** drunk drivers
**(C)** a road that may be slippery when wet
**(D)** a steep hill

Question 18 is about Picture 14. Based on the picture, decide which description—A, B, C, or D—best fits the picture, and write the letter of that choice on your answer sheet.

## Picture 14

18. The words on this sign mean the same as

   (A) Dead End, No Exit
   (B) One Way Traffic
   (C) Keep Out
   (D) Special Parking Rules Today, Do Not Park Here

## Picture 15

19. What is the vehicle in the picture?

20. Who are the passengers?

Question 21 is about words that might appear on a traffic sign. Decide which answer—A, B, C, or D—means most nearly the same as the phrase, and write the letter of that choice on your answer sheet.

21. Bridge Freezes Before Roadway

   (A) Bridge May Be Icy
   (B) Detour—Bridge Under Repair
   (C) Yield to Road Maintenance Crews
   (D) Cold Weather Forecast for Tonight

Question 22 is about Picture 16. Based on the picture, decide which description—A, B, C, or D—best fits the picture, and write the letter of that choice on your answer sheet.

### Picture 16

22. The words on the sign above mean that

   (A) 1000 people are working in the road
   (B) for the next 1000 feet, people will be working in the road
   (C) in 1000 feet, expect to find people working in the road
   (D) please help the people working in the road for the next 1000 feet

**Questions 23 and 24 have to do with filling in a chart. You are given the following information to put in Chart A.**

   Truck, license number 835 XZY, had a tune up at odometer reading 22,305.

   Truck, license number 673 PUR, received a new fuel pump at odometer reading 67,422.

   Truck, license number 441 RTG, had an oil change at odometer reading 46,098.

The information for the first truck has already been filled in. For question 23, write the information for the second truck in the proper columns in Chart A on your answer sheet. For question 24, write the information for the third truck in the proper columns in Chart A on your answer sheet.

**Questions 25 and 26 have to do with filling in another chart. You are given the following information to put in Chart B.**

   Driver, ID number 8723, took truck license number 997 IUP at odometer reading 88,141.

   Driver, ID number 6309, took truck license number 534 TRE at odometer reading 35,790.

   Driver, ID number 7342, took truck license number 256 TAE at odometer reading 56,798.

The information for the first driver has already been filled in. For question 25, write the information for the second driver in the proper columns in Chart B on your answer sheet. For question 26, write the information for the third driver in the proper columns in Chart B on your answer sheet.

**Questions 27 and 28 have to do with filling in another chart. You are given the following information to put in Chart C.**

Driver, ID number 3406, took his Jeep at odometer reading 12,562 and returned it at odometer reading 12,591.

Driver, ID number 9845, took his Jeep at odometer reading 54,970 and returned it at odometer reading 54,997.

Driver, ID number 4785, took her Jeep at odometer reading 43,054 and returned it at odometer reading 43,086.

The information for the first driver has already been filled in. For question 27, write the information for the second driver in the proper columns in Chart C on your answer sheet. For question 28, write the information for the third driver in the proper columns in Chart C on your answer sheet.

**Questions 29 and 30 have to do with filling in another chart. You are given the following information to put in Chart D.**

Vehicle license number 592 TJD had a grease job by mechanic ID number 8452.

Vehicle license number 447 IKT had its carburetor adjusted by serviceperson ID number 7092.

Vehicle license number 837 PRE had a tire changed by serviceperson ID number 6052.

The information for the first vehicle has already been filled in. For question 29, write the information for the second vehicle in the proper columns in Chart D on your answer sheet. For question 30, write the information for the third vehicle in the proper columns in Chart D on your answer sheet.

**Questions 31 and 32 have to do with filling in one more chart. You are given the following information to put in Chart E.**

Truck license number 042 RVB is to be driven into the yard by driver ID number 5842 and turned over to serviceperson ID number 4307 for service.

Truck license number 759 YUX is to be driven into the yard by driver ID number 8372 and turned over to serviceperson ID number 3987 for service.

Truck license number 943 WCG is to be driven into the yard by driver ID number 6241 and turned over to serviceperson ID number 4273 for service.

The information for the first truck has already been filled in. For question 31, write the information for the second truck in the proper columns in Chart E on your answer sheet. For question 32, write the information for the third truck in the proper columns in Chart E on your answer sheet.

Questions 33 and 34 are about pictures of lane-control lights. Each picture has a letter. You are to tell what each picture shows by writing a short description of the picture on your answer sheet.

33. What does Picture X show?

34. What does Picture Y show?

### Picture 17

35. Describe Picture 17 in the space on your answer sheet.

### Picture 18

36. The word on this sign means that the driver should

(A) stop
(B) turn around
(C) let merging traffic enter the roadway
(D) look carefully before proceeding

**Picture 19**

**37.** The meaning of this sign is

    **(A)** Right Turn Only
    **(B)** No Right Turn
    **(C)** No Left Turn
    **(D)** Left Turn Only

**Picture 20**

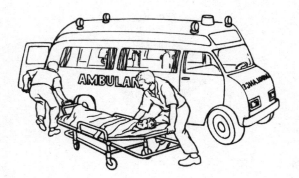

**38.** Describe what is happening in this picture.

**Picture 21**

**39.** What is happening in this picture? Write your description in the space on your answer sheet.

## Picture 22

**40.** The driver who approaches this sign must

**(A)** stop
**(B)** slow down and look both ways
**(C)** turn around
**(D)** back up

practice test

## Part B

### 40 QUESTIONS • 60 MINUTES

**Directions:** To answer the questions in Part B, you must use the answers from Part A. Refer *only* to your answer sheet for Part A to answer these questions. DO NOT look at the pictures in Part A. Mark the answers to questions 41–80 on the Part B answer sheet. Remember, you may not look back at the pictures in Part A while answering the questions in Part B.

**Question 41 is about question 1 of Part A, and question 42 is about question 2 of Part A.**

41. For number 41 on your answer sheet, mark space

    **(A)** if there are no vehicles in the picture
    **(B)** if there is one vehicle in the picture
    **(C)** if there are two vehicles in the picture
    **(D)** if there are three vehicles in the picture
    **(E)** if there are four vehicles in the picture

42. For number 42 on your answer sheet, mark space

    **(A)** if there is about to be a crash
    **(B)** if a vehicle just went through a stop sign
    **(C)** if a car is driving on the wrong side of the street
    **(D)** if there are no vehicles in the intersection
    **(E)** if one car has stopped at a stop sign

**Question 43 is about question 3 of Part A.**

43. For number 43 on your answer sheet, mark space

    **(A)** if a motorcycle is passing a car
    **(B)** if a motorcycle is directly behind a car
    **(C)** if a truck is behind a car
    **(D)** if two motorcycles are in the left lane
    **(E)** if there is nothing in the rearview mirror

**Question 44 is about question 4 of Part A, and question 45 is about question 5 of Part A.**

44. For number 44 on your answer sheet, mark space

    **(A)** if the man is likely to suffer internal injuries in case of a crash
    **(B)** if the man is wearing his seat belt properly
    **(C)** if the man is well protected in case of an auto crash
    **(D)** if the man is wearing his seat belt across his right shoulder
    **(E)** if the man is likely to be thrown from the car in an accident

**45.** For number 45 on your answer sheet, mark space

  **(A)** if the man's shoulder strap goes under his tie
  **(B)** if the man's lap strap is unfastened
  **(C)** if the man is likely to be thrown through the windshield in a crash
  **(D)** if the man is wearing his seat belt and shoulder harness properly
  **(E)** if the man is wearing a jacket

**Question 46 is about question 6 of Part A.**

**46.** For number 46 on your answer sheet, mark space

  **(A)** if you should blow your horn
  **(B)** if you should get out of your car and move the barrier
  **(C)** if you should come to a full stop and wait
  **(D)** if you should accelerate and continue
  **(E)** if you should stop, look, and proceed

**Question 47 is about question 7 of Part A.**

**47.** For number 47 on your answer sheet, mark space

  **(A)** if a car is about to hit a pedestrian
  **(B)** if a person is jaywalking
  **(C)** if a police officer is directing traffic
  **(D)** if a cyclist is going the wrong way on a one-way street
  **(E)** if a woman and child are crossing in the crosswalk

**Question 48 is about question 8 of Part A.**

**48.** For number 48 on your answer sheet, mark space

  **(A)** if the sign should be blue and orange
  **(B)** if the sign signifies that this is a slow-moving vehicle
  **(C)** if the sign means "pass when safe"
  **(D)** if the sign should be worn on the driver's back
  **(E)** if the sign means that you should yield the right of way to the vehicle to which it is attached

**For number 49 on your answer sheet, mark the space that has the same letter as the letter you wrote on the answer line for question 9 of Part A.**

**Question 50 is about question 10 of Part A.**

**50.** For number 50 on your answer sheet, mark space

  **(A)** if the arrow in one lane points in one direction and the arrow in the other lane points in the opposite direction
  **(B)** if the arrows in both lanes point to the right
  **(C)** if the arrows in both lanes point to the left
  **(D)** if there are arrows pointing in both directions in both lanes
  **(E)** if there is an arrow in only one lane

**Question 51 is about question 11 of Part A.**

51. For number 51 on your answer sheet, mark space

 (A) if it is raining
 (B) if there is one balloon on the ground
 (C) if there are three balloons
 (D) if there is heavy road traffic
 (E) if it would be wise for the motorist to pull over to the side of the road to watch the show

**Question 52 is about question 12 of Part A.**

52. For number 52 on your answer sheet, mark space

 (A) if the wear on the tire indicates the effect of overinflation
 (B) if the wear on the tire indicates the effect of excessive caster
 (C) if the wear on the tire indicates the effect of improper balance
 (D) if the wear on the tire indicates the effect of underinflation
 (E) if the wear on the tire indicates the effect of toe-out

**For number 53 on your answer sheet, mark the space that has the same letter as the letter you wrote on the answer line for question 13 of Part A.**

**Question 54 is about question 14 of Part A.**

54. For number 54 on your answer sheet, mark space

 (A) if you should look for hitchhikers
 (B) if you should look for schoolchildren
 (C) if you should look for a garage sale
 (D) if you should watch out for a flagman
 (E) if you should watch for deaf pedestrians

**Question 55 is about question 15 of Part A, and question 56 is about question 16 of Part A.**

55. For number 55 on your answer sheet, mark space

 (A) if a little boy is running across the street
 (B) if a little boy is sleeping
 (C) if a little boy is helping an old lady cross the street
 (D) if a little boy is lying in the street
 (E) if a little boy is getting out of the car

56. For number 56 on your answer sheet, mark space

 (A) if an ambulance has just pulled up
 (B) if a person is getting out of the car
 (C) if there has been a hit-and-run accident
 (D) if a crowd is gathering around the little boy
 (E) if a woman is crying

For number 57 on your answer sheet, mark the space that has the same letter as the letter you wrote on the answer line for question 17 of Part A.

For number 58 on your answer sheet, mark the space that has the same letter as the letter you wrote on the answer line for question 18 of Part A.

Question 59 is about question 19 of Part A, and question 60 is about question 20 of Part A.

59. For number 59 on your answer sheet, mark space

   (A) if the vehicle is a taxicab
   (B) if the vehicle is a bus
   (C) if the vehicle is a tractor-trailer
   (D) if the vehicle is a farm tractor
   (E) if the vehicle is a Jeep

60. For number 60 on your answer sheet, mark space

   (A) if the passengers are schoolchildren
   (B) if the passengers are campers
   (C) if the passengers are farmers
   (D) if the passengers are military personnel
   (E) if the passengers are adults

For number 61 on your answer sheet, mark the space that has the same letter as the letter you wrote on the answer line for question 21 of Part A.

For number 62 on your answer sheet, mark the space that has the same letter as the letter you wrote on the answer line for question 22 of Part A.

Questions 63 and 64 are about Chart A, which you filled in. Mark on your answer sheet the letter of the answer.

63. What is the license number of the truck that received a new fuel pump? Look at what you wrote on the chart. Do not try to answer from memory.

   (A) 673 PUR
   (B) 835 XZY
   (C) 441 RTG
   (D) 637 RUP

64. At what odometer reading did truck 441 RTG have its oil changed?

   (A) 46,908
   (B) 64,809
   (C) 46,098
   (D) 46,089

**Questions 65 and 66 are about Chart B, which you filled in. Look at what you wrote on the chart and mark your answer sheet with the letter of the correct answer.**

**65.** What was the ID number of the driver who took truck license number 534 TRE?

(A) 6390
(B) 6309
(C) 7342
(D) 7243

**66.** At what odometer reading did driver number 7342 take out his truck?

(A) 56,798
(B) 88,141
(C) 35,790
(D) 65,798

**Questions 67 and 68 are about Chart C, which you filled in. Look at what you wrote on the chart and mark your answer sheet with the letter of the correct answer.**

**67.** What was the odometer reading when driver number 9845 returned his Jeep?

(A) 54,997
(B) 54,970
(C) 15,591
(D) 43,086

**68.** What was the odometer reading when driver number 4785 took out her Jeep?

(A) 12,562
(B) 43,086
(C) 54,970
(D) 43,054

**Questions 69 and 70 are about Chart D, which you filled in. Look at what you wrote on the chart and mark your answer sheet with the letter of the correct answer.**

**69.** What service was performed on vehicle license number 447 IKT?

(A) lubrication
(B) replacement of air hose
(C) carburetor adjustment
(D) tire change

**70.** What was the ID number of the serviceperson who changed a tire?

(A) 837 PRE
(B) 6052
(C) 6025
(D) 7092

practice test

Questions 71 and 72 are about Chart E, which you filled in. Look at what you wrote on the chart and mark your answer sheet with the letter of the correct answer.

71. What was the ID number of the serviceperson to whom driver ID number 8372 turned over her truck?

(A) 3978
(B) 3987
(C) 3897
(D) 3879

72. What was the ID number of the driver who turned over her truck to serviceperson ID 4273?

(A) 943 WCG
(B) 5842
(C) 959 YUX
(D) 6241

Question 73 is about question 33 under Picture X of Part A, and question 74 is about question 34 under Picture Y of Part A.

73. For number 73 on your answer sheet, mark space

(A) if there are no lanes open in Picture X
(B) if there is only one lane open in Picture X
(C) if there are only two lanes open in Picture X
(D) if there are only three lanes open in Picture X
(E) if there is only one lane closed in Picture X

74. For number 74 on your answer sheet, mark space

(A) if there is only one lane closed in Picture Y
(B) if there are only two lanes closed in Picture Y
(C) if there are only three lanes closed in Picture Y
(D) if there are only four lanes closed in Picture Y
(E) if there are only five lanes closed in Picture Y

Question 75 is about question 35 of Part A.

75. For number 75 on your answer sheet, mark space

(A) if drivers approaching from the right cannot see any traffic signals
(B) if drivers approaching this light straight ahead have a green arrow pointing to the right
(C) if drivers approaching from the left are guided by five different traffic signals
(D) if drivers approaching this light straight ahead have a red arrow pointing to the left
(E) if drivers approaching this light straight ahead have a green arrow pointing to the left

**For number 76 on your answer sheet, mark the space that has the same letter as the letter you wrote on the answer line for question 36 of Part A.**

**For number 77 on your answer sheet, mark the space that has the same letter as the letter you wrote on the answer line for question 37 of Part A.**

**Question 78 is about question 38 of Part A.**

78. For number 78 on your answer sheet, mark space

    **(A)** if a person is being pushed in a wheelchair
    **(B)** if there has been a traffic accident
    **(C)** if two men are putting a person into an ambulance
    **(D)** if a police officer is directing traffic
    **(E)** if a woman is wringing her hands in despair

**Question 79 is about question 39 of Part A.**

79. For number 79 on your answer sheet, mark space

    **(A)** if there is a mail truck in the picture
    **(B)** if a car is about to enter an intersection
    **(C)** if three people are walking abreast
    **(D)** if children are playing in the street
    **(E)** if a man is walking with a woman

**For number 80 on your answer sheet, mark the space that has the same letter as the letter you wrote on the answer line for question 40 of Part A.**

## ANSWER KEY AND EXPLANATIONS

### Part A

1. Two.
2. The car on the left has stopped at the stop sign; the car on the right is passing through the intersection.
3. In the rearview mirror, the driver sees that there is a motorcycle directly behind the car.
4. The man on the left is wearing his seat belt incorrectly. The shoulder strap is under his arm instead of across his shoulder.
5. The man on the right is wearing his seat belt correctly.
6. Stop and wait for the train to pass and the barrier to be lifted.
7. The vehicles have stopped for pedestrians in the crosswalk.
8. The sign on the left should be mounted on the tractor. The sign is a warning to other vehicles on the road that the vehicle upon which it is mounted is a slow-moving vehicle.
9. (C)
10.

11. There is one car on the road. There are three hot air balloons in the sky. The sun is peeking from behind some clouds.
12. The tire is worn right down the middle.
13. (C)
14. Look for a flagman.
15. The young boy is lying in the roadway.
16. A person is getting out of a car.
17. (C)
18. (C)
19. The vehicle is a bus.
20. The passengers are a group of well-dressed men and women, some with briefcases.
21. (A)
22. (C)

### CHART A

|     | Truck License Number | Kind of Service | Odometer Reading When Serviced |
| --- | --- | --- | --- |
|     | 835 XYZ | tune up | 22,305 |
| 23. | 673 PUR | new fuel pump | 67,422 |
| 24. | 441 RTG | oil change | 46,098 |

### CHART B

|     | Driver ID Number | Truck License Number | Odometer Reading |
| --- | --- | --- | --- |
|     | 8723 | 997 IUP | 88,141 |
| 25. | 6309 | 534 TRE | 35,790 |
| 26. | 7342 | 256 TAE | 56,798 |

### CHART C

|     | Driver ID Number | Odometer Reading When Taken Out | Odometer Reading When Returned |
| --- | --- | --- | --- |
|     | 3406 | 12,562 | 12,591 |
| 27. | 9845 | 54,970 | 54,997 |
| 28. | 4785 | 43,054 | 43,086 |

### CHART D

|     | Vehicle License Number | Kind of Service | Serviceperson ID Number |
| --- | --- | --- | --- |
|     | 592 TJD | grease job | 8452 |
| 29. | 447 IKT | carburetor adjustment | 7092 |
| 30. | 837 PRE | tire change | 6052 |

### CHART E

|     | Truck License Number | Driver ID Number | Serviceperson ID Number |
| --- | --- | --- | --- |
|     | 042 RVB | 5842 | 4307 |
| 31. | 759 YUX | 8372 | 3987 |
| 32. | 943 WCG | 6241 | 4273 |

33. Picture X shows the left lane is open to traffic (shown by arrow) and the two lanes to the right are closed to traffic (shown by Xs).
34. Picture Y shows six traffic lanes. Starting from the left, lanes 1 and 2 are open to traffic, lanes 3 and 4 are closed to traffic, lane 5 is open, and lane 6 is closed.
35. There is a signal light at a three- or four-way intersection. Cars coming straight at the signal light can have a red, yellow, or green light, or a green arrow pointing left. Cars coming from left and right probably have only a red, yellow, or green light.
36. (C)
37. (B)
38. Two men are putting a person on a stretcher into an ambulance.
39. A man and a woman are walking together.
40. (A)

## Part B

| | | | | |
|---|---|---|---|---|
| 41. C | 49. C | 57. C | 65. B | 73. B |
| 42. E | 50. A | 58. B | 66. A | 74. C |
| 43. B | 51. C | 59. B | 67. A | 75. E |
| 44. A | 52. A | 60. E | 68. D | 76. C |
| 45. D | 53. C | 61. A | 69. C | 77. B |
| 46. C | 54. D | 62. C | 70. B | 78. C |
| 47. E | 55. D | 63. A | 71. B | 79. E |
| 48. B | 56. B | 64. C | 72. D | 80. A |

answers

practice test 8

answer sheet

# PRACTICE TEST 9: BASIC SKILLS

## Part A: Name and Number Comparisons

| | | | | |
|---|---|---|---|---|
| 1. Ⓐ Ⓑ Ⓒ Ⓓ Ⓔ | 11. Ⓐ Ⓑ Ⓒ Ⓓ Ⓔ | 21. Ⓐ Ⓑ Ⓒ Ⓓ Ⓔ | 31. Ⓐ Ⓑ Ⓒ Ⓓ Ⓔ | 41. Ⓐ Ⓑ Ⓒ Ⓓ Ⓔ |
| 2. Ⓐ Ⓑ Ⓒ Ⓓ Ⓔ | 12. Ⓐ Ⓑ Ⓒ Ⓓ Ⓔ | 22. Ⓐ Ⓑ Ⓒ Ⓓ Ⓔ | 32. Ⓐ Ⓑ Ⓒ Ⓓ Ⓔ | 42. Ⓐ Ⓑ Ⓒ Ⓓ Ⓔ |
| 3. Ⓐ Ⓑ Ⓒ Ⓓ Ⓔ | 13. Ⓐ Ⓑ Ⓒ Ⓓ Ⓔ | 23. Ⓐ Ⓑ Ⓒ Ⓓ Ⓔ | 33. Ⓐ Ⓑ Ⓒ Ⓓ Ⓔ | 43. Ⓐ Ⓑ Ⓒ Ⓓ Ⓔ |
| 4. Ⓐ Ⓑ Ⓒ Ⓓ Ⓔ | 14. Ⓐ Ⓑ Ⓒ Ⓓ Ⓔ | 24. Ⓐ Ⓑ Ⓒ Ⓓ Ⓔ | 34. Ⓐ Ⓑ Ⓒ Ⓓ Ⓔ | 44. Ⓐ Ⓑ Ⓒ Ⓓ Ⓔ |
| 5. Ⓐ Ⓑ Ⓒ Ⓓ Ⓔ | 15. Ⓐ Ⓑ Ⓒ Ⓓ Ⓔ | 25. Ⓐ Ⓑ Ⓒ Ⓓ Ⓔ | 35. Ⓐ Ⓑ Ⓒ Ⓓ Ⓔ | 45. Ⓐ Ⓑ Ⓒ Ⓓ Ⓔ |
| 6. Ⓐ Ⓑ Ⓒ Ⓓ Ⓔ | 16. Ⓐ Ⓑ Ⓒ Ⓓ Ⓔ | 26. Ⓐ Ⓑ Ⓒ Ⓓ Ⓔ | 36. Ⓐ Ⓑ Ⓒ Ⓓ Ⓔ | 46. Ⓐ Ⓑ Ⓒ Ⓓ Ⓔ |
| 7. Ⓐ Ⓑ Ⓒ Ⓓ Ⓔ | 17. Ⓐ Ⓑ Ⓒ Ⓓ Ⓔ | 27. Ⓐ Ⓑ Ⓒ Ⓓ Ⓔ | 37. Ⓐ Ⓑ Ⓒ Ⓓ Ⓔ | 47. Ⓐ Ⓑ Ⓒ Ⓓ Ⓔ |
| 8. Ⓐ Ⓑ Ⓒ Ⓓ Ⓔ | 18. Ⓐ Ⓑ Ⓒ Ⓓ Ⓔ | 28. Ⓐ Ⓑ Ⓒ Ⓓ Ⓔ | 38. Ⓐ Ⓑ Ⓒ Ⓓ Ⓔ | 48. Ⓐ Ⓑ Ⓒ Ⓓ Ⓔ |
| 9. Ⓐ Ⓑ Ⓒ Ⓓ Ⓔ | 19. Ⓐ Ⓑ Ⓒ Ⓓ Ⓔ | 29. Ⓐ Ⓑ Ⓒ Ⓓ Ⓔ | 39. Ⓐ Ⓑ Ⓒ Ⓓ Ⓔ | 49. Ⓐ Ⓑ Ⓒ Ⓓ Ⓔ |
| 10. Ⓐ Ⓑ Ⓒ Ⓓ Ⓔ | 20. Ⓐ Ⓑ Ⓒ Ⓓ Ⓔ | 30. Ⓐ Ⓑ Ⓒ Ⓓ Ⓔ | 40. Ⓐ Ⓑ Ⓒ Ⓓ Ⓔ | 50. Ⓐ Ⓑ Ⓒ Ⓓ Ⓔ |

## Part B: Reading Comprehension

| | | | | |
|---|---|---|---|---|
| 1. Ⓐ Ⓑ Ⓒ Ⓓ Ⓔ | 7. Ⓐ Ⓑ Ⓒ Ⓓ Ⓔ | 13. Ⓐ Ⓑ Ⓒ Ⓓ Ⓔ | 19. Ⓐ Ⓑ Ⓒ Ⓓ Ⓔ | 25. Ⓐ Ⓑ Ⓒ Ⓓ Ⓔ |
| 2. Ⓐ Ⓑ Ⓒ Ⓓ Ⓔ | 8. Ⓐ Ⓑ Ⓒ Ⓓ Ⓔ | 14. Ⓐ Ⓑ Ⓒ Ⓓ Ⓔ | 20. Ⓐ Ⓑ Ⓒ Ⓓ Ⓔ | 26. Ⓐ Ⓑ Ⓒ Ⓓ Ⓔ |
| 3. Ⓐ Ⓑ Ⓒ Ⓓ Ⓔ | 9. Ⓐ Ⓑ Ⓒ Ⓓ Ⓔ | 15. Ⓐ Ⓑ Ⓒ Ⓓ Ⓔ | 21. Ⓐ Ⓑ Ⓒ Ⓓ Ⓔ | 27. Ⓐ Ⓑ Ⓒ Ⓓ Ⓔ |
| 4. Ⓐ Ⓑ Ⓒ Ⓓ Ⓔ | 10. Ⓐ Ⓑ Ⓒ Ⓓ Ⓔ | 16. Ⓐ Ⓑ Ⓒ Ⓓ Ⓔ | 22. Ⓐ Ⓑ Ⓒ Ⓓ Ⓔ | 28. Ⓐ Ⓑ Ⓒ Ⓓ Ⓔ |
| 5. Ⓐ Ⓑ Ⓒ Ⓓ Ⓔ | 11. Ⓐ Ⓑ Ⓒ Ⓓ Ⓔ | 17. Ⓐ Ⓑ Ⓒ Ⓓ Ⓔ | 23. Ⓐ Ⓑ Ⓒ Ⓓ Ⓔ | 29. Ⓐ Ⓑ Ⓒ Ⓓ Ⓔ |
| 6. Ⓐ Ⓑ Ⓒ Ⓓ Ⓔ | 12. Ⓐ Ⓑ Ⓒ Ⓓ Ⓔ | 18. Ⓐ Ⓑ Ⓒ Ⓓ Ⓔ | 24. Ⓐ Ⓑ Ⓒ Ⓓ Ⓔ | 30. Ⓐ Ⓑ Ⓒ Ⓓ Ⓔ |

## Part C: Arithmetic Reasoning

| | | | | |
|---|---|---|---|---|
| 1. Ⓐ Ⓑ Ⓒ Ⓓ Ⓔ | 5. Ⓐ Ⓑ Ⓒ Ⓓ Ⓔ | 9. Ⓐ Ⓑ Ⓒ Ⓓ Ⓔ | 13. Ⓐ Ⓑ Ⓒ Ⓓ Ⓔ | 17. Ⓐ Ⓑ Ⓒ Ⓓ Ⓔ |
| 2. Ⓐ Ⓑ Ⓒ Ⓓ Ⓔ | 6. Ⓐ Ⓑ Ⓒ Ⓓ Ⓔ | 10. Ⓐ Ⓑ Ⓒ Ⓓ Ⓔ | 14. Ⓐ Ⓑ Ⓒ Ⓓ Ⓔ | 18. Ⓐ Ⓑ Ⓒ Ⓓ Ⓔ |
| 3. Ⓐ Ⓑ Ⓒ Ⓓ Ⓔ | 7. Ⓐ Ⓑ Ⓒ Ⓓ Ⓔ | 11. Ⓐ Ⓑ Ⓒ Ⓓ Ⓔ | 15. Ⓐ Ⓑ Ⓒ Ⓓ Ⓔ | 19. Ⓐ Ⓑ Ⓒ Ⓓ Ⓔ |
| 4. Ⓐ Ⓑ Ⓒ Ⓓ Ⓔ | 8. Ⓐ Ⓑ Ⓒ Ⓓ Ⓔ | 12. Ⓐ Ⓑ Ⓒ Ⓓ Ⓔ | 16. Ⓐ Ⓑ Ⓒ Ⓓ Ⓔ | 20. Ⓐ Ⓑ Ⓒ Ⓓ Ⓔ |

# Practice Test 9: Basic Skills

## PART A: NAME AND NUMBER COMPARISONS

**50 QUESTIONS • 8 MINUTES**

**Directions:** For each question, compare the three names or numbers and mark your answer:
**(A)** if **ALL THREE** names or numbers are exactly **ALIKE**
**(B)** if only the **FIRST** and **SECOND** names or numbers are exactly **ALIKE**
**(C)** if only the **FIRST** and **THIRD** names or numbers are exactly **ALIKE**
**(D)** if only the **SECOND** and **THIRD** names or numbers are exactly **ALIKE**
**(E)** if **ALL THREE** names or numbers are **DIFFERENT**

| | | | |
|---|---|---|---|
| **1.** | Thomas L. Kershaw | Thomas L. Kershaw | Thomas J. Kershaw |
| **2.** | Takahide E. Moro | Takahide E. Moru | Takahide E. Moru |
| **3.** | Carlota Cosentino | Carlotta Cosentino | Carlotta Constentino |
| **4.** | Albertina Andriuolo | Albertina Andriuolo | Albertina Andriuolo |
| **5.** | Francis J. Czukor | Francis Z. Czukor | Frances J. Czukor |
| **6.** | 7692138 | 7692138 | 7692138 |
| **7.** | 2633342 | 2633342 | 2633342 |
| **8.** | 2454803 | 2548403 | 2454803 |
| **9.** | 9670243 | 9670423 | 9670423 |
| **10.** | 2789350 | 2789350 | 2798350 |
| **11.** | Darlene P. Tenenbaum | Darlene P. Tenenbaum | Darlene P. Tanenbaum |
| **12.** | Maxwell Macmillan | Maxwell MacMillan | Maxwell Macmillian |
| **13.** | Frank D. Stanick | Frank D. Satanic | Frank D. Satanich |
| **14.** | J. Robert Schunk | J. Robert Schunh | Robert J. Schunk |
| **15.** | Fernando Silva Jr. | Fernando Silva Jr. | Fernand Silva Jr. |
| **16.** | 2797630 | 2797360 | 2797360 |
| **17.** | 6312192 | 6312192 | 6312192 |
| **18.** | 7412032 | 7412032 | 7412032 |
| **19.** | 2789327 | 2879327 | 2789327 |
| **20.** | 5927681 | 5927861 | 5927681 |
| **21.** | Wendy A. Courtney | Wendy A. Courtney | Wendy A. Courtnay |

**Directions:** For each question, compare the three names or numbers and mark your answer:
**(A)** if **ALL THREE** names or numbers are exactly **ALIKE**
**(B)** if only the **FIRST** and **SECOND** names or numbers are exactly **ALIKE**
**(C)** if only the **FIRST** and **THIRD** names or numbers are exactly **ALIKE**
**(D)** if only the **SECOND** and **THIRD** names or numbers are exactly **ALIKE**
**(E)** if **ALL THREE** names or numbers are **DIFFERENT**

| | | | |
|---|---|---|---|
| **22.** | Lambert Forman, MD | Lambert Forman, MD | Lambert Forman, MD |
| **23.** | Joseph A. Gurreri | Joseph A. Gurreri | Joseph A. Gurreri |
| **24.** | Sylnette Lynch | Sylnette Lynch | Sylnette Lynch |
| **25.** | Zion McKenzie Jr. | Zion McKenzie Sr. | Zion MacKenzie Jr. |
| **26.** | 6932976 | 6939276 | 6932796 |
| **27.** | 9631695 | 9636195 | 9631695 |
| **28.** | 7370527 | 7375027 | 7370537 |
| **29.** | 2799379 | 2739779 | 2799379 |
| **30.** | 5261383 | 5261383 | 5261338 |
| **31.** | J. Randolph Rea | J. Randolph Rea | J. Randolphe Rea |
| **32.** | W.E. Johnston | W.E. Johnson | W.E. Johnson |
| **33.** | Vergil L. Muller | Vergil L. Muller | Vergil L. Muller |
| **34.** | Atherton R. Warde | Asheton R. Warde | Atherton P. Warde |
| **35.** | E. Owens McVey | E. Owen McVey | E. Owen McVay |
| **36.** | 8125690 | 8126690 | 8125609 |
| **37.** | 2395890 | 2395890 | 2395890 |
| **38.** | 1926341 | 1926347 | 1926314 |
| **39.** | 6219354 | 6219354 | 6219354 |
| **40.** | 2312793 | 2312793 | 2312793 |
| **41.** | Alexander Majthenyi | Alexander Majthenyi | Alexander Majthenyi |
| **42.** | James T. Harbison | James T. Harbinson | James T. Harbison |
| **43.** | Margareta Goldenkoff | Margaretta Goldenkoff | Margaretha Goldenkoff |
| **44.** | Cornelius Detwiler | Cornelius Detwiler | Cornelius Detwiler |
| **45.** | Benjamin A. D'Ortona | Benjamin A. D'Ortoni | Benjamin D'Ortonia |
| **46.** | 1065407 | 1065407 | 1065047 |
| **47.** | 6452054 | 6452654 | 6452054 |
| **48.** | 8501268 | 8501268 | 8501286 |
| **49.** | 3457988 | 3457986 | 3457986 |
| **50.** | 4695682 | 4695862 | 4695682 |

# PART B: READING COMPREHENSION

**30 QUESTIONS • 60 MINUTES**

**Directons:** For each reading question, you will be given a paragraph that contains all the information necessary to answer the question that follows. Use only the information provided in the paragraph. Do not speculate or make assumptions that go beyond this information. Assume that all information in the paragraph is true, even if it conflicts with facts you may already know. Only one correct answer can be validly inferred from the information contained in the paragraph. Mark the letter of the correct answer on your answer sheet.

1. A member of the department shall not indulge in liquor while in uniform. A member of the department not required to wear a uniform and a uniformed member while out of uniform shall not indulge in intoxicants to an extent unfitting the member for duty.

The paragraph best supports the statement that a(n)

(A) off-duty member, not in uniform, may drink liquor to the extent that it does not unfit the member for duty.

(B) member not on duty, but in uniform and not unfit for duty, may drink liquor.

(C) on-duty member, unfit for duty in uniform, may drink intoxicants.

(D) uniformed member in civilian clothes may not drink intoxicants unless unfit for duty.

(E) civilian member of the department, in uniform, may drink liquor if fit for duty.

2. Tax law specialists may authorize their assistants to sign their names to reports, letters, and papers that are not specially required to be signed personally by the tax law specialist. The signature should read: "Jane Doe, tax law specialist, by Richard Roe, tax technician." The name of the tax law specialist may be written or stamped, but the signature of the tax technician shall be in ink.

The paragraph best supports the statement that

(A) if a tax law specialist's assistant signs official papers both by rubber stamp and in ink, the assistant has authority to sign.

(B) if a tax technician does not neglect to include his or her title in ink along with his or her signature following the word "by," the technician may sign papers that are not specially required to be signed personally by the tax law specialist.

(C) no signatory authority delegated to the tax technician by the tax law specialist maybe redelegated by the tax technician to an assistant unless so authorized in ink by the tax law specialist.

(D) if a tax law specialist personally signs written requisitions in ink, the technician is not required to identify the source of the order with a rubber stamp.

(E) when a tax technician signs authorized papers for a tax law specialist, the tax technician must write out the tax law specialist's signature in full with pen and ink.

3. Upon retirement from service, a member shall receive a retirement allowance consisting of an annuity that shall be the actuarial equivalent of his accumulated deductions at the time of retirement; a pension in addition to his annuity that shall be one service-fraction of his final compensation multiplied by the number of years of government service since he last became a member; and a pension that is the actuarial equivalent of their reserve-for-increased-take-home-pay to which he may then be entitled, if any.

The paragraph best supports the statement that

(A) a retirement allowance shall consist of an annuity plus a pension plus an actuarial equivalent of a service-fraction.

(B) upon retirement from service, a member shall receive an annuity plus a pension plus an actuarial equivalent of reserve-for-increased-take-home-pay if he is entitled.

(C) a retiring member shall receive an annuity plus reserve-for-increased-take-home-pay, if any, plus final compensation.

(D) a retirement allowance shall consist of a pension plus reserve-for-increased-take-home-pay, if any, plus accumulated deductions.

(E) a retirement allowance shall consist of an annuity that is equal to one service-fraction of final compensation, a pension multiplied by the number of years of government service, and the actuarial equivalent of accumulated deductions from increased take-home-pay.

4. If you are in doubt as to whether any matter is legally mailable, you should ask the postmaster. Even though the Postal Service has not expressly declared any matter to be nonmailable, the sender of such matter may be held fully liable for violation of law if he or she does actually send nonmailable matter through the mail.

The paragraph best supports the statement that if

(A) the postmaster is in doubt as to whether any matter is legally mailable, the postmaster may be held liable for any sender's sending nonmailable matter through the mail.

(B) the sender is ignorant of what it is that constitutes nonmailable matter, the sender is relieved of all responsibility for mailing nonmailable matter.

(C) a sender sends nonmailable matter, the sender is fully liable for law violation even though doubt may have existed about the mailability of the matter.

(D) the Postal Service has not expressly declared material mailable, it is nonmailable.

(E) the Postal Service has not expressly declared material nonmailable, it is mailable.

5. In evaluating education for a particular position, education in and of itself is of no value except to the degree in which it contributes to knowledge, skills, and abilities needed in the particular job. On its face, such a statement would seem to contend that general educational development need not be considered in evaluating education and training. Much to the contrary, such a proposition favors the consideration of any and all training, but only as it pertains to the position for which the applicant applies.

The paragraph best supports the statement that

(A) if general education is supplemented by specialized education, it is of no value.

(B) if a high school education is desirable in any occupation, special training need not be evaluated.

(C) in evaluating education, a contradiction arises in assigning equal weight to general and specialized education.

**(D)** unless it is supplemented by general education, specialized education is of no value.

**(E)** education is of value to the degree to which it is needed in the particular position.

**6.** Statistics tell us that heart disease kills more people than any other illness, and the death rate continues to rise. People older than 30 have a fifty-fifty chance of escaping, for heart disease is chiefly an illness of people in late middle age and advanced years. Because there are more people in this age group living today than there were some years ago, heart disease is able to find more victims.

The paragraph best supports the statement that

**(A)** if a person has heart disease, there is a 50 percent chance that he or she is older than 30.

**(B)** according to statistics, more middle-aged and elderly people die of heart disease than of all other causes.

**(C)** because heart disease is chiefly an illness of people in late middle age, young people are less likely to be the victims of heart disease.

**(D)** the rising birth rate has increased the possibility that the average person will die of heart disease.

**(E)** if the stress of modern living were not increasing, there would be a slower increase in the risk of heart disease.

**7.** Racketeers are primarily concerned with business affairs, legitimate or otherwise, and prefer those that are close to the margin of legitimacy. They get their best opportunities from business organizations that meet the need of large sections of the public for goods or services that are defined as illegitimate by the same public, such as prostitution, gambling, illicit drugs, or liquor. In contrast to the thief, the racketeer and the establishments he or she controls deliver goods and services for money received.

The paragraph best supports the statement that

**(A)** since racketeers deliver goods and services for money received, their business affairs are not illegitimate.

**(B)** since racketeering involves objects of value, it is unlike theft.

**(C)** victims of racketeers are not guilty of violating the law, therefore racketeering is a victimless crime.

**(D)** since many people want services that are not obtainable through legitimate sources, they contribute to the difficulty of suppressing racketeers.

**(E)** if large sections of the public are engaged in legitimate business with racketeers, the businesses are not illegitimate.

8. The housing authority not only faces every problem of the private developer, but it must also assume responsibilities of which the private developer is free. The authority must account to the community; it must conform to federal regulations; it must provide durable buildings of good standard at low cost; and it must overcome the prejudices of contractors, bankers, and prospective tenants against public operations. These authorities are being watched by antihousing enthusiasts for the first error of judgment or the first evidence of high costs that can be torn to bits before a Congressional committee.

The paragraph best supports the statement that

(A) since private developers are not accountable to the community, they do not have the opposition of contractors, bankers, and prospective tenants.

(B) if Congressional committees are watched by antihousing enthusiasts, they may discover errors of judgment and high costs on the part of a housing authority.

(C) while a housing authority must deal with all the difficulties encountered by a private builder, it must also deal with antihousing enthusiasts.

(D) if housing authorities are not immune to errors in judgment, they must provide durable buildings of good standard and low cost just like private developers.

(E) if a housing authority is to conform to federal regulations, it must overcome the prejudices of contractors, builders, and prospective tenants.

9. Security of tenure in the public service must be viewed in the context of the universal quest for security. If we narrow our application to the term of employment, the problem of security in the public service differs from that of private industry only in the need to meet the peculiar threats to security in governmental organizations—principally, the danger of making employment contingent upon factors other than the performance of the workers.

The paragraph best supports the statement that

(A) if workers seek security, they should enter public service.

(B) if employment is contingent upon factors other than work performance, workers will feel more secure.

(C) if employees believe that their security is threatened, they are employed in private industry.

(D) the term of employment in public service differs from that in private industry.

(E) the employment status of the public servant with respect to security of tenure differs from that of the private employee by encompassing factors beyond those affecting the private employee.

10. The wide use of antibiotics has presented a number of problems. Some patients become allergic to the drugs, so they cannot be used when needed. In other cases, after prolonged treatment with antibiotics, certain organisms no longer respond to them. This is one of the reasons for the constant search for more potent drugs.

The paragraph best supports the statement that

(A) because a number of problems have been presented by long-term treatment with antibiotics, antibiotics should never be used on a long-term basis.

(B) because some people have developed an allergy to specific drugs, potent antibiotics cannot always be used.

(C) since antibiotics have been used successfully for certain allergies, there must be a constant search for more potent drugs.

**(D)** if antibiotics are used for a prolonged period, certain organisms become allergic to them.

**(E)** since so many diseases have been successfully treated with antibiotics, there must be a constant search for new drugs.

11. The noncompetitive class consists of positions for which there are minimum qualifications but for which no reliable exam has been developed. In the noncompetitive class, every applicant must meet minimum qualifications in terms of education, experience, and medical or physical qualifications. There may even be an examination on a pass/fail basis.

The paragraph best supports the statement that if

**(A)** an exam is unreliable, the position is in the noncompetitive class.

**(B)** an applicant has met minimum qualifications in terms of education, experience, medical, or physical requirements, the applicant must pass a test.

**(C)** an applicant has met minimum qualifications in terms of education, experience, medical, or physical requirements, the applicant may fail a test.

**(D)** an applicant passes an exam for a noncompetitive position, the applicant must also meet minimum qualifications.

**(E)** there are minimum qualifications for a position, the position is in the noncompetitive class.

12. Two independent clauses cannot share one sentence without some form of connective. If they do, they form a run-on sentence. Two principal clauses may be joined by a coordinating conjunction, by a comma followed by a coordinating conjunction, or by a semicolon. They may also form two distinct sentences. Two main clauses may never be joined by a comma without a coordinating conjunction. This error is called a comma splice.

The paragraph best supports the statement that

**(A)** if the violation is called a comma splice, two main clauses are joined by a comma without a coordinating conjunction.

**(B)** if two distinct sentences share one sentence and are joined by a coordinating conjunction, the result is a run-on sentence.

**(C)** when a coordinating conjunction is not followed by a semicolon, the writer has committed an error of punctuation.

**(D)** while a comma and a semicolon may not be used in the same principal clause, they maybe used in the same sentence.

**(E)** a bad remedy for a run-on sentence is not a comma splice.

13. The pay in some job titles is hourly; in others it is annual. Official work weeks vary from 35 hours to 37½ hours to 40 hours. In some positions, overtime is earned for all time worked beyond the set number of hours, and differentials are paid for night, weekend, or holiday work. Other positions offer compensatory time off for overtime or for work during unpopular times. Still other positions require the jobholder to devote as much extra time as needed to do the work without any extra compensation. And in some positions, employees who work overtime are given a meal allowance.

The paragraph best supports the statement that if

**(A)** a meal allowance is given, there is compensation for overtime.

**(B)** the work week is 35 hours long, the job is unpopular.

**(C)** overtime is earned, pay in the job title is hourly.

**(D)** a jobholder has earned a weekend differential, the employee has worked beyond the set number of hours.

**(E)** compensatory time is offered, it is offered as a substitute for overtime pay.

14. All applicants must be of satisfactory character and reputation and must meet all requirements set forth in the Notice of Examination for the position for which they are applying. Applicants may be summoned for the written test prior to investigation of their qualifications and background. Admission to the test does not mean that the applicant has met the qualifications for the position.

The paragraph best supports the statement that if an applicant has

(A) been admitted to the test, the applicant has not met requirements for the position.

(B) not been investigated, the applicant will not be admitted to the written test.

(C) met all requirements for the position, the applicant will be admitted to the test.

(D) satisfactory character and reputation, the applicant will not have his or her background investigated.

(E) met all the requirements set forth in the Notice of Examination, the applicant will pass the test.

15. Although it has in the past been illegal for undocumented aliens to work in the United States, it has not, until now, been unlawful for employers to hire these aliens. With the passage of the Immigration Reform and Control Act of 1986, employers are subject to civil penalties and, ultimately, imprisonment if they knowingly hire, recruit, or refer for a fee any unauthorized alien. Similarly, it is also unlawful for employers to continue to employ an undocumented alien hired after November 6, 1986, knowing that he or she was or is unauthorized to work.

The paragraph best supports the statement that

(A) under the Immigration Reform and Control Act of 1986, it is no longer illegal for undocumented aliens to be denied employment in the United States.

(B) if an undocumented alien is not remaining on the job illegally, the worker was not hired after November 6, 1986.

(C) if a person wishes to avoid the penalties of the immigration law, the person must not knowingly employ aliens.

(D) if an employer inadvertently hires undocumented aliens, the employer may be subject to fine or imprisonment, but not both.

(E) if an unauthorized alien was able to find an employer who hired him or her after November 6, 1986, the alien was welcome to go to work.

16. The law requires that the federal government offer employees, retirees, and their families the opportunity to continue group health and/or welfare fund coverage at 102 percent of the group rate in certain instances where the coverage would otherwise terminate. All group benefits, including optional benefits riders, are available. Welfare fund benefits that can be continued under COBRA are dental, vision, prescription drugs, and other related medical benefits. The period of coverage varies from 18 to 36 months, depending on the reason for continuation.

The paragraph best supports the statement that

(A) the period of coverage continuation varies depending on the reason for termination.

(B) upon retirement, welfare fund benefits continue at a 102 percent rate.

(C) federal law requires employees, retirees, and their families to continue health coverage.

(D) COBRA is a program for acquiring welfare fund benefits.

(E) if retirees or their families do not desire to terminate them, they can continue group benefits at 102 percent of the group rate.

**17.** Historical records as such rarely constitute an adequate or, more important, a reliable basis for estimating earthquake potential. In most regions of the world, recorded history is short relative to the time between the largest earthquakes. Thus, the fact that there have been no historic earthquakes larger than a given size does not make us confident that they will not occur in the future. It may, alternatively, be due to the short length of available historical records relative to the long repeat time for large earthquakes.

The paragraph best supports the statement that

(A) if historic earthquakes are no larger than a given size, they are unlikely to recur.

(B) potential earthquakes do not inspire confidence in historical records as predictors of time between earthquakes.

(C) if the time span between major earthquakes were not longer than the length of available records, history would have greater predictive value.

(D) since there have been no historic earthquakes larger than a given size, we are confident that there will be a long time span between major earthquakes.

(E) in those regions of the world where recorded history is long, the time between the largest earthquakes is short.

**18.** A language can be thought of as a number of strings or sequences of symbols. The definition of a language defines which strings belong to the language, but since most languages of interest consist of an infinite number of strings, this definition is impossible to accomplish by listing the strings (or sentences). While the number of *sentences* in a language can be infinite, the rules by which they are constructed are not. This may explain why we are able to speak sentences in a language that we have never spoken before, and to understand sentences that we have never heard before.

The paragraph best supports the statement that

(A) if there is an infinite number of sequences of symbols in a language, there is an infinite number of rules for their construction.

(B) if we have never spoken a language, we can understand its sentences provided that we know the rules by which they were constructed.

(C) a language is defined by its strings.

(D) if the number of sentences in an unnatural language were not infinite, we would be able to define it.

(E) if sequences of symbols are governed by rules of construction, then the number of sentences can be determined.

**19.** An assumption commonly made regarding the reliability of testimony is that when a number of persons report the same matter, details upon which there is an agreement may generally be considered substantiated. Experiments have shown, however, that there is a tendency for the same errors to appear in the testimony of different individuals, and that, apart from any collusion, agreement of testimony is no proof of dependability.

The paragraph best supports the statement that

(A) if details of the testimony are true, all witnesses will agree to it.

(B) unless there is collusion, it is impossible for a number of persons to give the same report.

(C) if most witnesses do not independently attest to the same facts, the facts cannot be true.

(D) if the testimony of a group of people is in substantial agreement, it cannot be ruled out that those witnesses have not all made the same mistake.

(E) under experimental conditions, witnesses tend to give reliable testimony.

**20.** In some instances, changes are made in a contract after it has been signed and accepted by both parties. This is done either by inserting a new clause in a contract or by annexing a *rider* to the contract. If a contract is changed by a rider, both parties must sign the rider for it to be legal. The basic contract should also note that a rider is attached by inserting new words to the contract, and both parties should also initial and date the new insertion. The same requirement applies if they later change any wording in the contract. What two people agree to do, they can mutually agree not to do—as long as they both agree.

The paragraph best supports the statement that if

**(A)** two people mutually agree not to do something, they must sign a rider.

**(B)** both parties to a contract do not agree to attach a rider, they must initial the contract to render it legal.

**(C)** a rider to a contract is to be legal, that rider must be agreed to and signed by both parties, who must not neglect to initial and date that portion of the contract to which the rider refers.

**(D)** a party to a contract does not agree to a change, that party should initial the change and annex a rider detailing the disagreement.

**(E)** the wording of a contract is not to be changed, both parties must initial and date a rider.

**21.** Personnel administration begins with the process of defining the quantities of people needed to do the job. Thereafter, people must be recruited, selected, trained, directed, rewarded, transferred, promoted, and perhaps released or retired. However, it is not true that all organizations are structured so that workers can be dealt with as individuals. In some organizations, employees are represented by unions, and managers bargain directly only with these associations.

The paragraph best supports the statement that

**(A)** no organizations are structured so that workers cannot be dealt with as individuals.

**(B)** some working environments other than organizations are structured so that workers can be dealt with as individuals.

**(C)** all organizations are structured so that employees are represented by unions.

**(D)** no organizations are structured so that managers bargain with unions.

**(E)** some organizations are not structured so that workers can be dealt with as individuals.

**22.** Explosives are substances or devices capable of producing a volume of rapidly expanding gases that exert a sudden pressure on their surroundings. Chemical explosives are the most commonly used, although there are mechanical and nuclear explosives. All mechanical explosives are devices in which a physical reaction is produced, such as that caused by overloading a container with compressed air. While nuclear explosives are by far the most powerful, all nuclear explosives have been restricted to military weapons.

The paragraph best supports the statement that

**(A)** all explosives that have been restricted to military weapons are nuclear explosives.

**(B)** no mechanical explosives are devices in which a physical reaction is produced, such as that caused by overloading a container with compressed air.

**(C)** some nuclear explosives have not been restricted to military weapons.

**(D)** all mechanical explosives have been restricted to military weapons.

**(E)** some devices in which a physical reaction is produced, such as that caused by overloading a container with compressed air, are mechanical explosives.

23. The modern conception of the economic role of the public sector (government), as distinct from the private sector, is that every level of government is a link in the economic process. Government's contribution to political and economic welfare must, however, be evaluated not merely in terms of its technical efficiency, but also in the light of its acceptability to a particular society at a particular state of political and economic development. Even in a dictatorship, this principle is formally observed, although the authorities usually destroy the substance by presuming to interpret to the public its collective desires.

The paragraph best supports the statement that

**(A)** it is not true that some levels of government are not links in the economic process.

**(B)** all dictatorships observe the same economic principles as other governments.

**(C)** all links in the economic process are levels of government.

**(D)** the contributions of some levels of government do not need to be evaluated for technical efficiency and acceptability to society.

**(E)** no links in the economic process are institutions other than levels of government.

24. All property is classified as either personal property or real property, but not both. In general, if something is classified as personal property, it is transient and transportable in nature, while real property is not. Things such as leaseholds, animals, money, and intangible and other moveable goods are examples of personal property. Perma-

nent buildings and land, on the other hand, are fixed in nature and are not transportable.

The paragraph best supports the statement that

**(A)** if something is classified as personal property, it is not transient and transportable in nature.

**(B)** some forms of property are considered to be both personal property and real property.

**(C)** permanent buildings and land are real property.

**(D)** permanent buildings and land are personal property.

**(E)** tangible goods are considered to be real property.

25. The Supreme Court's power to invalidate legislation that violates the Constitution is a strong restriction on the powers of Congress. If an Act of Congress is deemed unconstitutional by the Supreme Court, then the Act is voided. Unlike a presidential veto, which can be overridden by a two-thirds majority vote of the House and the Senate, a constitutional ruling by the Supreme Court must be accepted by the Congress.

The paragraph best supports the statement that if an Act of Congress

**(A)** is voided, then it has been deemed unconstitutional by the Supreme Court.

**(B)** has not been voided, then it has not been deemed unconstitutional by the Supreme Court.

**(C)** has not been deemed unconstitutional by the Supreme Court, then it is voided.

**(D)** is deemed unconstitutional by the Supreme Court, then it is not voided.

**(E)** has not been voided, then it has been deemed unconstitutional by the Supreme Court.

**26.** All child-welfare agencies are organizations that seek to promote the healthy growth and development of children. Supplying or supplementing family income so that parents can maintain a home for their children is usually the first such service to be provided. In addition to programs of general family relief, some special programs for broken families are offered when parental care is temporarily or permanently unavailable.

The paragraph best supports the statement that

**(A)** it is not true that some organizations that seek to promote the healthy growth and development of children are child-welfare agencies.

**(B)** some programs offered when parental care is temporarily or permanently unavailable are not special programs for broken families.

**(C)** it is not true that no special programs for broken families are offered when temporary or permanent parental care is unavailable.

**(D)** all programs offered when parental care is temporarily or permanently unavailable are special programs for broken families.

**(E)** some organizations that seek to promote the healthy growth and development of children are not child-welfare agencies.

**27.** Information centers can be categorized according to the primary activity or service they provide. For example, some information centers are document depots. These depots, generally government-sponsored, serve as archives for the acquisition, storage, retrieval, and dissemination of a variety of documents. All document depots have the capacity to provide a great range of user services, which may include preparing specialized bibliographies; publishing announcements, indexes, and abstracts; and providing copies.

The paragraph best supports the statement that

**(A)** some information centers are categorized by features other than the primary activity or service they provide.

**(B)** some document depots lack the capacity to provide a great range of user services.

**(C)** no document depot lacks the capacity to provide a great range of user services.

**(D)** all information centers are document depots.

**(E)** some places that provide a great range of user services are not document depots.

**28.** Authorities generally agree that the use of hyphens tends to defy most rules. The best advice is to consult the dictionary to determine whether a given prefix is joined solidly to a root word or is hyphenated. One reliable rule, however, is that if an expression is a familiar one, such as "overtime" or "hatchback," then it is a nonhyphenated compound.

The paragraph best supports the statement that if an expression is

**(A)** a familiar one, then it is a hyphenated compound.

**(B)** a nonhyphenated compound, then it is a familiar expression.

**(C)** not a familiar one, then it is a hyphenated compound.

**(D)** a hyphenated compound, containing a suffix rather than a prefix, then it is not a familiar one.

**(E)** a hyphenated compound, then it is not a familiar one.

**29.** One use for wild land is the protection of certain species of wild animals or plants in wildlife refuges or in botanical reservations. Some general types of land use are activities that conflict with this stated purpose. All activities that exhibit such conflict are, of course, excluded from refuges and reservations.

The paragraph best supports the statement that

**(A)** all activities that conflict with the purpose of wildlife refuges or botanical reservations are general types of land use.

**(B)** all activities excluded from wildlife refuges and botanical reservations are those that conflict with the purpose of the refuge or reservation.

**(C)** some activities excluded from wildlife refuges and botanical reservations are general types of land use.

**(D)** no activities that conflict with the purpose of wildlife refuges and botanical reservations are general types of land use.

**(E)** some general types of land use are not excluded from wildlife refuges and botanical reservations.

**30.** Many kinds of computer programming languages have been developed over the years. Initially, programmers had to write instructions in machine language. If a computer programming language is a machine language, then it is a code that can be read directly by a computer. Most high-level computer programming languages use strings of common English phrases that communicate with the computer only after being converted or translated into a machine code.

The paragraph best supports the statement that

**(A)** all high-level computer programming languages use strings of common English phrases that are converted to a machine code.

**(B)** if a computer programming language is a machine language, then it is not a code that can be read directly by a computer.

**(C)** if a computer programming language is a code that can be read directly by a computer, then it is not a machine language.

**(D)** if a computer programming language is not a code that can be read directly by a computer, then it is not a machine language.

**(E)** if a computer programming language is not a machine language, then it is a code that can be read directly by a computer.

# PART C: ARITHMETIC REASONING

**20 QUESTIONS • 50 MINUTES**

**Directons:** Read each problem carefully and mark your answer sheet with the letter of the correct answer. If the correct answer is not given as one of the response choices, select choice (E), "none of these."

1. Twelve clerks are assigned to enter certain data on index cards. This number of clerks could perform the task in 18 days. After these clerks have worked on this assignment for 6 days, 4 more clerks are added to the staff to do this work. Assuming that all the clerks work at the same rate of speed, the entire task, instead of taking 18 days, will take
   - **(A)** 9 days
   - **(B)** 12 days
   - **(C)** 15 days
   - **(D)** 16 days
   - **(E)** none of these

2. In a low-cost public-health dental clinic, an adult's cleaning costs twice as much as the same treatment for a child. If a family of 3 children and 2 adults can visit the clinic for cleanings for a cost of $49, what is the cost for each adult?
   - **(A)** $7
   - **(B)** $10
   - **(C)** $12
   - **(D)** $14
   - **(E)** none of these

3. A government employee is relocated to a new region of the country and purchases a new home. The purchase price of the house is $87,250. Taxes to be paid on this house include the following: county tax of $424 per year, town tax of $783 per year, and school tax of $466 every six months. The aggregate tax rate is $.132 per $1000 of assessed value. The assessed value of this house is what percent of the purchase price?
   - **(A)** 14.52%
   - **(B)** 18.57%
   - **(C)** 22.81%
   - **(D)** 29.05%
   - **(E)** none of these

4. The Social Security Administration has ordered an intensive check of 756 SSI payment recipients who are suspected of having above-standard incomes. Four clerical assistants have been assigned to this task. At the end of six days at 7 hours each, they have checked on 336 recipients. In order to speed up the investigation, 2 more assistants are assigned at this point. If they work at the same rate, the number of additional 7-hour days it will take to complete the job is, most nearly
   - **(A)** 1
   - **(B)** 2
   - **(C)** 3
   - **(D)** 4
   - **(E)** none of these

5. A family spends 30 percent of its take-home income for food, 8 percent for clothing, 25 percent for shelter, 4 percent for recreation, 13 percent for education, and 5 percent for miscellaneous items. The remainder goes into the family's savings account. If the weekly net earnings of this household are $500, how many weeks will it take this family to accumulate $15,000 in savings, before interest?

(A) 200
(B) 175
(C) 150
(D) 100
(E) none of these

6. An Internal Revenue Service (IRS) officer is making spot-checks of income reported on income tax returns. A cab driver being audited works on a commission basis, receiving 42½ percent of fares collected. The IRS allocates that earnings from tips should be valued at 29 percent of commissions. If the cab driver's weekly fare collections average $520, then the IRS projects his reportable monthly earnings to be

(A) between $900 and $1,000
(B) between $1,000 and $1,100
(C) between $1,100 and $1,200
(D) between $1,200 and $1,250
(E) none of these

7. A department head hired a total of 60 temporary employees to handle a seasonal increase in the department's workload. The following lists the number of temporary employees hired, their rates of pay, and the duration of their employment:

One-third of the total were hired as clerks, each at the rate of $12,750 a year, for two months.

30 percent of the total were hired as office machine operators, each at the rate of $13,150 a year, for four months.

22 stenographers were hired, each at the rate of $13,000 a year, for three months.

The total amount paid to these temporary employees to the nearest dollar was

(A) $194,499
(B) $192,900
(C) $130,000
(D) $127,500
(E) none of these

8. An oil burner in a housing development burns 76 gallons of fuel per hour. At 9 a.m. on a very cold day, the superintendent asks the housing manager to put in an emergency order for more fuel oil. At that time, he reports that he has on hand 266 gallons. At noon on the same day, the superintendent again contacts the manager to notify him that no oil has been delivered. From that time, the maximum amount of time that he can continue to furnish heat without receiving more fuel oil is

(A) ½ hour
(B) 1 hour
(C) 1½ hours
(D) 2 hours
(E) none of these

9. The visitors' section of a courtroom seats 105 people. The court is in session 6 hours a day. On one particular day, 486 people visited the court and were given seats. What is the average length of time spent by each visitor in the court? Assume that as soon as a person leaves a seat it is immediately filled and that at no time during the day are any of the 105 seats vacant. Express your answer in hours and minutes, to the nearest minute.

(A) 1 hour 18 minutes
(B) 1 hour 20 minutes
(C) 1 hour 30 minutes
(D) 2 hours
(E) none of these

10. A worker is paid at the rate of $8.60 per hour for the first 40 hours worked in a week and time-and-a-half for overtime. The FICA (social security) deduction is 7.13 percent; federal tax withholding is 15 percent; state tax withholding, 5 percent; and local tax withholding, 2½ percent. If a worker works 48 hours a week for two consecutive weeks, she will take home

    (A) $314.69
    (B) $580.97
    (C) $629.39
    (D) $693.16
    (E) none of these

11. A court clerk estimates that the untried cases on the docket will occupy the court for 150 trial days. If new cases are accumulating at the rate of 1.6 trial days per day and the court sits five days a week, how many days' business will remain to be heard at the end of 60 trial days?

    (A) 168
    (B) 184
    (C) 185
    (D) 186
    (E) none of these

12. A criminal investigator has an appointment to meet with an important informant at 4 p.m. in a city that is 480 kilometers from his base location. If the investigator estimates that his average speed will be 40 mph, what time must he leave home to make his appointment?

    (A) 8:15 a.m.
    (B) 8:30 a.m.
    (C) 8:45 a.m.
    (D) 9:30 a.m.
    (E) none of these

13. A program analysis office is taking bids for a new office machine. One machine is offered at a list price of $1,360 with successive discounts of 20 percent and 10 percent, a delivery charge of $35, and an installation charge of $52. The other machine is offered at a list price of $1,385 with a single discount of 30 percent, a delivery charge of $40, and an installation charge of

$50. If the office chooses the less expensive machine, the savings will amount to just about

(A) 0.6 percent
(B) 1.9 percent
(C) 2.0 percent
(D) 2.6 percent
(E) none of these

14. An assignment is completed by 32 clerks in 22 days. Assuming that all the clerks work at the same rate of speed, the number of clerks that would be needed to complete this assignment in 16 days is

(A) 27
(B) 38
(C) 44
(D) 52
(E) none of these

15. The paralegals in a large legal department have decided to establish a "sunshine fund" for charitable purposes. Paralegal A has proposed that each worker chip in one-half of 1 percent of their weekly salary; paralegal B thinks 1 percent would be just right; paralegal C suggests that one-third of 1 percent would be adequate; and paralegal D, who is strapped for funds, argues for one-fifth of 1 percent. The payroll department will cooperate and make an automatic deduction, but the paralegals must agree on a uniform percentage. The average of their suggested contributions is approximately

(A) ¼ percent
(B) ⅓ percent
(C) ½ percent
(D) ⅝ percent
(E) none of these

16. A federal agency had a personal computer repaired at a cost of $49.20. This amount included a charge of $22 per hour for labor and a charge for a new switch that cost $18 before a 10 percent government discount was applied. How long did the repair job take?

   (A) 1 hour 6 minutes
   (B) 1 hour 11 minutes
   (C) 1 hour 22 minutes
   (D) 1 hour 30 minutes
   (E) none of these

17. In a large agency where mail is delivered in motorized carts, two tires were replaced on a cart at a cost of $34 per tire. If the agency had expected to pay $80 for a pair of tires, what percent of its expected cost did it save?

   (A) 7.5 percent
   (B) 17.6 percent
   (C) 57.5 percent
   (D) 75.0 percent
   (E) none of these

18. An experimental antipollution vehicle powered by electricity traveled 33 kilometers (km) at a constant speed of 110 kilometers per hour (km/h). How many minutes did it take this vehicle to complete its experimental run?

   (A) 3
   (B) 10
   (C) 18
   (D) 20
   (E) none of these

19. In one federal office, $\frac{1}{6}$ of the employees favored abandoning a flexible work schedule system. In a second office that had the same number of employees, $\frac{1}{4}$ of the workers favored abandoning it. What is the average of the fractions of the workers in the two offices who favored abandoning the system?

   (A) $\frac{1}{10}$
   (B) $\frac{1}{5}$
   (C) $\frac{5}{24}$
   (D) $\frac{5}{12}$
   (E) none of the these

20. A clerk is able to process 40 unemployment compensation claims in one hour. After deductions of 18 percent for benefits and taxes, the clerk's net pay is $6.97 per hour. If the clerk processed 1,200 claims, how much would the government have to pay for the work, based on the clerk's hourly wage *before* deductions?

   (A) $278.80
   (B) $255.00
   (C) $246.74
   (D) $209.10
   (E) none of these

practice test

# ANSWER KEY AND EXPLANATIONS

## Part A: Name and Number Comparisons

| | | | | |
|---|---|---|---|---|
| 1. B | 11. B | 21. B | 31. B | 41. A |
| 2. D | 12. E | 22. A | 32. D | 42. C |
| 3. E | 13. E | 23. A | 33. A | 43. E |
| 4. A | 14. E | 24. A | 34. E | 44. A |
| 5. E | 15. B | 25. E | 35. E | 45. E |
| 6. A | 16. D | 26. E | 36. E | 46. B |
| 7. A | 17. A | 27. C | 37. A | 47. C |
| 8. C | 18. A | 28. E | 38. E | 48. B |
| 9. D | 19. C | 29. C | 39. A | 49. D |
| 10. B | 20. C | 30. B | 40. A | 50. C |

1. **The correct answer is (B).** The first two names are exactly alike, but the third name has a different initial.

2. **The correct answer is (D).** In the second and third names, the surname is Moru. In the first name, it is Moro.

3. **The correct answer is (E).** The given name is alike in the second and third names only; the surname is alike in only the first and second names.

4. **The correct answer is (A).** All three names are exactly alike.

5. **The correct answer is (E).** The middle initial in the second name is different from that of the other two. In the third name, Francis becomes Frances.

6. **The correct answer is (A).** All three numbers are exactly alike.

7. **The correct answer is (A).** All three numbers are exactly alike.

8. **The correct answer is (C).** The "254" of the beginning of the second number is different from the "245" opening of the first and third numbers.

9. **The correct answer is (D).** The "243" ending of the first number is different from the "423" ending of the second and third numbers.

10. **The correct answer is (B).** The "2798" opening of the third number is different from the "2789" opening of the first and second numbers.

11. **The correct answer is (B).** In the third name, the surname changes from Tenenbaum to Tanenbaum.

12. **The correct answer is (E).** The surname is different in each of the three names.

13. **The correct answer is (E).** Again, all three surnames are different.

14. **The correct answer is (E).** "Robert J." of the third name is the reverse of "J. Robert" of the first two names; the spelling of the surname in the second name differs from that of the first and third.

15. **The correct answer is (B).** "Fernand" of the third name is different from "Fernando" of the first two.

16. **The correct answer is (D).** The "630" ending of the first number is different from the "360" ending of the second and third.

17. **The correct answer is (A).** All three numbers are exactly alike.

18. **The correct answer is (A).** All three numbers are exactly alike.

19. **The correct answer is (C).** The "287" beginning of the second number is different from the "278" beginning of the first and third numbers.

20. **The correct answer is (C).** The "861" ending of the second number is different from the "681" ending of the first and third.

21. **The correct answer is (B).** "Courtnay" of the third name is different from "Courtney" of the first and second.

22. **The correct answer is (A).** All three names are exactly alike.

23. **The correct answer is (A).** All three names are exactly alike.

24. **The correct answer is (A).** All three names are exactly alike.

25. **The correct answer is (E).** The second name is "Sr.," while the first and third names are "Jr."; the third surname begins with "Mac," while the first and second surnames begin with "Mc."

26. **The correct answer is (E).** The three numbers end "2976," "9276," "2796."

27. **The correct answer is (C).** The first and third numbers end "1695"; the second ends "6195."

28. **The correct answer is (E).** The three numbers end "0527," "5027," "0537."

29. **The correct answer is (C).** The first and third numbers are identical; the second number differs in a number of digits.

30. **The correct answer is (B).** The last two digits of the third number are reversed.

31. **The correct answer is (B).** "Randolphe" of the third name is different from "Randolph" of the first two.

32. **The correct answer is (D).** The surname of the second and third names, "Johnson," is different from the surname of the first name, "Johnston."

33. **The correct answer is (A).** All three names are exactly alike.

34. **The correct answer is (E).** The middle initial of the third name differs from the other two. "Asheton" of the second name differs from "Atherton" of the other two.

35. **The correct answer is (E).** The given name in the second and third names is "Owen" while in the first it is "Owens." The surname of the first two names is "McVey" while in the third it is "McVay."

36. **The correct answer is (E).** The three numbers end "5690," "6690," "5609."

37. **The correct answer is (A).** All three numbers are exactly alike.

38. **The correct answer is (E).** The last two digits are, respectively "41," "47," "14."

39. **The correct answer is (A).** All three numbers are exactly alike.

40. **The correct answer is (A).** All three numbers are exactly alike.

41. **The correct answer is (A).** All three names are exactly alike.

42. **The correct answer is (C).** The first and third names are exactly alike, but the second name inserts an "n" in the surname.

43. **The correct answer is (E).** The given name is different in all three names.

44. **The correct answer is (A).** All three names are exactly alike.

45. **The correct answer is (E).** The surname is different in each of the three names.

46. **The correct answer is (B).** In the third number, the fifth and sixth digits are reversed.

47. **The correct answer is (C).** In the second number, the fifth digit is "6" while in the other numbers the fifth digit is "0."

48. **The correct answer is (B).** In the third number, the last two digits are reversed.

49. **The correct answer is (D).** The last digit of the second and third numbers is "6"; the first number ends with "8."

50. **The correct answer is (C).** In the second number, the order of the fifth and sixth digits is reversed.

## Part B: Reading Comprehension

| | | | | |
|---|---|---|---|---|
| 1. A | 7. D | 13. E | 19. D | 25. B |
| 2. B | 8. C | 14. C | 20. C | 26. C |
| 3. B | 9. E | 15. B | 21. E | 27. C |
| 4. C | 10. B | 16. E | 22. E | 28. E |
| 5. E | 11. D | 17. C | 23. A | 29. C |
| 6. C | 12. A | 18. B | 24. C | 30. D |

1. **The correct answer is (A).** The essential information from which the answer can be inferred is found in the second sentence. Since *a uniformed member while out of uniform* (in other words, an off-duty member) *shall **not** indulge in intoxicants to an extent unfitting the member for duty,* it follows that the same member may drink liquor in moderation. Choice (B) is incorrect because it directly contradicts the first sentence. Choice (C) is incorrect because it introduces a concept not addressed in the paragraph—that of the uniformed member who reports unfit for duty. Choice (D) is wrong because it reverses the meaning of the second sentence—the uniformed member in civilian clothes may drink only to the extent that the member remains fit for duty. Choice (E) is incorrect because it raises a topic never mentioned in the paragraph—that of the civilian member of the department in a uniform.

2. **The correct answer is (B).** The paragraph makes the statement that the technician may sign that which it is not required that the specialist personally sign and states the rules that apply to the technician: name and title of tax law specialist followed by "by" and the name and title of the tax technician in ink. Choice (A) is incorrect in that the assistant does not have authority to sign all papers. Choices (C) and (D) are incorrect because they address topics not mentioned in the paragraph—redelegation and requisitions. Choice (E) is incorrect; the tax law specialist's name may be affixed by rubber stamp.

3. **The correct answer is (B).** The first clause states that the retiree is entitled to an annuity; the second clause tells of the pension that is the equal of one service-fraction of final compensation multiplied by number of years of government service; and the last clause describes an additional pension that is the actuarial equivalent of any reserve-for-increased-take-home-pay to which the retiree might at that time be entitled. Choice (A) is incorrect because it does not complete the explanation of the basis for the second pension. Choices (C), (D), and (E) are all hopelessly garbled misstatements.

4. **The correct answer is (C).** In effect, the paragraph is saying, "When in doubt, check it out." Ignorance of the nature of the material to be mailed or of how the law pertains to it does not excuse the mailer if the material was indeed subject to a prohibition. Choice (A) misinterprets the role of the postmaster. The postmaster is the final authority as to mailability. Choice (B) is incorrect in its direct contradiction of the paragraph, which states that ignorance is no excuse. Choices (D) and (E) both interpret beyond the paragraph. The paragraph places all burden on the mailer.

5. **The correct answer is (E).** The last sentence makes the point that *any and all training* is valuable, *but only as it pertains to the position for which the applicant applies.* Choices (A) and (D) miss the point. Any training or education is valuable if *it contributes to knowledge, skills, and abilities needed in the particular job.* Choices

(B) and (C) make statements unsupported by the paragraph.

6. **The correct answer is (C).** The second sentence tells us that heart disease is an illness of late middle age and old age. Choice (A) is totally wrong. Since heart disease is an illness of older people, the odds of a person with heart disease being older than 30 are much more than 50 percent. The fifty-fifty statement refers to the likelihood of persons older than 30 developing heart disease at some time. Choice (B) confuses death from *all other causes* with death from *any other illness*. Choice (D) makes an unsupported assumption that only the rising birth rate contributes to the number of people above a certain age. Actually, the longevity rate is much more crucial to this figure. Choice (E) makes a statement that, whether true or false, is in no way supported by the paragraph.

7. **The correct answer is (D).** If people want what they can't get through legitimate and entirely legal channels, they will turn to those who can supply those products or services. The consumers of less-than-legitimate products or services are unlikely to betray their suppliers. Choice (A) is incorrect. Since racketeers deliver goods and services for money received, they are not engaged in theft, but not all "non-thieves" are engaged in legitimate business. Choice (B) is incorrect because both racketeering and theft involve objects of value; the differences are along other dimensions. Choice (C) makes no sense at all. Choice (E) is unsupported by the paragraph.

8. **The correct answer is (C).** The first sentence tells us that the problems of the housing authority are numerous and that it faces all the problems of private developers and problems peculiar to a public authority. Being *watched by antihousing enthusiasts* is one of these problems. Choice (A) makes an unsupported statement.

The paragraph does not enumerate the problems of private developers. Choice (B) is incorrect. It is the antihousing authorities who watch for errors and cost overruns and then bring them to the attention of Congressional committees. Choices (D) and (E) make unsupported statements that do not make much sense as statements.

9. **The correct answer is (E).** *The peculiar threats to security in governmental organizations* to which the paragraph alludes are factors related to partisan, electoral politics. Other factors—job needs of the marketplace, interpersonal relationships, and internal power plays—affect private and public employees in about equal proportions. Choice (A) is unsupported by the paragraph. Choice (B) directly contradicts the paragraph. Choices (C) and (D) are entirely unsupported by the paragraph.

10. **The correct answer is (B).** Some people develop allergies to antibiotics so that although those specific antibiotics might be the drug of choice to counter illness, the antibiotics cannot be used for those people. Choice (A) makes a categorical statement that is unsupported by the paragraph. Choice (C) is incorrect because antibiotics do not cure allergies; they may cause allergies. Choice (D) is incorrect because the organisms do not become allergic to antibiotics (people become allergic). Choice (E) is incorrect because there would be no need to search for new drugs if the existing ones were unfailingly effective. We need new drugs precisely because some organisms have become resistant to current ones.

11. **The correct answer is (D).** The paragraph clearly states that *in the competitive class every applicant must meet minimum qualifications*.... There may or may not be a pass/fail examination, but there most definitely are minimum qualifications that must be fulfilled. Choice (A) is a distortion of the first sentence. The sentence means that

there are no reliable exams for non-competitive positions, not that noncompetitive positions are filled by unreliable exams. Choice (B) is incorrect because the paragraph states that there *may* be an exam, not that there will be an exam. Choice (C) is incorrect because if there is a test, the applicant must pass it. Choice (E) goes beyond the scope of the paragraph. The paragraph does not state that *all* positions for which there are minimum qualifications are in the noncompetitive class.

12. **The correct answer is (A).** The paragraph defines a comma splice as the joining of two main clauses by a comma without a coordinating conjunction. Choice (B) is incorrect because a run-on sentence is defined as two independent clauses sharing one sentence with no connective. Choice (C) is incorrect because the paragraph suggests that a semicolon used as a connective can stand alone. Choice (D) touches on a subject not addressed in the paragraph. Choice (E) reverses the intent of the paragraph. A comma splice *is* a bad remedy for a run-on sentence.

13. **The correct answer is (E).** In *some* positions overtime is earned for time worked beyond the set number of hours; *other* positions offer compensatory time for overtime. Compensatory time is an alternative to overtime pay. Choices (A), (B), and (C) make unsupported statements. Choice (D) combines the additional payments for two different classes of services. Overtime pay is for hours in excess of the standard number; weekend differentials are for work on weekends, even if within the standard number of workweek hours.

14. **The correct answer is (C).** The paragraph makes clear that applicants may take the test before their backgrounds and qualifications have been investigated. If qualification is not even prerequisite to testing, certainly a qualified applicant will not be barred from the exam. Choice (A) is incorrect in assuming that all persons admitted to the

test are unqualified. The paragraph indicates only that their qualifications need not have yet been verified. Choice (B) contradicts the paragraph. Choice (D) is incorrect. The investigation is made to verify satisfactory character and reputation. Choice (E) is unsupported by the paragraph.

15. **The correct answer is (B).** Since it is illegal to continue employing an undocumented alien hired after November 6, 1986, it must not be illegal to retain an employee who was hired before that date. Choice (A) is incorrect. It was never illegal to *deny* employment to undocumented aliens; it is now illegal to employ them. Choice (C) misinterprets the paragraph. The paragraph applies only to undocumented or unauthorized aliens. Aliens who have authorizing documents or "green cards" may be employed legally. Choice (D) is incorrect. Penalties are for *knowingly* hiring illegal aliens, not for inadvertent hiring. (You must limit your answers to the material presented in the paragraph, even though you may know of the burden on employers to verify documentation or face penalties.) Choice (E) contradicts the facts in the paragraph.

16. **The correct answer is (E).** COBRA provides for the continuation of health and welfare benefits upon payment of 102 percent of the group premium. Choice (A) misinterprets the variation in the length of continuing coverage to depend upon the reason for termination of coverage rather than upon the reason for continuation of coverage. Choice (B) is incorrect because it is the cost to the subscriber that jumps to 102 percent of the group rate, not the extent of the coverage. Choice (C) is incorrect because the law requires the employer to offer the opportunity to continue health coverage; it does not require employees, retirees, or their families to continue that coverage.

Choice (D) is wrong because under CO-BRA terminated employees and retirees can continue coverage, but they cannot acquire new benefits.

17. **The correct answer is (C).** Recorded history is short relative to the time span between major earthquakes; therefore, history is inadequate as a predictive tool. Either a much longer period of recorded history or a much shorter span between major earthquakes would enhance the predictive value of historical data. Choice (A) is not supported by the paragraph. Choices (B) and (D) are not only unsupported, but they also make no sense. Choice (E) makes an assumption that goes beyond the paragraph.

18. **The correct answer is (B).** Basically, the last sentence of the paragraph is saying that if we know the rules of construction of a language, we can understand it. Choice (A) contradicts the paragraph. The paragraph states that the number of rules is finite. Choice (C) twists the second sentence, which states that definition of a language by listing its strings is impossible because the number of strings is infinite. Choice (D) introduces unnatural languages, which are not a subject of the paragraph. Choice (E) makes an unsupported statement.

19. **The correct answer is (D).** Just as *agreement of testimony is no proof of dependability,* agreement of testimony is no proof of undependability. Choice (A) is incorrect because the thrust of the paragraph is that people's perceptions are sometimes in error. Choice (B) contradicts the paragraph. It is reported that a number of witnesses may report the same erroneous observation even apart from collusion. Choice (C) misses the point. Since witnesses can make mistakes, they are just as likely to have not noticed the truth as to have "observed" that which did not happen. Choice (E) is a misstatement.

20. **The correct answer is (C).** If a contract is changed by a rider, both parties must sign the rider. The basic contract should note that a rider is being attached, and both parties should initial and date the notice in the basic contract. Choice (A) is incorrect in that it creates a rider without necessarily having created a contract. A mutual agreement to refrain from an act may be a first point of agreement and not a change. Choices (B) and (D) are both incorrect because there can be no change unless both parties agree. Choice (E) is incorrect because if there is to be no change there is no call for a rider.

21. **The correct answer is (E).** The third sentence of the paragraph states that *it is not true that all organizations are structured so that workers can be dealt with as individuals.* From this statement we can infer that *some organizations are not structured so that workers can be dealt with as individuals.* Choice (A) contradicts both the third and fourth sentences by ignoring the information that *in some organizations, employees are represented by unions, and managers bargain with these associations.* Choice (B) is unsupported because the paragraph gives no information about working environments other than organizations. Choices (C) and (D) are incorrect because they generalize *some* to mean all.

22. **The correct answer is (E).** The third sentence states that *all mechanical explosives are devices in which a physical reaction is produced, such as that caused by overloading a container with compressed air.* From this we can safely conclude that *some* devices in which a physical reaction is produced, such as that caused by overloading a container with compressed air, are mechanical explosives. We cannot infer choice (A) because the paragraph does not provide sufficient information to enable the conclusion that all explosives that have been restricted to military weapons are nuclear weapons. It may be that other

explosives that are not nuclear weapons also have been restricted to military weapons. Choices (B) and (C) contradict the paragraph. Choice (D) is wrong because the paragraph provides no information at all about whether or not mechanical explosives are restricted to military weapons.

23. **The correct answer is (A).** The first sentence states that *every level of government is a link in the economic process.* It can be deduced that its contradictory statement, *some levels of government are not links in the economic process,* cannot be true. Choice (B) is not supported by the paragraph because it goes beyond the information given. It cannot be concluded that dictatorships observe more than one principle in common with other governments. Choices (C) and (E) represent incorrect interpretations of the information that *every level of government is a link in the economic process.* It cannot be inferred from this statement that *all links in the economic process are levels of government,* only that some are. We know that the category "all levels of government" is contained in the category "links in the economic process," but we do not know if other links in the economic process exist that are not levels of government. Choice (D) is not supported by the passage; there is nothing to suggest that the contributions of some levels of society do *not* need to be evaluated.

24. **The correct answer is (C).** The first sentence presents two mutually exclusive alternatives—*All property is classified as either personal property or real property, but not both.* The second sentence states that *if something is classified as personal property, it is transient and transportable in nature.* The fourth sentence states that *permanent buildings and land . . . are fixed in nature and are not transportable.* From that we can conclude that since permanent buildings and land are not transient and transportable in nature, they are not personal property; they must,

therefore, be real property. All other responses contradict the paragraph in some way.

25. **The correct answer is (B).** The essential information from which the answer is to be inferred is contained in the second sentence, which states that *if an Act of Congress is deemed unconstitutional . . . then the Act is voided.* In choice (B) we are told that an Act of Congress is not voided; therefore, we can conclude that it has not been deemed unconstitutional by the Supreme Court. Choices (A) and (C) are not supported because the paragraph does not indicate whether an Act of Congress is voided *only* when it has been deemed unconstitutional or if it could be voided for other reasons. Choices (D) and (E) contradict the paragraph.

26. **The correct answer is (C).** The last sentence states that *some special programs for broken families are offered when parental care is temporarily or permanently unavailable.* If this statement is true, then its negation cannot be true. Choice (A) contradicts the paragraph. Choices (B) and (D) cannot be validly inferred because the paragraph does not provide sufficient information to support the inferences made. Choice (E) is wrong because the paragraph states that *all child-welfare agencies are organizations that seek to promote the healthy growth and development of children.* There is no way of knowing from this statement whether or not there are organizations other than child-welfare agencies that seek to promote the healthy growth and welfare of children.

27. **The correct answer is (C).** This answer can be inferred from the information presented in the last sentence of the paragraph, which says in part that *all document depots have the capacity to provide a great range of user services.* In view of this statement, it is clearly the case that *no document depot lacks such a capacity.* Choice (A) goes beyond the information given in

the paragraph. Choice (B) contradicts the information presented. Choice (D) draws an overly general conclusion from the information presented. One can infer that *some* document depots are information centers, but one cannot infer that *all* information centers are document depots. Choice (E) goes beyond the information that is implicit in the last sentence.

28. **The correct answer is (E).** The last sentence says that *if an expression is a familiar one . . . then it is a non-hyphenated compound*. Therefore, if an expression is a hyphenated compound, it cannot be a familiar one. Choice (A) contradicts the information. Choice (B) is incorrect because the paragraph does not give us information about *all* nonhyphenated compounds, only those that are familiar expressions. Choice (C) is incorrect because the paragraph does not give us enough information about all unfamiliar expressions. Choice (D) cannot be correct because the paragraph provides no information about compounds that have suffixes.

29. **The correct answer is (C).** The second sentence tells us that *some general types of land use are activities that conflict with* the purpose of wildlife refuges and botanical reservations. The third sentence explains that *all activities that exhibit such conflict are . . . excluded from refuges and reservations*. Therefore, we can conclude that *some activities excluded from refuges and reservations* (the ones that conflict with the purpose of refuges and reservations) *are general types of land use*. Choice (A) is wrong because the paragraph does not give any information as to whether all activities that conflict with the purpose of refuges and reservations are general types of land use. Choice (B) cannot be inferred because the paragraph does not give enough information about *all* activities that are excluded. Choice (D) is incorrect because it is too inclusive. Choice (E) is based upon insufficient information.

30. **The correct answer is (D).** The third sentence states that *if a computer programming language is a machine language, then it is a code that can be read directly by a computer*. From this statement it can be seen that all machine languages are codes that can be read directly by a computer and that if a computer programming language is not such a code, then it is not a machine language. Choice (A) goes beyond the information presented in the paragraph. Choices (B) and (C) contradict the paragraph. Choice (E) is incorrect because the paragraph does not say whether or not computer languages that are *not* machine languages are codes that can be read directly by a computer.

answers practice test 9

## Part C: Arithmetic Reasoning

| | | | | |
|---|---|---|---|---|
| 1. C | 5. A | 9. A | 13. A | 17. E |
| 2. D | 6. C | 10. C | 14. C | 18. C |
| 3. B | 7. B | 11. D | 15. C | 19. C |
| 4. E | 8. A | 12. B | 16. D | 20. B |

1. **The correct answer is (C).** The first 12 clerks complete $\frac{6}{18}$, or $\frac{1}{3}$, of the job in 6 days, leaving $\frac{2}{3}$ of the job to be completed.

One clerk would require $12 \times 18 = 216$ days to complete the job, working alone. Sixteen clerks require $216 \div 16$, or $13\frac{1}{2}$ days for the entire job. But only $\frac{2}{3}$ of the job remains. To do $\frac{2}{3}$ of the job, 16 clerks require
$$\frac{2}{3} \times 13\frac{1}{2} = \frac{2}{3} \times \frac{27}{2} = 9 \text{ days}$$
The entire job takes 6 days + 9 days = 15 days.

2. **The correct answer is (D).** Let $x =$ cost of a child's cleaning
Then $2x =$ cost of an adult's cleaning
$$2(2x) + 3(x) = \$49$$
$$4x + 3x = \$49$$
$$7x = \$49$$
$$x = \$ \ 7$$
$7 is the cost of a child's cleaning; $2 \times$ $7, or $14, is the cost of an adult's cleaning.

3. **The correct answer is (B).** First determine the total annual tax:
$424 + $783 + (2)$466 = $424 + $783 + $932 = $2139
Divide the total taxes by the tax rate to find the assessed valuation.
$2139 ÷ .132 = $16,205
To find what percent one number is of another, create a fraction by putting the part over the whole and convert to a decimal by dividing.
$$\frac{\$16{,}205}{\$87{,}250} = \$16{,}205 \div \$87{,}250 = 18.57\%$$

4. **The correct answer is (E).** The correct answer is five additional days.
Four assistants completed 336 cases in 42 hours (6 days at 7 hours per day). Therefore, each assistant completed $336 \div 4$, or 84 cases in 42 hours, for a rate of 2 cases per hour per assistant.
After the first 6 days, the number of cases remaining is $756 - 336 = 420$.
It will take 6 assistants, working at the rate of 2 cases per hour per assistant, $420 \div 12$, or 35 hours, to complete the work. If each workday has 7 hours, then $35 \div 7$, or 5 days, are needed.

5. **The correct answer is (A).** Add what the family spends: 30% + 8% + 25% + 4% + 13% + 5% = 85%.
Since it spends 85 percent, it has 100% − 85% = 15% remaining for savings.
15% of $500 = .15 × $500 per week
                 = $75 per week
$15,000 ÷ $75 = 200 weeks

6. **The correct answer is (C).** Commission $= 42\frac{1}{2}\%$ of fares
$$42\frac{1}{2}\% \text{ of } \$520 = .425 \times \$520$$
                 = $221 commission
Tips = 29% of commission
29% of $221 = .29 × $221
                 = $64.09 in tips
Weekly earnings:
    $221.09
   +   64.09
    $285.18

Monthly earnings, based on four-week month:

$$\begin{array}{r} \$285.09 \\ \times\ \underline{\qquad 4} \\ \$1{,}140.36 \end{array}$$

Earnings, even in a month a few days longer than four weeks, clearly fall between $1,100 and $1,200.

7. **The correct answer is (B).** Take this problem one step at a time.

First, how many of each type were there?

Of the 60 employees, one third, or 20, were clerks; 30 percent, or 18, were machine operators; 22 were stenographers.

Then, how much did each of them earn?

The clerks earned $12,750 ÷ 12 = $1,062.50 per month

Machine operators earned $13,150 ÷ 12 = $1,095.83 per month

Stenographers earned $13,000 ÷ 12 = $1,083.33 per month

20 clerks × $1,062.50 × 2 months = $42,500.00

18 machine operators × $1,095.83 × 4 months = $78,899.76

22 stenographers × $1,083.33 × 3 months = $71,499.78

Finally, find the total amount paid to these temporary workers:
$42,500.00 + $78,899.76 + $71,499.78 = $192,899.54 total cost

8. **The correct answer is (A).** If 76 gallons are burned per hour and 266 gallons remain in the tank at 9 a.m., it will take 266 ÷ 76 = 3½ hours to use all the remaining fuel oil. From 9 a.m. to noon is 3 hours; therefore, at noon there is enough fuel for only ½ hour more.

9. **The correct answer is (A).** There are 360 minutes in a six-hour day. If each seat is occupied all day there are 105 × 360 = 37,800 minutes of seating time to be divided among 486 people. 37,800 ÷ 486 = 77.77 minutes of seating time per person = 1 hour 17.7 minutes per person.

10. **The correct answer is (C).** The worker earns $8.60 per hour for two 40-hour weeks or $8.60 × 80 hours = $688 and $12.90 per hour for an additional 16 hours ($12.90 × 16 hours = $206.40), so her gross pay is $688 + $206.40 = $894.40. From this, the following are deducted: FICA at 7.13% = $63.77 and the three withholding taxes at the combined rate of 22.5% = $201.24. Add the deductions: $63.77 + $201.24 = $265.01, and subtract the sum from the gross pay: $894.40 − $265.01 = $629.39.

11. **The correct answer is (D).** Since the court does one day's work per day, at the end of 60 days there will be 150 − 60 = 90 trial days of old cases remaining. New cases are accumulating at the rate of 1.6 trial days per day; therefore, there will be 60 × 1.6 = 96 trial days of new cases at the end of 60 days. 96 new trial days added to the backlog of 90 trial days would make the total backlog 186 trial days.

12. **The correct answer is (B).** A kilometer is $\frac{5}{8}$ of a mile.

480 km × $\frac{5}{8}$ = 300 miles; 300 miles ÷ 40 mph = 7.5 hours.

Subtract 7.5 hours from the required arrival time of 4 p.m. to find that he must leave at 8:30 a.m. (noon to 4 p.m. is 4 hours + 8:30 to noon is 3.5 hours).

13. **The correct answer is (A).** Calculate the cost of the first machine:
$1360 − 20% = $1360 × 80% = $1088 then
$1088 − 10% = $1088 × 90% = $979.20 + $35 + $52 = $1066.20.
Calculate the cost of the second machine:
$1385 − 30% = $1385 × 70% = $969.50 + $40 + $50 = $1059.50
The second machine is $6.70 less expensive than the first machine.
($1066.20 − $1059.50 = $6.70)
To determine the percent of savings by buying the second machine:
$6.70 ÷ $1066.20 = 0.6% savings.

**14. The correct answer is (C).** The proportion is $32 \times 22 = x \times 16$

$$16\,x = 704$$
$$x = 704 \div 16 = 44$$

**15. The correct answer is (C).** Add the suggested contributions and divide by the number of paralegals to get the average.

$$\frac{1}{2}\% = \frac{15}{30}$$
$$\frac{1}{1}\% = \frac{30}{30}$$
$$\frac{1}{3}\% = \frac{10}{30}$$
$$+\frac{1}{5}\% = \frac{6}{30}$$

$$\frac{61}{30}\% = 2\% \div 4 \text{ paralegals} = \frac{1}{2}\%$$

**16. The correct answer is (D).**
Compute the following:
$$\frac{49.20 - (18 - (18 \times .10))}{22} = x$$

$$x = \frac{33}{22} = 1.5 \text{ hours, or 1 hour}$$
30 minutes.

The cost of the switch after the government discount of 10% is applied is $18 - (18 \times .10)$ or $16.20. This amount, when subtracted from the total charge of $49.20, leaves $33, which represents the charge for labor. A charge of $33 at the rate of $22 per hour represents 1.5 hours, or 1 hour 30 minutes, of work.

**17. The correct answer is (E).** The correct answer is not given as one of the response choices. The answer can be obtained by computing the following:

$$\frac{\left(\dfrac{80}{2} - 34\right)}{40} = x$$

$$x = \frac{6}{40} = .15$$

$$.15 \times 100 = 15\%$$

The expected $80 cost for a pair of tires would make the cost of a single tire $40. The difference between the actual cost of $34 per tire and the expected cost of $40 per tire is $6, which is 15% of the $40 expected cost.

**18. The correct answer is (C).** Obtain the answer by setting up a simple proportion:

$$\frac{110 \text{ km}}{60 \text{ min}} = \frac{33 \text{ km}}{x \text{ min}}$$

Solving this proportion, we obtain $110x = 1980$; $x = [1980 \div 110] = 18$.

**19. The correct answer is (C).** Compute the following:

$$\frac{\left(\dfrac{1}{6} + \dfrac{1}{4}\right)}{2} = x$$

This simple arithmetic averaging of two fractions can be accomplished by first finding their lowest common denominator:

$$\frac{1}{6} = \frac{2}{12} \text{ and } \frac{1}{4} = \frac{3}{12}$$

The sum of $\dfrac{2}{12}$ and $\dfrac{3}{12}$ is $\dfrac{5}{12}$. This fraction, when multiplied by $\dfrac{1}{2}$ (which is the same as dividing by 2) gives the correct answer:

$$\frac{5}{12} \times \frac{1}{2} = \frac{5}{24}$$

**20. The correct answer is (B).** Compute the following:
(1) $0.82S = 6.97$
and
(2) $\dfrac{1200}{40} \times S = Y$

The clerk's net pay of $6.97 per hour represents .82 of his or her gross pay (100% − 18% =82% or .82). Solving equation (1) we find that the clerk's hourly salary *(S)* before deductions is $8.50. Substituting this figure in equation (2), we compute the total number of hours of work involved (1200 forms divided by 40 forms per hour equals 30 hours of work), and then multiply 30 hours by an hourly wage of $8.50 to get $255.00, the amount the government would have to pay for the work.

# PART IV
## GLOSSARY

# Glossary

**Base salary:** A *basic salary* with *COLA* added.

**Basic salary:** Annual, daily, or hourly rate of pay, as indicated by the salary schedule for the employee's assigned position; excludes *COLA*.

**Career appointment:** An appointment to the Postal Service without time limitation.

**Casual appointment:** A noncareer, limited-term appointment to a Postal Service position.

**COLA:** see *Cost-of-Living adjustment*.

**Cost-of-Living Adjustment (COLA):** Increase in pay based on increases in the Consumer Price Index (CPI) over a base month; this increase is specified in bargaining unit agreements.

**Entrance examination:** Test given to establish eligibility for employment.

**Grade:** Pay category.

**In-service examination:** Test administered to substitute rural carriers and career Postal Service employees to determine eligibility for advancement and *reassignment;* also used to establish qualification for enrollment in certain postal training courses.

**Merit Promotion Program:** Provides the means for making selections for promotions according to the relative qualifications of the employees under consideration.

**Performance test:** A procedure in which the applicant is directed to carry out a certain work activity related to the position under consideration.

**Promotion:** The permanent assignment, with or without relocation, of an employee to an established position with a higher grade than the position the employee previously held in the same schedule or in another schedule.

**Quality step increase (QSI):** An increase in addition to a periodic *step increase,* granted on or before the expiration of a required waiting period, in recognition of extra competence.

**Rated application:** Application and other required documents that provide a basis for evaluation against an established rating standard. Based on this application, a final rating is established for each competitor.

**Reassignment:** The permanent assignment, with or without relocation, to another established position with the same *grade* in the same schedule or in a different schedule.

**Register:** A file of eligible employees' names arranged in order of relative standing for appointment consideration.

**Step increase:** An advancement from one step to the next within a specific *grade* of a position; this is dependent on satisfying certain performance and waiting period criteria. See also *quality step increase*.

**Temporary appointment:** A noncareer, limited-term appointment, up to but not exceeding one year in a position that includes the performance of duties assigned to nonbargaining units.

**Temporary assignment:** The placement of an employee in another established position for a limited period of time to perform duties other than those in the position description.

**Veteran preference:** Points granted to eligible applicants to be added to the ratings on examinations.

# NOTES

# NOTES

**NOTES**

# Peterson's
## Book Satisfaction Survey

## Give Us Your Feedback

Thank you for choosing Peterson's as your source for personalized solutions for your education and career achievement. Please take a few minutes to answer the following questions. Your answers will go a long way in helping us to produce the most user-friendly and comprehensive resources to meet your individual needs.

When completed, please tear out this page and mail it to us at:

> Publishing Department
> Peterson's, a Nelnet company
> 2000 Lenox Drive
> Lawrenceville, NJ 08648

You can also complete this survey online at **www.petersons.com/booksurvey.**

1. **What is the ISBN of the book you have purchased? (The ISBN can be found on the book's back cover in the lower right-hand corner. )** _____

2. **Where did you purchase this book?**
   - ❑ Retailer, such as Barnes & Noble
   - ❑ Online reseller, such as Amazon.com
   - ❑ Petersons.com
   - ❑ Other (please specify) _____

3. **If you purchased this book on Petersons.com, please rate the following aspects of your online purchasing experience on a scale of 4 to 1 (4 = Excellent and 1 = Poor).**

|  | 4 | 3 | 2 | 1 |
|---|---|---|---|---|
| Comprehensiveness of Peterson's Online Bookstore page | ❑ | ❑ | ❑ | ❑ |
| Overall online customer experience | ❑ | ❑ | ❑ | ❑ |

4. **Which category best describes you?**
   - ❑ High school student
   - ❑ Parent of high school student
   - ❑ College student
   - ❑ Graduate/professional student
   - ❑ Returning adult student
   - ❑ Teacher
   - ❑ Counselor
   - ❑ Working professional/military
   - ❑ Other (please specify) _____

5. **Rate your overall satisfaction with this book.**

| Extremely Satisfied | Satisfied | Not Satisfied |
|---|---|---|
| ❑ | ❑ | ❑ |

6. **Rate each of the following aspects of this book on a scale of 4 to 1 (4 = Excellent and 1 = Poor).**

| | 4 | 3 | 2 | 1 |
|---|---|---|---|---|
| Comprehensiveness of the information | ❏ | ❏ | ❏ | ❏ |
| Accuracy of the information | ❏ | ❏ | ❏ | ❏ |
| Usability | ❏ | ❏ | ❏ | ❏ |
| Cover design | ❏ | ❏ | ❏ | ❏ |
| Book layout | ❏ | ❏ | ❏ | ❏ |
| Special features (e.g., CD, flashcards, charts, etc.) | ❏ | ❏ | ❏ | ❏ |
| Value for the money | ❏ | ❏ | ❏ | ❏ |

7. **This book was recommended by:**
   - ❏ Guidance counselor
   - ❏ Parent/guardian
   - ❏ Family member/relative
   - ❏ Friend
   - ❏ Teacher
   - ❏ Not recommended by anyone—I found the book on my own
   - ❏ Other (please specify) _____

8. **Would you recommend this book to others?**

| Yes | Not Sure | No |
|---|---|---|
| ❏ | ❏ | ❏ |

9. **Please provide any additional comments.**

_____

_____

_____

_____

_____

Remember, you can tear out this page and mail it to us at:

Publishing Department
Peterson's, a Nelnet company
2000 Lenox Drive
Lawrenceville, NJ 08648

or you can complete the survey online at **www.petersons.com/booksurvey.**

Your feedback is important to us at Peterson's, and we thank you for your time!

If you would like us to keep in touch with you about new products and services, please include your e-mail address here: _____